SO-AEE-498

Communication

Communication
Embracing Difference

Daniel M. Dunn
Purdue University–Calumet

Lisa J. Goodnight
Purdue University–Calumet

Allyn and Bacon
Boston   New York   San Francisco
Mexico City   Montreal   Toronto   London   Madrid   Munich   Paris
Hong Kong   Singapore   Tokyo   Cape Town   Sydney

Executive Editor: Karon Bowers
Development Editor: Ellen Darion
Editorial Assistant: Jennifer Trebby
Marketing Manager: Mandee Eckersley
Production Editor: Christine Tridente
Editorial-Production Service: Colophon
Composition Buyer: Linda Cox
Manufacturing Buyer: Megan Cochran
Cover Administrator: Kristina Mose-Libon
Text Design and Electronic Composition: Glenna Collett

For related titles and support materials, visit our online catalog at www.ablongman.com.

Library of Congress Cataloging-in-Publication Data
  Communication : embracing difference / Daniel M. Dunn, Lisa J. Goodnight.
    p. cm.
  Includes bibliographical references and index.
  ISBN 0-321-08823-9 (alk. paper)
    1. Oral communication.   I. Goodnight, Lisa J.   II. Title.
  P95 .D86 2003
  302.2'242—dc21   2002026121

Printed in the United States of America
10 9 8 7 6 5   06 05

For

Linda and Laura
—D. M. D.

Lee and Hannah
—L. J. G.

Contents

Listening   45

Verbal Communication   63

UNIT TWO Interpersonal Communication

Preface

We teach a very diverse population of students. Our students range widely in age, ethnicity, race, religion, sexual orientation, social role, and socio-economic status. Many are first generation college students and often attend our colleges or universities part-time while holding a full-time job. They are mothers, fathers, grandparents, and teenagers. *Communication: Embracing Difference* is written for them. It is also written for you, teachers of all different types of students. It reflects the full lives of our students in their work, family life, community, and here at school. This text is a tool that will help you provide students with opportunities to explore and celebrate the richness of their lives and the overall richness of difference and diversity in society.

Themes of the Book

Humans approach communication and communication situations from diverse and unique positions. Because communication is an interdependent process that includes at least two people, multiple approaches to any given communication situation exist. Understanding the diversity of communication approaches leads to a greater overall understanding of others. By understanding and celebrating difference, students become more effective communicators in a variety of settings and, ultimately, feel more confident. They are better able to navigate successfully in an increasingly diverse society.

In this book, we want to move beyond the narrow definition of diversity, often defined as "political correctness." Thus, the theme of embracing difference is integrated throughout the text in all of its features and includes every aspect of students' lives.

This book is also based on the premise that although students need to learn and understand theories of human communication, it is the practical application of communication skills that helps students become effective communicators. In other words, applied communication skills help students learn and create effective strategies. Students must be able to effectively interpret, adjust, and respond to a variety of different approaches and situations. These skills can and should be practiced in several settings, including interpersonal, small group, and public communication.

Organization of the Book

Communication: Embracing Difference includes three units containing sixteen chapters. Unit One, The Process of Communication, includes chapters on perception, language, nonverbal behavior, and listening. Unit Two, Interpersonal Communication, emphasizes theories and skills of interpersonal communication including self-disclosure, conflict, and an entire chapter on communication climate. A chapter on interviewing covers the principles and practices of interviewing with special attention to informative and employment interviewing. The unit also includes an overview of small-group communication, small-group decision making, and leadership. Unit Three, Public Communication, discusses the process and practice of public speaking in six chapters. Topics such as speech topic selection, research, audience analysis, delivery, presentational aids, informative speaking, and persuasive speaking are covered in depth.

Pedagogical Features

The theme of **embracing difference** is integrated into every aspect of the text. The following pedagogical features will help students to reflect on, apply, and critically think about communication:

Chapter Opening Scenarios

Each chapter begins with a scenario that describes a real-life communication situation faced by our students. These stories not only resonate with our students' lives at work, home, and school, they also highlight the increasing diversity of student populations across the country.

Ethics in Communication

This feature brings students back to the situation presented at the beginning of the chapter, following up on the ethical dilemmas posted there. It helps students to see and understand the ethical choices people make in a variety of real-life circumstances. The feature may be used as a starting point for class discussion or for a reflection assignment such as a journal.

Communication and Technology

This feature discusses how technological advances have changed the way we communicate. Topics such as email and computer-mediated communication, the use of the Internet for research, the role of presentational software in public speaking, and working in virtual teams are discussed.

Student-Oriented Pedagogy

Generously sprinkled throughout each chapter are activities designed to help students think about and practice effective communication. These include:

- **Self-Assessment activities:** Self-reflection activities that allow students to analyze, understand, and refine their own communication skills.

- **Skill Building activities:** Opportunities for students to develop and practice the skills taught in the text and apply them to real-life situations.

- **Critical Thinking activities:** Opportunities to analyze the communication of others in a variety of settings and situations and to strategize about these communication challenges.

- **Learning Objectives** help students focus on overall concepts, theories, and skills discussed in the chapter.

- **Checklists** in each chapter summarize the most important theories or skills.

- **Chapter summaries** review the main themes of each chapter.

- **Review questions** help students reflect on the chapter material and can also be used for study guides, quizzes, or exams.

- **Glossary of Terms** serves as a helpful reference tool at the end of the text.

Instructor Supplements

Print

- **Instructor's Manual** by Patricia Mellon, Purdue University–Calumet
  This Instructor's Manual includes chapter objectives, chapter outlines, and a wealth of thought-provoking discussion topics and activities.

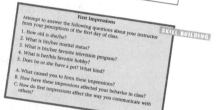

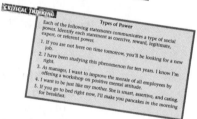

- **Test Bank** by Erin Okamoto Protsman, Purdue University–Calumet
  This Test Bank contains hundreds of challenging multiple-choice, true–false, short answer, and essay questions, along with an answer key. The questions closely follow the text chapters and are cross-referenced with corresponding page numbers.

- **Computerized Test Bank**
  The printed Test Bank is also available electronically through Allyn & Bacon's computerized testing system, TestGen EQ. The fully networkable test generating software is now available on a multiplatform CD-ROM. The user-friendly interface enables instructors to view, edit, and add questions; transfer questions to tests; and print tests in a variety of fonts. Search and sort features allow instructors to locate questions quickly and arrange them in a preferred order.

- **A Guide for New Teachers of Introduction to Communication** by Susanna G. Porter, Kennesaw State University
  This instructor's guide is designed to help new teachers effectively teach the introductory communication course.

- **The ESL Guide for Public Speaking** by Debra Gonsher Vinik, Bronx Community College of the City University of New York
  This guide provides strategies and resources for instructors teaching in a bilingual or multilingual classroom. It also includes suggestions for further reading and a listing of related web sites.

- **Allyn & Bacon Public Speaking Transparency Package**
  This set, produced using PowerPoint, includes 100 full-color transparencies.

- ***The Blockbuster Approach: Teaching Interpersonal Communication with Video, 2/e,*** by Thomas E. Jewell, Marymount College
  This guide provides lists and descriptions of commercial videos that can be used in the classroom to illustrate interpersonal concepts and complex interpersonal relationships. Sample activities are included.

- ***Great Ideas for Teaching Speech*** by Raymond Zeuchsner, California Polytechnic State University
  This book provides descriptions of and guidelines for assignments successfully used by experienced public speaking instructors in their classrooms.

Electronic Supplements

- **Allyn & Bacon Digital Media Archive for Communication, Version 2.0**
  This CD-ROM offers still images, video clips, and assorted lecture resources that can be incorporated into multimedia presentations in the classroom.

- *PowerPoint* **Presentation for** *Communication: Embracing Difference* (available on the Web—www.ablongman.com/ppt). This text-specific package consists of a collection of lecture outlines and graphic images keyed to every chapter in the text.

- **Allyn & Bacon** *PowerPoint* **Presentation for Introduction to Communication** (available on the Web—www.ablongman.com/ppt).

- **Allyn & Bacon** *PowerPoint* **Presentation for Public Speaking** (available on the Web—www.ablongman.com/ppt).

- **Allyn & Bacon Student Speeches Video Library**
  Instructors have their choice of one video from a collection of seven videos that includes three 2-hour American Forensic Association videos of award-winning student speeches and four videos with a range of student speeches delivered in the classroom. Some restrictions apply.

- **Allyn & Bacon Public Speaking Key Topics Video Library**
  This library contains three videos that address core topics covered in the classroom: Critiquing Student Speeches, Speaker Apprehension, and Addressing Your Audience. Some restrictions apply.

- **Allyn & Bacon Public Speaking Video**
  This video includes excerpts of classic and contemporary public speeches and student speeches to illustrate various aspects of the public speaking process.

- **Allyn & Bacon Communication Video Library**
  A collection of communication videos produced by Films for the Humanities and Sciences. Contact your local Allyn & Bacon sales representative for ordering information. Some restrictions apply.

- **Allyn & Bacon Interpersonal Communication Video**
  This interpersonal video contains three scenarios illustrating key concepts in interpersonal communication with a guide featuring transcripts and teaching activities. A separate video guide is available as well.

- **Video: Interpersonal Communication with Guidebook**
  Eight interpersonal scenarios examine a wide range of interpersonal issues. An extensive guide provides a script, class discussion questions, and exercises for each of the episodes.

Student Supplements

Print

- *Preparing Visual Aids for Presentations,* **3/e,** by Dan Cavanaugh
  This 32-page booklet provides ideas to improve presentations, including suggestions for planning a presentation, guidelines for designing visual aids and storyboarding, and a *PowerPoint* presentation walk-through.

- *Public Speaking in the Multicultural Environment,* 2/e, by Devorah Lieberman, Portland State University
  This booklet helps students learn to analyze cultural diversity within their audiences and adapt their presentations accordingly.

- *Speech Preparation Workbook* by Jennifer Dreyer and Gergory H. Patton, San Diego State University
  This workbook takes students through the various stages of speech creation—from audience analysis to writing the speech—and provides supplementary assignments and tear-out forms.

- *Outlining Workbook* by Reeze L. Hanson and Sharon Condon, Haskell Indian Nations University
  This workbook includes activities, exercises, and answers to help students develop and master the critical skills of outlining.

- *iSearch for Speech Communication*
  This resource guide for the Internet covers the basics of using the Internet, conducting Web searches, and critically evaluating and documenting Internet sources, as well as Internet activities and URLs specific to the discipline of speech communication. The book also contains an access code for ContentSelect, our online research database.

Electronic

- **Interactive Speechwriter Software, Version 1.1 (Windows)** by Martin R. Cox
  This interactive software package for student purchase provides supplemental material, writing templates (for the informative, persuasive, and motivated sequence speeches, as well as for outlines), sample student speeches (text only), and more! This program enhances students' understanding of key concepts discussed in the text and is available for Windows and Macintosh.

- **Speech Writer's Workshop CD-ROM, Version 2.0**
  This interactive software assists students with speech preparation and enables them to write better speeches. The software includes four separate features: (1) a speech handbook with tips for researching and preparing speeches plus information about grammar, usage, and syntax; (2) a speech workshop that guides students through the speech-writing process and includes a series of questions at each stage; (3) a topics dictionary containing hundreds of speech ideas—all divided into subcategories to help students with outlining and organization; and (4) a citation database that formats bibliographic entries in MLA or APA style.

- **Companion Website with Online Practice Tests (http://www. ablongman.com/dunn)** by Elsa Peterson
  This site includes chapter objectives, weblinks, and a wealth of questions and assignments, including multiple-choice, true–false, and essay options.

- **ContentSelect**
  This free research database (available via an access code in *iSearch for Speech Communication*), searchable by key-word, gives you immediate access to hundreds of scholarly journals and other popular publications. Ask your local representative for details.

Acknowledgments

We are indebted to many people for their help with this book. First, we thank the Purdue University–Calumet community for its support of this project and especially our colleagues in the Department of Communication and Creative Arts. We also want to especially thank our students for providing us with the inspiration for writing this book and for sharing their real-life experiences with us. A special thanks goes to all the past and present graduate teaching assistants in Communication and Creative Arts at Purdue University–Calumet for their ideas, inspiration, and assistance, especially Shelly Robertson, Patricia Mellon, and Erin Okamoto Protsman.

We also thank the reviewers of this text, who provided many helpful ideas and suggestions: Kelly Albada, East Carolina University; Rusalyn Andrews, Cottey College; Katrina Bell-Jordan, Northeastern Illinois University; Martin H. Brodey, Montgomery College; Diane Casagrande, West Chester University; Michael Eaves, Valdosta State University; Michael R. Elkins, Texas A&M–Kingsville; Penny Eubank, Oklahoma Christian University; Jane Flesher, Chippewa Valley Technical College; Parthenia H. Franks, Morehouse College; Donna Friess, Cypress College; Anne Gillespie, University of Central Arkansas; Kim Gyuran, Modesto Junior College; Debbi Hatton, Sam Houston State University; Debra S. Jones, Chattanooga State Technical Community College; Ray E. Karrer, Paris Junior College; Donnell King, Pellissippi State Technical Community College; Colleen Keough, University of Southern California; Steven Miura, University of Hawaii–Hilo; James McNamara, Alverno College; Kristine Mirrer, Kean University; Donna Munde, Mercer County Community College; Majia Holmer Nadesan, Arizona State University West; Alkis Papoutsis, Borough of Manhattan Community College; Kathleen Perri, Valencia Community College; James E. Reppert, Southern Arkansas University; Thomas E. Ruddick, Edison Community College; Jack Sargent, Kean University; Candice Thomas-Maddox, Ohio University–Lancaster; and Darla Williams, Millersville University.

Of course, this book would not have been completed without the editors and support staff at Allyn & Bacon. We are indebted to Karon Bowers, Executive Editor, for her support and encouragement. We thank Mandee Eckersley for her marketing expertise, Christine Tridente for steering the book through production, and Jennifer Trebby for handling reviews and many other tasks along the way. We are especially indebted to Ellen Darion, Senior Development Editor, for sharing the overall vision of the book and truly believing in the project. Her creativity, inspiration, and sense of humor helped make this book better than it would have otherwise been.

Finally, we would like to thank our families. This project took us away from the ones we love the most, and we are grateful for their patience, support, and encouragement. This book is dedicated to them. Special thanks to Nancy and Joseph Goodnight.

An Overview of Communication

At the conclusion of this chapter, you should be able to:

- Define communication.
- Explain the various components of the communication process.
- Describe the functions of communication.

- Explain the significance of intrapersonal communication to both interpersonal and public communication.
- Describe the difference between dyadic communication and small-group communication.

Sue, Jose, Alicia, and Cory are sitting in a classroom waiting for class to begin. They have been in their communication class together for two weeks and tonight the first journal assignment is due.

Sue is a mother of two small children and can only come to campus two nights a week. Her husband does shift work in the local factory, so Sue must schedule her classes around his work schedule. She has enjoyed interacting with her fellow classmates and is excited about learning new ideas. Sue's youngest daughter had an ear infection this week, so Sue was not able to finish the journal assignment.

Jose is an older returning student. He works all day at one of the local steel mills and is taking classes with the hopes of getting a promotion. By the time he gets to campus, he is tired and would rather not interact with other students. He likes the class sessions when he can just listen and take notes. Jose completed his assignment, but fears he has not done it correctly.

Alicia just graduated from high school and is excited about attending the local university. She and her parents have been saving for her education for several years, and she will be the first one in her family to attend college. Alicia was an honor student in high school and hopes to major in biology and eventually go to medical school. She is working part-time on campus in the financial aid office and has already joined several student organizations. She is a bit anxious about giving speeches, but is looking forward to learning about communication. Her journal assignment has been done since the day after it was assigned. She has revised it twice but is still nervous about turning it in.

Cory also just graduated from high school and doesn't know what he wants to do. He has been unable to find a well-paying job, so his parents are forcing him to take classes. He works part-time for a computer company repairing hardware. Cory is shy and does not want to interact with others. He would rather be at home surfing the Internet. So far the class hasn't been too boring, but Cory thinks the assignments require too much work. He did not do the journal assignment due tonight.

All of these students are looking for something different from this communication course, and each has approached the first assignment differently. Each will approach learning in a unique and different way. Obviously, Sue, Jose, Alicia, and Cory will send and receive messages differently. This chapter discusses how diversity in age, gender, ethnicity, family roles, learning styles, religion, and approach affect the communication process.

The Communication Process

It takes a significant amount of work and energy to communicate effectively with others. One measure of our effectiveness stems from our understanding of ourselves and of others, a subject that is treated at length in the following chapter. Several factors contribute to our effectiveness as communicators, namely, our ability to listen, our verbal communication skills, our nonverbal communication skills, our understanding of our relationships with others, our ability to analyze an audience, and our knowledge of the way to research, prepare, and deliver a public speech. All these topics (and more) are covered in subsequent chapters. Communicating effectively, more broadly, stems from an overall understanding that people are simultaneously different and similar. We approach communication and each communication situation from diverse perspectives. In the beginning of the chapter we see four different people who have diverse expectations about their communication course experience. Sue, for example, is anxious to meet new people and wants to learn new ideas. Cory, on the other hand, is shy and not at all excited at the prospect of having to meet his fellow students. Yet, these two seemingly different people share some things in common. They are in the same communication class and live in the same geographic area. These two things alone can form the basis for common ground and the foundation for effective communication. The theme of "difference" will be explored throughout the text. First, however, to pave the way for these discussions, we must understand the nature of the communication process.

We used to think of communication as a one-way process. This was called the **linear model** of communication. The linear model argued that communication can only move in one direction, from the sender to the receiver. The receiver played a passive role in the overall process. Over the years, scholars have added to and revised the linear model. We now describe communication as an ongoing, dynamic process. The **transactional model** describes communication as an interdependent process whereby the speaker and receiver are simultaneously sending and receiving messages. With this in mind, let's turn to a more detailed definition of communication.

Communication is the interdependent process of sending, receiving, and understanding messages. This definition implies that the components

Each person in this family has a unique approach to the communication process.

of the communication process (discussed later in this section) cannot be examined separately. Rather, the relationship that exists between the sender and the receiver, as well as the environment of the communication event, must be viewed as a whole. According to this perspective, if any of the components or circumstances change (that is, the number of individuals involved in the interaction, the seating arrangements, or the time of day), the communication event is altered.

Communication is an ongoing process; we never stop sending and receiving messages. In fact, we do both simultaneously. For example, when we tell our supervisor about how all our overtime is hurting our grades, we also observe the supervisor's reaction to what we are saying—we simultaneously send a message *and* receive the supervisor's message (that is, his or her concern, or surprise, or apparent lack of concentration on what we are saying).

Even though we may not deliberately or directly communicate with another person, we constantly send out information about ourselves. Our clothing, our behavior toward others (children, spouses, lovers, colleagues, and so on), and the amount of eye contact we establish all communicate information about ourselves. People make inferences about our behavior, just as we interpret what we observe about others.

As you will discover, communication is a dynamic process, a process that changes from one communication setting to the next. Although it is difficult to predict the ways your ideas will be interpreted by others, certain components are always present in the communication process: people, a message, encoding, decoding, the channel, feedback, the context, and noise (Figure 1.1). Understanding these components will give you both an awareness of the communication process and a working vocabulary to help you formulate and dissect messages.

People

People are an integral part of the communication process. Today's technology offers sophisticated telecommunication and computer systems. Yet this technology simply facilitates human communication, which includes conversations between individuals, public speeches delivered to an audience, employee interviews, small-group discussions, knowing glances between friends or partners, and so on. None of these situations is possible without the involvement of people.

Each of us is unique in many ways. Our ethnicity, race, sexual orientation, gender, socioeconomic status, age, values, and many other characteristics make up who we are, how we feel, and, more importantly, how we approach communication. These aspects together create our frame of reference. **Frame of reference** allows us to create and interpret messages. It is our unique view of the world and everything in it. Think about the other students in your class. What things do you share with them? Are you all the same age? How many men and women are in the class? How about ethnic-

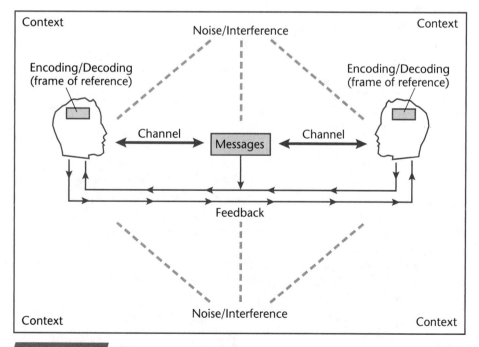

FIGURE 1.1 **The Communication Process**

ity and race? Paying close attention to the frames of reference of your classmates will help you become a more effective communicator this semester.

Human interaction places the individual in two roles: the source and the receiver. The **source** is the person who creates and sends a message, whereas the **receiver** is the individual to whom the message is sent. The receiver also sends messages back to the source, so the entire process bounces back and forth. For example, Joan (the receiver) listens to Karl (the source) explain how his overtime on the job is affecting his grades at school. She remarks, "I understand, and let's try to work something out with your schedule for next week." What she has done, momentarily, is send a message of her own. For that instant, Karl becomes the receiver. When people communicate with each other, messages are sent and received simultaneously.

SELF-ASSESSMENT   **Your Frame of Reference**

Listed below are some items that are components of your frame of reference and, consequently, you as a communicator. Take a few moments to reflect on your frame of reference by answering the following questions.

1. What is your family like? Do you have sisters and brothers? Are you married? Do you have children? Are you part of a step-family?

2. What education or special skills do you have? How long have you been attending college? Do other members of your family have a college degree or graduate degree? Do you have specialized training?

3. Where do you call home? What is the neighborhood like? Is your family's original home in another country? Is your neighborhood dominated by one ethnic background?

4. What is your religious background? Are you affiliated with a religious group? Were you raised in this religion? What are the major beliefs of your religious group?

5. Are you interested in local, national, or world politics? What is your party affiliation, if any? Have you taken an active part in campaigning for a cause or a candidate?

6. What is your work experience? What is your current job, if any? If you could have any job, what would it be? If you have decided on a major, what most influenced you in making that choice?

7. What is your ethnic background? How much contact with other ethnic groups or races have you had in your community? How

do you celebrate holidays? What are some of the stereotypes about your ethnic group?

8. Are you male or female? How does gender affect your communication? What is the gender of most of your friends? What is your sexual orientation?

9. How old are you? How does your age affect your communication? Is it more difficult to communicate with those older or younger than you?

10. What special interests do you have? How do you spend your free time? Do you have any hobbies? Do you play or watch sports? What kind of music do you listen to?

Message

The **message** is the thought, feeling, or action that is sent from the source to the receiver with the use of symbols. When we create messages, we have a choice of code systems, such as verbal or nonverbal and oral or nonoral (see Chapters 4 and 5). Thus, messages can be communicated either verbally or nonverbally, intentionally or unintentionally. Verbal messages are composed of words: "I was so offended by Larry's comments that I thought I was going to scream at him!" Nonverbal messages are composed of gestures, facial expressions, vocal inflection, touch, and so on. Nonverbally, we might communicate our anger at Larry's comments by glaring at him or turning red. The content of our messages can reflect a great deal of preparation or structure (as in public speeches), a casualness (as in a conversation with a good friend), or no forethought at all (as in many of our nonverbal messages).

We can also strategically alter our message to be better understood by the receiver. For example, a speaker will want to do extensive audience analysis before giving a public speech to ensure that the audience understands the message. We can alter our message through language choice, delivery style, and many other variables we will discuss in later chapters.

Encoding

Encoding is the process of putting thoughts, ideas, or feelings into meaningful symbols that another person can understand. Symbols represent things—our feelings, names for the objects around us, explanations for behaviors, and so on. We are most familiar with the concept of words (language) as our primary symbol system (more about this in Chapter 4). When we want to send a message, we rely on our frame of reference to choose the appropriate symbol. For example, the words chosen for this message would be easily understood by the receiver: "I'm really glad to see you. I've missed you so much these past two weeks." Nonverbal symbols also convey our messages effectively. A hug, for example, symbolizes an expression of warmth toward another person. In both these examples, the symbols used to convey the message (verbal expression using words, nonverbal expression using a hug) are easily discerned by the receiver.

Decoding

Decoding is the process of interpreting or attaching meaning to another person's message. Communication often stops because people decode messages differently based on their frame of reference. Because of diverse attitudes, knowledge, and past experiences, receivers often interpret messages differently from the way they were intended by the senders. Take the example of Shelly and Tom:

> Shelly and Tom have been dating for the past two years. They are ready to go off to different colleges this fall. Shelly will be attending the large state university several hours away, while Tom is staying home to attend the local college and work part-time. Shelly feels it is time to see other people and wants to break off their relationship. She calls Tom and says she has something important to talk to him about and they set up a place and time to meet. Tom, however, believes that he will do better in school because he is in a committed and loving relationship with Shelly and knows they will be able to visit one another on the weekends, exchange daily emails, and phone calls. When Shelly called to say she had something important to discuss, Tom assumed they would discuss when they would announce their engagement to their families. Obviously, Tom has decoded the meaning of Shelly's message differently than she intended.

Channel

The **channel** is the vehicle by which the message is communicated from the source to the receiver. Familiar channels include the various types of media—television, radio, movies, newspapers, magazines, computer chat rooms, and tapes—as well as letters, reports, email, and our voices.

Sight and sound are the primary channels we use to communicate with others. We can see people's facial expressions and read the written word. The sound of our voices can travel thousands of miles by telephone, can be recorded on tape, or can be broadcast via radio or television. Another one of our senses, touch, also can act as the channel. We might place our hand on a friend's shoulder to communicate our concern for the loss of a loved one. At such times the use of touch can communicate much more than words.

Feedback

Another important component in the communication process is feedback. **Feedback** is the receiver's response to the sender's message; it provides information about the way the message is being interpreted. For example:

> Tameka is working with several of her colleagues on a new procedure to order office supplies. There have been several instances of over-ordering and it has cost the company thousands of dollars. Tameka and her team have been asked to determine the best way to control office supply ordering. After many weeks of discussion, each team member presents his or her idea to the group. The group discusses each idea and then decides on the best procedure to recommend to their supervisor.

The group's discussion of each idea is an example of feedback.

Often we are unaware of the feedback we send to others. For instance, Candi may tell Jorge that she is interested in hearing about his trip to Cincinnati, but she may be nonverbally communicating her boredom by glancing at the clock or stifling a yawn. In this example, the verbal feedback and the nonverbal feedback differ; Candi's verbal expression of interest is not supported by her nonverbal yawn. At other times, what we say is supported by our nonverbal response. For example, Glen might tell Kevin that he understands Kevin's instructions, and he reinforces this verbal feedback by nodding his head.

As senders we sometimes have difficulty interpreting the feedback we get from a receiver. For instance, we might interpret the feedback from an audience as being negative, when in reality it is positive. Consider the following:

> Cathy is a student who likes to sit in the front row. She feels this helps her stay involved in the class. She never misses class and also enjoys listening to speeches; however, because she finds direct eye contact difficult, she looks down at her class notes frequently. When Sean gives his speech, he may misinterpret her behavior as a negative response to his message.

Cathy's behavior toward the speaker is motivated by her own discomfort, not by her disapproval of the presentation. Now consider another student:

> James sits in the front row for a different reason. He hopes to make a positive impression on both his instructor and his peers. He consistently gives Sean nonverbal approval by nodding his head after the presentation of each idea. Occasionally as he nods, he is daydreaming about the upcoming weekend. So, even though James is providing Sean with positive feedback, he is not really listening.

Listening is covered in Chapter 3.

The preceding examples illustrate the difficulty we can face when attempting to interpret the feedback given by receivers. Because we use feedback to alter our subsequent messages, problems can arise when our interpretations are incorrect. Remember, we are using our frame of reference to encode a message, and the receiver is using his or her different frame of reference to decode the message. If, for example, the speaker interprets Cathy's lack of eye contact as disapproval of his or her presentation, then his or her future interactions with Cathy might be less than friendly. The importance of interpreting messages accurately is stressed throughout this book.

Context

The conditions surrounding communication with others are referred to as the **context** of the interaction. What types of conditions are there? The **physical setting** in which the communication occurs can have a substantial impact on communication. Consider the difference between discussing a business proposal with a few clients over lunch at a posh restaurant and discussing the same proposal with the same clients in your firm's conference room. The location influences the degree of formality in the interaction. Such factors as seating arrangements, time of day, degree of privacy, room size, temperature, and lighting affect how people communicate with each other.

A second aspect of context is the **psychological climate** of the interaction. This refers to the attitudes and feelings we have about ourselves and the other people involved in the communication. These feelings can affect how we respond to others. For example:

> Sherry is an English major and has a difficult time in Professor Anderson's course. Sherry's assignments in Professor Anderson's course have caused her considerable anxiety because she perceives Professor Anderson's comments about her writing to be overly critical. Sherry brings these negative feelings about Professor Anderson to every class meeting; as a result, the psychological climate of each class session is tense.

A positive psychological climate, on the other hand, can contribute immensely to the interaction between people. Consider the following:

> Beth, a student in the basic speech class, is terrified of public speaking. Because her instructor offers encouragement to all the students, Beth gradually feels a genuine warmth develop within the class. After several weeks Beth gains confidence and actually looks forward to coming to class. She notices changes in her classmates as well. As the semester progresses, Beth's speeches, as well as those of her classmates, show significant improvement.

Chapter 7 includes a more detailed discussion of communication climates, both supportive and defensive.

Noise and Interference

Noise, any intended or unintended stimulus that affects the fidelity of a sender's message, disrupts the communication process. Noise is often thought of as **interference** to the communication process. Noise can be external or internal, and it can influence our ability to process information. **External noise** includes sounds or visual stimuli that draw our attention away from the intended message. Imagine how difficult it would be to deliver a speech with construction workers drilling outside the classroom; it would be equally difficult for the audience to concentrate on the speaker's message. Similarly, a strange man who walks into the room can distract the audience, especially if he calls attention to himself.

Internal noise includes our own thoughts or feelings that prevent us from processing a sender's message—such thoughts as our plans for the upcoming weekend, bills that need to be paid and mailed, the fact that we have not had anything to eat since we woke up this morning, the fact that we really dislike the campus newspaper, and so on. When we find ourselves concentrating on such stimuli instead of devoting our full attention to the sender's message, we say that noise is interfering with the communication process. In Chapter 3 we will tackle the subject of listening interference in greater detail.

The Communication Process   SKILL BUILDING

1. Try to explain your last difficult encounter with someone by using the following terms:

a. Source	e. Channel	i. Decoding
b. Frame of Reference	f. Feedback	j. Noise
c. Receiver	g. Context	k. Feedback
d. Message	h. Encoding	

2. How do the source and receiver's different approaches to communication affect the outcome of the interaction?

Functions of Communication

Why do we communicate? By nature, we are social beings who need others to survive and thrive in our society. Communication allows us to form societies, create our identities, and accomplish a variety of tasks. Most importantly, we use communication to bridge the gap between people and to form common ground. Communication functions in five specific ways.

Ethics in Communication

Different Approaches

In the beginning of the chapter, we learned about four students in a communication course. Sue, Jose, Alicia, and Cory have been in class together for two weeks, and their first assignment is due tonight. Each has taken a different approach to the assignment and to how each communicates about the assignment with the instructor.

Sue has been taking care of her daughter this week. Her daughter had an ear infection, and Sue spent hours in the doctor's office and then standing in line at the pharmacy. Her daughter has not slept through the night for several days, and Sue is exhausted. She did not have time to complete her journal assignment. Sue decides the best thing to do is to call her instructor before class and let her know that she can't turn in her assignment. She hopes the instructor will grant her a two-day extension, but she knows that the course policy states that no late assignments will be accepted. Although the instructor may not grant the extension, Sue is choosing to openly and honestly communicate with her instructor.

Jose has been working overtime, but he completed his journal assignment. He was somewhat confused by the assignment, so Jose emailed the instructor, as the syllabus suggested he do. He felt uncomfortable calling her and felt an email would be more appropriate. Jose's instructor did not acknowledge the email with a reply after three days, so Jose finished the assignment, but is not sure if he did it correctly. Like Sue, Jose chose to openly and honestly communicate with his instructor. The instructor, on the other hand, by intentionally not replying to the email, is acting unethically.

Alicia is concerned about her first assignment. As a matter of fact, she has revised it twice and is still not sure if she has done it correctly. Alicia has created a "time management" study schedule so that she can have enough time to work and study. She thought about stopping by the instructor's office hours to clarify the assignment, but decides to "just finish it" and hope it is done correctly. Had Alicia gone to her instructor with her questions, she might not feel as uneasy about her assignment. The instructor has no way of knowing that Alicia needed help because Alicia never communicated her feelings.

Finally, Cory has taken a very different approach to the assignment. Feeling forced into taking college classes, Cory is not motivated to complete the assignment. He believes that the assignment requires too much work, and he would rather be doing anything else but studying. Cory chooses not to talk to his instructor about the assignment and simply does not turn it in. Perhaps Cory's instructor could have recommended a career counselor or a family counselor if she had known about Cory's situation. Choosing not to communicate only makes the situation worse for Cory, as he will probably fail the class if he continues in this way.

When we communicate, we have many choices to make. Who we talk to and what we talk about are two important considera-

tions. Sometimes the choices are easy, and other times we must overcome our uneasiness or fear and share our feelings and thoughts. Sometimes it is better not to share information. If we intentionally do not communicate when we know we should (in the case of the instructor and email), we may be acting unethically. Each of us communicates differently, and each communication situation involves a question of ethics.

1. *Communication creates and maintains our sense of self or our identity.* From the moment we were born, we were engaged in the communication process. Our parents talked to us, read books to us, and played games with us. It is through communication that we learned our name and gender; we learned about love, frustration, and fear; and we learned how to be part of a family. Specifically, communicating with others helped us to create who we are. For example, what does it mean to be a girl in our society? Well, that all depends on who you ask. In some families, it means to take care of all the household chores like cooking, cleaning, and laundry. Although social expectations are changing and some families share all the household responsibilities, in many homes, gender stereotypes dictate who does what. What else does it mean to be a girl? One study shows that even at birth, gender expectations shape who we become. Baby congratulations cards for girls are pink, show bunnies or birds, and portray the baby as sleeping or immobile. Boy cards are primarily blue, show cars and sports equipment, and portray the baby as active in play (Willer, 2001). These stereotypes are subtle and we may hardly notice them, but they play a role in what is expected of us and how we create our identity.

2. *Communication helps us create communities.* Of course, we all live in a community of some kind just by virtue of living in a house, apartment, or dorm. But communities are more than geographic locations. Communities are also created by shared meanings for symbols. These shared meanings bind people together in support or work networks. So, someone who lives hundreds or thousands of miles from you could be part of your social community because you both share a similar language or symbol system. For example, people who talk in computer chat rooms share meanings for special symbols, and if you don't know what the symbols mean, you can't communicate. Do you know what LOL means? Laughing out loud. How about BBN? Bye Bye for Now. These are examples of how shared meanings allow us to communicate and thus create communities.

Communication allows us to form and strengthen our relationships at home, school, and work.

3. *Communication forms and strengthens relationships.* Through communication, we form human bonds that, in turn, form our friendships, families, and work relationships. We fall in love using communication. We solve problems at work by communicating with our co-workers, and we create lasting friendships by sharing stories, experiencing new things, and being supportive of one another. It is through communication that we share our emotions and feelings.

4. *Part of being in a relationship is the ability to influence the other person.* Communication is how we do this. Communication allows us to sell products, campaign for an issue or candidate, debate a topic in class, or get the television remote from our significant other. Persuasion is an integral part of our lives because we are not only the sources of persuasive communication, but are also the receivers of over 5,000 persuasive messages per day (Larson, 2000).

5. *Communication conveys and creates information.* How many times a day do you check the Internet for some form of information like the weather report, sports score, or late-breaking news? Communication allows us to find information that will help us fulfill our needs. For example:

> Alex was planning her vacation to Michigan. Alex's family will be spending a week at a cottage on Lake Michigan, and Alex wants to know several things before they go. What is the weather forecast (do I need a jacket, jeans, umbrella)? What is the fastest route to the cottage (should we take the toll road or the expressway)? What kind of restaurants are nearby (fast food or more formal)? What kind of shopping is available

(grocery, clothing, sports)? These are all questions Alex needs answered before she packs her suitcase and leaves for her vacation.

Communication also helps us create information and knowledge. Have you ever worked in a group and found that you were coming up with new ideas and concepts as your discussion progressed? Through communication, we create information and knowledge. We learn from one another and use that information to develop new ideas and concepts.

Functions of Communication   CHECKLIST

Communication

- creates and maintains our identity.
- helps us create communities.
- forms and strengthens relationships.
- allows us to influence and persuade others.
- conveys and creates information.

Types of Communication

Intrapersonal

Communication takes place when we interact with one other person, when we interact with a small group, and when we speak to an audience. A special type of communication, intrapersonal communication, is an integral part of any communication event. **Intrapersonal communication** is communication with ourselves; it is an ongoing process that includes such activities as evaluating ourselves and our relationships with others, planning for the future, and doing some internal problem solving. We engage in intrapersonal communication all the time—as we get ready for work or school, during our three-mile jog, as we prepare dinner for ourselves, and before our presentation at a business meeting. The following sections discuss two other types of communication: interpersonal communication and public communication.

Interpersonal

Interpersonal communication is the informal exchange that occurs between two or more people. It usually occurs on two levels: dyads (groups of two) and small groups.

Dyadic communication is the interaction between two people. It can focus on safe topics, such as our day at the office, or on highly sensitive issues, such as our love for a particular person. Dyadic communication tends to be informal, and therefore requires little or no preplanning. Interviews are the exception; they are generally formal in nature. (Chapter 8 is devoted to this topic.) Through dyadic communication we can learn a great deal about ourselves and our relationships with others.

Small Group

Small-group communication includes those interactions with three to eight people present. In most instances, small-group communication is less intimate than dyadic communication and less formal than public speaking. Small-group communication can occur as an informal discussion of such social issues as gun violence or shelters for runaway adolescents or serve as a vehicle for problem solving in organizations. Small group communication is discussed in more detail in Chapters 9 and 10.

Public

Public communication involves having an individual share information with a large group; the usual structure has a speaker presenting ideas

Hillary Rodham Clinton (D-NY) engages in public communication daily.

to an audience. Public communication is more formal than interpersonal communication; it therefore requires more preparation on the sender's part. Usually, speakers have a limited amount of time in which to share their ideas; this forces them to plan and organize what they want to say in advance. Chapters 11 to 16 treat the area of public communication in depth, addressing such subjects as topic selection, researching, organizing, and delivering a public speech.

Understanding Difference, Diversity, and Communication

For many people, the primary goal of a communication course is to broaden their understanding of the communication process and to become better at something they have been doing since birth: communicating with others. If we reflect for a moment about our communication with others, we realize that some encounters are easier for us than others. For instance, we might feel relaxed talking with a close friend or spouse, but we are self-conscious and nervous when we are introduced to someone new, especially someone who is different from us in some way. This anxiety is familiar to all of us—who among us has not been in a situation in which we have felt uncomfortable and wished that we could be more at ease?

The intent of this book is to help you become a confident, effective communicator by teaching you about the complex nature of communication and by presenting a variety of skills that can help you improve your communication. The application of these skills in both your interpersonal and public communication encounters can transform you into a competent communicator.

Humans approach communication and communication situations from diverse and unique positions. The differences we have should be understood and celebrated because they lead to greater understanding and thus more effective communication. As we learned earlier in the chapter, our frame of reference is made up of many different variables, including our age, gender, ethnicity, race, religion, family roles, work experience, geographic location, sexual orientation, learning style, and socioeconomic status. Our frame of reference is unique and thus makes us different from others. We may look different, sound different, and think and feel differently. The variables that create our frame of reference affect the communication process. For example, when we see someone who looks or sounds different from us, we may become defensive and close ourselves off from any interaction with this person. But if we instead value the differences and strive to understand this person, then we can have a greater understanding and more effective communication. Specifically:

During the first week, students in a communication class are placed in study groups by their instructor. Noelle, an 18-year-old freshman who is

COMMUNICATION and TECHNOLOGY

Changing the Way We Communicate

Technology has changed the way we communicate with one another. An explosion of technological advances has made communication cheap, easy, and immediate. Cell phones and computers have become an integral part of our daily lives. These statistics tell the story:

- 109.5 million people had cell phones in 2000 (Skertic, 2001, E2).
- 259 billion minutes were used on cell phones in 2000 (Skertic, 2001, E2).
- According to the U.S. census, two thirds of households with school-aged children have a computer (U.S. Census).
- 94 million people used the Internet at home in 2000 (U.S. Census).
- One in three adults has used email, and one in four has used the Internet to search for information (U.S. Census).
- According to Juniper Communications, the average online user received more than 2,100 emails in 2000 (Davich, 2001, C1).

The advent of these technological advances has made communicating easier, but it has also created new communication obstacles. Two major problems with cell phones are "cell yell" and "stage-phoning," according to Eric Taub. Cell yell is "a tendency of many cell phone users to speak into their phones more loudly than necessary, unwittingly involving surrounding strangers in their personal business" (Taub, 2001, 4:3). When we are standing in line at the grocery store, for example, we get to hear about a stranger's love life or his or her medical results because he or she is screaming into the cell phone.

Another problem is stage-phoning, which Taub defines as "making unimportant calls in public just to impress others" (2001, 4:3). This may also include wearing the cell phone so everyone can see the phone or placing the phone on the table in a restaurant. Sadie Plant, a researcher for Motorola, argues that when men and women dine together, men are more likely to place their phones on the table while women will leave their phones in their purse (Taub, 2001, 4:3).

The Internet and email create another set of problems for communicators. Email lends itself to "bad manners." Using all capital letters, indicating that the sender is yelling, or not using emoticons or smileys (see Chapter 4) to indicate the tone of the message are two popular mistakes made by emailers. Also, we are more likely to send a message with negative comments than we are to actually say them to the person's face (see Chapter 7). Lastly, most of us think of email as being a form of private communication. Not so, according to a 2000 study by the American Management Association. "Nearly three fourths of the country's largest corporations eavesdrop on their employee's e-mail use," and "twenty eight percent have dismissed people for misusing office equipment" (Davich, 2001, C2).

We can enhance our relationships and overall communication with the use of technology. We just need to be careful about how and when we decide to make a cell phone call or send an email.

DILBERT © UFS. Reprinted by Permission.

African-American is grouped with Mo (short for Mohamed), also 18 years old and a freshman; Katie, who is 25, a senior, white, and a working single mother; and Cathy, who is 45, a junior, white, and a returning student who works full time. Noelle thinks to herself, "How am I going to be able to work and study with this group? I don't have anything in common with them." When the group begins to work together, Noelle discovers that she and Katie live in the same town, that Mo knows Cathy's youngest son, and that they all are nervous about doing presentations in front of the class.

At first Noelle saw only the differences between herself and her group members. But after taking the time to get to know them, Noelle found they all had much in common.

The first part of this chapter discussed the nature and components of the communication process. Building on this foundation, future chapters will explore the numerous aspects of both interpersonal and public communication, including our perceptions of ourselves and others, listening, nonverbal communication, improving the communication climate, selecting speech topics, analyzing the audience, and organizing speeches.

Each chapter presents an explanation of the topic and then suggests specific skills that can be used to improve your effectiveness as a communicator. An increased understanding of the communication process may help you to see the role you (and others) play in that process. For example, after reading Chapter 7 on improving the communication climate, you will be better acquainted with the subject of supportive climates; as a result, you will be better able to see how you can play an active role in creating this type of climate. At the same time, you will be able to recognize when you and others act defensively.

In each chapter both the discussion of the topic and the suggested skills will help you to become an active participant in the communication process. Your involvement in a particular activity (Skill Building, Critical Thinking, or Self-Assessment), whether it is gathering evidence for a persuasive speech or observing the nonverbal behavior of an interviewer, has a positive effect as it forces you to practice what you have learned. We hope this text will help you to enhance your ability to interpret, adjust, and respond to others in a variety of communication situations with people who are just like you and, more importantly, with people who are different from you.

Summary

Communication is the interdependent process of sending, receiving, and understanding messages. Although it is an ongoing, dynamic process that changes from one communication setting to the next, there are certain components that are always present: people, a message, encoding, decoding, the channel, feedback, the context, and noise.

Communication functions in several ways. It can create our sense of self, form relationships and communities, be used to persuade, and convey and create information.

Communication can take place when we interact with one other person, when we interact with a small group, and when we speak to an audience. In all these situations, intrapersonal communication (communication with ourselves) can be expected. Interpersonal communication is the informal exchange that occurs between two or more people; the interaction

between two people is called dyadic communication, whereas an interaction involving three to eight people is called small-group communication. A final type of communication, public communication, involves having an individual share information with a large group.

The last section of this introductory chapter included a discussion of difference and diversity and their relationship to communication. First encounters with new people and public speaking are two common causes of anxiety, yet there are ways for us to become better, more effective communicators. Most importantly, we must celebrate and appreciate the different approaches to communication we all have as a means of improving our communication effectiveness. Throughout this book specific techniques for improving our communication will accompany the discussions of each communication topic.

Review Questions

1. Define communication.
2. Explain the difference between encoding and decoding.
3. How can people use nonverbal communication to give a sender feedback?
4. Differentiate between external and internal noise.
5. How does communication create our sense of self?
6. Describe the different types of communication.

2

Perception

At the conclusion of this chapter, you should be able to:

- Describe the three steps involved in processing information.
- Explain self-concept and self-esteem.
- Explain how feedback from others helps shape our self-concept.
- Discuss the factors that influence our perception of others.

- Describe two forms of stereotyping: "allness" and "halo and horns."
- Explain the importance of developing accurate perceptions of ourselves and others.

The Border Tool and Dye Company employs fifty people. It is a small company, and everyone seems to work well together. A vice president's position has opened up, and the company's four managers are being considered for the promotion. The four managers include:

Tony, who is in his mid-thirties, has worked for the company since high school. Although he has been promoted several times in the past few years, this year he did not receive a merit raise. He comes from a traditional family and attends church regularly with his wife and five children. Amy, Tony's wife, stays home to take care of their children.

Connie, who is single and in her early forties, has lived with her partner for the past three years. They adopted a child last year and share all the parenting responsibilities. Connie earned her college degree several years ago after attending classes at night. She was promoted to manager after receiving her degree in management.

Anita, who is a recent immigrant from the Middle East, is in her late twenties. She has a college degree in manufacturing and has only worked at the company for a few months. In her short time in this country, she has had difficulty adjusting to the different communication styles of her co-workers and to the culture overall. She lives alone in a studio apartment and works more hours than any of the other managers.

Tom, who is over fifty years old, has been a manager the longest. He earned his degree in communication almost thirty years ago and was hired as a manager when the company opened ten years ago. He is divorced from his wife, but sees his two daughters every weekend.

Each of these people has his or her own view of himself or herself and of the other managers. These views, or perceptions, affect the way in which each communicates. How do you think each of these managers views himself or herself? How do you think each views the others? In this chapter, we will discuss how our differences affect our perceptions of others and self and, ultimately, how these perceptions effect our interpersonal communication and public communication.

As we learned in Chapter 1, people are very different. Look at the people described in the beginning of this chapter. They are certainly different in many ways. Our past experiences, age, gender, societal roles, and many other characteristics make each of us unique. These differences need to be understood and accepted in order for us to become more effective communicators. One important result of our differences is the unique way each of us views the world around us. This is called perception. **Perception** is the process of assigning meaning to stimuli. The way we select stimuli from the environment, organize them, and eventually interpret their meaning play an important role in the way we communicate in relationships and in public-speaking situations. In this chapter we shall learn more about the process of perception, how we perceive ourselves, and how we perceive others. Finally, we shall look at some strategies for developing accurate perceptions about ourselves and others.

The Process of Perception

None of us perceives the world objectively. Our perception of each new situation is tempered by our preconceived ideas, our current physiological and psychological states, our interest or attention, and our goals. This is called our frame of reference (see Chapter 1). Essentially, all our perceptions are subjective and unique. Understanding that each of us operates from such a base is the first step in making our communication more effective. Let's discuss the way we select, organize, and interpret the stimuli in our environment—that is, the process of perception.

Selective Attention

We are constantly bombarded by stimuli. Since we cannot respond to all the information we are exposed to, we are forced to exercise a degree of selectivity. The process of determining what we pay attention to and what we ignore is called **selective attention.** Of the dozens of shows broadcast on television at any given hour, we are likely to respond to only a few; this is an example of selective attention. Specifically, think about how you watch TV. Do you "flip" through the channels looking for something interesting to watch? What determines what channels you watch and what

Selective attention is the process of determining what we pay attention to and what we ignore.

channels you ignore? How we select stimuli from our environment is a uniquely personal phenomenon that depends on our interests and needs.

One important factor in selecting stimuli is our level of interest in it. We are often drawn to topics that directly affect us. For instance, we would probably pay particular attention to student gossip regarding a tuition increase because such a change would have an immediate impact on us. Similarly, the more intriguing we find a topic, the more likely we will be motivated to select it and focus our attention on it. For instance, if Erin is very interested in political communication, she is likely to stop on channels such as CSPAN, CNBC, or CNN. The content of these channels stimulates Erin's interest enough to make her want to listen to the shows' ideas. On the other hand, if Charles has very little interest in government or politics, it will take more than the political content of the shows to keep him involved. Other factors, such as Charles's desire to see how his stocks are doing or to get the latest score for the Chicago Cubs baseball game, might encourage him to pay attention to those channels.

Needs, physical or emotional desires that grow out of circumstances in our immediate environment, also motivate us to select and assign meaning to certain stimuli, as reflected in the preceding example of Charles. Consider this example as well: If our secondhand car completely "dies," we suddenly find ourselves paying particular attention to television advertisements for good "buys." Our need for reliable transportation motivates us to look for a new vehicle.

Needs are triggered by all sorts of circumstances—hunger, security, longing to be part of a group, desire for recognition, self-fulfillment. Abraham Maslow's hierarchy of needs, discussed more thoroughly in Chapter 11, can be used as a framework for understanding needs shared by all of us. We are especially sensitive to those stimuli in our environment that we perceive as having the potential to satisfy our needs. For example, until we purchase another used car, we will continue to read the ads in the local newspaper. After the purchase, however, we no longer have either the need or interest to scan the classified section of the paper (assuming, of course, that the car we bought is satisfactory).

Selective Attention

SELF-ASSESSMENT

Pay close attention to what you attend to for 24 hours. Keep a log.

1. What television channels do you watch the most? Describe the kinds of shows that you seek out.

2. When you read a newspaper, what section of the paper do you read first? Second? Third?

3. What radio stations do you listen to? Describe the content.

4. Why do you think you pay attention to these things? How do these reflect your frame of reference?

Organization

Before we can begin to interpret the stimuli we have selected from our environment, we must be able to place them in a structure that allows us to make sense of them. **Organization** is simply another phase of the perception process; in other words, we perceive that certain items belong together, and we therefore tend to organize them that way. Consider the organization found in any grocery store. We expect that all types of cereal will be stocked in the same aisle, and nearly without exception, they are. How frustrated we would be if this were not the case; we would need to wander from aisle to aisle in search of our favorite kind. Similarly, stimuli can be organized into patterns that make sense. Three elements of organization aid this process: similarity, proximity, and closure.

Similarity

Stimuli that resemble one another are commonly grouped together. Their **similarity** dictates that they be treated in this way. The preceding description of a grocery store's organization demonstrates the idea of similarity. So too does the organization of a library's book collection. Specifically, cook-

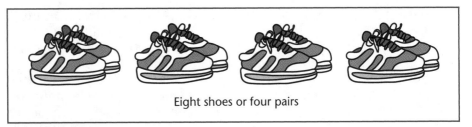

Eight shoes or four pairs

FIGURE 2.1   **Example of Proximity**

books are shelved in one section, biographies in another, photography books in another, and so on. The arrangement is by subject; therefore, books about similar topics are likely to be catalogued and shelved in the same area.

Proximity

Stimuli also can be organized according to their proximity, or closeness to one another (Figure 2.1). When we group two events together because of the closeness of their occurrence, we are applying the principle of proximity. For example, we can probably recall someone talking about the significance of a particular event because it happened "right after my grandfather died" or "the night my daughter was born." We also might recall when a newspaper account of an automobile accident caught our attention because the accident happened next to the high school we attended. Such associations help to organize the stimuli we have selected from our environment.

Closure

Finally, the element of **closure** contributes to the way we organize stimuli. That is, when we are familiar with an idea or topic, we tend to "fill in the gaps" when pieces are missing. In formulating an opinion about someone, for example, we sometimes make assumptions based on our observations. For instance, if we see an elegantly dressed woman step out of a shiny Mercedes, we assume that this person is wealthy. Closure also affects how we listen to a speaker. Sometimes we inadvertently fill in a speaker's words before he or she actually articulates them; we are so familiar with a phrase that we know what the speaker will say even though he or she has not completed the thought. For instance, many of us could complete a reference to Patrick Henry's famous words, "Give me liberty . . . ."

A number of potential problems can develop as we attempt to organize information as described so far. For example, referring to people's similarities can lead to stereotyping, a concept discussed at length later in this chapter. With closure, our inclination to "fill in the gaps" or "fill in the missing words" might actually cause us to make false assumptions about a person or that person's message. For example:

> Chantel's father has always been a strong supporter of liberal candidates and causes. She has heard him go on and on about the need for increased funding for public schools or about how to save the environment. Recently at dinner, Chantel's father began to talk about President Bush and his policies. Chantel, thinking that she knew exactly what her father was going to say, tuned him out and thought about the meeting she had that day with a potential client. On the contrary, Chantel's father was arguing for the Bush tax cut and how it might help stimulate the economy.

Chantel used closure to fill in the gaps of her father's message and assumed she knew what he was going to say. Thus, Chantel missed the meaning of her father's message.

Finally, because individuals perceive things differently, the way they organize information is likely to be widely varied too. The uniqueness of our perception can result in a breakdown in communication/understanding between people. This phenomenon is discussed more thoroughly in the next subsection.

Interpretation

It is during the interpretation phase of the perception process that we communicate our perceptions to others. As we discussed in Chapter 1, during the encoding and decoding process, we use our frame of reference to make sense of the stimuli. Several factors affect how we interpret what we have perceived: our past experiences, our attitudes, personal constructs and prototypes, and attribution.

Our past experiences play a fundamental role in the way we **interpret** information, especially since it can determine how we look at both the present and the future. Joan, hearing the meteorologist announce that a snowstorm is beginning to hit the city, decides to phone the babysitter to let her know that both Joan and her husband will probably reach home later than usual because of slow traffic. Joan's past experience driving in snow enables her to anticipate these conditions.

Unlike the positive effect of Joan's past experience in the preceding example, clinging to the past can create problems for an individual who cannot seem to let go of a negative experience. Consider this example:

> Keisha, a skilled and competent civil engineer, is scheduled to have an interview with a new engineering firm. She is quite nervous, in part because it has been four years since her last employment interviewing experience. She landed her present job after earning her engineering degree, but she still recalls one miserable interview in which she fumbled her responses and did not get the job she wanted most. Although she comes to this interview with four years of experience, she cannot seem to

shake her fear of repeating her previous performance. These thoughts prevent her from interpreting the present interview more positively.

Past experience often shapes our attitude about a particular subject. Certainly Keisha's case is an example of this phenomenon. **Attitude,** a predetermined position regarding a person, event, concept, or object, affects the way we interpret data. For instance, our attitude toward a speaker can determine the way we respond to that person's speech. If we like the speaker's voice or admire his or her confidence, we may interpret the presentation as more powerful. Likewise, our attitude toward the speaker's topic may play a significant role in the way we assess its treatment. Someone who works for Greenpeace, for instance, is likely to be critical of a speech that praises the oil industry, even if the speech is well organized and well presented.

Our attitude concerning a stimulus can change with time. This transformation occurs when we reinterpret the meaning of information because of changed circumstances. Consider the following example:

Alison has just graduated from high school and is really looking forward to attending the local university. In high school, Alison was a cross country and track star. She lettered in both sports and was a finalist at the state cross country tournament. Alison never really socialized with the "theater" people and thought they were strange because of the way they dressed and talked. Upon entering her communication class on the first day, Alison sees several people who look like the theater people she knew in high school. She decides to avoid them and sit next to students who look more like her. As the class progress and Alison is forced to interact with all the students in her class, she realizes that the theater people are really creative, intelligent, and fun. She is thrilled when she gets a chance to work with Dennis and Cynthia, two students involved in the arts program on campus, on their group project for class.

Altered circumstances forced Alison to reinterpret her thoughts and attitudes about her fellow students.

Connected to personal experiences and attitudes, personal constructs and prototypes guide our interpretation of people. **Personal constructs** are the characteristics we use to judge others. We form our interpretation of them and their behavior by assessing specific qualities such as appearance, intelligence, or friendliness on a continuum from positive to negative. For example, we might see someone as fitting somewhere between pretty and ugly or smart and dumb or warm and cold. **Prototypes** are representatives of our ideal. We use this ideal as a means of comparison. We have an image of the "perfect" boss or the best basketball player. When we interpret someone or someone's behavior, we judge them against our ideal image. This comparison helps us to make judgments about people.

Attribution can also play a significant role in our interpretation of behavior. **Attribution** involves assigning causation to our behavior and the behavior of others. We use our frame of reference to interpret human action. How we perceive the cause for an action will affect our overall perception of self or other. Specifically, if an important task at work is not completed, we can blame a specific person by interpreting the incomplete work as a sign of laziness. Or, we may blame the incomplete work on the poor computer software program. These are examples of external attribution (outside forces or influences such as computer software, the weather, and poor management) and internal attribution (inside forces or influences such as personal characteristics, including laziness, meanness, and incompetence). **Self-serving bias** is a form of attribution. Self-serving bias occurs when we see ourselves in a positive light by blaming others or external forces for problems. But, when the same problem happens to others, we perceive the reason for the problem as internal, or some type of personal flaw. For example:

> Sue and Lynda work in the same office as assistants to the Director of Personnel. Andrew, the Director of Personnel, asked Sue to book his air travel to the national meeting last month. Sue booked the wrong flight, which resulted in a three-hour layover for Andrew and several others in their department. Lynda told her husband, "Sue is just so sloppy and careless. She just didn't pay attention to the flights she booked." Last week, Andrew asked Lynda to book his flight for another trip. She also booked the wrong flight with a long layover. This time, however, Lynda said to her husband, "Andrew did not give me all the information I needed to book the trip. If he had been specific about his meeting schedule, I would have booked the correct flight."

Lynda's perception of Sue's behavior and her own is an example of self-serving bias. While she blames Sue's mistake on some flaw in Sue's work habits, Lynda blames Andrew for her mistake.

Perceptions of Ourselves

Our discussion so far has focused on the process of perception. We have learned that perception is highly selective and that it affects the way we organize and interpret the stimuli in our environment. How does this process of perception relate to the way we see ourselves?

TABLE 2.1	The Process of Perception
Selective attention	Determining what we pay attention to and what we ignore
Organization	Categorizing stimuli into patterns
Interpretation	Making sense of the stimuli with the use of our frame of reference

Self-Concept

Central to the way we perceive the world is the way we see ourselves. Our perception of ourselves dictates the way we send and receive messages. **Self-concept** is our perception of ourselves, or how we picture ourselves in a very broad sense. In other words, how you would "define" your self. For example, Andrea might define herself this way: "I am a daughter, partner, friend, student in business management, president of my church council, and avid runner." All the roles Andrea plays help to define who she is and help her to understand her self-concept. Self-concept is a complex phenomenon that has significant implications for communication. Its key role in the communication process can be attributed to the fact that much of the way we interact with others stems from our self-concept. Perhaps an example will clarify this point:

> As an attorney, Victor considers himself to be a specialist in the area of wills and estates. His self-confidence is reflected in his communication with those clients who seek his professional help in such matters. He is forceful, knowledgeable, and dynamic. However, when Victor agrees to handle a divorce settlement for his neighbor, his communication with his client is less effective. He speaks softly and often uses "tag" questions such as "That's right, isn't it?" This can be attributed to his decreased feeling of confidence in the area of divorce law.

The way in which we send and receive messages, then, is affected by our own beliefs about ourselves. Since we all have different experiences, knowledge, and attitudes, we possess different strengths and weaknesses that provide the basis for our unique self-concept. Our self-concept is also situational; that is, there are certain situations in which we feel comfortable with the role that we play, while other situations present a greater challenge for us. The preceding example of Victor is a case in point. Here is another: Dan, one of the authors, feels comfortable teaching a basic communication class, but finds it threatening to take his car into the garage for service. This is a result of his level of competence in one area and lack of confidence in another.

Self-Esteem

Self-esteem is our measure of self-worth; as such, it is the evaluative dimension of our self-concept. For example:

> Deena's grandmother was a nurse, and Deena believes that nursing is a noble profession. So, when Deena decided to go back to college, she chose nursing as her major. Deena feels great about her decision to attend college part-time while working and about choosing nursing as a career. Deena's positive feelings about herself help to elevate her self-concept.

By permission of Tony Cochran and Creators Syndicate.

While not actually a part of our self-concept or self-esteem, the feedback we receive from others significantly affects how we see and feel about ourselves. Moreover, it is the way we perceive that feedback that will have the greatest impact on our self-concept and self-esteem. For instance, if we receive large doses of positive feedback from our family, we are likely to perceive ourselves in a positive light. This, in turn, affects the way we present ourselves to others.

Because we all have different strengths and weaknesses, it is important not to judge others according to our own positive and negative points. Two factors that affect our self-concept are the self-fulfilling prophecy and significant others. Both are discussed in the following section.

SELF-ASSESSMENT

Understanding Your Self-Concept

Describe your self-concept using the following categories:

- your role within your family
- your career goals
- your relationships with your school peers
- your ethnicity, gender, and age
- your physical traits
- your personality traits.

Now, evaluate your self-concept in each of the preceding categories. In other words, how do you feel about your self (self-esteem) concerning each of the categories?

Self-Fulfilling Prophecy

In a **self-fulfilling prophecy,** our behavior matches someone else's expectations. For example, when an individual perceives us to be a certain way, he or she begins to treat us according to that preconceived notion, and eventually we act out or fulfill the way we are being perceived. The following example demonstrates how the self-fulfilling prophecy operates:

> John comes from a highly critical home environment. His parents have difficulty expressing positive feelings toward him, which reinforces his feelings of inadequacy. Moreover, they constantly push him to take on new challenges. The same theme is reinforced on the job; John's boss frequently gives him challenging assignments, but in the same breath communicates his doubts about John's ability to complete the tasks.
>
> As John begins to internalize the image that others have of him, his confidence diminishes. Inevitably, his behavior reflects that loss of self-esteem. He stops sharing his ideas with others and reevaluates his goals for the future. His communication becomes guarded; he avoids interaction with others.

Although usually thought of in negative terms, the self-fulfilling prophecy also can have a positive effect on our self-concept. This happens when we are exposed to positive feedback from others. Such feedback suggests that we are capable, talented, and admired. If this feedback is reinforced over a period of time, we naturally begin to believe it.

Significant Others

The development of our self-concept is also influenced by **significant others,** those individuals to whom we are emotionally close and whom we allow to influence our lives. We often feel that it is necessary to gain acceptance from these people because we think their approval will enhance our self-concept. At times we place greater importance on the opinions and advice of our significant others than we do on our own:

> During high school, Martie envisioned herself becoming a great chef. She even gathered information about various cooking schools, both in the United States and abroad. However, instead of filling out applications for these schools, Martie mailed applications to several liberal arts colleges and universities. The reason? Martie's father wanted her to become a medical doctor, and Martie eventually decided not to disappoint her dad.

CRITICAL THINKING   Self-Fulfilling Prophecy

Kathy is the supervisor of the Accounting Department of Midwest Electronics' Minneapolis Division. Avery has just been transferred to her unit. In reviewing Avery's personnel file, Kathy discovers that Avery has a history of difficulty in communicating with his supervisors. Although prior supervisors commented favorably about his capabilities as a CPA, they also noted his inability to take directions. Other members of the company also have discussed Avery's reputation with Kathy. She is nervous about supervising Avery because she anticipates having a difficult time.

1. How might the self-fulfilling prophecy operate in future interactions between Kathy and Avery?
2. Has the self-fulfilling prophecy ever operated in any of your relationships? Describe how it affected your communication within the relationship.

Reflective Appraisal

The overall image of ourselves is based on our view of how we believe other's see us. This image is called a **reflective appraisal** (Sullivan, 1953). Reflective appraisals are also called the "looking glass self" because we see ourselves through other people's eyes (Cooley, 1912). For example:

> Edwina always wanted to be a teacher, but was convinced she was not smart enough to finish the required course work and student teaching to receive her teaching license. During her sophomore year, Edwina was chosen to do an internship with an elementary school, helping students with learning disabilities to read. The students at Homan Elementary School loved Edwina and encouraged her to pursue her dream of being a teacher. Edwina began to see herself through her students' eyes and felt confident enough about her abilities to change her major to education.

Families and peers are two groups of significant others that have a strong effect on the development of our self-concept.

Family

During our childhood and adolescence we are in constant contact with **family** members. Consequently, parents play an overwhelming role in the development of our self-concept. The example of Martie and her father illustrates this point. As youngsters, we are dependent on our parents; this relationship is likely to change as we grow older and begin to challenge and question our parents' judgments and values.

In some cases, family influence can be devastating to our self-concept. If we grow up in a home where little warmth and love are demonstrated, we may believe that we are not lovable; if our parent's scream and shout to

Interactions with our parents greatly influence the development of our self-concept.

vent their frustrations, we may grow up thinking we are the cause of their problems.

Of course, the opposite also can occur. We may grow up in a family environment that is overprotective, one in which individuals are not given the opportunity to explore and take risks. Parents often want to protect their children from the outside world, hence their love is overly possessive. The children, in turn, may feel guilty when they do not want to return the smothering affection shown by their parents. In both these family environments the feedback received from the parents is likely to have a negative impact on the self-concepts of the children involved.

Under ideal circumstances, our families can represent a highly constructive influence on the development of our self-concept. When our home life is warm and the environment is conducive to expressing and sharing feelings, our self-concept is positive. Furthermore, when problems arise and the necessary time is taken to discuss them openly, this also can have a positive impact on our self-concept.

Peers

Peers, another group of significant others, also can profoundly influence our self-concept. Some people go out of their way to gain the acceptance of their peers in order to boost their own self-concept; however, we sometimes let our peers play a disproportionate role in our lives because we feel it is vital to be accepted as part of the group.

A by-product of peer pressure can be the exhibition of counterproductive behavior. For example, a young teenager might join a violent street

COMMUNICATION and TECHNOLOGY

Presentation of Self on the Internet

According to Sherry Turkle in her book *Life on the Screen,* when we enter cyberspace, we create virtual identities (1995). In other words, we can reconstruct our "self" or "selves" as we communicate on the World Wide Web in chat rooms, bulletin boards, through email, and on personal web pages. She says, "Many more people experience identity as a set of roles that can be mixed and matched, whose diverse demands need to be negotiated" (1995, p. 180). Thus, our email "style" is different when sending a memo to our boss than it is when we send a joke to our best friend. We have always adjusted our "self" or image to more effectively communicate. Because of the nature of technology, however, we can create or reconstruct our image and identity specifically for cyberspace. As Turkle argues, "your image is a textual description. So, the obese can be slender, the beautiful plain, the nerdy sophisticated" (1995, p. 12).

One popular way to reconstruct identity is through personal web pages. These web sites present to the world the image of yourself you want to send. So, you don't have to worry about your clothing, hair, or speaking style. In other words, "On the Internet, you can't smell my breath, catch the tremor in my voice, or realize that I'm watching the rest of the party over your shoulder" (Miller, 1995, p. 4). According to Hugh Miller, per-

sonal web pages may contain the following categories:

1. *An introduction of self.* This could include a photograph of yourself or family members (children), a background about where you live and work, and a listing of personal interests or hobbies.
2. *"This is what I think is cool."* These pages are a subset of the introduction and provide links to interesting web pages, chat rooms, music, video, or other web material.
3. *Electronic resume or curriculum vitae.* This is used as a tool to find employment. These sites could be picked up with an effective search engine and might be seen by potential employers. Also, you could send potential employers to the page as a way to communicate your skills and abilities.

Miller cautions that the personal web page can be easily fabricated. "The homepage provides a locus for the electronic self. There's more possibility for misrepresentation than in email because web pages are carefully set up before presentation to the world, and are only slightly interactive" (1995). So, whether you are setting up your own page or viewing others, be aware that the personal homepage is a presentation of self and that self is constantly changing and adapting to the ever-changing technological world.

gang in order to be accepted by his or her peers. In this case, the peer pressure is potentially detrimental to the teen's self-concept, because he or she will look to others for self-esteem. In fact, the tension he or she feels from a diminished self-concept may motivate him or her to seek a group that shares his or her insecurities.

On the other hand, peers, like families, can be a positive force in shaping self-concept. Associations with people who are capable of providing support and positive feedback help to boost self-esteem. For example, a friend may encourage you to apply for a job by giving you a "pep" talk: "Your experience as a welder gives you an edge over the other candidates. What better qualification is there for selling and demonstrating how welding equipment works than the experience you have acquired during the past four years?"

Perceptions of Others

The same factors (discussed earlier) that apply to the process of perception also apply to our perceptions of others. In other words, certain aspects of another person either draw our attention or are ignored, depending on our own interests and needs. We sort out these facts and then make an effort to interpret them based on our past experience, attitudes, personal con-

Friends can provide support and positive feedback that can boost our self-esteem.

structs, and prototypes. During the process, we develop a perception of this person that subsequently affects our communication with him or her.

Whether our perception of another person is generally positive (he or she is friendly, attractive, talented, knowledgeable, kind, and so on), negative (he or she is overbearing, critical, stubborn, stupid, grouchy, and so on), or neutral (he or she is okay), we react to that perception. It is this reaction that affects our communication with the person. In sum, our perceptions of others could serve to filter messages so we only hear what we want to hear. Attribution can play a significant role in our interpretation of others and their behavior.

Attribution involves assigning causation to our behavior and the behavior of others. We use our frame of reference to interpret our actions. How we perceive the cause for an action will affect our overall perception of ourselves or others.

First Impressions   **SKILL BUILDING**

Attempt to answer the following questions about your instructor from your perceptions of the first day of class.

1. How old is she/he?
2. What is his/her marital status?
3. What is his/her favorite television program?
4. What is her/his favorite hobby?
5. Does he or she have a pet? What kind?

A. What caused you to form these impressions?
B. How have these impressions affected your behavior in class?
C. How do first impressions affect the way you communicate with others?

Stereotyping

Stereotyping, placing or categorizing people, places, objects, or events into groups based on generalized characteristics, also contributes to the way we perceive others. Although stereotyping helps us "order" stimuli, it can distort reality because it fails to recognize individual differences among people and objects. Our perception of others is commonly the result of "allness" stereotyping or "halo and horns" stereotyping. We shall take a look at each of these practices next.

With **allness stereotyping,** we attribute a particular characteristic to a group of people; for the purpose of this discussion, we shall use bankers as our select group. Based on our limited contact with bankers, we generalize that this group is a conservative lot. When we find out that someone we have just met is a banker, we then make the assumption (frequently wrong) that this person is also conservative. By superficially categorizing people into groups, we severely diminish the possibility of perceiving the unique differences among people.

The following situation aptly demonstrates the narrow-mindedness that commonly results from allness stereotyping:

> Years ago, Vernon worked for one summer as a construction laborer building garages. He liked interacting with the other workers, but found most of them "pretty dumb." Now he and his wife are having a deck built on the back of their home. Every day before he leaves for work, Vernon says hello to the construction workers, but does not engage them in any substantive conversation. After a few days, a member of the crew, Marshall, asks Vernon if he or someone on the crew has done something to offend Vernon because Vernon seems to ignore them. Vernon is surprised at how articulate Marshall is and through their conversation learns that Marshall and several other members of the crew all studied engineering in college.

Vernon used allness stereotyping and assumed that all construction workers are "pretty dumb." Obviously, he was mistaken and had to revise his perceptions of the crew.

How many times have you heard someone pass judgment on another person without first interacting with that individual? We have all made judgments about a person's behavior by placing that person in a racial, ethnic, social, or sexual group without knowing much, if anything, about the actual person. The tendency to place people in a group and make generalizations about their behavior because of their group membership illustrates how allness stereotyping can distort reality. A related form of stereotyping, **halo and horns stereotyping,** happens this way: Based on our observations of an individual in a particular situation or setting, we develop either a positive or negative perception about that person; we then allow our initial perception to transfer to other situations. The significance of halo and horns stereotyping is that we see an individual in either a consistently positive or consistently negative light, which effectively eliminates the sounder practice of assessing the individual's other characteristics on their own merits. Consider the following:

> Tamara loves yoga. She has been taking a class for the past year and has just been asked to join the advanced class by Stan, the supervising yoga instructor. Stan also asks Tamara if she might be interested in teaching a class for beginners on Saturday mornings. "You have mastered all the techniques and are my best student, Tamara," Stan tells her. "I think you would make an excellent teacher."

What's wrong with Stan's logic in this example? Is he making an objective assessment of Tamara's potential as a teacher? Would Tamara have the patience to teach others? How might she interact with students who don't take yoga seriously? Making positive or negative judgments about a person's behavior based on limited information often hinders the communication process.

Developing Accurate Perceptions of Ourselves and Others

Accurate perceptions of both ourselves and others mean better communication and understanding between individuals, something all of us desire. In other words, we want to match our perceptions with those of others to ensure we share the same meanings. In previous sections of this chapter we discussed not only the process of perception, but also specific factors that influence our perception of ourselves and our perceptions of others. Some of these factors, such as self-esteem and stereotyping, actually cause us to form perceptions that are different from our partner's. In this final section we shall suggest how to develop accurate perceptions of ourselves and others.

Our perception of ourselves is strongly tied to the notion of self-concept. As defined earlier, self-esteem is a reflection of the way we view our worth or value. For instance, our work with the Meals-On-Wheels program raises our self-esteem because we view our efforts as worthwhile. On the other hand, our self-esteem diminishes when we judge ourselves to be clumsy in athletics. What should be apparent to us (but frequently is not) is that our self-concept is situational—our estimate of ourselves varies according to the circumstances of the particular situation. To perceive ourselves accurately, then, we must realistically evaluate our behavior in a given situation and take into account the feedback we receive from others. Our perceptions become blurred when we begin to generalize that we behave or communicate a particular way "all the time." This estimation is usually inaccurate.

Impression Management

How we want others to perceive us is called **impression management.** Our self-concept and self-esteem greatly effect how we present ourselves to our friends, family, and work colleagues. Depending on the situation, we take on roles just as actors do, and we then interact with others to create an image of ourselves. For example, when Lisa, one of the authors, teaches, she wears "professional" clothes and answers her phone by saying, "This is Dr. Goodnight." She does this because she wants to project an image of professionalism and competence. At home, Lisa wears jeans and answers the phone, "Hello." In each situation, she is playing a different role and projecting a different kind of image.

Accurate perceptions of others are sometimes hindered by clinging to first impressions and by stereotyping. In order to develop accurate perceptions of others, we must avoid relying on first impressions and stereotypes; instead, we should be open to altering our perceptions when new information about a person warrants such a change.

We sometimes form an initial impression of someone and then stick to it. Because many people feel uncomfortable when they first meet someone, and therefore may act shy or nervous, a first impression may not be an accurate one. This means that distortion and misunderstanding of the other person's behavior can easily occur. Consider the following:

> Bob's behavior is loud and obnoxious at the party where Cristy first meets him. His crude jokes call a great deal of attention to him. After several minutes, people start to whisper about his inappropriate behavior and try to avoid him. Cristy decides that he is a jerk.
>
> At another party two weeks later, Cristy runs into Bob again. This time he behaves much differently. He is more natural and does not try to "put on a show." Instead, he appears relaxed and is easy to talk to. In fact, Cristy is comfortable enough to ask him why he behaved the way he did at the first party. He tells her that he gets so nervous about meeting and talking to new people that he feels he has to impress everyone.

Luckily, Cristy did not adhere to her initial impression of Bob, whose earlier communication behavior grew out of his own discomfort. It took a second encounter and asking questions of Bob for Cristy to realize that her first impression had, indeed, been unfair. Armed with additional information, she was ready to alter her former perception of Bob.

The public-speaking situation is another area where we must be careful about clinging to first impressions. As people get more confident about making speeches, there are undoubtedly significant changes in the way they present themselves. Consider the case of Natalie:

> Natalie has just been hired as the new director of the local YWCA. Part of her job includes soliciting contributions from various businesses in the community. Her initial fund-raising effort involves talking to officials of the town's largest bank. She is nervous about her presentation, and consequently, she does not make a particularly strong impression on the bank trustees. A few of these individuals, however, recognize the importance of the agency's service to the community and subsequently show their support with monetary gifts.
>
> Four months later Natalie is serving on a community task force with two bank officers. In the intervening months she has gained confidence in her new position, which is evidenced by her effective participation on this committee. The bank trustees note the changes in Natalie's public image and dismiss their earlier doubts about her capabilities.

Once again, first impressions proved to be inaccurate.

Stereotypes, much like first impressions, are the result of having either too little or inaccurate information about someone. Based on brief observations and insufficient information, we think we know how another person will behave. Is our perception likely to be accurate? Probably not. For example, it is illogical to think that because Sam is single, he is also shy. We must get to know him better before we can make such a statement (while it is possible that Sam is shy, there is an equal chance that he is not). Our communication with others depends, to a large degree, on the way we perceive them. When our perceptions are inaccurate, the possibility of misunderstandings between ourselves and others increases. We must always realize that we are all different in many ways, and as a competent communicator, our job is to verify our perceptions and strive to understand the other person. In order to do this, we can use perception checking.

Perception Checking

Using questions to clarify our understanding of the message is called **perception checking.** To do this, we must assume that our first impression is not always correct and we need further clarification. Your perception is based on your frame of reference, so your perception may be different from the perception of the person you are communicating with. We can reach mutual understanding with perception checking. Here are a few guidelines for asking questions:

1. State your observations as clearly as possible. Be descriptive about what you have seen or heard. Example: "You seem pretty upset about your math quiz grade. You sat through class without taking any notes or participating in the discussion after we received our grades."

2. Ask if the other person sees or hears the same thing. Example: "Are you upset?"

3. Offer a few possible interpretations. Example: "Is it your grade, or is something else bothering you?"

Be sure to perception check in a nonthreatening way to minimize defensiveness. The goal of perception checking is to clarify meaning, not put the other person on the spot. We will discuss more about perception checking in Chapter 3.

Developing Accurate Perceptions   CHECKLIST

- Realistically evaluate our behavior in a given situation.
- Take into account feedback we receive from others.
- Avoid relying on first impressions and stereotypes.

- Be open to altering our perceptions.
- Practice perception checking.

In the chapters that follow we shall see that perception plays a key role in nearly all aspects of the communication process: in listening, in verbal communication, in nonverbal communication, in our relationships with others, and in public speaking.

Ethics in Communication

Understanding Self-Concept and Self-Esteem

In Chapter 1 we discussed how our differences enrich and sometimes deter effective communication. Let's look at how the managers in the beginning of this chapter may view themselves. They are certainly different from one another and have their own unique way of seeing themselves and the world around them. Their self-concepts and self-esteems will have an impact on how they communicate intrapersonally and interpersonally.

Tony is a father, husband, church member, and manager. He receives positive support and feedback from his wife, children, and friends. At home, his self-esteem is quite positive. He communicates freely with his family and friends about his dreams, ambitions, fears, and feelings. At work, however, despite his past promotions, Tony feels a bit insecure. The lack of a merit raise this year was seen by Tony as negative feedback on his job performance. He finds himself more and more hesitant to speak up at meetings, for example, because he feels intimidated by his college-educated colleagues. Tony's self-esteem at work is not as high as it is at home.

Connie is a mother, partner, college graduate, and manager. Like Tony, she receives love and support from her family and friends. She and her partner have developed and nurtured an egalitarian relationship where they share in all the joys and responsibilities of their family's life. At home, then, Connie feels great about herself and the roles she plays. After completing her college degree, Connie was promoted and given a large pay raise. She worked hard for her degree by attending classes at night, part-time, for six years. At work, she feels confident about her abilities and knowledge and freely communicates her ideas and concerns.

Anita is single, a recent immigrant, college graduate, and manager. At work, Anita is self-assured and assertive. She was at the top of her graduating class and is confident about her knowledge and expertise in manufacturing technology. Anita is dedicated to her job and works long hours to ensure that her division is the most productive. Like Connie, Anita is not shy about voicing her ideas and concerns, but this was not always the case. When Anita first joined the company, she was intimidated by her co-workers' "aggressive" communication styles and hesitated to offer her opinions. After several weeks, however, Anita received lots of positive feedback on her ideas and overall work performance from her colleagues and superiors. In her personal life, however, she has not received much positive feedback and still feels shy and insecure.

Tom is a father, divorcee, college graduate, and manager. He is older than the other managers and has been at the company the longest. On and off the job, Tom has low self-esteem. At work, Tom is intimidated by the younger managers because he fears they may know more than he does about technology. Unlike Tony, who is quiet, Tom is loud and aggressive in meetings. He hopes his aggressive communication style will keep the others away and will hide his insecurity. At home, Tom is adjusting to living alone. He misses his

daughters and the companionship of a partner. Just as he does at work, Tom communicates aggressively with his daughters and ex-wife as a way to cover up his fears and insecurities.

These four managers have been affected greatly by the feedback of others. Colleagues and superiors at work as well as their families and friends have impacted the perceptions each has about himself or herself. Positive feedback from her boss certainly affected the way Anita communicates on the job. Perceived negative feedback from his boss affected Tony's communication. These four managers also illustrate that self-concept is situational. At home and at work, we can feel quite differently about ourselves.

Ethical communication begins with accurately and realistically evaluating our behavior in any given situation while taking into account the feedback of significant others. We need to be honest with ourselves and with others about our perceptions and be willing to adjust our first impressions.

Summary

Perception is a dynamic process in which we assign meaning to stimuli. This process involves three critical stages: selective attention, organization, and interpretation.

We first select stimuli from the environment through a process called selective attention. What we pay attention to is generally determined by our interests and needs. Next, we attempt to organize the information we have selected from the environment. To make the stimuli more

understandable, we can group them according to similarity or proximity. In addition, the element of closure contributes to the way we organize stimuli. Finally, we are ready to interpret the stimuli. Factors that affect how we interpret what we have perceived include our past experiences, attitudes, personal constructs, prototypes, and attribution.

A key ingredient in the way we perceive the world is the way we see ourselves. Self-concept is the total perception we have of ourselves. Self-esteem is the way we measure our self-worth. Furthermore, the way we perceive feedback from others greatly affects our self-concept and self-esteem. Factors such as the self-fulfilling prophecy and significant others (including families and peers) contribute to the development of our self-concept.

Our perception of others affects how we communicate with them. Factors such as power and stereotyping (including allness stereotyping and halo and horns stereotyping) play a major role in the way we see other people.

Improving the accuracy of our perceptions requires that we avoid such practices as clinging to first impressions and stereotyping. The degree to which we are successful can be measured by our improved communication with others.

Review Questions

1. Describe the three-stage process of perception.
2. What is attribution?
3. Define self concept and self-esteem.
4. How does feedback from others affect the way we view ourselves?
5. What is self-fulfilling prophecy?
6. How does stereotyping distort reality?
7. How can we ensure our perceptions of self and others are accurate?

3

Listening

At the conclusion of this chapter, you should be able to:

- Differentiate between hearing and listening.
- Explain how noise interferes with listening.
- Explain how delivery interferes with listening.
- Explain how language interferes with listening.

- Explain how perceptions interfere with listening.
- Describe the types of listening.
- Use the skills of questioning, paraphrasing, and interpreting.

ecently at a local discount store, two customers are attempting to return the same defective toaster oven. William and Olga had bought their toaster ovens on sale, but found that they did not heat properly. Each wants a refund.

William enters the store and quickly goes to the customer service counter. He is dressed professionally, in a suit and tie, as he is coming home from a long day at the office. Jamal, the clerk on duty, informs William that he can only exchange the toaster oven for a new one because William does not have the receipt. William asks to speak to the manager. When the manager, Angela, arrives, she listens intently to William's description of the defective toaster oven. She asks him to repeat the details so she can take careful notes. Angela empathizes with his story and issues him a full refund. She offers him an apology and hopes he will shop again at the store.

Just as William leaves the counter, Olga approaches with the same toaster oven. Olga, a recent immigrant from Russia, speaks broken English and is not very well dressed. She tries to explain to Jamal that she would like a refund for the toaster oven because it is defective. He interrupts her in the middle of her explanation and states that she cannot have a refund without the receipt. Olga, like William before her, asks to speak with the manager. When Angela arrives, she tries to listen to Olga, but is distracted because she should have left for her lunch break twenty minutes ago and is anxious to leave the store. In addition, another customer is waiting to talk to her on the phone about another problem. Angela gets short with her when Olga struggles to find the right words to explain the problem with the toaster oven. Angela reluctantly offers only to exchange the toaster oven. She does not take notes and offers no apology or offer to shop again at the store as she picks up the phone to talk to the waiting customer.

Why is Angela treating these two customers with the same problem differently? She appears to listen intently to William, but interrupts Olga. In this chapter, we will discuss the communication skill of listening and how our frame of reference can affect our ability to listen. We will also discuss how we can improve our listening skills in order to improve our overall communication.

One part of the communication process that we take for granted is listening. Perhaps the reason for this is the attention we so often place on sending messages. Mention that you are taking a communication class to someone, and his or her response is apt to be, "Oh, aren't you scared to death to give a speech in front of a class? I dread getting up in front of others." You are not likely to hear, "Don't you worry about being an effective listener?" While you may chuckle over this illustration, the fact is that listening needs to be taken seriously. Remember, communication is an interdependent process that requires both the sender (speaker) and receiver (listener) to be engaged in the interaction. In this chapter, we focus on the skill of listening and ways to improve our listening skills.

In recent years, both the business community and numerous professions have recognized the importance of effective listening. According to the International Listening Association, more than thirty-five business studies have indicated that listening is the "top skill needed for success in business." Because of this, listening workshops are commonplace in business and industry today. This effort seems entirely appropriate when we consider how much time we spend each day listening to colleagues, friends, family, television, radio, and so on. In fact, we spend about 45 percent of our day listening, according to the International Listening Association.

Becoming an effective communicator begins with listening. As we discussed in Chapter 1, effective communicators value diverse approaches to communication. Thus, valuing diversity begins with effective listening skills. As a skilled listener, you can better understand your audience and his or her message and offer appropriate feedback.

Hearing and Listening

What is the difference between hearing and listening? Hearing is one's physical ability to perceive sounds; listening is the process of giving thoughtful attention to what we hear. Listening is more complex than hearing because it demands that we concentrate on what others say to us. To listen effectively, we must take the focus off of ourselves and focus on the other person. This is difficult to do. We sometimes assume that when we send a message, the other party will listen to it and understand its meaning. If this were true, we would not have conflict or misunderstandings when we communicate with others. Clearly, we don't always lis-

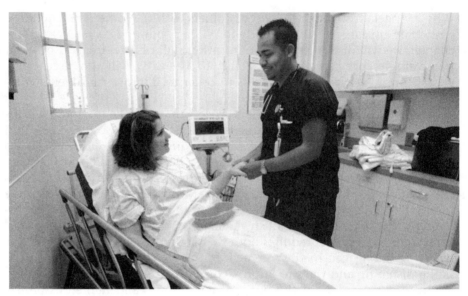

We listen not only with our ears, but with our eyes and heart, as well.

ten, and even when we do, we may not understand the meaning of the message.

Listening takes more than just the use of our ears. We must also listen with our eyes and heart. The Chinese symbol for listening includes the ears, eyes, and heart. Effective communicators are able to take the focus off of themselves and use their frame of reference to listen to the message. Manny is an example of an effective listener:

> Manny has been working as an emergency room nurse for five years. He is very close to finishing his bachelor's degree in nursing. One of the skills that makes Manny an excellent nurse is his listening skills. He is able to focus on the patient's message, but also pays close attention to the patient's body movement, clothing, and other nonverbal messages. Recently, a woman with a broken wrist was brought into the emergency room by her boyfriend. The patient said she fell down the stairs. Manny asked her to tell him the story of how it happened. As she spoke, Manny noticed that her voice was shaking and her lip was cut. She also did not make eye contact with her boyfriend. Manny deduced that the woman had not just fallen, but was probably pushed by her boyfriend. He informed the doctor, and they were able to find help for the patient from the local battered women's shelter. Had Manny not used his effective listening skills, he would not have been able to help his patient.

In order to be an effective listener, Manny had to focus on his patient and not himself. He had to ignore all the internal and external noise. Many factors influence our ability to be effective listeners.

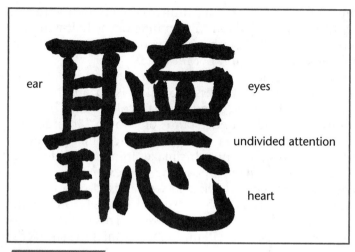

ear

eyes

undivided attention

heart

FIGURE 3.1 **The Parts of the Chinese Character That Symbolize the Verb "to listen"**

Factors That Interfere with Listening

An important part of being an effective communicator is to develop skills in the area of listening. These skills help us to understand the messages others send and ensure that our responses to these messages are appropriate. Later in this chapter we discuss specific skills for effective listening. First, however, we shall consider a number of variables that can interfere with our ability to listen: noise, delivery, language, message overload, and perceptions. A basic understanding of these obstacles will help us to implement the skills described later in this chapter.

Noise

Noise can interfere with our ability to listen because it prohibits us from actually hearing the message, and it can be intentional or unintentional. Incidents of noise fall into two categories: external and internal noise. **External noise** consists of sounds or visual stimuli that draw our attention away from an intended message. For example, if a road crew is repairing the street directly below the lecture hall where your class is underway, you and your fellow students may have difficulty hearing the professor because of the noisy equipment. Eventually, you all may give up the struggle and simply quit listening to the message.

Internal noise consists of our own thoughts or feelings that prevent us from listening to someone else's message. In the weekly progress meeting, you are thinking about last night's dinner conversation with your spouse about whether to take a vacation this summer or the half-written report sitting on your desk at work. In either case, you are thinking about something other than your supervisor and her message.

Similarly, internal noise can hinder our interactions or conversations with others. For example, Professor Shelley is so absorbed in his own thoughts about his daughter going away to college that he resorts to pat verbal responses, like "Yes, I understand" or "Go on," in order to appear to be involved in his conversation with his student Kamal. Professor Shelley's preoccupation with his own thoughts makes it impossible for him to listen to Kamal's questions about the upcoming unit exam.

In order to become effective listeners, we must do our best to ignore all external and internal noise. Our focus should always be on the speaking situation and especially the speaker and message. This is difficult to do, but if we pay attention to noise, we will undoubtedly miss the speaker's message.

Delivery

Another factor that affects our ability to listen is the speaker's delivery style. Many times we can be distracted by the speaker's voice, bodily movement, dress, or appearance. We fail to listen to the message and instead focus on the delivery, good or bad, of the message. Take the speaker who uses "ums," "ya knows," or "like" throughout the presentation. You may find yourself listening for the next "um" instead of listening for the main ideas. Or, you may find the speaker's voice and appearance so credible and authentic that you do not critically listen to the message, but instead accept it because of the speaker's delivery style. Either way, you are not focusing on the message, but the speaker's delivery style. Competent listeners don't ignore the speaker's style, but focus primarily on the content of the message.

Language

Have you ever tried to discuss a problem with a colleague or friend, but his or her choice of words only resulted in your becoming angry, not solving the problem? This is an example of language interfering with the listening process. Messages that include words or phrases that offend us, such as ethnic or racist slurs, slanderous comments, sexist and homophobic comments, profanity, or condescending references, often trigger a negative reaction that actually prevents us from listening to the sender's complete message.

In addition to offending listeners, language can alienate, frustrate, or annoy listeners, and by doing so, diminish our ability or desire to listen. For instance, **jargon**—highly specialized words used and understood by specific groups of people—might intimidate or frustrate listeners unfamiliar with the profession or activity associated with such language. Bankers talk about "Fanny-Maes," "balloon versus fixed rates," and negative amortizations" when describing loans; however, to those who have never applied for a home or business loan, these terms may be intimidating. Feeling like an outsider can affect how we listen: "I'll never be able to understand what they're talking about. Why should I listen?"

When we are faced with this kind of interference, we should strive to understand the message by taking detailed notes (discussed later in the chapter) so that we can ask questions of the speaker later. We can also confront the speaker about his or her use of phrases or words that offend us. Perhaps the speaker never intended to offend us and perceives the meaning of a specific word or phrase differently.

Message Overload

Message overload can also hinder us from becoming effective listeners. Message overload refers to our attention to details instead of the main ideas of the message. The extent to which we concentrate on the details of the message, instead of the major points, can actually interfere with our ability to listen. Consider the following situation:

> Adel's manager has mandated that all employees become proficient in all company software, including PowerPoint, Word, and Excel. Adel decides to attend the beginner's workshop on word processing, primarily because he feels intimidated by the prospect of working with computers. As soon as the instructor begins her introduction, Adel starts taking copious notes. By doing so, he fails to listen for her main ideas, which form the foundation of word processing. At the end of the workshop, Adel's notes are filled with details, yet his understanding of word processing remains sketchy.

Adel is experiencing message overload. He needs to listen for the central ideas of the presentation and the connections between the ideas to discern the major theme.

Avoiding Message Overload   SKILL BUILDING

Pick a class in which you take extensive notes.

1. During the next lecture, make an effort to listen for the instructor's major points. Record these in your notes, along with any important subpoints.
2. After class, review your notes. Rewrite the major themes.
3. Before the next class, review the major themes to help plant the ideas in your head.
4. How does focusing on the overall themes help you to avoid the practice of listening only for details?

Perceptions

How does our self-perception act as a barrier to listening? In simple terms, if we find the communication setting or the message threatening in some way, we may become defensive, which, in turn, causes us to do a poor job

Ethics in Communication

The Skill of Listening

In the beginning of the chapter, we read about Angela, the store manager, and her interactions with two customers, William and Olga. Each wants to return a defective toaster oven and asks for a full refund. Angela gives William his money back, but only offers to exchange Olga's toaster oven. Let's take a closer look at Angela's listening skills.

In her conversation with William, Angela is a very effective listener. Specifically, she:

- uses active listening. She asks questions of William and paraphrases his message in order to check her perceptions. Angela wants to make sure she understands William's problem.
- takes careful notes as a tool to remember the details of their conversation.
- shows William empathy and provides supportive feedback.
- focuses on William and his message by avoiding all internal and external noise.

Clearly, Angela has a positive impression of William. Her positive perception may be based on his gender, professional dress, and his ability to clearly articulate the problem with the toaster oven.

Conversely, several factors interfere with Angela's ability to listen effectively to Olga. Perhaps one of the problems is Angela's

negative perception of Olga. Remember, negative perceptions hamper our ability to listen. Specifically, Angela:

- listens passively and does not use any of the responsive listening skills (questioning, paraphrasing, and interpreting).
- shows no empathy and offers no support to Olga.
- is clearly focusing on Olga's delivery, such as her dress and ability to articulate the problem, and not on the message.
- is focusing on Olga's struggle with language and not the content of the message.
- is distracted by internal and external noise (wanting to go to lunch and a phone call waiting for her).

Angela's frame of reference influences how she listens to these two customers with the same problem. She sees only the differences between William and Olga, such as their outward appearance and ability to articulate their problem. Angela fails to see the similarities and lets their differences dictate how she communicates with them. Ethical listening requires that we strive to understand the other, despite their differences, and actively participate in the interaction by ignoring distractions and using our responsive listening skills.

of listening. Defensive communication is our response to threatening interpersonal or public-speaking situations. (The subject of defensive communication is treated in detail in Chapter 7.) These threatening situations can take many forms, but a common factor is that we feel insecure or inadequate. When these feelings surface, they affect our ability to listen. For an example, let's go back to the issue of jargon, a form of language interference. Nearly all of us have been in situations where others used jargon, whether it is doctors spouting medical terms, lawyers talking "legalese," or actors critiquing a performance in their own special language, and we have felt like an outsider. What sometimes accompanies this feeling of being on the outside is feelings of frustration or intimidation, which may trigger self-doubt or a lowered self-esteem. "I'm not as smart as these doctors. I'll never understand what they're talking about or feel comfortable around them." If we dwell on our lowered self-esteem, we may drift from the conversation or speech and stop listening.

In addition, the way we perceive others affects our desire to listen to them. Simply stated, if our perception of someone is basically a positive one, we are likely to want to listen to that person; a negative perception hampers our desire to listen. President George W. Bush, for instance, is perceived as being a conservative. As a result, many people avoid listening to his speeches and press conferences because they think they "know exactly what he's going to say." The liberal community may not listen to his message because it assumes he will see issues from a purely conservative perspective. Conversely, if we respect a professor, we are more likely to listen to him or her and act on his or her advice to read a particular book or to pursue an advanced degree.

Perception and Listening   SELF-ASSESSMENT

1. Identify an individual with whom you feel uncomfortable.

2. How do you react when this person speaks to you?

3. Evaluate how you listen to this person. Do you interrupt this person? Do you let your mind drift?

4. Name someone whom you admire.

5. How do you react when this person speaks to you?

6. Evaluate how you listen to this person.

7. Describe the differences in how you listen to this person and to the individual identified in #1.

8. What accounts for the difference in the way you listen?

PEANUTS © UFS. Reprinted by Permission.

Effective Listening

Despite the stumbling blocks to effective listening we have discussed so far—noise, delivery, language, message overload, and our perceptions of ourselves and others—it is possible to become a good listener. What is necessary is an understanding of the factors that contribute to effective listening, accompanied by our commitment to develop the ability to listen effectively. These factors include recognizing the importance of active listening and implementing responsive listening skills. First, let's discuss the types of listening: active and passive.

Active and Passive Listening

Active listening is listening with a sense of purpose and involvement. This is a sharp contrast to passive listening, in which the only party involved in the message is the sender. Watching television, for example, requires no

Listening to the radio while we drive is an example of passive listening.

more of you than that you be a passive listener; there is no need to provide feedback regarding the message being televised. With active listening, you decide in advance that it is important for you to focus on the sender's message; you therefore make every effort to stay involved in the interaction. For example:

Paul is beginning his new job today as an internal sales representative for a pipefitting firm. Part of his first day includes extensive orientations

COMMUNICATION and TECHNOLOGY

Listening to Talk Radio

In a 1996 study, one in five adults has "reported listening to a call-in political program more than once a week; these listeners are politically active and regular consumers of news media" (Rubin and Step, 2000, pp. 635–636; Annenberg Public Policy Center, 1996). According to Hofstetter and Gianos, about 850 radio stations in the United States are all talk or news and talk (1997). Obviously, talk radio is popular and commands the radio airwaves. How and why do we listen to talk radio? Scholars have found that we listen actively, not passively to talk radio and that we are motivated to listen to gain personal contact, information, and entertainment.

We often think of listening to the media as passive, not active. But scholars have found that talk show listeners actively listen and participate in the interaction. Hofstetter and Gianos contend, "the most involved talk radio listeners appear to be active listeners who are not simply passively consuming the host's view points, but appear to be fully capable to make critical judgments about politics perhaps stimulated by what has been heard on talk radio but fully independent of whatever the host may advocate" (1997, p. 512). More specifically, "When a listener is interested in the discussion topic and can

relate that topic to direct experiences, he or she becomes more involved with the programming. To become a more active participant, the listener may call the program" (Armstrong, Rubin, and Rubin, 1989, p. 84). Thus, talk show listeners get involved in the communication process and provide feedback to the show through phone calls.

We listen to talk radio to gain personal contact, information, and entertainment. First, talk radio becomes a form of interpersonal communication that can alleviate loneliness and offer companionship (Armstrong, Rubin, and Rubin, 1989). Armstrong, Rubin, and Rubin argue, "The telephone interactions between callers and program hosts provide companionship, a form of social network, and a forum for their ideas" (1989, p. 84). Second, talk radio provides us with an opportunity to seek and share information, according to Armstrong, Rubin, and Rubin (1989). Lastly, we listen for the entertainment value, because talk radio can be exciting and humorous (Rubin and Step, 2000).

Talk radio is a media phenomenon with favorite hosts and ideological points of view. As studies have shown, we are certainly attending to and actively listening to talk radio.

from personnel (to discuss employee benefits), the safety marshall (to discuss emergency operations), and the office manager (to discuss office procedures and regulations). Paul comes to the orientation with a large three-ring binder, legal pad, and several pens. As each speaker presents his or her material, Paul takes careful notes, asks questions, and files all the handouts in his binder.

Paul knows that he must stay focused on the message by taking notes and staying organized. There are three specific types of active listening. They are informative, critical, and empathetic. We will discuss each in some detail.

Informational Listening

One of the primary reasons we engage in communication (as we learned in Chapter 1) is to learn new ideas or to transmit information. In these situations, we use informational listening. **Informational listening** allows us to focus on the content of the message in order to gain knowledge. We use this kind of listening in the classroom, for example. Paul, in the preceding example, is using informational listening in his orientations from personnel, the safety marshall, and the office manager. Informational listening requires that we keep an open mind while we listen to the entire message. This can be difficult, especially if a message argues against something we feel strongly about. Another difficulty with informational listening, as we discussed earlier in the chapter, is message overload. Be sure to focus on the main ideas or arguments of the message.

Critical Listening

Critical listening begins with informational listening. Before we listen to evaluate, we must first listen to the message. **Critical listening** asks us to evaluate the speaker's message or intent. For example:

> Wendy has been selected to sit on her first jury. Wendy is nervous about the idea of making a final judgment of guilt or innocence. As the lawyers present their opening arguments, Wendy listens carefully to each presentation, paying close attention to the facts and arguments. Although she thinks the defendant may be guilty, she forces herself to suspend judgment until all the facts have been presented.

With critical listening, you may also be asked to offer constructive feedback to the speaker. Like Wendy, be sure to postpone judgment until you've heard the entire message. Also, be sure that your feedback is focused and will ultimately be helpful to the speaker. As you listen to evaluate, pay close attention to your frame of reference and your perceptions of the speaker and his or her message. Your biases could cloud your judgment. As with informational listening, try to keep an open mind and suspend your judgment until you have heard the entire message.

Empathetic Listening and Being Supportive

Empathy, the ability to understand what someone else is feeling, involves looking at a situation from the other person's perspective. Empathetic listeners strive to take the focus off themselves, to avoid being judgmental, and to display sensitivity to the sender's nonverbal communication. As empathetic listeners, our utmost concern is to understand the sender's message, even though our efforts might dictate that we hold in check our own feelings about a topic. Consider the following:

> Sarah has just found out that her eighteen-month-old son, Michael, has autism (a neurological disorder). She is devastated by the news and fears that her son will never have a full and normal life. She calls her best friend, Darla, to share her news. Darla listens intently and tries to imagine herself in Sarah's position.

In this example, Darla's ability to take the focus off herself enables her to listen carefully to Sarah.

Part of empathy involves being nonjudgmental. As empathetic listeners, we try to avoid judging the statements of others; instead, we strive to keep an open mind while the other party is speaking (there is always time afterward to evaluate the entire message). If we mentally criticize what the other person is saying, we risk missing part of the message.

Listening with empathy also demands that we pay attention to the sender's nonverbal communication. Nonverbal communication is communication without words (this topic is discussed in Chapter 5). Active listeners look for nonverbal messages that support verbal statements. Such efforts help them get to the heart of the sender's message. For example:

> Libby is telling her neighbor, Elana, about a job performance appraisal she has scheduled for tomorrow with her supervisor. Elana can see that Libby is nervous about the appraisal not only by listening to what she says about her supervisor and about the job she has done, but also by the fact that she is talking faster than usual and she keeps jumping up from the kitchen table where they are having a cup of coffee.

By taking into account nonverbal as well as verbal communication, the active listener can construct a more accurate picture of the sender's message.

Supportive behavior is communication designed to assist or encourage speakers to express their feelings. It communicates to them that we are involved in the interaction and that we are making an effort to understand their position. In fact, according to Wendy Samter (1994), supportive or comforting communication is considered one of the most important interpersonal communication skills.

Supportive listeners are involved verbally and nonverbally. Additionally, they avoid making judgments about the sender's feelings; instead, supportive listeners communicate a sense of caring or empathy. For instance, the remark, "I understand why you acted the way you did" lends support to the person who has just finished telling you why she broke up with her boyfriend. This statement does not judge the other person's actions.

We also can offer support to others through the use of nonverbal communication. Appropriate nonverbal communication demonstrates our involvement in the listening process. One way to show that we care about another person's message is to use direct eye contact. Along with a supportive nod, direct eye contact demonstrates our support and communicates to others that we are listening.

Remembering: An Essential Part of Active Listening

Active listening requires that we take the focus off of ourselves and pay attention to the message and the speaker. With effective listening, we hope to gain knowledge, evaluate a message, or offer support to a friend. In each situation, it is necessary for us to retain the message for later use. Eight hours after hearing a message, we only remember 35 percent of the information (Wood, 2000). Taking notes can help us to remember a speaker's message. Although this may not be practical with empathetic listening, note taking is a useful tool in other listening situations. Whether you are listening to a professor's lecture, a supervisor's report about company profits, or sitting on a jury, note taking can increase your ability to remember information. Note taking requires that you become an active participant in the process. It also helps you to stay focused on the speaking situation and avoid internal noises. Here are some guidelines for effective note taking:

1. Write down any words or terms you don't understand.
2. Try to determine the speaker's argument or thesis statement. In other words, what does the speaker want you to remember?
3. Determine the speaker's main ideas.
4. Write down anything the speaker repeats several times or has on a visual aid. Repetition signals that something is important.
5. Formulate questions about the message that you could ask the speaker later.
6. Don't get caught up in all the details. Look for the overall message (Rademacher, 2001).

SKILL BUILDING   Listening with Empathy

1. Select a partner in class.
2. Choose one of the following topics to discuss with your partner:
   a. Should preschool education be mandatory for all four-year-olds?

b. Should the government outlaw research on human embryos?

c. Is affirmative action still a viable solution to discrimination in hiring practices?

3. Evaluate your listening according to the following points:

a. Did you look at the topic from your partner's perspective?

b. Was your listening judgmental?

c. Did you pay attention to your partner's nonverbal communication?

4. How can you improve your listening effectiveness?

Responsive Listening Skills and Checking Our Perceptions

We have just concluded a section that described active listening and the techniques to accomplish this skill. There are other skills that can enhance your listening effectiveness. These are known collectively as responsive listening skills and require us to interact with the sender. In other words, as listeners, we provide the sender with feedback about the message by questioning, paraphrasing, and interpreting his or her statements and by offering support that encourages the sender to speak. In addition, these skills help us to check our own perceptions of the meaning of the speaker's message (see Chapter 2).

Questioning

Questioning is a communication skill designed to help us understand another person's message. It also keeps us involved in the interaction. Questions should be specific about the speaker's message. Consider the following situation:

> Carlos is a mortgage loan officer at First American Savings and Loan. He is scheduled to speak at this month's library program, "Refinancing Your Home." In his talk he explains the different types of mortgages—fixed rate, adjustable, FHA—and points out the advantages and disadvantages of each. He also mentions closing costs and other related service fees. Taylor has done her best to avoid message overload and has listened for all the central ideas, but she still is confused by some of the terminology. At the conclusion of the presentation, Taylor asks Carlos a few questions: "How does the lending institution determine the points charged to the buyer?" "Under what circumstances is an adjustable mortgage most advantageous?"

The questions asked by Taylor help her to clarify the information in Carlos's presentation. In addition, the feedback provided by Taylor's questions indicates to Carlos how well the material is understood by the audience.

Paraphrasing

Paraphrasing means restating another person's message in our own words. Paraphrasing forces us to digest the sender's message and then ask for confirmation that we have understood that message. The benefit of this skill is that we receive immediate feedback from the other person—either we have understood or misunderstood the message. This process gives us a better understanding of the sender's message. Consider the following interaction between Dave and Kevin. Kevin is Dave's supervisor at a large engineering firm. They are meeting to discuss Kevin's recent evaluation of Dave.

Dave: I have a question about this evaluation.

Kevin: O.K. (pause). Is there a problem?

Dave: I don't understand what you mean by this comment, "I am concerned about Dave's attitude." Are you saying I have an attitude problem?

Kevin: No, not at all. I think you are a very dedicated worker.

Dave: Then are you saying that I'm too focused on the work and not enough on my relationships with my colleagues in the office?

Kevin: No. I'm saying that we need to stop spreading you so thin; we need to give you an opportunity to focus more on your work, instead of trying to handle so many other responsibilities.

Dave: So you are saying that the company realizes the stress I've been under and wants to help me reduce the stress?

Kevin: Yes. It's the company's responsibility to hire additional employees so that you can work in your area of expertise.

Dave: Gotcha. I had interpreted your comment as a criticism. I'm sure glad I asked you about it. Thanks.

In this interaction, both parties paraphrased the other's questions and concerns. By doing so, they were able to listen more effectively and understand each other better.

Interpreting

Interpreting a message is similar to paraphrasing. **Interpreting** requires that you clarify the meaning of a message, but also allows you to offer an alternative perception. Because we all view things differently, an interpretation could help the speaker see things from your point of view. For example:

Shaunna and her best friend Tasha are sitting in the campus cafeteria discussing their computer class and their instructor Professor Howard. Shaunna says, "I know he doesn't like me. I have stayed after class the last two sessions to ask him a question about using Powerpoint, and he just blows me off and tells me to stop by during his office hours. He really doesn't want to help me." Tasha responds, "I heard you two talking,

Interpreting helps us to see a different view of a situation.

and I also noticed that he was looking at his watch. It did seem like he was in a hurry and couldn't spend the time helping you. But, don't you remember he told us on the first day that he teaches two classes back to back and the classes are in different buildings? He's probably not able to help you because he had to run to his next class. Why don't you go during his office hours and see if he can help you then?"

Tasha is offering an alternative view of the situation to Shaunna. Tasha's interpretation may help Shaunna to see her interaction with Professor Howard differently.

All the responsive listening skills just discussed increase our understanding of another person's message by directly involving us in the communication process. The opportunity to express our understanding communicates to the sender that we have been attentive listeners. We are able to check our perceptions of the message and clarify any misunderstandings. Furthermore, as listeners through questioning, paraphrasing, and interpreting, speakers find out how effectively they have communicated their message.

CHECKLIST   Responsive Listening Skills

- Use questioning by asking for additional information or clarification.
- Use paraphrasing by restating another person's message in our own words.
- Use interpreting to clarify the meaning of a message, but also offer an alternative perception.

Summary

Listening is the process of giving thoughtful attention to what we hear. It goes beyond hearing, which is our ability to perceive sounds. Poor listening skills can create a lack of understanding between the sender and receiver. Variables that interfere with our ability to listen effectively include noise, delivery, language, message overload, and perceptions of self and others.

Despite the barriers discussed in the first part of the chapter, it is possible to become an effective listener. One way to achieve this is by becoming an active listener, which means listening with a sense of purpose and involvement. Passive listening requires nothing from the receiver. There are three types of active listening: informational, critical, and empathetic. Informational listening is used to gain knowledge. Critical listening requires us to evaluate the speaker's message or intent. Empathetic listening requires that we take the focus off of ourselves, avoid being judgmental, and display sensitivity to the sender's verbal and nonverbal communication. It is essential to all active listening that we listen to remember the message for later use. Note taking can help us do this.

Responsive listening skills help us to become effective listeners. These skills include questioning, paraphrasing, and interpreting and require listeners to interact with the sender.

Review Questions

1. What are the differences between hearing and listening?
2. Describe the factors that interfere with our ability to listen?
3. Why is remembering the message an essential part of active listening?
4. What is the goal of informational listening?
5. Why is it important to listen to the entire message before passing judgment?
6. List some ways you can be an empathetic listener and offer support to another.
7. Define paraphrasing and interpreting. How are they similar? Different?

Verbal Communication

At the conclusion of this chapter, you should be able to:

- Explain why language is symbolic.
- Discuss the relationships between words, thoughts, and objects.
- Explain how language communicates power.
- Explain the difference between the connotative and denotative meanings for words.
- Explain how such cultural influences as ethnic background, race, and geographic regions affect the meanings of words.
- Explain the relationship between perception and language.

- Describe the problems with language.
- Use descriptive language to improve verbal communication.
- Use dating to improve verbal communication.
- Use indexing to improve verbal communication.
- Understand the need to avoid profanity and generic language.
- Show respect for others through language.

One of the requirements for April's communication course is to observe and critique a public speech by Dr. Calvin Smith, a well-known expert in philosophy. Dr. Smith's presentation will take place in the campus auditorium, and the campus and local communities are invited to attend. April is excited about the speech because she loved her introductory philosophy course, in which she read some of Dr. Smith's work. She loved the way the class challenged her to think about her identity and the way we all choose to present ourselves to the outside world.

Five minutes before the presentation was to begin, the auditorium was almost full. April found a seat near the back. She saw several of her classmates and thought she might catch some of them at the end to compare notes and discuss the overall speech. At six o'clock, Dr. Moriarity, the Dean of Liberal Arts, introduced Dr. Smith. The Dean read a long list of the books Dr. Smith had written and distinguished awards he had received. April was even more excited to hear what Dr. Smith had to say after such an impressive introduction. After the applause died down, Dr. Smith began to speak. He said:

> The title of my presentation is "Living the Human Life: A Philosophical Exploration." I hope we can explore the philosophical implications of the examined life. To begin, let me pose a question. What is the epistemological position of a subjective relativist? If we consider the ontological or cosmological construction of such a being, we can understand that this person has no epistemological stance, from a philosophical standpoint, of course. Furthermore, let us juxtapose the essence of this person by understanding the binary opposition of being and not being. In order to do this, however, we must first understand, as Sartre said, the phenomenolologial journey of praxis and consciousness.

April was completely lost. She continued to listen for another hour and still did not understand anything Dr. Smith had said. None of her classmates were able to understand the presentation. In her critique of his presentation, April wrote that she did not know what many of his words meant. She had never heard them before, and Dr. Smith did not define them during his presentation.

Clearly, Dr. Smith was not able to communicate his ideas to April or any of her classmates. In this chapter, we will discuss how language can hinder and enhance our communication. We will also discuss how our differences—such as gender, age, ability, ethnicity, culture, and approach—can make communication difficult. Finally, we will offer some suggestions on how to improve communication by being aware of our language choices.

Our word choices can make a tremendous difference in how successfully we convey our thoughts and emotions. The more precise and vivid our language is, both in interpersonal and in public communication settings, the greater impact our messages will have. Consider the following responses Latisha gives when asked by her friend Amy, "What's wrong?"

Response A: Oh, I'm just really depressed.

Response B: John and I are both distraught over the layoff notice he received yesterday from the mill. We just don't know if he'll be able to find a job with comparable pay. We're worried about making ends meet, about what this is going to do to our lives, especially for the kids.

After listening to the second response, Amy feels great compassion for her friend. Latisha's use of precise language in the second response does a better job of communicating her thoughts and concerns. In public speaking, messages are communicated more effectively when the language is vivid and precise. A few days after the terrorist attacks on the World Trade Center in New York and the Pentagon in Washington, D.C., President Bush addressed the nation. His vivid language helped to make his message powerful and effective:

We have seen the state of our Union in the endurance of rescuers, working past exhaustion. We have seen the unfurling of flags, the lighting of candles, the giving of blood, the saying of prayers—in English, Hebrew, and Arabic. We have see the decency of a loving and giving people who have made the grief of strangers their own. (2001)

As we discussed in Chapter 1, we are all unique, and our differences sometimes make it difficult to communicate effectively. Many communication misunderstandings begin with our choice of language or our interpretation of language. In this chapter, we first discuss the nature of language and meaning, then move to a description of the problems with language. Finally, we offer some suggestions about how to improve our use of language in order to more effectively communicate with our partners, co-workers, and audiences.

The Nature of Language and Meaning

One of the chief ways we express our thoughts, feelings, and attitudes is through verbal communication. Verbal messages are constructed first by

President George Bush chose his words carefully when he spoke to the nation on September 11, 2001.

selecting words and then by sending them. Words are **symbols** that represent things—our feelings, names for the objects around us, and explanations for behaviors. Words collected together and understood by a large group form a language. Knowledge of this language makes it possible for us to recognize the symbols (words) others use to send their messages. Language is an arbitrary system of symbols that is governed by rules and conveys power.

Language Is Symbolic

Symbols represent something else. As we learned in Chapter 1, nonverbal messages are symbolic even though they may not contain words. Words are symbols that represent our thoughts, feelings, and ideas in a specific context or relationship. How do you tell someone you love about your feelings? You could send the message nonverbally (see Chapter 5) through a kiss, hug, or tender touch. Verbally, you could just say, "I love you." Sometimes, however, this seems like such a dramatic statement, especially the first time you say it. Thus, we can communicate our feelings with other symbols such as "I care about you" or "I missed you while you were away." Depending on the relationship and the context, these symbols could certainly communicate "love."

Words help us to communicate effectively because they represent both abstract and concrete things. In our society, we have *freedom, democracy,* and *justice.* These words represent abstract principles. Words such as *school, computer,* and *dog* represent concrete things that we can actually see, touch, or hear.

Language Is an Arbitrary System of Symbols

Language is arbitrary because its meaning can change depending on the speaker, audience, and context. The meanings for words are constantly changing and evolving. In addition, new words are created every day. In fact, the *Oxford English Dictionary* "records about 90,000 new words (and meanings of old words) that have entered the English language in the last 100 years" (Johnson, 2000, p. 6). Furthermore, we can choose to alter the meanings of words. Let's look at Professor Nadesan's class.

Professor Nadesan pointed to a table at the front of the room and asked, "What is this?" The students said, "It's a table," "It's a desk." Professor Nadesan sat on the table and said, "Now what is it?" A student replied, "It's a chair." Then she stood on it as if to change a light bulb and the class said, "Now it's a step stool." Professor Nadesan said, "Okay, which label is the right one?" The class was stumped. All the labels seemed like the right one. "Correct," she said. "All the labels are correct. It just depends on the context."

ZITS   *BY JERRY SCOTT AND JIM BORGMAN*

© Zits Partnership. Reprinted with special permission of King Features Syndicate.

COMMUNICATION and TECHNOLOGY

Communicating on the Internet

New words are created every day. We create words and symbols to adapt to our changing society. In the past decade, we have developed a whole new language for communicating via email and in chatrooms. Two specific kinds of language have been created to make our communication on the Internet more effective. These are called acronyms and email shorthand, and smileys and emoticons. According to Netlingo.com, acronyms and email shorthand are used "because it's quicker and easier to type out a few letters, rather than typing out the full expression." A smiley is "a sequence of characters on your computer keyboard" and tells the receiver "what you really mean when you make an offhand remark," according to Netlingo.com. Smileys are also called emoticons because they convey emotions that might not be known through the use of just words. Here are a few examples of acronyms and emoticons:

Acronyms or Email Shorthand

AWGTHTGTTA	Are we going to have to go through this again?	CUL8R	See you later
		HAK	Hugs and kisses
B4	Before	IDK	I don't know
B4N	Bye for now.	ILY	I love you
BBN	Bye bye for now.	J/K	Just kidding
BS	Big smile	LOL	Laughing out loud
CSL	Can't stop laughing	THX	Thanks

Smileys or Emoticons

:-s	confused	:->	sarcastic
:'-(	crying	:-V	shouting
:-e	disappointed	:-/	undecided
:")	embarrassed	'-)	winking
:-*	kiss	I-o	yawning
x-(	angry or mad	:-(o)	yelling

Meanings for words have changed over the years and within groups. For example, think about the words *cool* and *bad*. *Cool* once only meant a type of temperature. One might say, "This soup is supposed to be hot, but it is cool." Now, however, *cool* means something we like, and we might say, "The new Mellencamp CD is cool." The meaning for *bad* also has evolved. Once we might have said, "This soup tastes bad. There is too much salt in it." Now, you might hear, "This soup tastes bad. Can I have some more?" Each use of the word means something different depending on the sender, the receiver, and the context.

Language Is Rule Governed

We learn how to use language by watching and listening to our parents or caregivers from the day we are born. Rules guide our use of language. We learn rules about how to pronounce words and how to spell words. Do you remember learning that the "e" is silent at the end of words such as *cake, ate,* and *kite*? Do you recall learning that "i comes before e except after c"? These rules govern the way we write and speak every day.

There are also rules about how to use language in particular contexts. When is it okay to interrupt your boss? When can you raise your voice to your spouse? What topics can we discuss? These unspoken rules guide our use of language and are called **regulative rules.** For example:

> Tyrone was hired two weeks ago to deliver internal mail throughout a large law firm. He delivers the mail twice a day to all the secretaries in the building. Within the first week, Tyrone learned that he was to be "seen, not heard" by the partners of the firm. He noticed that only the other lawyers and specific secretaries were "allowed" to initiate conversation with the partners. Also, Tyrone learned that he should leave his personal life out of the office. When two secretaries were discussing a family illness, one of the lawyers ordered them back to work and to "discuss your personal problems at lunch."

Language Communicates Power

We will learn in Chapter 6 that power is the ability to influence others and that power is a perception. Someone's perception of us is often based on the language we use, and that perception can have an effect on the overall communication process. Power can be communicated through language.

We form our perceptions of others based, in part, on their language usage.

Powerless language is characterized by disclaimers such as "I don't think this is the right answer, but . . ." and tag questions such as "I really like this class, don't you?" These statements communicate a sense of uncertainty and tentativeness. The speaker appears more uncertain than assertive (Grob, Meyers, and Schuh 1997, p. 287). Powerful language, on the other hand, is characterized by assertive statements and certainty. In our society, "powerful language is perceived as more persuasive and credible than powerless language" (Burrell and Koper 1994, p. 252). Thus, a person using powerful language will be perceived as credible, believable, and more capable.

Studies have shown that in dyadic or interpersonal situations, women tend to use more powerless language, while men use more powerful language. But in a study on small-group interaction, men and women used similar language choices: both used powerful and powerless language (Grob, Meyers, and Schuh, 1997).

The Meaning of Words

An important theory that explores the relationship between our thoughts and the words we choose to convey those thoughts was developed by C.K. Ogden and I.A. Richards (1923). They maintain that words are symbols and that these symbols are given meaning when they are placed together to make statements. For example, when we ask someone seated at the same table to "pass the salt," that person is likely to respond by picking up the salt shaker and handing it to us. He or she would not in all likelihood toss it down to our end of the table as if it were a football being passed for a touchdown.

According to Ogden and Richards, our thought process is the direct link between the object and the word; consequently, if the word for a particular object is not part of our personal vocabulary, then the word for that object will have no meaning to us. This very thing happens all the time with small children (who are still busy acquiring language). For example, if you were to ask your three-year-old daughter to bring you the dictionary from the kitchen table, she would likely be stumped by your request. You would need to describe and define the term for her, using words that she already understands; that is, "It's the large book that has small holes on one side, by the pages. Each one has a letter of the alphabet on it to help people look up the words they want quickly and easily."

Of course, adults also encounter this type of situation. For instance, Alice, Majia's grandmother, might recognize the term *CD*, having heard it before, yet she might think it refers to a "certified deposit" from a bank or credit union. Because of this, she would not understand Majia when she says, "I would really like some new CDs for Christmas this year, Grandma." Alice would need to ask Majia for an explanation or try to figure out what

Majia is talking about by listening to her subsequent comments. There can be no true understanding of a message if the words that compose that message are not a part of our symbol system. In this example, Alice did not understand Majia's statement regarding CDs (compact discs) because the word *CD* was not part of her symbol system (Figure 4.1).

Denotative meaning is the specific reference of a word; it is what we would find if we looked in a dictionary. Denotative meanings are usually shared or understood within a given culture. For instance, most individuals would define *book* as something that is read, and most dictionaries would offer a similar definition for this word.

Multiple meanings occur with denotation on occasion, and these can cause confusion. Take, for example, the word *aggressive*. *Webster's New Collegiate Dictionary* offers the following definitions: "1 a: tending toward or practicing aggression <aggressive behavior> b: marked by combative readiness <an aggressive fighter> 2 a: marked by driving forceful energy or initiative: ENTERPRISING <an aggressive salesman> b: marked by obtrusive energy." After hearing the comment, "Nancy is aggressive," we might wonder which definition of *aggressive* the person had in mind. Is Nancy someone who shows a lot of initiative in her work? Or is Nancy the type of person who displays her aggression by trying to dominate or lash out at others? It is easy to see how we might be confused.

A word's **connotative meaning** is that which is determined by someone's experiences, values, and culture. It is the personalized definition we

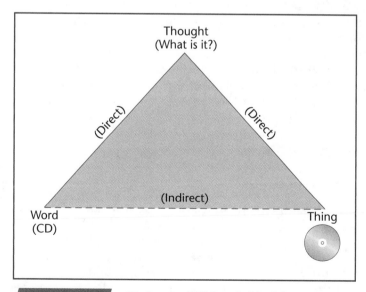

FIGURE 4.1   **Ogden and Richards Model**

assign to a word. *Aggressive,* for example, is a word used to describe someone's personality or behavior. This description may mean something entirely different to different people. For instance, a positive connotation for *aggressive* might indicate a person who is enterprising, a go-getter; a negative connotation would indicate one who is overbearing or who tries to dominate others. Our individual experiences determine the way we use and interpret the word *aggressive.*

CRITICAL THINKING   **Denotative and Connotative Meanings**

For each of the following words, describe its denotative and connotative meanings. You may use a dictionary to develop the denotative meanings.

1. Home
2. Baby
3. School
4. Table
5. Love

6. Freedom
7. Communication
8. Disrespect
9. Family
10. Feminism

In our examination of verbal communication, we also will discover that our thought processes are central to our choice of words. More precisely, our choice of words grows out of our environment, that is, our cultural background, experiences, knowledge, and attitudes. Our differences make communication a complicated process when choosing words as the sender and when interpreting words as the receiver. In the next section, we shall explore how cultural influences, ethnic/racial/social influences, geographic location, and our perceptions affect our choice of words and the ways in which we interpret the words of others.

Factors That Influence Our Language Use

Cultural Influences

Cultural studies routinely include language as one area of research. By **cultures** we mean the customary beliefs and attitudes of a racial, religious, or social group. The customs practiced by a group help shape the language used to communicate with others. Furthermore, the language used by a particular culture has its own set of meanings and often sets the group apart from others. For example, college students desiring membership in a

Our culture greatly influences the meanings we have for symbols.

fraternity or sorority quickly learn the language associated with fraternity life: Pledging, rushing, hazing, and the Greek alphabet are part of the customs practiced by these social groups. Their language makes them part of an inner circle on campus. Of course, not everyone who is part of the culture chooses to participate in the language, ideas, and beliefs of the culture. For example, not all Jewish Americans share the same ideas about the Middle East and Israel. Not all fraternities practice hazing.

Ethnic, Racial, and Social Influences

A country such as the United States is composed of many subcultures. The dozens of groups can be defined as ethnic (Polish Americans, Italian Americans, Irish Americans), racial (blacks, Hispanics or Latinos, Native Americans), and social (fraternities, steel workers, Goeths). The identities of these groups is in some measure maintained by the language they speak. For instance, one would expect to hear Polish spoken in a neighborhood populated predominantly by first-generation Polish Americans. Their language binds them together as a group, but at the same time, their language can act as an insulator. In order for them to be understood outside the confines of their homes, they need to be able to speak the same language as the majority of the population. If they cannot understand a news program broadcast in English, they must rely on others to translate the information for them. And, if their children choose to remain in the neighborhood and speak only Polish, they too will become part of the group.

Some speakers deliberately use language to appeal to a particular group. Stokely Carmichael, during the 1960s, for example, attempted to explain the meaning of *Black Power* to different audiences. When describing the meaning of the term to a primarily white audience, he highlighted the sociological implications this way:

> Traditionally, for each new ethnic group, the route to social and political integration into America's pluralistic society has been through the organization of their own institutions with which to present their communal needs within the larger society. This is simply stating what the advocates of Black Power are saying. The strident outcry, particularly from the liberal community, that has been evoked by this proposal can only be understood by examining the historic relationship between Negro and white power in this country (1969, p. 102).

The language Carmichael used in his explanation was intentionally analytical, clinical, and academic. He wanted to communicate that Negroes (a deliberate word choice) had to take the same steps as other ethnic groups trying to legitimately establish themselves in this country.

On the other hand, when describing *Black Power* to a primarily black audience, Carmichael adopted a more emotional language style:

> Now we've got to talk about this thing called the serious coalition. You know what that's all about? That says that black folks and their white liberal friends can get together and overcome. We have to examine our white liberal friends. And I'm going to call names this time around. We've got to examine our white liberal friends who come to Mississippi and march with us and can afford to march because our mothers, who are their maids, are taking care of their house and their children; we got to examine them [applause]. Yeah; I'm going to speak the truth tonight. I'm going to tell you what a white liberal is. You are talking about a white college kid joining hands with a black man in the ghetto, that col-

lege kid is fighting for the right to wear a beard and smoke pot, and we fighting for our lives [cheers and applause]. We fighting for our lives [continued applause] (1969, p. 91).

In explaining the term to supporters of the movement, Carmichael used a particular type of language to rally the audience. His language served to keep the members focused as a group, separate from the white liberals he alluded to. The meaning derived from Carmichael's messages to these racially different audiences was vastly different because of his choice of words and his language style.

Geographic Influences

Geographic location often accounts for language differences. For instance, you are probably familiar with the regional variations for carbonated beverages; *soda* is spoken along the East Coast, whereas *pop* is the term used by Midwesterners. The first time Jill heard her cousin order a soda while visiting her in Baltimore, she was surprised to see a glass of cola served by the waitress instead of a drink with ice cream in it. Although her understanding of *soda* was something different from her cousin's, obviously the waitress spoke the same language. This simple example of geographic influence demonstrates how easily language affects understanding between communicators. When the meaning of words is different for the parties involved, understanding is not complete.

Perceptions

Our perceptions are defined by the language we acquire as a result of our cultural background—our education, our family environment, our neighborhood, the geographic area where we grow up, and the social groups we belong to. All these factors shape how we look at the world and at the same time provide us with a language to express what we see as reality.

A theory developed by Edward Sapir (1921) and Benjamin Whorf (1956) suggests that our perception of reality is dependent on the language system that supports our thought processes. Specifically, our language is the tool by which we assign meaning to events we encounter. We tell the doctor in the hospital emergency room, for example, that we think we broke a finger playing racquetball. She responds by telling us that an x-ray will determine whether the injury is a skeletal, comminuted, or compound fracture. Her medical training accounts for the difference in her perception of the situation. Her language, acquired as part of her medical education, reflects her perception. Her superior knowledge of this subject is reflected by a more sophisticated vocabulary.

Here's another example of this hypothesis in action: Ralph invites his friend Charlie over for a couple of beers. Ralph turns on the television set and begins to watch a baseball game. Although Charlie has no interest in the sport and has never learned much about the game, he watches along with his friend. Charlie makes the following comment midway through the third inning: "Too bad that ball was caught. It almost went into the stands." Ralph responds by saying, "Charlie, that player hit a perfectly executed sacrifice fly, which advanced the runner from second to third." Ralph's heightened knowledge about baseball dictates that he describe the "out" this way.

The significance of the Sapir-Whorf hypothesis is that people both perceive and describe events differently, in part because of their language. As communicators, we must realize that the understanding of our verbal messages (and the verbal messages of others) depends on the language system of the listener.

SELF-ASSESSMENT   **Meanings Are in People, Not in Words**

Answer the following questions:

1. List as many dirty words as you can.
2. Name the clean parts of the body.
3. Name three good people.
4. Name three bad foods.
5. What do the words *dirty, clean, good,* and *bad* mean to you?
6. How might your meanings for these words be different from those of your classmates?
7. What has influenced your meanings for these words?

Problems with Language

Language itself is often problematic for communicators. The preceding section pointed out that language is dependent on our perceptions. Additionally, problems of understanding arise because others do not perceive our words in the way we intend for them to be understood. Something that is clear to you, for instance, may be "clear as mud" to someone else. To better explain this idea, three general problems of language will be discussed: vague language, abstraction, generations, multiple meanings, technical language or jargon, and slang.

Vague Language

Vague language is language that lacks directness and specificity; it is void of details. Responses spoken in vague terms can leave the other person wondering what you mean. Consider this interaction between Marge and Pamela at the grocery store:

Marge: When did you get back from your vacation?

Pamela: Last Thursday.

Marge: Did you enjoy it?

Pamela: We were rather disappointed; so were the kids.

Unless Marge pursued her questioning (that is, "What was disappointing about the trip?"), she would probably wonder about her neighbor's vacation.

Abstraction

Abstraction is the use of broad terms to explain ideas or concepts. For example, if you simply mentioned someone's generosity, you would be talking in an abstract sense; to be more definite, you could mention the large donation that person makes annually to the American Cancer Society. Abstraction becomes a problem when the receiver or audience does not comprehend the sender's message because of the language used. Most students, for example, have experienced walking out of a classroom with absolutely no idea of what the instructor was trying to communicate. If he or she had attempted to more clearly define the terms used, the ideas might have been better understood.

Generalization

Similar to the problem that occurs when abstract language is used to define concepts is the problem of **generalization:** the use of nonspecific language to describe objects, events, and feelings. It is easier for misunderstandings to occur when others listen to us speak in generalities. Conversely, specific language forces us to be more clearly focused on our subject. Consider the following conversation between Phillip and his supervisor at the hardware store. In it, the supervisor's comments lack directness:

Supervisor: I need to talk to you.

Phillip: Sure. About what?

Supervisor: I think you're having a difficult time with your work. I'm not really satisfied with your performance.

Phillip: What do you mean?

Supervisor: It seems to me that you don't enjoy your work.

Phillip: What makes you say that?

Supervisor: I think you need to be friendlier to the customers.

Phillip: How do I do that?

Supervisor: Well, I just think you need to be more outgoing. Spend more time around them.

Phillip: What do you mean, talk to them more?

Supervisor: Well, yes, that would be a start.

CRITICAL THINKING   **Vague Language**

Use the example of Phillip and his supervisor to answer the following questions:

1. What would your response be to the supervisor's feedback?
2. Can you clearly understand the position taken by the supervisor?
3. Identify the vague language in the preceding dialogue.
4. Rewrite the dialogue between Phillip and his supervisor, eliminating the vague language.
5. How does vague language hinder communication with others?

Multiple Meanings

If someone you have just met says to you, "I have an interest in the city's downtown renovation project," does he mean that he has a financial interest in the enterprise or that he is concerned about the project's chances of revitalizing an area that he considers his home? In this example, use of the word *interest* is confusing. In order to determine precisely what the speaker meant by *interest,* either you would have to know the individual well enough to realize what he was implying, or you would need to ask him an additional question or two to better understand the comment. Some words have special meanings to individuals; therefore, it is not always easy to discern what someone else's message means. On the other hand, there are many words that have universal meaning. These make it easier for us to communicate with others.

Technical Language or Jargon

Technical language or **jargon,** the specialized terms associated with a particular discipline, skill, or career, is another factor that contributes to a lack of understanding between people. Technical language is most effective when used with people who are familiar with the terminology. Refer back to the opening story about April and Dr. Smith. Dr. Smith's use of jargon and technical language created a communication barrier that prohibited April from understanding his presentation. An attorney, for example, would know what a quasicontract is or would readily understand its definition:

In the civil law, a contractual relation arising out of transactions between the parties which give them mutual rights and obligations, but do not involve a specific and express convention or agreement between them. The lawful and purely voluntary acts of a man, from which there results any obligation whatever to a third person, and sometimes a reciprocal obligation between the parties. (Black, 1979, p. 293)

After hearing (or reading) this definition, anyone who is not a law student or practicing attorney is likely to be confused. Other words used in the definition also need defining: *mutual rights, obligations, specific convention.* Rather than grasping the meaning, we would probably need someone to translate the technical language, or jargon, into everyday terms.

Technical language, in addition to contributing to increased difficulty in understanding, also can be intimidating. Consider, for example, the anxiety experienced by parents who rush their child to the hospital for an emergency admission. Their anxiety is heightened further when they cannot understand the technical medical terms used by the pediatrician and the emergency room doctor and nurses. They become frightened when they hear the doctor order a blood culture and direct the nurses to start an IV, as well as by mention of the child's dangerously elevated white count and possible septicemia. The language is intimidating, producing more stress. A perceptive physician would recognize the parents' distress and try to alleviate their fears by explaining the child's condition in terms better understood by the average person. While the language used in the emergency room is undoubtedly an effective way for the medical team to communicate, it can create a higher degree of anxiety for anyone who is not in the medical profession.

Slang

Like technical language, slang is used by a specific group. It is used by a co-culture and can be geographic or generational. Are there any specific terms that relate to where you live and are really only understood by those who live there? In Northwest Indiana, we often refer to ourselves as "da region," and the people who live here are called "region rats." These terms reflect our geographic location as the Northwest Indiana region (as the rest of the state refers to us) and our ability to live and thrive in a dirty and polluted environment (close to the steel mills) like rodents. People who visit here generally do not refer to us as region rats. It is a term we have adopted for ourselves as a form of our identity.

Every generation has its own terms and meanings for those terms. Teen culture in the United States has always had its own language. Words like *groovy* or *hip* meant something desirable to the teens that used them thirty years ago. Today, teens have new words or phrases. Some examples include:

My bad   My mistake or taking the blame for something
                            that is not right

So	To emphasize something: "We are going to so win tonight's volleyball match."
Whack or whacked	Something bad or not cool: "Tom is whacked. He is not even going to the dance."
Wassup?	Another way to say "What is up?" or "What are you doing?"
Scrub	Unattractive boy

If you do not belong to the group, you may not know what the words mean. In this case, slang is used as a way for those of the same group to communicate with one another without "outsiders" understanding the meaning. In the preceding example, teens can use slang to exclude their parents and teachers from the conversation.

Euphemisms

Euphemisms are words that substitute for other words because they are more pleasant. For example, we call older people "senior citizens" or we refer to larger sizes of clothes as "plus size." Euphemisms are used to spare someone's feelings or to lessen the impact of the words. When someone dies, for example, we may say that the person has "passed away" or "is no longer with us."

Euphemisms, however, may be confusing and, at times, misleading. When politicians call for "revenue enhancement" or "increased revenue," they are calling for a tax increase. The nuclear industry calls nuclear waste "spent fuel" as a way to make us less fearful. Even though euphemisms can be helpful as a way to spare someone's feelings, be aware that they also can confuse or even mislead the listener.

Racist, Sexist, and Other Insensitive Language

Effective communicators need to be aware that our language choices might offend our partner, group members, or audience. Racist and sexist statements are the most obvious language choices that will certainly offend your listener, but there are others we need to avoid. We must also be aware of comments that are ageist (degrading of someone's age), for example, "That old man could never run a marathon"; homophobic (degrading comments about someone's sexual orientation), as in "She looks like a dyke in that leather jacket"; and comments about someone's abilities, like "She's handicapped since the car accident."

These comments not only serve to insult and alienate your audience, but also encourage others to see the person in a negative way. So, when you call someone a "fag," "spic," "gimp," or "old geezer," you are not just using a label, you are showing how little you value the person. These terms are a sign of disrespect and will certainly put an end to the interaction.

Improving Verbal Skills

In the preceding section we identified specific problems concerning language and our communication with others. How do we combat the potential problems associated with vague language, abstraction, generalization, multiple meanings, technical language, and slang?

First and foremost, we need to always be aware of the context in which a message is presented. By *context,* we mean the environment or conditions surrounding the communication between two parties. For instance, the responses of two athletes to a sportscaster's question, "What do you think was the key play of the game?" are bound to be tempered by whether or not the players were on the winning or losing side. Knowledge of the circumstances surrounding the interaction gives us a more complete understanding of the message.

In addition, we can learn specific techniques to help diminish language barriers. These techniques include being descriptive, dating, indexing, avoiding profanity and vulgar language, eliminating sexist language, and showing respect for others.

Being Descriptive

Descriptive language employs specific words that represent observable behavior or phenomena. Being descriptive directs our communication to actions that are observable, and at the same time it avoids drawing inferences or making judgments about those actions.

For example, consider the difference between these two statements:

Statement A: Heather doesn't look directly at me when we speak.

Statement B: Heather avoids direct eye contact with me because she does not like me.

Statement A is simply an observation made by the individual who is speaking. Statement B goes beyond description; it tries to offer an explanation for Heather's behavior. By doing so, the individual is confronted with a problem addressed earlier in this chapter—making generalizations. In fact, Heather's lack of direct eye contact may be attributed to other factors: perhaps she is shy, or perhaps she actually likes this person and is too nervous to establish direct eye contact.

Being descriptive helps us communicate more clearly and accurately, and it reduces the misunderstandings that occur between people. At the same time, being descriptive can make our speech more interesting.

Dating

Dating is the use of a specific time reference to clarify a message. By interjecting a specific date, we make a statement that is based on fact. The following set of statements illustrates the difference between a general comment and one that is more specific as a result of dating:

Russell: I don't get along with my in-laws.

Russell: I don't get along with my in-laws during the holidays.

SKILL BUILDING   Dating

1. Examine the following statements. Rewrite them using the skill of dating to increase their accuracy.

   a. I can't get along with my boss.

   b. Bill never cleans his room.

   c. Professor Williams's classes are always boring.

   d. I always have a good meal at the Peking House.

   e. The Chicago Cubs are the best baseball team.

2. How does the use of dating improve verbal communication?

The first statement is very general; it does not take into account that the situation may have changed at some point. By dating the second statement, Russell avoids making a generalization about the relationship he has with his in-laws.

Without dating, statements made by one party can cause confusion or hard feelings for both parties. Consider this dialogue between Sheila and Jim (dating is not used):

Sheila: I just bought a two-bedroom house in Highland.

Jim: What section of town is the house located in?

Sheila: It's just a few blocks west of the downtown area.

Jim: I've heard that that area of town has a bad flooding problem.

Sheila: You're kidding! The realtor never mentioned that problem to me!

What Jim failed to do in the preceding exchange was to tell Sheila that the flooding problem happened over three years ago. By including this date in his conversation with Shelia, Jim would not be making a misleading statement, and in this case, his comments certainly would not be as upsetting. Dating lends accuracy to our communication with others.

Indexing

Indexing is a technique that takes into account the individual differences among people, objects, and places. The use of indexing helps us to focus on the unique qualities of each person or thing. For example, to say that car sales representatives are dishonest would be generalizing or stereotyping. To prevent making such an irresponsible statement, it would be better to say, "The sales representative at Downtown Automotive failed to honor the price he quoted me two days ago, but the sales representative at Suburban Auto came up with the same figures when I went back to put a deposit on a car." This is a more accurate statement because it points out the individual differences between the sales representatives; in this case, one was dishonest, but the other was not. Since language and perception are interconnected, the use of indexing can more accurately reflect our perceptions of people, events, or objects.

Avoiding Vulgar Language and Profanity

We have all used or heard "four-letter words." Most of the time, these words are used inappropriately and alienate our audience or partner. Profanity and vulgar language are commonplace and we hear them all the time. Like all language, profanity is learned by watching and listening to others. One father told this story about his daughter's use of profanity:

> Clara was about two years old and we were riding in the car. I was in a hurry to get home after a long day at work and was not being very patient. When a car cut in front of us and we missed a long stop light, I said, "S_ _t!!" A few moments later, Clara repeated the word and laughed. I was horrified.

Profanity and vulgar language can be used to convey strong emotions or to make a point. It is also used to "shock" audiences, as Howard Stern and other "shock jocks" have illustrated. For us, however, profanity and vulgar language can cause more damage than it can help to clarify your message.

Eliminating Generic Language

We once agreed that "he" referred to any person or that "man" referred to all people. This is called generic language. Fortunately, this is no longer the case, and dictionaries, newspapers, and textbooks do not use the generic "he" or "man" to refer to men and women. Generic language is a problem because it only pretends to include women, when in fact it only refers to men. Language must be inclusive when it is referring to an entire population. Specifically:

1. Avoid the generic "he" when you want to talk about all people. *"A person taking a prescription medication should be sure **he** knows the side effects before taking the first dose."* This sentence is sexist because it only refers to one sex. Think for a moment . . . when you heard this sentence, how did you visualize the person? Was the person a man or woman? Most of us would answer a man because the use of "he" leads us to that picture. The masculine pronoun "he" does not refer to women and men. Instead, try to use a plural (*"**People** taking a prescription medication should be sure **they** know the side effects before taking the first dose"*), or use both the male and female pronouns (*"A person taking a prescription medication should be sure **he** or **she** knows the side effects before taking the first dose"*).

2. Avoid using words with "man" when you want to talk about men and women or when you are referring to a woman. Think about all the words that include "man." *Mankind, man-made, policeman, fireman,*

Ethics in Communication

Appropriate Language Use

In the chapter-opening story, April can't understand a word of Dr. Smith's speech. His presentation to the campus community was confusing and almost everyone in the audience failed to understand his message. Of course, some of the faculty members understood the presentation, but the students and community members could not. What went wrong with the presentation?

Dr. Smith, a well-known philosopher, was invited to the campus to discuss the topics of identity, self, and society. Dr. Moriarity, Dean of Liberal Arts, personally asked Dr. Smith to present his ideas in a way for all to understand. When Dr. Smith sent Dr. Moriarity a preview of the speech, Dr. Moriarity was troubled by the language choices and asked Dr. Smith to limit his use of specialized terms that the audience would not know. Dr. Smith refused to make any changes or to take his audience into account. He answered Dr. Moriarity, "I will not water down my ideas for students. If they can't understand the terms, then they should get a dictionary."

Dr. Smith's speech, then, failed before it began. His use of technical terms or jargon served to confuse and alienate the audience. Although the language may have been appropriate for the small number of faculty in the audience, Dr. Smith intentionally used language that was inappropriate for his overall audience. It is no wonder that April and her classmates were confused.

and *chairman* are just a few examples. How can a woman be a policeman? She certainly can be a police officer, but calling her a policeman seems silly. Find alternative words for sexist labels as we have done with *policeman* and *police officer*.

Avoiding generic language will help you to relate to the receivers of your message and will ensure that you do not alienate them.

Improving Verbal Skills

CHECKLIST

- Being descriptive
- Being concrete
- Dating
- Indexing
- Avoiding profanity and vulgarity
- Eliminating sexist (generic) language

Summary

This chapter explored the role of language in the communication process. Words are symbols that represent such things as our feelings, names for the objects around us, and explanations for behaviors. Language is an arbitrary system of symbols and is rule governed. Language also communicates power.

C.K. Ogden and I.A. Richards (1923) developed a theory to explain the relationship between our thoughts and the words we select to express those thoughts. Cultural influences, including ethnic/racial/social groups and geography, and perception are factors that affect our choice of words and our interpretations of others' words. The Sapir-Whorf hypothesis maintains that our perception of reality is dependent on the language system that supports our thought process.

Problems of understanding sometimes arise because others do not perceive our words as we intend for them to be understood. These problems stem from the use of vague language, including abstraction and generalization, the use of words having multiple meanings, and the use of technical language or jargon, and the use of slang.

We can improve our verbal communication by using such techniques as being descriptive, dating, and indexing. We should also avoid profanity and generic forms of language to ensure we don't offend or alienate our listeners. Lastly, we should show respect for others through our language choices.

Review Questions

1. What is the relationship between the word, the thought, and the thing?
2. Describe how ethnic/racial/social influences and geographic influences affect the meanings of words.
3. Describe powerful and powerless language.
4. What is the relationship between perception and language?
5. Explain the difference between connotation and denotation.
6. Describe ways to improve your verbal communication.
7. How can dating lead to more accurate verbal communication?
8. How can indexing help you avoid stereotyping?
9. Why should we avoid profanity and generic language?
10. How can we show respect for our audiences through our language choices?

5

Nonverbal Communication

At the conclusion of this chapter, you should be able to:

- Explain the nature of nonverbal communication.
- Compare and contrast five types of bodily movements.
- Explain why people react differently to touch.
- Explain how paralanguage operates in nonverbal communication.
- Discuss how our silence can send a message.
- Define four levels of personal space.

- Explain the significance of territory in nonverbal communication.
- Explain how our personal appearance and clothing can be used to create an image.
- Discuss how our use of time sends messages.
- Apply four techniques to improve interpretation and use of nonverbal messages.

Carla, a biology lab instructor, watches her students as they arrive. One by one they enter the room and take a seat at one of the many lab stations. Several students who are dressed like Carla smile and say "hello" as they take their seats. Carla smiles back. A young woman in her early twenties in medical scrubs arrives. Carla says to herself, "Well, at least there will be one smart student in the class. She can help me with some of the slower students."

Right behind the "nurse," a very well dressed woman in her late thirties enters the classroom. She is carrying a briefcase and the course textbook. "I bet she's good at business, but I'll be anxious to see what she does with the labs."

A very young man dressed in ragged jeans and a t-shirt hurries into the classroom. He has several earrings in both ears and a nose ring. Several tattoos cover his forearms and hands. "A loser," says Carla. "He will surely need help with every aspect of the course. Maybe he can be lab partners with the "nurse" and she can help him get through the course: that is, if he is motivated to do so. I doubt he is!"

The last student to enter, five minutes late, is a man in his forties dressed in a mechanic's uniform that is very soiled from the day's work. Carla says to herself, "He could at least get to class on time. He doesn't care very much. Obviously he works with his hands all day, which will be helpful with the lab equipment, but I know I'll have to spend time with him on the lab reports. Maybe I can partner him with the 'business' woman. She will need help with the labs, and she can help the mechanic with the reports."

Carla is making several assumptions about her students' knowledge, motivation, and ability before she really knows anything about them. How is the students' dress effecting Carla's perception of the students? What messages are the students sending by the way they are dressed? Do you think these messages are intentional? Do you think they realize they are sending these messages? In this chapter, we look at nonverbal communication and how we communicate without using language or symbols. Specifically, we will see how our differences affect our sending and interpreting nonverbal messages.

Nonverbal communication encompasses the broad spectrum of messages we send without verbalizing our thoughts or feelings. Included in this definition are bodily movements, space, touch, personal appearance, paralanguage, silence, and time. We communicate nonverbally in our interpersonal relationships, within small groups, and in public-speaking situations. In addition, part of our listening includes nonverbal responses. When we consider the widespread use of nonverbal communication, it becomes evident that this subject warrants further study.

Nonverbal messages are an integral part of our communication. In fact, 65 to 70 percent of the meaning of our messages is delivered nonverbally (Anderson, 1999). That means that when you are talking to your friend about the difficult test you just took, your friend is getting most of the meaning of your message from your voice, bodily movements, and other nonverbal channels. Thus, nonverbal messages work with verbal messages to communicate our thoughts and feelings. Effective communicators understand and appreciate the unique and different ways we use nonverbal messages in every communication situation. In this chapter, we will discuss the nature of nonverbal communication, the types and functions of nonverbal behavior, and finally, ways to improve our use of nonverbal communication.

The Nature of Nonverbal Communication

We have just learned how important nonverbal messages are to the overall communication process. Nonverbal communication is also intentional and unintentional, ambiguous, multichanneled, and culturally bound.

Nonverbal communication can be **intentional** or **unintentional.** In other words, we can decide to send a message using our body, voice, or use of time. Or we can send messages we are unaware we are sending or don't mean to send. For example, when a mother yells at a child because the child ran into the street, she intentionally uses her voice to emphasize the verbal message, "Don't go into the street." But when she tells the story a few minutes later to her husband, her voice shakes. This is unintentional use of voice to convey the message that she was afraid their child would be hit by an oncoming car.

Nonverbal messages are ambiguous. It is very difficult for anyone to accurately interpret the meaning of nonverbal communication. Does a wave mean hello or good-bye? What do two hands in the formation of a T mean? A time-out? A technical foul? To understand the meaning, we need to know the context of the communication and the relationship between the sender and receivers. Of course, nonverbal behavior that indicates our emotional state is somewhat easier to interpret accurately. For example, we know that someone crying and sobbing is in some kind of pain or that someone laughing loudly is happy. Well, most of the time. Take the example of Sarah. Sarah was sitting in her hospital bed crying and sobbing almost uncontrollably. When her friend Kristen entered the room, she rushed to her side and said, "Oh my goodness, what has happened? I thought you and the baby were okay." Sarah said, "We are really great. I am just so happy our new little girl is healthy, and I am relieved that the delivery went well." Sarah was not crying because she was sad or in pain, but because she felt intense relief and joy at the birth of her daughter.

We send nonverbal messages through many different channels. Unlike language (see Chapter 4), which only provides us with one channel (symbols), nonverbal communication is **multichanneled.** We can use our body, voice, and appearance to convey the same message. For example:

> Mike is getting ready for his first date with Allyssa. They are going to a movie and then out for pizza. He decides to wear his favorite Tommy Hilfiger sweater and jeans (he bought at the outlet mall). He takes great care to carefully shave his chin (to avoid any cuts) and brush his teeth. He leaves several minutes before he needs to, to be sure he isn't late. On the way to Allyssa's apartment, he picks up a bouquet of flowers. When he arrives at her door, five minutes early, he greets her with a big smile and the flowers.

What message has Mike sent by his dress, use of time, and facial expression? Obviously, Mike wants Allyssa to know he cares about her and wants her to like him. Mike did not have to say this with words, he used several channels to convey his message.

As we learned in Chapter 1, each of us is unique and different in many ways. Our use of nonverbal communication is one aspect that makes us unique and different because nonverbal behavior is **culturally bound.** In other words, the meanings and functions of nonverbal communication are derived from our culture. According to Anderson, "one of the most basic and obvious functions of nonverbal behavior is to communicate one's culture" (1999, p. 75). As we said earlier, many times we are unaware of our nonverbal behavior and are unintentionally sending messages. What we sometimes fail to understand is that a nonverbal message in one culture may mean something entirely different in another. For example, the A-OK sign (making a circle with the thumb and index finger), which we in the United States use all the time to mean "fine" or "okay," means something very different in South America:

Culture dictates the appropriate use of nonverbal behaviors.

When Richard Nixon visited Venezuela as the U.S. vice president in 1956 and gave two A-OK signs to a crowd of demonstrators in Caracas, a huge riot erupted. Nixon was later informed that the A-OK sign actually had a different meaning in Venezuela, similar to an upraised middle finger in America (Anderson, 1999, p. 78).

Each culture has its own set of nonverbal behaviors and meanings. Some cultures have unwritten rules that dictate when touching behavior is appropriate. In European societies, for example, it is commonplace for men to embrace in public as a way of greeting each other, whereas in the United States greetings are usually done with a handshake. Public embraces are less common. How we use time or touch, what is considered beautiful, and how far apart we stand all communicate our culture.

Types and Functions of Nonverbal Communication

We have learned about the nature of nonverbal communication, and now we turn to a discussion about the specific types of nonverbal behavior and its functions as a part of the overall communication process. Specifically, we will discuss bodily movement, touch, paralanguage, silence, space, personal appearance, and the use of time.

Bodily Movement

Kinesics is the study of bodily movements. As mentioned at the beginning of this chapter, we communicate a great deal about how we feel in a given situation by our nonverbal actions. Paul Ekman and Wallace V. Friesen developed a classification system that helps us understand our nonverbal communication (1969). Their system identifies the different types of kinesic behaviors: emblems, illustrators, affect displays, regulators, and adaptors. A definition and a discussion of each will help us see how bodily movements affect our communication.

Emblems

Emblems, according to Ekman and Friesen, are body motions that take the place of words (1975). For instance, holding up your hand, palm flattened, signals "stop" to someone standing across the room from you. Likewise, a basketball coach motioning "time out" with his hands communicates to a player on the court that the player should signal the referee to stop play so that the team can discuss a new strategy. In order for emblems to be an effective form of nonverbal communication, both parties must readily understand the motions being used. A spectator unfamiliar with sports might not understand the "time out" motion used by those involved in the game and therefore might question why the referee officially signaled time out. Emblems also can be used effectively when there are obstacles to verbal communication. The example of the basketball game applies here as well; the coach may signal to a player to call for time out because the crowd is generating too much noise for the coach to be heard by the player.

Illustrators

Illustrators are nonverbal symbols that reinforce a verbal message. While emblems take the place of a verbal message, illustrators enhance the verbal message. A tight squeeze that accompanies your saying, "I missed you so much these past two weeks," illustrates the sincerity of your verbal message. Similarly, after screaming at your boyfriend or girlfriend, "I never want to see you again," slamming the door further demonstrates your anger. Illustrators must be natural in order to be effective. Consider the effect of slamming a door ten minutes after you have concluded an argument with someone—the effect would be rather hollow. Effective public speakers frequently use illustrators to emphasize their points. For them it is a natural behavior to raise an arm or point a finger when they become passionate or emphatic about their topic.

Affect Displays

Affect displays are nonverbal signs of our emotional state. Giving someone a cold stare, for example, would indicate that we are angry or displeased. Conversely, a smile would indicate that we are happy or pleased with our immediate environment. According to Ekman and Friesen, facial expressions are used as affect displays (1975). Emotions such as sadness, happiness, fear, surprise, anger, and disgust can be communicated using our faces.

In many cases, we are unaware of the affect displays we use; they tend to be automatic. For instance, Sherry does not realize that she is twisting her hair as she delivers her speech, yet her behavior belies the nervousness she is experiencing.

On the other hand, there are times when we deliberately control our affect displays in order to hide our feelings. What does this mean for the person who observes our behavior? Basically, affect displays can be misleading because they do not always portray how we feel. Perhaps an example will clarify this point. We might smile after a prospective employer informs us that we were not selected for the position; despite our disappointment, we do not want to let the other person know how much we had hoped to get the job. Perhaps the situation has made us feel self-conscious; we perceive that our image will suffer, so we behave accordingly. Other factors that influence the way we use affect displays include the upbringing we received from our family (for example, some children are taught to display little emotion in public) and gender expectations (for example, men should always appear strong).

Regulators

Regulators are nonverbal behaviors used to control, or regulate, communication between people. These cues indicate whether or not it is appropriate for the sender to continue his or her message. Scholars have found, for instance, that when two people are having a conversation, the listener maintains eye contact 70 percent of the time (perhaps indicating that he or she is listening) and the speaker only 40 percent of the time (Knapp and Hall, 1992). Furthermore, if we notice someone smiling at us or nodding his or her head in agreement, we might be encouraged to continue speaking. Catching someone glancing at his or her watch or gazing across the room, however, might indicate that we are not holding the attention of our listeners. As public speakers, we can benefit from reading audience regulators. Often these regulators indicate when adjustments need to be made: whether it is time to move on to the next point or whether we should conclude our speech.

As receivers, we may wish to control the direction or focus of a conversation. One way to achieve this is by using regulators. If we approve of what is being said, we can demonstrate our support by nodding our heads. This communicates to the sender, "Yes, that's right. Please continue." If we wish to change the direction of the communication, we might shake our heads or pound our fists on the table in an attempt to say, "I disagree" or "You're mistaken. Let me tell you how it really is!"

Who uses regulators? Both people with acknowledged influence, such as company executives, parents, or clergy, and individuals who feel uncomfortable expressing themselves verbally. They might effectively control a discussion by using such nonverbal cues. For example, a student listening to an instructor lecture about Chaucer's *Canterbury Tales* may be totally uninterested in the subject, but she realizes that it would be unacceptable to tell the instructor how bored she is. Instead, she can effectively communicate her sentiments by thumbing the pages of a book, yawning, or glancing at the clock on the wall. These regulators represent the student's effort to control the instructor's communication.

Adaptors

Adaptors are nonverbal behaviors individuals use to adjust to or cope with uncomfortable communication situations. They help us relieve the tension we may be feeling. For example, Dean is extremely anxious about his upcoming job interview. What he would really like to do is bound out of his chair, make a mad dash for the elevator, and forget about the whole thing. Instead, he taps his feet nervously on the tile floor, waiting to be called.

Although adaptors are meant to help us through stressful situations, they can pose problems for public speakers. An audience who notices a public speaker wringing his or her hands or twisting a strand of hair can easily be distracted by this behavior; their attention shifts from the speaker's message to watching the nonverbal behavior. Once the speaker is made aware of the problem, he or she can practice controlling the distracting behavior during the delivery. The speaker can work at incorporating natural gestures into the delivery to take the place of adaptors. Repeated efforts should result in the speaker actually feeling more comfortable before the audience and in delivering a more effective speech.

CRITICAL THINKING   **Use of Bodily Movements**

Watch one of your favorite television dramas ("The West Wing," "ER," "CSI: Crime Scene Investigation") without the sound on.

- Focus your attention on the characters' use of their bodies to communicate. List their use of emblems, illustrators, regulators, affect displays, and adaptors.

- Could you determine the entire meaning of their messages without the verbal part of the message? Why or why not?
- What parts of the message could you determine?
- How did the characters' use of bodily movement clarify their message? Provide examples.

Touch

Touch is a form of nonverbal communication that conveys a wide range of emotions. Usually, spontaneous touching behavior communicates such emotions as tenderness (a caress), concern (a hand on someone's shoulder, joy (a hug), anger (a slap or punch), or passion (a kiss). Sometimes it is easier to convey our feelings by touching someone than by finding the appropriate words to express our feelings. In such instances, touching is just as effective as a verbal message.

People react differently to touch. Many people respond positively to physical affection because it communicates concern and offers security. Others feel uncomfortable or nervous when touched—to them it is a question of having their personal space violated. As communicators, we need to be sensitive to these differences in people and to respect the feelings of others.

Two variables play a role in the way touching is interpreted: our socialization and the context of the situation. Our socialization affects the way we respond to touch in that we tend to react more positively to touch if we have been exposed to touching behavior during our upbringing. On the other hand, if our childhood included minimal touching, we are likely to be more uncertain or uncomfortable with touching as adults.

The context of the communication situation also can affect the way we use touch. For instance, a person may outwardly display affectionate touching behavior to an individual in private, yet the same behavior would be an intrusion of that person's privacy if done in public. Consider, too, that in a work environment intimate touching rarely occurs between colleagues. Under different circumstances, however, these same employees

TABLE 5.1	Types of Bodily Movements
Emblems	Body motions that take the place of words
Illustrators	Nonverbal symbols that reinforce a verbal message
Affect displays	Signs of our emotional state
Regulators	Nonverbal behaviors that attempt to control communication
Adaptors	Nonverbal behaviors that grow out of our discomfort

might embrace each other: A wedding or an announcement of a child's birth are two such occasions.

Paralanguage and Silence

Paralanguage is the vocal aspect of delivery that accompanies speech and other nonverbal utterances. It can include pitch (tone), volume (loudness), rate (speed), and quality (richness of one's voice), all of which work in conjunction with the spoken word. Chapter 14 presents a more detailed discussion of these factors.

What can we learn about someone from this special form of nonverbal communication? Pitch can bring with it certain associations. We sometimes associate youth or immaturity with a high-pitched voice. Of course, this is not necessarily the case; certain people maintain a high-pitched voice throughout their lives. A deep, resonant voice often communicates just the opposite, the image of someone who has a mature, steady, or dramatic nature.

The *volume* of a message communicates something extra. For example, when we desire to speak to someone on an intimate level, we often use a soft voice. Conversely, we use a loud voice to say "I want your undivided attention" or simply to ensure that our voice is heard in a noisy, crowded room.

The *rate* of our speech can convey our emotional state. When we feel nervous, for example, we tend to speak more rapidly. This happens in both interpersonal and public-speaking situations. Have you ever phoned someone you do not know very well and blurted out the purpose of your call in the first ten seconds? The interaction goes this way because you are nervous. Contrast this behavior with the normal speed at which we talk. A normal pace communicates that we are more comfortable with our surroundings.

The *quality* of one's voice is highly subjective. Generally speaking, someone with a nasal or grating voice is more annoying to listen to than someone who has a resonant voice.

One aspect of paralanguage that people universally find annoying is the use of **fillers** or **vocal interruptions,** sounds used to fill in the gaps between the words that comprise our messages. Words such as *you know, like, uh, uh,* or *um* are examples of commonly used fillers. It is more effective to pause between ideas than to repeatedly use fillers.

CRITICAL THINKING　　　　　　　　　　**Paralanguage**

Ron has been working at the local paint store for eighteen months. His boss, Mr. Washington, owns the store. For the past two months Ron has thought about asking Mr. Washington for a raise. He thinks he deserves one; he is punctual, pleasant to the customers, and good at mixing paints. He is nervous about approaching Mr. Washington with his request, however. How might his voice reflect his nervousness? Specifically:

- Does Ron talk fast or slowly?
- Is the pitch of his voice different than usual?
- Do you notice any change in the volume of Ron's voice?
- Does he use any fillers during his interaction with Mr. Washington?
- What does paralanguage communicate to others?

We have discussed the use of voice as a type of nonverbal behavior. Not using your voice is also paralanguage. **Silence** is the absence of using your voice. When we choose not to speak, we are sending a strong message to others. Silence can communicate anger, disappointment, embarrassment, and even affection. We often think of the "silent treatment" when our partner, a family member, or friend refuses to talk because of a disagreement. By refusing to talk, we take control of the communication and assert our power (see Chapter 6). Silence can also communicate uneasiness or discomfort. For example, during Albert's visit to his partner's Steve's parents' home, it was clear that Steve's parents were not very comfortable meeting Albert, even though they said they were happy to meet him. During his short visit, several minutes were spent in silence as each tried to think of something to say.

But silence can also send a positive message. We can listen intently to show respect. Or, have you ever sat with someone you love and just held hands? The silence between you can be comforting and affirming.

Space

What is your reaction when someone you have just been introduced to moves within a few inches of you to begin a conversation? Do you take a step back? If you are feeling uncomfortable, you might wonder, "Why is this person invading my space?" Factors such as your cultural upbringing play a part in how you respond to someone else's communication. **Proxemics** is the study of physical space as it relates to human interaction. This section discusses two types of space: personal space and territory.

Personal Space

Personal space is the area that exists between ourselves and others. While we are not always conscious of the amount of personal space we need, our communication behavior is likely to change in response to fluctuations in that space. When we feel that someone has infringed on our personal space, for example, we will likely display defensive behavior. In his book, *The Hidden Dimension,* Edward Hall (1969) discusses how people use space to insulate and protect themselves. He identifies four distances that correlate with the levels of space that people need in various communication settings. These include intimate distance, personal distance, social distance, and public distance.

Intimate distance is that distance at which it is appropriate for highly personal communication encounters to occur. This area ranges from actual touching to a distance of approximately eighteen inches. These encounters are usually private and are reserved for communicating very special feelings. When we put an arm around the shoulder of a friend whose sister has just died, we are within the area known as intimate distance. The nature of this relationship dictates the appropriateness of our behavior. When a stranger stands within a few inches of us on a crowded bus during rush hour, however, we are likely to feel that our personal space has been invaded. To us it seems inappropriate for a stranger to be within this intimate distance.

According to Hall, **personal distance** is that area most appropriate for interpersonal interactions dealing with personal matters, that is, approximately eighteen inches to four feet. In interpersonal relationships, the closer the parties remain, the more private is the discussion. As people move farther apart physically, the likelihood is greater that the dialogue is becoming less personal. During an interview, for example, two parties usually sit across a table or desk from each other while having their discussion. If a person from another department enters the room, it is quite likely that the interview would temporarily cease while another type of interaction takes place. Perhaps the interviewer would stand up, introduce the other two individuals to each other, and establish a less personal conversation. Having a third party in the picture changes the dynamics of the interaction; personal distance is no longer appropriate or feasible for this new dialogue.

Social distance is that distance most appropriate for communication of a nonpersonal nature. A boardroom business meeting, a family picnic, a literature study group meeting in a member's home, or four couples enjoying an evening together playing bridge are all examples of situations where communication occurs at a social distance, that is, from approximately four to twelve feet. Social distance is the one category that cuts across both interpersonal and public communication. Of the examples just listed, the communication at a family picnic is purely interpersonal, yet it is entirely possible for a public presentation to be made by someone at a meeting of company executives.

Public distance, a distance exceeding twelve feet, is most appropriate for public communication. Situations involving public distance are usu-

When waiting to use an ATM machine, we try to maintain social or public distance.

ally more formal or defined by an audience and a speaker. For instance, when we purchase tickets for the performance of a popular comedian, we expect to watch his or her act as part of the audience. If, however, the comedian were to come down off the stage and mingle with the audience and even single out individual members to use in a few jokes, we might feel that the comedian has taken advantage of the personal space we perceive to be appropriate for this situation. We feel uncomfortable because the comedian has acted differently than we expected.

Territory

Territory is the space we stake out as our own. At home, we may have a special chair in the den or family room that we think of as our own; at work, our desk and the area immediately surrounding it are part of our territory. Because we often attach a special significance to territory, it is not uncommon for us to become protective of it. Whether it is a teenager communicating that her bedroom is off limits to other family members; an employee who defines his territory by specially arranging his desk, posters, pictures, and plants; or a vice president who furnishes her office in order to convey a particular level of status or power, territory is an expression of our feelings and attitudes.

SELF-ASSESSMENT   Territory

- Do you or any members of your family have a particular chair, room of the house, and so on, that you or he or she consider special?
- How do you or he or she communicate to others that the territory is special?
- What happens when someone invades this space? Be specific.
- What does this say about the importance of territory in our communication with others?

Physical Appearance and Clothing

In our Western culture, appearance matters. People's perceptions of our outward appearance make a big difference in our opportunities to establish relationships, find jobs, and succeed in school. Studies have shown that we care about appearance, and attractive people, overall, find it easier to make friends, gain employment, and earn good grades. What messages are you sending by wearing several earrings or piercing your nose or belly button? In some social groups, this is a sign of being cool or stylish. How might a future employer at a bank, for example, perceive the body piercings? Our physical appearance matters, and we need to be aware that others may view us differently because of it.

The way we dress becomes part of the message we send to others, whether we intend it to or not. Our clothes and style of dress contribute to the way we see ourselves and the way others perceive us. Our style of clothing also reflects our ability or willingness to adjust to a variety of social situations. In other words, what we choose to wear can reflect our desire to gain acceptance within a given social situation. For instance, if we want to "fit in" among the other guests at a formal dinner party, we would wear a tuxedo or an appropriate evening dress. Moreover, our choice of dress reveals information about ourselves and affects our impact in both interpersonal and public communication settings.

What specifically does our clothing communicate? One thing it can indicate is our age or an age we wish to project. If, for example, we want to appear youthful, we would dress according to the latest styles or trends. Beware, however, that we can inadvertently give away our age by wearing clothes considered to be out of date.

Certain types of dress identify individuals as members of particular groups or professions. When we see someone dressed in a blue uniform, we presume (usually correctly) that he or she is a member of a police department. Other examples include black collars worn by priests, military uniforms worn by men and women in the armed forces, uniforms represent-

The striped shirt worn by this referee communicates his power to control the basketball game.

ing different sports, leather jackets worn by members of motorcycle gangs, and native dress representing foreign nations (sarongs worn by Indian women, for example).

Sometimes we wear clothing specially selected to project an image that is different from the one we have ourselves. Consider these examples: (1) Ken, a college student, copies the style of a popular TV star in order to appear sexy; (2) Fred, a recent graduate, wears a three-piece suit to his interview with a prestigious law firm in order to project an air of maturity and professionalism; and (3) Nicole, a career woman, dresses in a business suit and carries a leather briefcase to her training seminar for local bank managers.

In selecting our clothing, we should keep the following in mind: Our clothes should not draw negative attention to ourselves. Whether we are speaking before an audience or interacting with only one or two other people, we should dress appropriately for the occasion. If we wear something

COMMUNICATION and TECHNOLOGY

Nonverbal Communication and Business

A television commercial for Southwest Airlines in late 2001 said:

"You can't pat a back with a fax."
"You can't shake a hand with an email."
"Some things are just better in person."

Despite the advent of technology and its effect on the way we communicate, business professionals still believe that "some things are just better in person." In other words, technology is not a substitute for nonverbal communication. As Michael Begeman, manager of the 3M Meeting Network in Austin, Texas, says, "Communication across all media is increasing. Videoconferencing is doubling year to year, and we're seeing an explosion of dataconferencing. At the same time, people are spending more time than ever in face-to-face meetings and say they don't plan on that changing" (Boss, 1999, p. 15). In fact, according to Shira Boss, "the more ways there are to communicate long distance, the more business people insist on face-to-face meetings" (1999, p. 15). Specifically, according to the National Foundation of Women Business Owners, "Businesswomen, especially, value personal business contacts" (Boss, 1999, p. 15).

Why is this the case? Why do business professionals insist on face-to-face meetings when communicating using technology is easier, faster, and cheaper? It is the personal touch that secures business and seals the deal. Platt states, "You may receive many emails, voice mails, and phone calls, but you are missing significant amounts of data that would normally be available to you in face-to-face working relationships" (1999, p. 15). Problems are harder to detect without the nonverbal cues such as eye contact, facial expressions, and tone of voice. Most of all, trust is developed through nonverbal communication. Terry Neese, former president of the National Association of Business Owners, argues that "technology hasn't changed the fact that relationships are built on trust," and "the eye contact develops the integrity, sincerity, and relationship-building process, and you can't do that via phone, fax, or email" (Boss, 1999, p. 15).

So, despite the expense of face-to-face interaction, which includes transportation and lodging, businesses are insisting on meeting their clients in person instead of using technology. Neese argues, "It's absolutely more expensive, but being able to sit across the table from a potential customer, in my opinion, raises the possibility of putting any kind of business deal together around 70 percent" (Boss, 1999, p. 15). Nonverbal communication is important to any communication situation, and business professionals understand this. Marti Smye, president of People Tech Consulting, sums it up this way: "People need to physically come together in groups and interact. Technology will never take the place of person to person contact" (Hunt, 1996, p. 23).

outlandish, no one will pay attention to our message; they will be too busy studying our attire.

Time

The study of how we use time is called **chronemics.** In our culture, time is viewed as a commodity or thing we can trade or buy. Think about the words we use to describe time: We *save* time by taking a short cut; we *budget* our time by working longer hours on Thursday so we leave early on Friday; our group *invested* so much time in this project in order to get our grade up; and we *waste* time by watching television. As Anderson says, "Psychologically and rhetorically, most Americans treat time like their most prized possession or like money itself: something to be earned, saved, spent, and treasured" (1999, p. 63).

Think about the messages we send with our use of time. What does being prompt or on time mean? What about being late? If you are consistently late for class, what might the instructor think about you and your attitude toward the course? Probably not very positively. We value promptness because it communicates professionalism, caring, and respect. Spending a lot of time with someone is also considered a sign of caring and respect. In one study, the amount of time spent with someone was the leading predictor of relational satisfaction and understanding (Stelzner and Egland, 1995).

Time can communicate status. Think about the people who can keep you waiting. We often wait thirty minutes to an hour to see a physician. We accept that our supervisor, instructor, or other authority figure can and will make us wait because their time is perceived as more valuable.

Improving Nonverbal Communication

As you have discovered throughout this chapter, the chief difficulty associated with nonverbal communication is its interpretation by others. It is easy to misunderstand the nonverbal cues you receive, yet it is more difficult to question these behaviors than it is to ask questions about particular verbal statements. As a result, you need to proceed cautiously when drawing conclusions about nonverbal communication. By using the following suggestions, you can increase your ability to accurately interpret nonverbal messages.

Explore All Possible Meanings of Nonverbal Messages

Because nonverbal messages can have a variety of meanings, it is easy to misinterpret them. This is one of the difficulties of nonverbal communication. To combat that problem, we should strive for greater accuracy in our interpretation of messages.

How do we achieve this? One way is to try to remain open minded about the different meanings nonverbal behavior can suggest. For instance, if someone fails to establish direct eye contact with us, this might mean (1) that the person is extremely shy, (2) that the person is distracted because he or she has something else on his other mind, (3) that the person is not interested in the conversation, or (4) that be person is showing respect as taught in his or her culture (a more detailed discussion of eye contact appears in Chapter 14). Before an accurate conclusion can be reached, all the possibilities should be explored.

Look for Nonverbal Messages That Are Consistent with Verbal Statements

Nonverbal communication that supports verbal statements helps confirm the validity of the verbal message. Since nonverbal messages are more spontaneous than verbal messages, they more accurately reflect our feelings. Thus, if the verbal message is supported by the nonverbal behavior, we are probably interpreting the sender's message correctly. However, when the verbal and nonverbal messages are inconsistent, it is generally wiser to check your perception and ask for clarification.

Use Questions and Descriptive Feedback to Achieve Accuracy

We will be able to communicate more effectively if we learn to focus on the behaviors of others and accurately describe what is observable without making unwarranted inferences. Asking questions about observable behavior may help us to avoid the trap of prematurely evaluating others. This process is known as perception checking. **Perception checking** is a verbal statement that reflects our understanding of a nonverbal message (see Chapters 2 and 3). If we can confront nonverbal behavior by asking specific questions about that behavior, we may find it easier to clear up misinterpretations and avoid unnecessary conflict. Look at the following example of Bob and Nancy on their first date:

> *Bob:* I've noticed that you keep looking at your watch. You must be really bored!
>
> *Nancy:* No, I'm not. It's just a habit of mine. I'm having a good time, but I'm just a little nervous.
>
> *Bob:* Me too, I want to get to know you better, but it's always so hard in the beginning. That's probably why I'm rambling so much!

In this example we can see how perception checking helped clarify the communication between Bob and Nancy. Bob's comments focused on the behavior he observed without being critical.

Monitor Your Own Use of Nonverbal Communication

Self-reflection is always the first step to understanding and practicing effective communication. Think about what messages you may be sending intentionally or unintentionally with your bodily movement and paralanguage, use of space and time, and your appearance and clothing. Keep in mind that others may interpret your nonverbal messages differently from the way you had intended. Also, be aware that your verbal and nonverbal messages may be inconsistent. Strive to have your nonverbal communication complement and enhance your verbal messages.

Improving Nonverbal Communication Skills   CHECKLIST

- Explore all possible meanings of a nonverbal message.

- Look for nonverbal messages that are consistent with verbal statements.

- Use questions and descriptive feedback to achieve accuracy.

- Monitor your own use of nonverbal messages.

Improving Nonverbal Communication   SKILL BUILDING

When Aaron does not arrive home from work at his usual time, his wife, Brenda, begins to wonder what's keeping him. Forty-five minutes later he storms through the front door. His wife responds by saying, "Where have you been? When you didn't call to tell me how late to expect you, I began to think something awful happened. Is everything OK?" "Everything's fine," Aaron replies, but he avoids direct eye contact. He leaves the room a moment later, slamming the door behind him. When Brenda approaches him again, he backs away from her touch.

1. Come up with three explanations for Aaron's nonverbal behavior.

2. Share your reasons with a classmate.

3. Does your partner have the same explanations as you? Note any other interpretations.

4. How do these multiple meanings create confusion for the receiver?

5. Reexamine the preceding dialogue, and develop a list of questions a receiver might ask Aaron in order to better understand his behavior. These questions should focus on Aaron's nonverbal communication.

Ethics in Communication

Nonverbal Behavior

Review the story at the beginning of the chapter about Carla, the biology lab instructor, and her students. This story is a clear example of what we discussed in Chapter 2. People make judgments about others based on their own perceptions, and our perceptions are based on our frames of reference.

In the scenario, Carla is obviously judging her students and their ability to succeed in her class based solely on their nonverbal behavior. For example, because a student is wearing medical scrubs, Carla assumes she will excel in the biology lab. Carla goes on to assume that the student in ragged jeans and a t-shirt is "a loser" and will need help in the class. Lastly, the student who arrives five minutes late and is dressed like a mechanic is judged as unmotivated and unable to write, according to Carla.

Based on Carla's frame of reference, she has judged these students and may have acted unethically. Her ability to effectively communicate and teach these students will be greatly affected by her perceptions. She fails to see that each of her students is different and may have much to offer the class. By suspending her judgment and checking her perceptions (see Chapter 2), Carla could be an effective communicator and teacher. As we said earlier in the chapter, she needs to explore all possible meanings of the nonverbal messages (perhaps the student was late because he couldn't find the classroom, for example) and she needs to ask questions.

The students, however, must also realize that their nonverbal behavior sends messages. Although these messages may be unintentional, they impact the overall communication process. We all need to be aware and monitor our nonverbal behavior and to keep in mind that others may interpret our behavior differently than we had intended.

Summary

Nonverbal communication is that area of communication in which messages are sent without the use of words. This area includes kinesics, touch, paralanguage, silence, space, personal appearance and clothing, and time.

Ekman and Friesen developed a classification system that divides bodily movements into five categories: (1) emblems (motions that take the place of words); (2) illustrators (nonverbal symbols that reinforce a verbal message); (3) affect displays (nonverbal signs of our emotional state); (4) regulators (nonverbal behaviors used to control or regulate communication between people); and (5) adaptors (nonverbal behaviors used to adjust to or cope with uncomfortable communication situations).

Through touch we communicate a wide range of emotions, including such feelings as tenderness, concern, and anger. How we use touch to communicate nonverbally and how we respond to touch depends on several variables, including our socialization and the context of the communication situation.

Paralanguage, another component of nonverbal communication, is the vocal aspect of delivery that accompanies speech. It can include pitch, volume, rate, and quality, all of which work together with the spoken word. Silence is the absence of using your voice, and it communicates such emotions as anger or contentment.

Proxemics is the study of physical space as it relates to human interaction. We need varying degrees of personal space, the area that exists between ourselves and others, for different communication encounters. Edward Hall identifies four distances that correspond to the levels of space people require: intimate distance, personal distance, social distance, and public distance. In addition to personal space, territory (the space we stake out as our own) is a factor in our nonverbal communication.

How we look and dress become part of the message we send to others. Our clothing can reveal such things as our age, our profession or membership in a particular group, or an image we wish to project.

Our use of time sends a nonverbal message. In our culture, time is viewed as a commodity like money. Time can also communicate our status and power.

Most problems with nonverbal communication center around misinterpretation. There are a number of techniques, however, that can increase our ability to accurately interpret nonverbal messages: explore all possible meanings of nonverbal messages, look for nonverbal messages that are consistent with verbal statements, and use questions and descriptive feedback to achieve accuracy. We should also monitor our own use of nonverbal communication in order to send clear and consistent messages.

Review Questions

1. Explain why nonverbal communication is ambiguous.
2. Why is nonverbal communication culturally bound? Give an example.
3. Describe the five types of bodily movement.
4. Describe two instances in which you have touched a person and gotten different responses. What might account for the difference?

5. How does paralanguage reveal our feelings about a given situation?
6. List and describe the four categories of personal space.
7. How does clothing contribute to an individual's efforts to create a public image?
8. List and describe the four skills that help us improve our interpretation and use of nonverbal communication.

6

Understanding Ourselves and Others

At the conclusion of this chapter, you should be able to:

- Define interpersonal communication.
- Understand the importance of intimacy and power in relationships.
- Explain the stages of a relationship.
- Describe the four quadrants of the Johari window.
- Explain the benefits of self-disclosure.
- Name the cautions associated with self-disclosure.

- Apply cost-benefit theory to one of your own interpersonal relationships.
- Explain three interpersonal needs.
- Explain four problems associated with interpersonal conflicts.
- Apply four techniques to improve your ability to resolve conflicts.

At a local utility company, two very diverse people work together. Ivan, a second-generation Russian, is religious, adheres strictly to very traditional family values, and is shy. When problems arise at work, he avoids them at all costs. Ellen is a single parent by choice and is quite liberal in her views about families, politics, and social issues. She verbally attacks her co-workers, especially Ivan, when she feels threatened.

Ivan and Ellen's boss, Lee, rewards good work performance at the end of the year with bonuses and other incentives such as travel. Ellen believes that Lee continuously favors Ivan and she makes sure everyone knows how she feels. Ivan believes that Ellen's criticisms are proof she is after his job. Lee is unable to deal with their feelings because he has family problems at home.

In this chapter, we discuss how our self-concept affects our ability to see how others view us. We all have interpersonal needs that manifest themselves in our communication with others. Remember, each of us approaches each and every communication situation differently. It is this diversity in approach that makes communication fulfilling, and sometimes frustrating.

If given the option of living in complete isolation or living in the company of others, the majority of us would choose a life that is shared with others. This selection does not imply that such a life would be easy; on the contrary, communicating with others demands considerable time, energy, and understanding.

In the preceding chapters we explored several fundamental components of the communication process. Each of these plays a significant role in our communication behavior with others. Chapter 2 focused, in part, on our self-concept—how it affects our perception of others and how it affects the way we send and receive messages. In Chapter 3 we discovered skills to help us become effective listeners, including such techniques as listening with empathy, questioning, and being supportive. After focusing our attention on the meaning of words and some of the problems we encounter with language, Chapter 4 went on to discuss skills for improving our verbal communication. Finally, in Chapter 5 we explored the complex nature of nonverbal communication, including such topics as nonverbal behaviors; how such factors as space, touch, clothing, time, and paralanguage affect our nonverbal messages; and what we can do to become more skillful at interpreting nonverbal messages.

Taken as a whole, we have amassed a strong foundation of principles and skills that can now be used to assess our relationships with others. In this chapter we shall explore ways to improve our relationships by increasing our understanding of ourselves and the way we interact with others, by becoming aware of the benefits and risks of sharing with others, and by exploring ways to confront conflict within our relationships.

The Nature of Interpersonal Relationships

As we learned in Chapter 1, **interpersonal communication** is the informal exchange that occurs between two or more people. This can occur in dyads (two people) or in small groups. We will discuss small-group communication in Chapters 9 and 10. Through dyadic communication, we can learn about ourselves and about our relationships with others. Specifically, we will discuss four elements of dyadic relationships: content and relational messages, intimacy, power, and the stages of development and dissolution of relationships. Let's begin with a look at content and relational messages.

Content and Relational Messages

When we communicate, we are sending two types of messages. The **content message** is the obvious message. It is the words or language we use. For example, the question "What time will you be home tonight?" asks the receiver to answer with a specific time reference, such as "Five o'clock." There is also a more hidden message embedded in the question. This is called the relational message. These **relational messages** are usually sent nonverbally through tone of voice, body language, or use of space (see Chapter 5). Let's look at the above question again. If I emphasize the word *time* and use a sarcastic tone when I ask my partner, "What *time* will you be home tonight?" I would certainly be sending the message that I am angry or annoyed. This may be due to past behavior (my partner's coming home late) and my feeling neglected or jealous. But, if I use a very soft tone of voice and whisper in my partner's ear, "What time will you be *home* tonight?" I am certainly sending a different kind of message. In this instance, I want my partner to come home and I want him or her to know I will eagerly await his or her return.

We send messages intentionally and unintentionally. As we discussed in Chapter 1, our frame of reference will help us decode our partner's message. As senders, we may not even be aware of the relational messages we send. As effective communicators, we must pay close attention to our content and relational messages, keeping in mind that others may decode our messages differently than the way we intended.

Intimacy

When two people share a special private bond, they have intimacy. **Intimacy** is characterized by a sense of closeness and trust we share with another. In our society, we immediately think of physical intimacy, but there are other types of intimacy as well. *Physical intimacy* is not strictly limited to sexual activity. Anytime we share a physical closeness with another (mother and child, close friends or athletes), we can have intimacy. Emotional intimacy is created through self-disclosure. When we share our feelings for one another and they are returned, we create intimacy. *Intellectual intimacy* is shared when abstract concepts or other intellectually challenging ideas are discussed. Jo and Doug illustrate intellectual intimacy.

> Jo and Doug are both graduate students and love to read. On their first dates, they shared ideas about the meaning of life, religion, music, art, and politics. They loaned each other books and would later debate the theories and ideas embedded in the author's arguments. Although they often disagreed, Jo and Doug were energized by their conversations and looked forward to their time together.

Lastly, two people can share *spiritual intimacy*. People can share their strong faith in God or other higher powers. The partners may attend religious

Athletes share physical intimacy.

services, study groups, meditations, or other activities to share their spiritual intimacy.

Intimacy is a necessary component of interpersonal relationships. Through communication, namely self-disclosure (discussed later in this chapter), we form private bonds with others.

Power

When we perceive that a person has power, control, authority, or influence over others, our perception dictates how we will communicate with that person. Each relationship we enter has some dimension of power in it. The significance of power rests with one person's ability to influence another's behavior. In interpersonal situations, the person's perceived power motivates others to communicate or behave in a specific way. For example, because certain professional athletes are admired by thousands of children, organizations believe that children will pay close attention to what these athletes say; hence, on television, we hear them telling kids to stay off drugs and stay in school.

Adults also react positively to those people they consider role models or mentors. For example, consider the following:

Yvonne is completing an internship at a public relations firm where Sharon is her boss. She has observed how Sharon takes charge of an advertising campaign and is amazed at Sharon's many talents, such as her ability to conceptualize the entire campaign, her skillful interactions with clients, her directions to the production staff, and so on. Yvonne's

COMMUNICATION and TECHNOLOGY

Intimacy Online

Jonathan Coleman of *Newsweek* magazine says, "Cell phones, beepers, headsets, watches that both tell time and give good email— smart, sleek, technological fashion statements that enable you to be reached any time, any where; devices that allow you to keep up and keep track and that keep you tethered to the daily grind" (2000, p. 12). As a matter of fact, as we learned in Chapter 1, we send over 2.2 billion emails a day. Why? Some scholars argue that we use the Internet primarily for interpersonal communication (Jackson, 2001).

Email and the Internet have become essential tools for communication. Ninety percent of Internet users say they use the Internet to communicate with family and friends (Jackson, 2001). People are seeking intimacy online. "Survey research suggests that people feel more socially connected and engaged in more communications with more people as a consequence of Internet use," according to scholar Linda Jackson (2001). For example, we can find people with the same interests or hobbies online. We were once limited to finding friends in our geographic area, but no more. Thomas Moore, a professor at MIT, says "he feels closer to some people he has met over the net than he did even to friends he made growing up in a small town in New Mexico. Those relationships were mere accidents of geography; he and his new friends chose each other through common interest" (Kupfer, 1995, p. 94).

Another type of relationship being formed online is the romantic or sexual relationship. Scholars argue that these relationships are so intense because of the anonymity. We lower our inhibitions and feel free to self-disclose information we wouldn't tell someone face to face. Jane Gackenback, a professor of psychology, says, "Because of the large amount of self-disclosure involved in an online relationship, it can seem more real or important. Someone can be married to their spouse for 20 years, but still feel horribly alone. Finding someone online who you can share very intimate feelings with can be very powerful. The medium itself enhances this effect" (Gackenback, 1998). Thus, we tell our deepest darkest secrets, including sexual fantasies, to someone we have never seen or heard. Kupfer argues, "The Internet is making it acceptable for a man to exchange explicit sexual fantasies with a strange woman—or with someone who claims to be a woman" (1995, p. 94). Therein lies the danger . . . deception. As we discussed in Chapter 2, we can easily change or mask our identity on the Internet.

Thus, we seek all types of relationships online. Friendships, family relationships, romantic and sexual relationships begin and are maintained through email and chatrooms every day.

ZITS   *BY JERRY SCOTT AND JIM BORGMAN*

© Zits Partnership. Reprinted with special permission of King Features Syndicate.

perception of Sharon's abilities is overwhelmingly positive. As their relationship grows, Yvonne finds that she wants to be like Sharon, and Sharon encourages Yvonne to choose a career in public relations.

These examples illustrate positive influences of power. Power can also be intimidating or threatening. Consider the following:

> Mary has been working at Shear Magic for two years. She loves her job as a hair stylist, but dislikes the pressure from the owners to attend out-of-town workshops to develop her skills. Mary has attended all the local workshops, but the owners now want her to attend a weekend seminar two hours away from her home. Mary is very uncomfortable about leaving her eighteen-month-old son, Ryan. But Mary also feels uncomfortable about talking to the owners about her feelings because she is afraid they may fire her or cut her hours. She suffers in silence, fearful of losing her job, but also uneasy about leaving her son.

Social power is the "potential for changing attitudes, beliefs, and behaviors of others" (Verderber and Verdeber, 1995, p. 284). Each of us has some power, whether we are aware of it or not. French and Raven (1968) have described for us the different types of social power that affect our interpersonal communication. **Coercive power** is derived from one's perceived ability to control another person's behavior through negative reinforcement and intimidation. Coercive power can be communicated through threats or nonverbally by tone of voice, invasion of personal space, or even physical contact. **Reward power** is one's perceived ability to provide things such as money, objects, or love and affection. Reward power is communicated through promises, for example. **Legitimate power** is derived from one's position of authority. People with legitimate power have been given the responsibility (by election or appointment) to assert influence over others. Legitimate power is seen in the use of space, for example. The CEO of a company has the largest office, biggest desk, and a beautiful view from the window. These indicate that the person has legitimate power over others in the company. **Expert power** is one's superior knowledge in a particular field. Expert power is influential when the person has a skill or information that you need. Many experts communicate their power through titles such as Doctor or Reverend. We can easily be intimated by expert power and therefore fail to ask questions, for example. Lastly, **referent power** is derived from one's feelings of identification with another. Someone's image or personality may influence us. In the preceding example, Sharon has referent power in her relationship with Yvonne. Yvonne identifies with Sharon and wants to be like her.

Each relationship has some level of power that affects the communication between the two friends, lovers, or co-workers. Many times, we may feel powerless in a relationship. **Powerlessness** means that we feel as if we have no say in the relationship or that the other is making all the decisions. We may feel as if we are not in control. No one wants to feel this way. In all relationships, we need to strive to be empowered and to empower our partner. **Empowerment** is the ability to make choices. We want to be able to choose even small things like what movie to see or where to eat dinner. More importantly, in each relationship we want to choose a partner, to choose whether or not to stay in the relationship, and to create a relationship that is based on mutual respect and equality. When both partners are empowered, our self-concept and self-esteem are higher and we feel more confident and secure in the relationship. Let's look at Miguel and Samantha:

> Miguel and Samantha will be graduating from college this spring. Miguel is looking for a job in journalism, while Samantha is seeking a position in human relations. Each has his or her own set of friends and socializes without his or her partner at least once a week. Miguel and Samantha

TABLE 6.1	Types of Social Power
Coercive power	One's ability to control another person's behavior through negative reinforcement
Reward power	One's ability to provide things such as money, objects, or love
Legitimate power	One's position of authority
Expert power	One's superior knowledge in a particular field
Referent power	One's feelings of identification with another

both work while attending college and share the costs of all their activities, such as eating out or listening to music at the local coffeehouse. Although they are independent, Miguel and Samantha are dependent on one another for intimacy and support. Recently, Miguel failed an exam in his senior seminar in journalism. He was very upset, but Samantha was able to comfort him and together they developed new study strategies for Miguel's next exam. They compromise often in order to ensure that each has his or her needs met in their relationship.

CRITICAL THINKING   **Types of Power**

Each of the following statements communicates a type of social power. Identify each statement as coercive, reward, legitimate, expert, or referent power.

1. If you are not here on time tomorrow, you'll be looking for a new job.
2. I have been studying this phenomenon for ten years. I know I'm right.
3. As manager, I want to improve the morale of all employees by offering a workshop on positive mental attitude.
4. I want to be just like my mother. She is smart, assertive, and caring.
5. If you go to bed right now, I'll make you pancakes in the morning for breakfast.

Stages of Relationship Development

Romantic relationships and close friends develop in a similar fashion. Mark Knapp and Anita Vangelisti (1992) created a model for the development of these relationships, and the type of communication that takes place between the two people characterizes each stage (Figure 6.1). Relationships you may have with family members and work colleagues will evolve and dissolve differently than this model shows.

Initiating

The first stage is called the initiating stage because the relationship begins with one person making "first contact" or initiating the interaction. Initiating is characterized by safe, surface topics such as, "How about this weather?" or "Isn't this a great party?" The most important part of this phase is the first impressions we have about the other. Obviously, if our first impression is not favorable, the relationship may not progress.

Experimenting

Experimenting, the second stage, allows the two people to get better acquainted. We may discuss topics more in-depth, but the topics would still be considered "small talk." This stage could last a few minutes, but could also last the length of the relationship. Some relationships just don't progress any further. For example:

> Every year at Christmas time, Rebecca and her husband Andrew must attend Rebecca's company's holiday party. Although they always enjoy the dinner and dancing, Andrew does not like having to make small talk with the other spouses. One husband in particular, Randy, always corners Andrew and wants to discuss the stock market and politics. During the first holiday party several years ago, Andrew sat and talked with Randy for over an hour and decided he did not want to become friends. So, every year at this party, Andrew just exchanges small talk with Randy.

Intensifying

When two people begin to express their feelings for each other, verbally and nonverbally, they have entered the intensifying stage. This is most clearly seen in romantic couples, although friends also can enter this stage. The two people begin to think of themselves as a couple and spend more time together. The couple may exchange small gifts, and touching becomes a part of the relationship. They may even address one another as "Honey" or "Sweetheart."

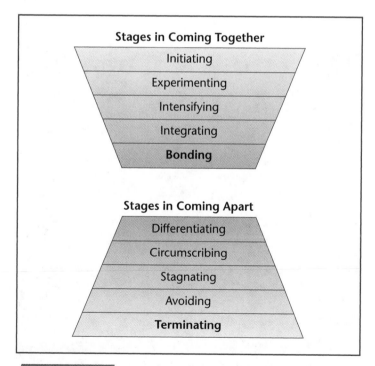

FIGURE 6.1   **Knapp's Relational Development Model**

Integrating

When society sees the two people as a couple, the integrating stage has occurred. The couple will spend holidays together, meet each other's families, and begin buying things together. They may even live together. The two begin to depend on one another for comfort, support, and intimacy. The integration with the other helps us to change and become someone new. We may change our attitude about life, we may become better listeners, or we may even change the way we look.

Bonding

The traditional wedding ceremony is the most popular way to seal the bond between two romantic partners. Of course, gay couples do not have the opportunity to legally wed in most states, but many still have weddings or commitment ceremonies. This stage is the most public of the stages as the couple promises to stay together and love one another in front of friends and family. The couple's bonding generates support from their family and friends. The commitment can put new pressure on the relationship, and it certainly changes the nature of the relationship.

Differentiating

The differentiating stage is characterized by the need for independence and autonomy. Now that the two people have become a committed couple,

A wedding ceremony is an example of the bonding stage in relationship development.

each will feel the need to regain their independence. Thus, each person finds ways to differentiate himself or herself from the other. The partners may find hobbies to pursue alone, such as playing softball, taking an aerobics class, or just going out with friends. This stage can cause tension, as one partner may feel threatened by the other's need to be independent. Partners must walk a thin line between staying committed to the relationship and finding autonomy.

Circumscribing

Not all relationships will last a lifetime. Most romantic relationships fail, and in the circumscribing stage, partners communicate less and less. Defense mechanisms (see Chapter 7) characterize the communication as the partners avoid discussing problems or become overly critical of each other. The couple is less interested in maintaining the relationship. For example:

> Heather and Lydia have been a couple for two years. They have lived together for the last eighteen months. Heather and Lydia are both lawyers and share many of the same interests, such as civil rights law, traveling, and training their golden retriever, Chestnut. Lately, however, Lydia has been working longer hours and has canceled their planned trip to India. When Heather asks, "Is there something wrong? Have I done something to make you angry?" Lydia just says, "No, of course not. I'm just overloaded at work and feel under stress." Lydia does not verbalize how her feelings have changed toward Heather and believes it is better to just not talk about their relationship.

Stagnating

When a relationship stops growing, it is in the stagnating stage. The partners "go through the motions" without much feeling or enthusiasm. The couple may not love one another anymore and are staying together out of convenience, fear, or for others, such as their children. The intimacy of the past is gone, and self-disclosure has stopped.

Avoiding

The avoiding stage is characterized by distancing. The partners spend little time together, and almost all communication has ceased. It is just too difficult and uncomfortable to be together. Some people will make excuses to not see one another: "I have to study for my biology exam" or "I need to spend time with my friends," or one may just say, "I don't think we should see one another for awhile." In the television program "Friends," Ross and Rachel had been seeing one another for a long time, but Rachel was beginning to feel overwhelmed by the closeness. In one episode, she says, "I think we need a break." Ross says, "Yeah, you are right. Let's go get some ice cream." Rachel says, "No, I mean a break from each other."

Terminating

Relationships end. The terminating stage includes ending the relationship sometimes very quickly or perhaps over weeks or months. The ending of the relationship does not have to be painful or negative. Some relationships do not work and only bring pain to the partners. It is much better for both people to find other partners. The terminating stage is not inevitable. Some couples can communicate their feelings and problems and return to the intimacy of the past.

Self-Disclosure within Relationships

As we assess our relationships with others, we might ask ourselves, "Where is this relationship headed?" Are we involved in a growth relationship, or is the relationship going to remain at a superficial level? If we think we are in a blossoming relationship, we are likely to share increased information about ourselves. At the same time, we are interested in the other person's feedback.

We can improve the quality of relationships through self-disclosure. **Self-disclosure** is the conscious decision to share personal information about ourselves. Its purpose is to help others get to know and understand us better. What we disclose about ourselves can be of little or high risk, or somewhere in between. For example, voicing an opinion about the weather would probably be nonthreatening for us, whereas telling a friend that you don't particularly like her new boyfriend would involve some degree of risk. Likewise, revealing to a spouse that our emotional needs are not being met is certainly a more difficult task. The degree to which we self-disclose depends on how we feel both about ourselves and our relationship with the other person.

Johari Window

One way to illustrate the ways we communicate with others is the Johari window. Joseph Luft and Harry Ingham developed this model, which is designed to be a visual presentation of the self (Luft, 1970). It can be used to explain our communication behaviors with others. Specifically, our interactions are classified as being (1) open, (2) blind, (3) hidden, or (4) unknown. Each of these behaviors represents part of the self, yet in any given interaction one of these behaviors outweighs the others. For example, Antonia openly discloses her career plans with her parents, yet she chooses to hide the seriousness of her relationship with Mike when her parents raise the question. In the first situation, Antonia willingly shares her feelings; in the second, the opposite is true. The way we communicate, then, depends on our relationship with the other party. By assessing our

Johari window, we can gain a better understanding of the way we present ourselves to others.

Of the four quadrants that comprise the Johari window, the open window represents that aspect of our self that we knowingly share with others and that others can readily determine about us. Information we are willing to divulge to others, such as our feelings about a political candidate, a piece of artwork, our job, or a movie we saw last week, comprises this open side of our self.

The **blind quadrant** of the Johari window represents that part of our self that we either unconsciously reveal to others or are actually unaware of, yet others have knowledge about. In social interactions, for example, our unconscious behavior can sometimes be annoying or distracting. Traci drums her fingers and sways from side to side when she delivers a speech. These unconscious gestures reveal her nervousness to members of the audience. Luther does not know that he is adopted, yet everyone else assembled for the family reunion is aware of the fact. If either Traci or Luther were made aware of the "unknown factors," the information would move from the blind to the open part of the self.

The third quadrant of the Johari window represents the hidden self. The **hidden quadrant** represents the part of us that we are aware of but do not want to share or have not yet shared with others. This may include our dislike of Mexican food, our discomfort over participating in any athletic activity, our fear of being asked a question during class, or our fear of confronting a loved one about wanting to dissolve a relationship.

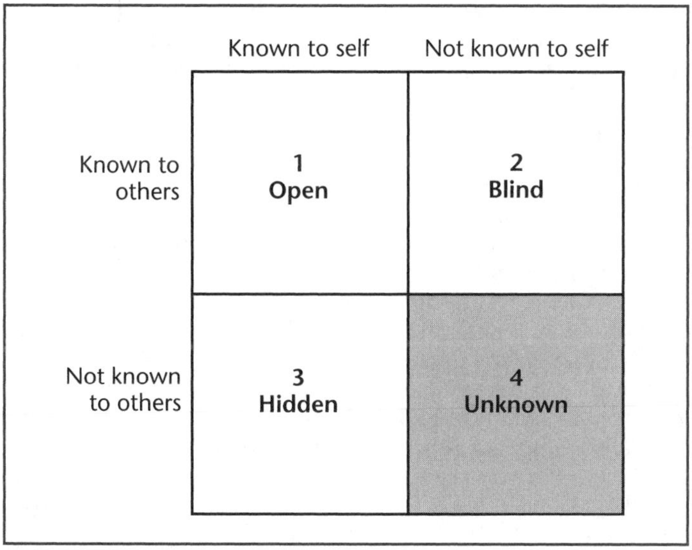

	Known to self	Not known to self
Known to others	1 **Open**	2 **Blind**
Not known to others	3 **Hidden**	4 **Unknown**

FIGURE 6.2   **Johari Window**

The last **quadrant** of the Johari window is that part of us that is **unknown** to both ourselves and to everyone else. We can think of this area as including our untapped potential or hidden talents, or simply that part of our self that remains unexplored. For example, we may not realize that we have an aptitude for speaking foreign languages, a special talent for gardening, or the agility to be a good tennis player because we have never pursued these areas.

Benefits of Self-Disclosure

The process of self-disclosure has a number of benefits, namely, an increased understanding of ourselves, the ability to express our feelings, and an increased likelihood that others will be more open with us. The end result is that our understanding of our interpersonal relationships grows.

One benefit of self-disclosure is an increased understanding of ourselves. By communicating our feelings to someone else, we are forced to acknowledge these feelings and even analyze why we feel a particular way. Simply stated, in the process of sharing with others, we end up taking a better look at ourselves. Our strengths, weaknesses, beliefs, and ambivalences are not only shared with others, they are reaffirmed for us as well.

Another potential benefit of self-disclosure is the relief we experience from letting our feelings out. In general, we are more inclined to self-disclose with someone whom we trust or know well. After doing so, we generally feel better about ourselves and the possible strengthening of our relationship.

A third benefit of self-disclosure is the increased likelihood that the other party will begin to share his or her feelings and concerns with us. When both parties feel comfortable enough to do this, understanding between individuals is strengthened and intimacy is achieved. An example will clarify this point:

> Stephanie and her neighbor Linda are discussing their three-year-old sons, Chad and Ian. During the course of their conversation, Linda reveals that she sometimes has tremendous feelings of guilt because she works full time and therefore has less time to spend with Ian. She worries that he is being denied a "full-time" mother. Linda is surprised by Stephanie's response. Stephanie, too, doubts how good a job she is doing as a mother. Although she does not have a job outside her home, Stephanie wonders if her influence is too controlling or smothering. She also admits that she often feels that she would have a better attitude about motherhood if she had some outside activity, such as a job.

By sharing with each other, each woman sees that she is not alone in her concerns; both have similar feelings of guilt over not being the "perfect" mother. Their understanding of each other is increased because of this shared information.

Cautions of Self-Disclosure

Trust is a prerequisite for self-disclosure in relationships. We would not consider an open discussion of our feelings with someone we barely know, nor would we expect an acquaintance to disclose something highly personal or sensitive to us.

It is conceivable to trust someone, yet not feel comfortable enough with this person to reveal private feelings. Basically, we look for someone whom we believe will be both a good listener and responsive to our needs. Empathy is often a key ingredient in these interactions. We want the other party to be an uncritical listener who shows support and understanding for our position and ultimately feels comfortable enough to share some of his or her own feelings with us. This give and take between two individuals promotes better understanding of each other and improves communication.

Finally, in order for self-disclosure to be a meaningful process, it should occur in an environment or setting that is natural. For example, if we want to discuss our anger over the way our daughter's teacher handled a situation at school, we would make an appointment with the teacher. We would not bring up the subject if we saw the teacher waiting in line with her husband at a crowded restaurant; the time and place would be all wrong. Instead of resolving the problem, we would likely put the teacher on the defensive and create a potentially more uncomfortable situation. Consider the individual and the communication climate (discussed in Chapter 7) before making a decision about self-disclosure.

Self-Disclosure   **SELF-ASSESSMENT**

Describe a significant relationship. Include in your description the length of the relationship, the type of relationship, and some general background information about the two of you.

1. How does self-disclosure function in your relationship?
2. Describe how much information is disclosed and the types of information both of you disclose.
3. Do you feel the self-disclosure is reciprocal? Why or why not?

Theoretical Explanations of Interpersonal Communication

Several communication theories help to explain the dynamics of our interpersonal relationships. In this part of the chapter we shall discuss two of them. First, Schutz's theory of interpersonal needs outlines our needs and explains the varying degrees of fulfillment; second, cost-benefit theory assesses why we choose either to remain in a relationship or to exit from it.

Interpersonal Needs Theory

William Schutz (1966) developed a theory based on the nature of our interpersonal needs. His theory argues that people have certain needs that affect their communication in interpersonal relationships: the need for inclusion, the need for control, and the need for affection.

Inclusion

Inclusion needs, according to Schutz, deal with our desire to be part of a group and lead to a division of people into three categories: undersocial individuals, oversocial individuals, and ideal individuals. **Undersocial individuals** find it difficult to participate in groups, usually because they believe they are not capable of effective social interaction. Among the members of this group are those individuals who consider themselves to be shy, those who fear they will appear to be inarticulate or boring, and those

We all share the need to belong to a group.

who see themselves as significantly different from other members of the group. In order to cope with their lack of confidence, such individuals communicate by avoiding or retreating from group interactions.

Surprisingly, **oversocial individuals** also feel extremely uncomfortable in social interactions. Rather than shy away from social interaction, however, these individuals push full-speed ahead as a means of compensating for their anxiety. Many of us, for example, know a person like Sabrina, whose social calendar rivals that of a corporate executive. She is a member of several political organizations and three church committees, and she volunteers each Saturday morning at the hospital gift shop. Typically, such excessive group participation indicates an attempt to prove that we are capable of functioning comfortably in these situations.

Ideal individuals, according to Schutz, feel comfortable enough to participate in social groups, but do not feel a need to participate in all groups. More important, these individuals are comfortable with themselves in social interactions. They are likely to be skilled at presenting ideas to others and at the same time eager to listen to the ideas of others.

Control

Control needs refer to our desire to have power, influence, or responsibility for our social environment. In terms of control, we may be characterized as abdicrats, autocrats, or democrats. **Abdicrats** find it extremely difficult to participate in the decision-making process because they are afraid of the possible consequences that accompany some decisions. They lack confidence, so they try to refrain from making either definitive or controversial decisions. For example, Edward is a classic "fence sitter"; he waits until others communicate their positions before he shares his. His reluctance encompasses a variety of decision-making situations. Internally, he may question his ability to make appropriate or wise decisions, so he avoids all kinds of decisions. Edward exhibits the communication pattern associated with the abdicrat.

At the other end of the scale is the **autocrat,** an individual who also may feel uncomfortable with decision making, but whose anxiety manifests itself in the opposite way. Instead of retreating from decision making, autocrats attempt to dominate the process. In an effort to camouflage their true feelings, autocrats believe that by making numerous decisions they will prove that they can be influential. Unfortunately, this type of behavior has an extremely negative effect on others. Autocrats do not listen to the ideas of others because they are too absorbed in their role of trying to be influential in the discussion. Many of us have encountered autocrats, perhaps at work or in our own families. These individuals seem obsessed with "having the final say" when making decisions, which, according to Schutz, stems from their efforts to prove that they are really capable of making decisions.

The ideal manifestation of control needs is displayed by the democrat. **Democrats** can cope with the responsibilities of decision making, yet they do not feel the need to have the final say in every decision-making session. They can assume a leadership role when necessary, but they also can function in a less active role without difficulty. These individuals are generally open to a variety of alternatives; they are receptive to ideas that differ from their own and are comfortable with having others participate in the process.

Affection

The third interpersonal need identified by Schutz is the desire for intimacy (see the related discussion earlier in this chapter). An **underpersonal individual,** according to Schutz, will shy away from developing close, intimate relationships with others. Underpersonal individuals may avoid personal discussions or steer conversations to "safe" topics. They frequently have poor self-concepts and believe that they are not capable of sustaining intimate relationships. Consider the following:

> Many consider Kim to be someone who is difficult to get to know. When individuals attempt to get close to her, an invisible wall is erected that communicates "stay away." This pattern of communication surfaces in a variety of situations. At work, she spends very little time socializing with people. When she does socialize with others, she keeps the conversation at a safe level, being cautious not to reveal much about herself.

Kim's desire to protect herself suggests a fear of intimacy. She engages in little sharing with others because she may not feel that she is capable of participating in close relationships.

The fear of intimacy also can cause another type of behavior, exemplified by the **overpersonal individual.** Overpersonal individuals try to compensate for their anxiety by establishing many relationships. In an effort to feel better about themselves, they try to be closely involved with several people. In addition, these individuals are typically possessive of their relationships, which is often stifling and aggravating for all parties involved. A phone call to ask "Why haven't you called lately?" represents the sort of behavior caused by such anxiety. These individuals have an excessive need for support that is both draining and seemingly unending.

Personal individuals feel comfortable with their ability to handle close personal relationships. They realize that relationships are constantly changing and can adjust to this fact. As relationships grow more distant, well-adjusted individuals can, in time, let go without guilt. That is, they will not blame the other person, and more important, they will not feel guilty when the nature of a particular relationship changes. Such individuals realize that sometimes people grow closer together, but at other times people grow apart, and that change is a function of the dynamics of the relationship, not the result of a guilty party's actions. Individuals whose needs for affection are neither deficient nor excessive are better equipped to cope with intimacy.

Schutz's theory of interpersonal needs can contribute to our understanding of the ways people's needs dictate their behavior within different communication situations. Our ability to recognize both deficient communication (*deficient* meaning either undersocial, abdicratic, or underpersonal) and excessive communication (*excessive* meaning oversocial, autocratic, or overpersonal) enables us to better understand the dynamics of a particular relationship. Furthermore, such understanding allows us to step back and analyze the communication of others. Being able to explain another person's communication behavior helps us to avoid personalizing the unmet needs of that person. Accordingly, our responses to interpersonal communication situations are likely to be more sensitive.

Cost-Benefit Theory

A theory developed by John Thibaut and Harold Kelley attempts to explain how people assess their relationships (1959). **Cost-benefit theory** (also called *cost-reward theory* or *exchange theory*) suggests that people choose to maintain or exit relationships based on the rewards they receive within those relationships. If the rewards (which may be either emotional, psychological, financial, or physical) are perceived to outweigh the costs (which can include emotional stress, financial expense, amount of time spent in the relationship, or physical abuse), then an individual will likely remain in the relationship. If the costs are perceived to outweigh the rewards, he or she will probably leave the relationship. Consider the following:

> Judd examines the rewards versus the costs in working for his father-in-law. He acknowledges that the salary he receives constitutes the chief reward in the relationship, yet he is bothered by the costs and drawbacks: lack of independence, the social stigma associated with working for a relative, and the tension that it sometimes creates in his marriage to Elaine.

According to Thibaut and Kelley's theory, if Judd believes the costs outweigh the benefits, he will sever the relationship. Conversely, if Judd determines that the benefits (in this case, financial security) outweigh the costs, he will probably decide to remain in his father-in-law's employ. Furthermore, he may work to increase his involvement in the business, perhaps by assuming a greater role in decision making or by striving to become a partner.

Relationships are seldom as simple as the one just outlined. There are times, for example, when we choose to remain in uncomfortable relationships because the alternative is even less desirable. Judd's decision to remain in his father-in-law's firm, despite his frustrations over feeling financially dependent, may be colored by the fact that the employment outlook for architects is bleak in the city where he lives. In this case, the alternative is less appealing than remaining in the relationship.

Cost-benefit theory can be a valuable tool in understanding how we assess relationships. When we feel frustrated in a relationship, we may choose to leave the relationship, or we may try to discuss the problem in an effort to improve the relationship. For example, Judd might attempt to change the dynamics of his working relationship with his father-in-law if his goal is to reap additional rewards. After discussing the situation with his father-in-law, he might be able to identify an area of the business that needs developing and then concentrate his efforts in that direction. If he is successful, he will have achieved a measure of independence that he desired all along. By doing so, Judd has improved his relationship with his father-in-law.

Although it cannot explain all the complexities of human relationships, applying cost benefit theory to relationships may help us understand some of our relationships more fully, why they are satisfying or dissatisfying to us, and whether or not they are worth trying to improve.

Conflict within Relationships

Conflict is a natural and common occurrence within relationships, but by its very nature it produces discomfort for the parties involved. An area that builds on several of the communication skills discussed in this and previous chapters is *conflict resolution*. According to Joyce H. Frost and William W. Wilmot, **interpersonal conflict** is "an expressed struggle between at least two interdependent parties who perceive incompatible goals, scarce rewards, and interference from the other parties in achieving their goals" (1978, pp. 9–14). In this definition, *expressed struggle* refers to the fact that both parties acknowledge that a problem exists; by contrast, there is no conflict if only one party perceives that there is a problem. Consider the following: Simon is angry with Althea because she did not phone him; however, because Althea is unaware of his frustration, she does not perceive that there is a conflict.

In expressing feelings, people send either verbal or nonverbal messages. Laura, for example, raises her voice when she is upset about something, whereas Jayne shows her discontent by "glaring" at others. When Laura and Jayne express their feelings to each other, the conflict is brought out into the open and they can attempt to resolve it.

What is meant by *incompatible goals*? Basically, in order for one party to gain, there is a perceived loss to the other party. In other words, one party gains at the other party's expense. If your neighbor announces, for example, that he plans to erect a five-foot fence along your adjoining properties, you might tell him that you are against such a proposal. Your neighbor may want privacy, but you would like the neighborhood to remain open so the children can run between the houses when they play. However, if the neighbor succeeds in getting the necessary papers to allow this action, you might perceive yourself to be the loser, while your neighbor perceives himself to be the winner.

Frequently, conflicts arise over scarce rewards. You and your partner may only have one night out per month. You would like to have an elegant dinner and go dancing. Your partner would rather go to the local bar and grill to eat chicken wings and play Internet trivia. Both of you cannot have your "reward" of a night out. Look again at the story in the beginning of the chapter. Ellen and Ivan have a conflict over the allocation of travel and bonuses. The resources are scarce and someone will lose.

Several factors contribute to the difficulties people experience when involved in conflicts, such as denial, suppression, aggression, passive aggression, and status. These factors inhibit our attempts to resolve conflicts because they stifle open communication between parties.

Denial

Denial is our refusal to acknowledge that a problem exists. When we refuse to see a problem, it generally creates tremendous frustration on the part of the second party, who may wish to resolve the problem. For example:

> Martina usually resorts to yelling when she and her husband, Eric, disagree over an issue. Eric has a serious problem accepting Martina's communication style (that is, her yelling), yet he cannot convince Martina that she has a problem; she contends that venting emotions by yelling is a perfectly natural and acceptable behavior. By denying the problem, Martina makes it difficult for Eric to take any further steps to resolve their differences.

Suppression

With **suppression,** we acknowledge that a problem exists, but we attempt to minimize its importance. Our fear is that confronting the problem may result in consequences that are too difficult or painful for us to address. Like denial, the amount of frustration experienced by the other person can be substantial. For example, Gloria's anger increases each time Joel's mother criticizes their home and Joel fails to talk to his mother about it. Instead, Joel tries to make light of the problem with Gloria.

Aggression

Aggression is a problem in conflicts because we are hostile toward the other party and try to intimidate him or her into a resolution that is clearly more advantageous to us. Consider the following:

> Alec and his wife, Audrey, discuss on a daily basis Alec's desire to move from their current neighborhood to a suburb populated predominantly by successful young professionals. Despite Audrey's pleas that she will

not feel comfortable living in the more affluent suburb, Alec insists that the move is right for them. After four months of these persuasive talks, Audrey finally consents to give it a try. The resolution of Alec and Audrey's conflict is only temporary, because from Audrey's point of view, Alec pressured her into something she genuinely opposed. Furthermore, if her discontent about the move persists, she will continue to harbor angry sentiments toward her husband, and the underlying conflict will go unresolved.

Another problem related to aggression is passive aggression. **Passive aggression** is a subtle and covert form of aggression. On the surface, it may appear that the person is complying with a request, compromising, or offering a compliment, but upon closer examination, he or she is acting aggressively. For example, a co-worker will agree to a meeting and then stand you up, or your roommate may "forget" to give you a phone message. Each of these people is angry or upset about something. But instead of discussing the problem, they choose to act in a subtle, covert aggressive manner.

Status

A final problem that interferes with conflict resolution is **status.** Status is the relative standing of one party in relation to the other. An individual's status can be either achieved or dictated by society. In interpersonal conflicts, status can act as an inhibitor in two ways: (1) we can use our perceived status to intimidate others, or (2) we can feel intimidated by others who use their status to control interactions. For example:

Kammi is extremely upset over her principal's decision to cut funds for the remedial reading program she supervises at the middle school, yet feels too intimidated by the principal's superior status to strongly voice her objections. The principal, on the other hand, sensing that he will have a difficult battle over the issue, firmly announces that he has given the matter considerable thought and will not reverse his decision to cut

TABLE 6.2	Factors That Contribute to Conflict
Denial	We refuse to acknowledge that a problem exists.
Suppression	We acknowledge a problem, but we minimize its importance.
Aggression	We are hostile toward the other party and try to intimidate him or her into a resolution.
Passive aggression	We appear to be agreeable, but then act in a subtle, covert, aggressive manner.
Status	Either we or the other party uses status to intimidate.

the program. He uses his status to prevent an open discussion of the conflict with Kammi.

As with denial, suppression, aggression, and passive aggression, the problem with status is that conflicts are left unsatisfactorily resolved.

Improving Our Efforts to Resolve Conflicts

After learning about the problems that impede conflict resolution, it is natural to wonder how we can best approach the area of conflict resolution. While no simple formula exists, primarily because each relationship has unique characteristics, several skills can help us deal with conflict in our relationships. These skills include dealing with feelings, keeping the discussion focused on the problem, being a sensitive listener, and being flexible.

Deal with Feelings

When we suspect we are having a conflict with someone, the first step is to examine our own feelings concerning the problem. This self-examination helps us better understand exactly what it is that is making us angry, hurt, or frustrated. Once we have acknowledged our feelings, we can more effectively express what is bothering us to the other person. Let us examine the following situation:

> Lorna is furious with her son Adam for staying out past midnight. Initially, she decides to "let him have it" when he comes walking through the front door; then she reconsiders this tactic. She decides that her chief feeling is not anger, but concern for his safety. When Lorna realizes this, she pledges that she will calmly express her feelings to Adam rather than yell at him for being late.

Adam arrives home ten minutes later and finds his mother waiting for him just inside the front door. He begins to apologize for being so late, but he allows his mother to speak instead. In getting her feelings out, Lorna is surprised and pleased with herself for not turning the situation into a shouting match. By remaining calm, she succeeds in having an open discussion with Adam. Furthermore, they are able to resolve this conflict together.

Find a Special Time to Meet

Have you ever felt like you were "attacked" by your significant other? You walked in the door and were confronted by an angry parent, spouse, partner, or roommate. Adam probably thought that's what he was about to face when he came home late. Of course, the natural posture we take is to become defensive and either avoid the situation or get angry, too. Making a special time to meet or making a "date" to solve the problem can significantly improve the chances of resolving the conflict. Both partners should have a chance to think about the problem and then agree to set time aside to discuss it.

Keep the Discussion Focused on the Problem

When we discuss our conflict with another person, the most beneficial strategy is to remain focused on the problem. How? The easiest way is to try to describe our feelings about the issue, about the other person's behavior and how it offends or angers us. We should avoid attacking the other person; rather, we should focus on observable behavior that contributes to the problem. By doing so we avoid the pitfall of getting too personal.

Use Perception Checking and Empathetic Listening

As we discussed in Chapter 2, we all have different perceptions based on our frames of reference. It is essential to check our perceptions of the other person's messages (content and relational) by using questioning, interpreting, and paraphrasing (Chapter 3). Also, looking at a conflict from the other person's perspective can lead to greater understanding of the problem. As indicated in Chapter 3, **empathy** means being able to look at something from someone else's viewpoint. In our attempt to understand the other person's position, we can use the skills associated with effective listening, such as paraphrasing, listening without being judgmental, and being supportive.

Empathy also can help diffuse a conflict. When we take the time to reconstruct the other person's position, we gain insight into why that person communicates the way he or she does. A by-product is that we take a better look at our own reactions to this person's communication. The overall effect is to have a more positive understanding of each other.

Finally, by being a sensitive, supportive listener, we encourage the other party to more freely express his or her feelings. This is a desirable way to get at the core of a conflict. If anger, resentment, doubts, or pain remain unspoken, the conflict cannot be resolved and the communication between the individuals will continue to be strained.

Find a Solution for Both Parties: Be Flexible

Interpersonal conflicts are more easily resolved when the individuals involved are flexible. Being flexible means having the ability to adapt to a variety of situations. Flexibility suggests that there is more than one way to work through a conflict. Consider the following:

> Claire and her son Jonathon disagree over the type of punishment Jonathon should receive for denting the family car. Claire would like to bar him from driving for one month, particularly because he took the car

without her knowledge and permission, whereas Jonathon argues that no punishment is warranted because the accident was the other driver's fault. Realizing that their individual stands are narrow minded, they decide to openly discuss the matter in order to arrive at a better solution. In this case, Claire and Jonathon reach a compromise: Claire agrees to let Jonathon continue to drive the car, and Jonathon agrees to get his mother's okay before taking the car in the future.

This is an ideal situation, because both parties walk away from the conflict having "won" something. Their willingness to talk about the problem and cooperate with each other by collaborating on the solution demonstrates their flexibility.

Ethics in Communication

Resolving Conflicts

Conflicts occur in every relationship. When we resolve our conflicts, our relationships can be enhanced by increased trust and intimacy. In the beginning of the chapter, Ellen, Ivan, and Lee are in the midst of several connected conflicts.

Ellen uses aggression in her communication with Ivan to intimidate him and others. Ivan avoids problems or denies they exist. He chooses to ignore Ellen's aggression and keeps his thoughts and feelings to himself. Lee knows there are problems in the office, but chooses to minimize their importance (suppression) in order to concentrate on the conflicts at home.

Despite their hurt feelings and lack of self-disclosure, Ellen, Ivan, and Lee could resolve their conflicts by following a few guidelines. First, each must deal with his or her own feelings. Self-examination will help each better understand their feelings about the others. Without self-examination, Ellen, Ivan, and Lee will not be able to clearly express their feelings. Second, as the supervisor and the one with legitimate

power, Lee must set aside time to discuss the problems in the office with Ivan and Ellen. He needs to give them advance notice of any meetings and to be sure to establish a supportive and nonthreatening atmosphere for all of them to self-disclose their feelings. Third, everyone needs to focus on his or her perceptions of the problems in the office. Ellen must concentrate her comments on the distribution of incentives (travel and bonuses). Ivan needs to discuss his feelings of job insecurity and why he thinks Ellen wants his job. Lee should discuss his past inability to deal with their conflicts because he has been focused on his family. Finally, each needs to use questioning, paraphrasing, and interpreting as a means of checking their perceptions (see Chapters 2 and 3). Also, each should practice empathetic listening by looking at the problem from the others' point of view (see Chapter 3). They should keep in mind that everyone has a different perspective and that they need to strive to understand and respect the others' views.

CHECKLIST Improving Our Efforts to Resolve Conflicts

- Deal with feelings.
- Make a special date.
- Keep the discussion focused on the problem.
- Use perception checking and empathetic listening.
- Find a solution for both parties: be flexible.

SKILL BUILDING Conflict Resolution

1. With a partner, create a hypothetical situation in which a conflict needs to be resolved.
2. Together, use the following skills to work through a solution:
   a. Deal with feelings.
   b. Keep the discussion focused on the problem.
   c. Be a sensitive listener.
   d. Be flexible.
3. Apply these same skills to a conflict you are having in one of your personal relationships.

Summary

People need people—for sharing feelings, for support, for confirmation of their beliefs. Our interpersonal relationships teach us much about ourselves and the way others communicate. Four elements characterize dyadic relationships. Content messages are the words or language we use, and relational messages are the intentional or unintentional nonverbal messages. Intimacy is the sense of closeness and trust shared with another. Power is the perceived control or authority over others. There are several types of social power, including coercive, reward, legitimate, expert, and ref-

erent. We should also strive to empower our partners and to feel empowered in our relationships. Romantic relationships develop in stages, according to Mark Knapp. Each stage of the relationship is characterized by the communication behavior of the two partners.

Self-disclosure, the conscious decision to share personal information, is one way to improve the quality of our relationships. Its benefits include an increased understanding of ourselves, the ability to express our feelings, and an increased likelihood that others will be more open with us. Despite these benefits, a few cautions exist; namely, (1) we need to be selective with whom we share, and (2) self-disclosure should occur under natural conditions. The Johari window, developed by Joseph Luft and Harry Ingham, classifies our interactions as either open, blind, hidden, or unknown. This theory represents a visual presentation of self.

Two interpersonal theories help us understand our communication in dyads: Schutz's theory of interpersonal needs and cost-benefit theory. William Schutz's theory of interpersonal needs argues that our needs for inclusion, control, and affection have an impact on our communication in interpersonal relationships. Finally, John Thibaut and Harold Kelley's cost-benefit theory explains how we assess our satisfaction within a given relationship.

Conflict is an integral part of interpersonal relationships. A number of factors inhibit our attempts to resolve conflicts, including denial, suppression, aggression, and status. In order to improve our efforts in this area, the following skills are recommended: deal with feelings, find a special time to meet, keep the discussion focused on the problem, use perception checking and empathetic listening, and find a solution for both parties by being flexible.

Review Questions

1. Define interpersonal communication.
2. What are content and relational messages?
3. List the four types of intimacy and provide an example of each.
4. What role does power play in relationships?
5. Why is it important for both partners to feel empowered?
6. What causes tension in the differentiating stage?
7. What is the most public stage of a relationship?
8. Describe the benefits of self-disclosure.
9. Why is it important to be selective when engaging in self-disclosure?
10. Distinguish among the four quadrants of the Johari window: open, blind, hidden, and unknown.
11. What are the similarities between undersocial and oversocial behavior?
12. Apply cost-benefit theory to one of your current relationships.
13. Differentiate between denial and suppression.
14. How does being an empathetic listener help resolve an interpersonal conflict?

7

Creating a Positive Communication Climate

At the conclusion of this chapter, you should be able to:

- Explain why people communicate defensively.
- Identify eight types of defensive communication.
- Explain how altering a defensive climate can improve our communication with others.

- Identify the six pairs of communication behaviors in the Gibb study.
- Compare and contrast the six pairs of communication behaviors in the Gibb study.
- Explain the benefits of stepping back from defensiveness.

n a recent meeting, Lee, the director at a local utility company, presents his budget to the new vice president, Carolyn. Also in the meeting are Ivan and Ellen (from Chapter 6) and several other supervisors. Everyone present has a copy of the budget, and Lee asks for comments or questions.

Ellen believes the budget favors Ivan's department at the expense of hers. She aggressively protests the perceived inequity by attacking Ivan and his performance as a supervisor. Ivan responds, not by verbally attacking Ellen, but by withdrawing from the discussion. He does not attempt to defend himself and when asked for his opinion, he declines the invitation to participate. Lee tries to mediate a discussion, but is unsuccessful because everyone is tense and uncomfortable. Embarrassed, Lee ends the meeting.

Afterward, Ivan and another supervisor meet for coffee. Ivan spends the entire time complaining about Ellen and Lee's inability to "control" her. At home, Ellen tells her partner about the meeting and complains about Ivan's work performance and how it makes more work for the rest of the supervisors.

In this chapter, we discuss the kinds of communication behaviors exhibited by Ivan, Ellen, and Lee. We also discuss some strategies for improving interpersonal communication.

Have you ever felt the way Ellen, Ivan, and Lee do? It is difficult to know how to react in a communication setting where you feel threatened. When feelings of self-doubt or insecurity surface, people attempt to protect themselves. This self-protection often manifests itself in the form of defensive communication. **Defensive communication** is a person's reaction, either verbal or nonverbal, to a communication situation in which he or she feels personally threatened or uncomfortable. Many times we feel threatened or insecure when we must communicate with others who are different from us in some way. Instead of taking the focus off of ourselves, we focus on the other person and how he or she may not look or talk like we do. The differences among us can be scary and cause us to communicate defensively. But, as we have discussed in earlier chapters, in order to communicate effectively, we need to focus on the similarities we share with others and begin to value our differences.

The people in our story focused only on themselves and failed to value the others in the room. Likewise, a public speaker who exhibits "forced" humor in front of an audience is also reacting defensively to the fact that he or she is uncomfortable in the situation. The communication we use to protect our "public" self places a shield between ourselves and others. This protective shield, however, creates a number of problems that affect our communication, including an inability to effectively confront problems. Consider, too, that it requires a tremendous amount of energy to simply maintain these protective walls.

Although defensiveness is an understandable reaction to an uncomfortable situation, learning how to cope with defensive communication, both our own and that of others, can lead to greater confidence as a communicator. Becoming aware of the different defense mechanisms is a major step toward self-improvement. One important lesson is learning not to take personally the defensiveness of others. Equally important is learning how to implement a positive communication climate, which may lead to a reduction of defensiveness and an improvement of our communication with others. These objectives are the subject of this chapter.

Understanding Defense Mechanisms

When we feel threatened by a situation or by another person, we often engage in defensive communication, which is simply our effort to protect ourselves. We can exhibit a variety of defensive communication behaviors, and these are called defense mechanisms. Developing an understanding of the different defense mechanisms people use should help us to recognize the types of feedback we receive from others. Several defense mechanisms are explained in this section: avoidance, psychological withdrawal, distancing, reaction formation, sarcasm, outdoing others, overly critical communication, and formula communication.

Avoidance

Avoidance occurs when we retreat from a problem in a relationship. We are troubled about something, but we decide not to confront the problem or the person associated with the problem. Instead, we convince ourselves that the problem will go away. Avoidance is evident in the following example:

> Jasmine and Raphael have been married for five years. Both are in their mid-twenties and were raised by very traditional working-class families. Raphael is a postal carrier and is the primary financial supporter of the family. Jasmine is a full-time server at a local restaurant, but attended the local community college part-time before they were married. Raphael, feeling some pressure from his parents, is ready to start a family. Jasmine, however, wants to return to college full-time in order to finish her degree in psychology. Last week, Jasmine made an appointment to meet with an academic counselor to schedule her classes. Raphael is very upset that Jasmine, in his opinion, has put her desire to finish school before his desire to have a child. Raphael chooses not to discuss this with Jasmine and avoids any discussion of Jasmine's enrollment in college and his disappointment.

A satisfactory resolution to the problem is not achieved because this couple will not discuss the resentment Raphael feels toward Jasmine.

In significant relationships, avoidance also can pose a problem. In some work environments or in families, for example, problems are never worked through because the individual members are unwilling to discuss their feelings. Minor incidents are seen as insignificant events and are dismissed or repressed. The frustration associated with these minor episodes may build over the years, resulting in bad feelings among co-workers or family members. When these feelings finally surface, the interaction is often a heated shouting match, the result of buried frustrations.

Psychological Withdrawal

Closely related to avoidance is the defense mechanism known as psychological withdrawal. **Psychological withdrawal** occurs when we feel terribly uncomfortable in a particular situation but at the same time feel forced to be physically present. Because we are unable to leave the social setting, we mentally attempt to escape from it. This type of behavior is different from daydreaming during a lecture. Daydreaming can be attributed

When we are uncomfortable in social situations, we might escape by using psychological withdrawal.

to boredom or preoccupation with other thoughts; psychological withdrawal can be attributed to uncomfortable feelings. For example:

> Donald and Regina have been separated for eight months. After a year of marriage counseling, they realized that their marriage was over, and Donald moved out of their apartment. Donald is Jewish while Regina is Catholic, and their inability to resolve their religious differences is the primary reason for their separation. Donald had always been close to Regina's brother Thomas, and when Thomas asked a few months ago if Donald would be an usher at his upcoming wedding, Donald accepted. Now that he and Regina have separated, Donald feels uncomfortable seeing Regina and his soon-to-be-ex-relatives at the wedding. Donald keeps his commitment and acts as usher, but he withdraws psychologically, not mingling or socializing at the wedding.

People also use this defense mechanism in professional settings. Ivan, from the beginning of the chapter, for example, experiences extreme discomfort each time he attends staff meetings. Because he is usually shy and quiet, he believes that others will not listen to his ideas. Rather than risk rejection, he withholds his comments and avoids direct eye contact with others.

Distancing

Distancing is a defensive response that communicates "Do not get close to me." It is our way of shielding or hiding our perceived weaknesses from others. Adjectives sometimes used to describe such people include *conceited, cold,* and *aloof.* In reality, people who use distancing are shy and afraid of opening themselves up to criticism. Distancing communicates that we do not wish to be approached. Dominique is a good example:

> Dominique has just been promoted to a managerial position in the purchasing department she has worked in the past five years as a data entry operator. A single mother of a small daughter, Dominique went to college at night and weekends in order to earn her degree in business management. She worked hard for her degree and is well qualified for the promotion. Because she feels unsure of herself in her new role with the same people she once worked with, she decides to make herself inaccessible to those employees she now supervises. She explains in an email that her new responsibilities will keep her busy for the next several weeks and that all requests to see her should be cleared with her secretary.

Dominique's actions communicate to her employees that she wishes to distance herself from them. At the same time, her behavior reveals her lack of confidence in her new position.

Reaction Formation

In **reaction formation,** we behave contrary to the way we really feel. This behavior grows out of our need to present an image that is completely different from the one we believe is true. For example, an individual who exhibits reaction formation may feel uncomfortable in certain situations but will put on an act to appear confident. Consider the case of the class clown. This person actually feels uncomfortable in a group setting; however, in order to compensate for that feeling, he or she strives to "prove" to everyone else that he or she enjoys being the center of attention:

> Richard is the oldest member of his communication class. He is married with an adult child still living at home. This class is his first upon returning to college to finish his degree in construction technology. During the day, Richard is a supervisor of a crew of ten workers and has much responsibility. On the construction site, Richard is confident and very self-assured. At school, however, Richard is the class clown. His daily efforts at humor are contrived and predictable. He consistently tries to get the instructor's attention. It does not take long for Richard's classmates to realize that his communication behavior is extreme; they sense that it is unnatural for someone to always crave the attention he seems to demand.

Richard's communication is not intended to be annoying; rather, it represents an effort to be accepted by others. He believes that his instructor and fellow classmates will not like the "real" Richard and that he must pretend to be someone else while he is in class.

SKILL BUILDING   **Reaction Formation**

Joe always seeks center stage during class discussions, yet he behaves awkwardly in small-group activities. On several occasions, you have observed Joe's lack of direct eye contact when he talks to others.

1. Explain the difference between Joe's communication during class discussion and his communication in small groups.

2. Can you identify someone from your own circle of friends or family who communicates as Joe does? If so, how does recognizing this defensive behavior help you communicate more effectively with this person?

Sarcasm

Sarcasm is the use of a biting sense of humor designed to keep people at a distance and to maintain control in a situation. Humor is meant to be spontaneous and nonmalicious. The sarcastic person, however, often plans his or her next retort, intent on making others uncomfortable or simply putting them down. The sarcasm is intended to hurt the other person. Initially, we may find the sarcastic person to be humorous or witty; after repeated contact with this person, however, we may feel on guard or tentative. Consider the following:

> *Deneen:* Can you clarify the difference between interpersonal and intrapersonal communication?
>
> *Professor Casey:* Were you vacationing? What do you think I have been lecturing about for the past five days?

Professor Casey's remarks in this example demonstrate how sarcasm can play a detrimental role in communication. Because the professor is in a position of authority, Deneen may take his remarks personally and begin to question her own intelligence. Moreover, the professor's sarcastic remarks can adversely affect other class members.

In general, the sarcastic person appears unapproachable. As a result, other people tend to avoid interactions with that person. Let us take another look at the effects of Professor Casey's defensive communication. Danielle, an extremely quiet student, may decide never to speak up in class after the preceding incident, reasoning that she will again be put down. If other class members develop a similar attitude and stop asking questions, what has Professor Casey been able to accomplish? The use of sarcasm allows the professor to place a shield around himself and at the same time makes it difficult for students to question and challenge him. This technique enables the professor to maintain distance between himself and his students; he stays in control by remaining unapproachable.

Outdoing Others

Outdoing others happens when we feel the need to constantly top the achievements of others. We tend to define our self-worth in relation to others. When we exhibit "one-upmanship," we rarely listen to the communication we receive, because we are too busy worrying about our role in the interaction. Thus, we communicate superficial information instead of communicating important information about our feelings. Despite an inability to take the focus off ourselves, we are not self-centered; rather, our discomfort in interactions causes us to see only how things personally affect us. For example:

> Lorraine had a difficult time with math in high school, and her grades reflected this. Now that she is in college, Lorraine is struggling with a math course that is required for all elementary education majors. She works two nights a week with a tutor because she is motivated to be the first one in her family to earn a college degree. For Amanda, math is easy, but English is very difficult. Amanda's difficulty with English has begun to erode her self-confidence in all her school work. The following dialogue illustrates this point.
>
> *Lorraine:* I studied the entire weekend for my math test, and I think it was worth it because I received 82 percent on the exam. I finally think I understand what we've been learning this past semester.
>
> *Amanda:* I got 91 percent on the test. I'm really pleased because I didn't have to stay home over the weekend to study. I'm glad math comes so easily to me.

While Lorraine was attempting to share her good news, Amanda felt the need to overshadow her friend's achievement. The dialogue started out by focusing on Lorraine, but it transferred to Amanda in the end. No real self-disclosure took place, and Lorraine is left feeling defeated.

Overly Critical Communication

Overly critical individuals judge the behavior of others; they compare the accomplishments of others to their own feelings of inadequacy and believe that by criticizing others, their own self-esteem will be enhanced.

Their critical style of communication reflects their own critical nature. Consider the following:

> Serina's mother never worked outside the home because she gave up her dream to become a writer when she met Serina's father, married, and had three children. She resents her choice, although she loves her husband and Serina. Serina put herself through school by working full-time at a local bank while attending college at night. Both Serina and her husband work full-time and their sons go to day care. Serina tries to see her mother at least once a week and often invites her to dinner with her children. Despite Serina's efforts, her mother can be overly critical with her communication.
>
> *Serina:* I'm going to apply for the position in management that just opened up. I see it as a significant advancement for my career.
>
> *Serina's mother:* Do you really think you are talented enough to be promoted? I think you would be better off keeping your present position. You haven't been terribly successful as a supervisor, so how do you expect to be a capable manager?

Serina's mother is critical because her self-esteem is weak. If Serina's mother is repeatedly critical in her communication with others, it is probably the result of a negative self-concept. Her critical communication in this example would explain her attempt to boost her self-esteem. Clearly, Serina's mother does not value Serina or her siblings for who they are and what they have accomplished as adults.

Formula Communication

Formula communication is safe, nonthreatening communication that involves little or no risk on the part of the communicator. It is often evident in the superficial dialogue that people exchange. There is the potential for greater depth in these relationships, but the people involved are hesitant to share their feelings. Consequently, the barriers remain and the communication stays at a superficial level. For example:

> Bob and Emily have been married for six years. Emily has never lived up to her mother-in-law, Beth's, expectations. Their home was never clean enough or decorated correctly. The meals she prepared for herself and her husband were not nutrious enough and "not what Bob likes," according to Beth. For the first year of Bob and Emily's marriage, Emily tried to please Beth, to no avail. Then during their third year of marriage Bob changed jobs, so the two of them relocated. They still, however, make regular trips back home to see everyone. The beginning of each visit is devoted to small talk and bringing everyone up to date. Afterwards, the conversation wanes; dialogue seems stuck at this superficial level. Emily and her mother-in-law are grateful for the television that fills the long moments of silence; this "third party" gives them a welcome excuse to keep their conversation to a minimum.

When we first meet someone, we generally engage in safe, nonthreatening communication.

Although the parties believe there is more to their relationship, no one is willing to take the risk to change the communication pattern. Thus, the parties continue to rely on superficial communication to survive the weekend. Table 7.1 presents a summary of defense mechanisms.

TABLE 7.1	Defense Mechanisms at a Glance
Avoidance	We retreat from a problem in a relationship.
Psychological withdrawal	We feel uncomfortable in a particular situation, yet feel forced to be physically present.
Distancing	We prevent others from getting close to us.
Reaction formation	We behave contrary to the way we really feel.
Sarcasm	We use a biting sense of humor to keep people at a distance and to maintain control in a situation.
Outdoing others	We feel the need to top the achievements of others.
Overly critical communication	We judge or criticize the behavior of others.
Formula communication	We engage in superficial dialogue as a means of self-protection.

SELF-ASSESSMENT   Defense Mechanisms

1. Review Table 7.1, which describes the defense mechanisms.
2. Identify one defense mechanism you recognize in your own communication.
3. During the next two days, record those instances when you exhibit this defensive behavior. Include the following information:
   a. the circumstances that triggered your defensiveness
   b. the names and your relationships to the individuals involved
4. Is there a noticable pattern to your defensive communication? Explain.

Coping with Defensiveness

As discussed in the preceding section, people communicate defensively in an attempt to protect themselves. Although their frustration is often with themselves, they defend themselves by directing their frustration, anger, or anxiety toward others.

As a result of our discussion about defense mechanisms, we should be able to recognize defensive communication. The next logical step is to learn how to communicate more effectively when we encounter defensive behavior. Realistically, there is no escaping defensive communication; therefore, it helps to know how to combat defensiveness when we encounter it. Our increased understanding of defensiveness will help us break through the walls others erect in order to shield themselves. Our reward for having accomplished this significant task is a level of communication that is more meaningful. Meaningful communication leads to more fulfilling relationships at home, work, and school. Ultimately, we can begin to understand and value the other person's point of view.

The Nature of Communication Climates

We bring a particular state of mind with us when we engage in the act of communicating. This emotional atmosphere is known as the **communication climate.** It includes such factors as our feelings toward the person or persons with whom we are interacting, our attitude about the subject under discussion, and how we feel about ourselves in the particular interaction. The climate, therefore, often determines the degree of comfort we experience while interacting with others.

Jack Gibb (1961) differentiates between supportive and defensive communication climates. A **supportive climate** is one that encourages a free and open interaction between individuals. We can be ourselves and appreciate the differences of others. For instance, a family gathering in which members pore over photo albums and talk nostalgically of bygone days represents a supportive climate. Inhibitions lessen as the individuals get caught up in their reminiscences. The family members focus on their shared experiences and feelings. A **defensive climate,** on the other hand, inhibits the interaction between individuals. We attempt to hide our thoughts, feelings, and ideas as a means of self-protection. In addition, we tend to focus on the "otherness" of the people with whom we are communicating. Consider the following situation:

Morgan, who is twenty-one years old and single, loves her job as a customer service clerk at the local Kmart. The job is interesting because she gets to meet so many different people every day. She is working on a degree in retail marketing and would like to move into management at her store someday. While behind the customer service desk, Morgan usually greets each customer with a smile and pleasant, "Hello, how can I help you today?" But, during the holidays, it is difficult to be so polite because everyone is rushed and long lines are constant. Morgan must deal with all different types of merchandise returns during the holiday season. Many customers want a refund without offering a receipt. Store policy clearly states that a receipt is necessary for a cash refund. One rather busy afternoon, Morgan begins each interaction by asking, "Do you have a receipt?" This question sets the tone for the conversation and instantly puts the customer on the defensive.

A supportive climate invites self-disclosure and an appreciation for the differences of others.

In this example, Morgan creates a defensive climate, which makes the customer feel abused and unappreciated and less likely to shop at Kmart again.

The Gibb study identifies six "pairings" of behaviors that contribute to a defensive/supportive climate. In other words, for each of the six behaviors Gibb associates with a defensive climate, there is a counteractive behavior that contributes to a supportive climate. The follow subsections will focus on the Gibb pairings: evaluation versus description, control versus problem orientation, strategy versus spontaneity, neutrality versus empathy, superiority versus equality, and certainty versus provisionalism.

Evaluation versus Description

Highly evaluative communication contributes to a defensive climate. **Evaluative behavior** is judgmental; it attacks the individual rather than that person's actions. In the following example, Holly and Jim have just moved in together after dating for six months. They met at work and have spent every free moment together since their meeting. Both are divorced. Holly has two married adult children, while Jim has no children. They decided to move in together to see if they are compatible and to try to avoid some of the mistakes they believe they made in their first marriages. During the first few weeks of sharing a home together, they find it difficult to communicate their frustrations. Both are used to living alone and having their own things just so. In a particular stressful moment, parties resort to evaluative communication:

> *Jim:* Why don't you ever pick your stuff up around here? You're so lazy! I'm always the one who cleans up this place. You never care about anyone but yourself.
>
> *Holly:* I'm not lazy! You're the one with the problem. You're always criticizing! Everything has to be "just so" all the time. You know what? You're impossible to please!
>
> *Jim:* I can't believe how nasty you are!
>
> *Holly:* How about you?!

In this exchange, both Holly and Jim become defensive, which is reflected by their communication with each other. In order to ensure a more supportive climate, Jim needs to use a technique known as **descriptiveness,** the ability to focus on observable behavior. If Jim were to explain to Holly why he has a problem with their messy apartment, the interaction would probably go more smoothly, perhaps something like this:

> *Jim:* Holly, it bothers me that this place is so messy. Since we're having company this weekend, I was wondering if you could do some cleaning. How long will it take you to finish what you are doing?

Holly: Well, I don't know. I'm really busy today, but I'll try to get everything straightened up by tomorrow evening.

Jim: I'd really appreciate that.

In this dialogue, Jim attempts to focus on the problem he has with his partner's sloppiness rather than attacking Holly personally. When we have difficulty with others, it usually deals with their behavior; therefore, it makes sense to have our feedback focus on those actions.

Evaluative versus Descriptive Communication **SELF-ASSESSMENT**

Consider an interpersonal relationship that is important to you.

1. Identify an aspect of the other person's behavior that you find irritating.

2. Write down your observations. Try to avoid using evaluative language.

   Evaluative: Bob always interrupts me because he has to be the center of attention.

   Descriptive: Bob interrupted me three times last night when I was telling the story of my first night of classes at the university.

3. Share your observations with a classmate. Practice descriptive statements about the observable behavior of others with your partner.

4. What are the advantages of descriptive language?

5. How can you use descriptiveness to improve your relationship with the person identified at the beginning of this activity?

Control versus Problem Orientation

Sometimes we try to resolve a conflict with a one-sided solution. When this approach is taken, one party decides it is the other party who needs to change. **Control** is a means of making the other party conform to our way of thinking. Furthermore, it suggests that there is only one way to see a problem. Consider the following:

Melanie was rebellious as a teenager. She repeatedly challenged the authority of her parents by piercing her tongue and getting several tattoos, which contributed to tense family communication. Her parents both worked full-time and had little time to spend with her. When dialogue did occur, shouting and screaming were typical. Melanie's parents felt that she was the one with the problem, that she was the one who needed to change. They encouraged her to seek therapy, yet they refused to participate in family counseling.

With a **problem orientation,** the parties involved realize that several people contribute to the problem and that adjustment of behavior is necessary on all fronts. The focus of the discussion rests with the assumption, "We have a problem. Let's try to resolve it." This is illustrated in the following case:

> Debbie is Melanie's age. Like Melanie, she went through a rebellious stage during her teens. There was considerable tension in her household, yet Debbie's family did not assume that the problem was entirely hers. Instead, the whole family participated in counseling sessions. Over a period of several months the problems between Debbie and her parents improved. This meant, however, that all the parties involved eventually altered their communication.

Strategy versus Spontaneity

Efforts to manipulate interactions between people indicate that some **strategy** is in motion. This frequently creates a defensive climate between parties. Sometimes when we have a conflict with another person, we try to preplan the dialogue, often with disastrous results. When we discuss our differences with the other party, our comments can lack spontaneity and sincerity. Consider the following situation:

> A conflict is brewing between Paula and Ruth. They have been friends for over twenty years. The two friends met in high school and were two of only a few African-American students in a predominantly white school. They went to college together and remained in contact when Ruth was promoted at her job and had to move to another state. Ruth recently moved back to her hometown. At first, the friendship returned to its old intensity and openness. But lately, Paula has stopped calling and inviting Ruth to movies or shopping. Ruth, in return, has increased her invitations, only to be turned down by Paula. Paula always offers an excuse. Ruth has been troubled over the tension that has developed between them, so she invites Paula out for lunch. Ruth is nervous about the meeting and stays up until 2:00 A.M. planning what she wants to say. When they meet, Paula surprises Ruth by bringing up some unexpected points. Ruth's preplanned comments are inappropriate for their current conversation. The outing is a failure for both women.

Spontaneity is the opposite of strategy. **Spontaneity** refers to an open discussion of feelings. You know the major points you wish to bring up in a discussion, but you do not have an exact script for the interaction that is about to take place. "I feel bad about the present strain in our relationship and I hope we can repair the damage" will go much farther than a preplanned script.

Neutrality versus Empathy

Neutrality implies indifference toward another individual. This apparent disinterest can be interpreted as a lack of caring and can therefore have a negative effect on the communication climate. For example:

Allan and Barbara have been taking classes together since they met in their first college class four years ago. As study partners, they have helped one another with tests, math homework, and physics labs. They have both returned to college after many years with the full support of their spouses and families. As full-time workers and part-time students, Allan and Barbara have depended on each other for support and friendship. Allan has decided to continue his education and go to law school. He wants to share his news with Barbara. When he sees Barbara in the college cafeteria, he can't wait to tell her. Barbara, however, shows little interest, prompting Allan to wonder why he was excited about telling her.

Empathy, the ability to look at something from someone else's perspective, is the antithesis of neutrality. Empathy communicates an understanding of the other person's viewpoint. In essence, it means taking the focus off yourself so that someone else's position can be readily seen. Consider the following circumstances:

Jan's two children have been home from school for the past two and a half weeks because of a teachers' strike. Jan is angered by the disruption the strike has caused her boys' education, their family's daily schedule, and so on. Roberta, one of Jan's closest friends, teaches in the school district. Roberta visits Jan one afternoon following another unproductive negotiating session. She is frustrated by the long ordeal, but she firmly believes the strike is justified. Despite her differing views, Jan allows Roberta to discuss her feelings and explain her reasons.

The empathy displayed by Jan in this example creates a communication climate in which Roberta feels free to express her views because she knows they will be valued by Jan.

Neutrality versus Empathy   CRITICAL THINKING

Using the example of Jan and Roberta, answer the following questions:

1. What evidence is there that Jan is able to take the focus off herself?

2. How does Jan's behavior make it easier for Roberta to disclose her feelings?

3. How do you use empathy in your relationships to create a supportive communication climate? Give specific examples.

Superiority versus Equality

Superiority communicates an attitude that an individual is better, more important, or more valuable than someone else. Designed to intimidate others, superiority discourages people from expressing themselves freely and therefore can contribute to a defensive communication climate. Consider the following:

> Carol, a graduate teaching assistant, is lecturing to fifty first-year students in her Introduction to Philosophy course. This is the first time Carol has taught this course, and she is somewhat unsure of herself. A student raises his hand and asks Carol a question. Instead of answering the student's question, Carol cites her degrees in philosophy and describes her latest research project. This tactic is chosen intentionally to intimidate the students and to make them feel embarrassed to ask a question.

This reply sets the tone for the remainder of the semester—a tense, defensive climate in which ill feelings dominate.

Equality, treating others on a par with ourselves represents a supportive climate. The dialogue between individuals tends to be much freer and more supportive because the status of the individuals does not interfere with the interaction. For example, if Carol had responded to the student's question by first acknowledging the importance of asking questions, the class as a whole would likely have proceeded more productively.

Certainty versus Provisionalism

We have all encountered individuals who believe that their way is the only way to proceed. Gibb refers to this type of person as one who has a high degree of **certainty,** one who believes that others cannot possibly contribute new knowledge to the situation. He or she does not see the value in differing approaches, viewpoints, or opinions. This individual frequently promotes defensiveness in others by inhibiting others from describing their ideas.

Provisionalism, on the other hand, is a willingness to explore new ideas. Individuals in this category realize that theirs is not the only way to look at a situation; they welcome input from others. For example:

> Karen and Angie are both receptionists for Dr. Johnson, D.D.S. Karen has worked for Dr. Johnson for three years. She is the senior member of the office. After eight weeks on the job, Angie suggests a different method for handling insurance claims to Karen. Rather than being threatened by Angie's suggestion, Karen recognizes the merit of the proposed change and decides to approach Dr. Johnson about implementing it. With Dr. Johnson's approval, Angie's idea saves the office several hours of work per week and the insurance claims are filed faster. Provisionalism, as illustrated in this example, creates a supportive communication climate that encourages an open exchange of ideas.

COMMUNICATION and TECHNOLOGY

Email Flaming and Defensiveness

More and more of us are using email to communicate with friends, family, and co-workers. Email is fast, inexpensive, instantaneous, and easy. We can even send photographs, reports, and other documents as attachments to our email. Email is a great way to send and receive information and stay in touch with friends or family who are far away. But, if used haphazardly, it can create defensiveness. Have you ever opened an email from a co-worker or friend and found an insulting or mean message that hurt your feelings or made you very angry? An email like this is called a flame. A flame is an example of defensive communication. Its goal is to hurt the other person's feelings, not to convey information. These messages are usually sent without real thought and as a reaction to the sender's immediate feelings. Flames do not solve problems or conflict and can only serve to intensify existing hurt feelings.

In order to avoid using flames and to use email to create a positive communication climate, follow these guidelines:

1. Carefully proofread every message you send. A misspelled word or typo could mean, for example, that the receiver misses an important meeting (the email says 1:00 and the meeting is actually at 2:00). The receiver is sure to be embarrassed and angry for missing the meeting and for receiving misinformation. One typo could cause defensiveness and conflict.
2. Allow time to pass before you send a message. Give yourself some time to reread and review your email before pressing the "send" icon. You may feel differently about the problem or conflict tomorrow. It is easy to write something to someone when you don't have to deliver the message face to face. Never write anything you would be unwilling to communicate in person.
3. Remember that email is not a private communication between you and the receiver. It is a permanent and sometimes public record of your message. If you don't want your message to be public, don't use email. Messages you send today could come back to haunt you tomorrow.
4. Ask yourself if email is the best way to deliver this message. Would it be better to use the telephone or discuss the problem face to face? Many of us use email to avoid conflict or to deliver messages that are unpleasant news. If you were the receiver, would you want to open your email and find this message?
5. Lastly, remember that the receiver will provide the emotion to the message. In other words, email is devoid of facial expressions, voice quality, and bodily movement—all things that help the receiver to interpret our message and provide some clues to the sender's meaning. Sarcasm, for example, is difficult to communicate via email. Whenever appropriate, use characters like :) and ;) to communicate a joke or happy/funny message (see Chapter 4).

SKILL BUILDING   **Writing Email**

Review the story of Ivan, Ellen, and Lee. After identifying the defensive mechanisms used by each, do the following:

1. Choose one of the characters.
2. With a partner or on your own, write two emails to one of the other characters in the story. The first email should be a flame. In other words, write an email that creates further defensiveness and conflict. The second email should follow the guidelines listed on page 153 to create a supportive communication climate.
3. Compare the emails. Which email was easier to write? Why? Which email will allow the parties to meet again and resolve their conflicts? Explain.

CHECKLIST   **Creating a Supportive Communication Climate**

- Be descriptive.
- Try to resolve the problem together.
- Openly discuss feelings.
- Value the other person's point of view.
- Treat others on a par with yourself.
- Show a willingness to explore new solutions.

CRITICAL THINKING   **Understanding Defense Mechanisms**

1. Reread the vignette at the beginning of the chapter.
2. Describe the defense mechanisms used by Ellen, Ivan, and Lee.
3. Why do you think they are using these defense mechanisms?

Stepping Back from Defensive Communication

If we find ourselves responding to someone else's defensive communication by behaving defensively in turn, it is time to step back and take stock of our actions or risk developing a habit of defensive communication. By analyzing the interaction, we can gain insight into the communication behavior of both parties and choose a more productive course of action

Ethics in Communication

Creating a Positive Communication Climate

In the vignette at the beginning of the chapter, Ellen and Ivan engage in defensive communication. Their use of defense mechanisms leads not only to ineffective communication, but also to low productivity for the company. It is also unethical. Ellen's shouting and personal attacks serve only to hurt Ivan's feelings and alienate her supervisor, Lee. Ivan's withdrawal from the interaction in the meeting and his subsequent discussions with other supervisors behind Ellen's back do not solve the problems they have and are also not fair to Ellen.

Clearly, Ellen and Ivan's communication is ineffective and unethical. How could they change the ways in which they communicate so that their conversations are productive and honest? The Gibb study provides us with some clues. First, Ivan and Ellen need to understand equality versus superiority. Each is communicating in a way that says his or her ideas are better than the other's. Neither Ellen or Ivan appreciates the unique opinions and viewpoints of the other. Second, both communicate with certainty instead of under-

standing provisionalism, or are open to new ideas. Neither is able to take the focus off of himself or herself and focus on the task at hand and the other people involved. Third, problem orientation is ignored by Ellen and Ivan. Both seek to control the situation, in this case the meeting and the budget, without focusing on the needs of the individual.

A positive communication climate could be created by observing the following suggestions. The first step for Ivan and Ellen is to recognize their use of defense mechanisms. Self-reflection should help each to recognize their reliance on and reason for their defensiveness. Also, they must identify the defense mechanisms used by the other. Second, the most important step for Ellen and Ivan is to respect and understand diverse approaches to problem solving and conflict. An appreciation for each person's unique and different communication styles will go a long way toward helping them to solve their problems. If Ellen and Ivan are willing to take these steps, their communication will be both effective and ethical.

than that provided by a defensive response. In the example at the beginning of this chapter, Ellen, Ivan, and Lee all exibited defensive communication behaviors. All three left the meeting feeling undervalued and unappreciated. If each had taken the time to reflect upon their relationships and their communication, they might have been more willing to step back from their defensiveness and attempted to create a more positive communication climate. For example, Lee could have said to Ellen, "I realize that you are angry about your department's budget cuts, but that is no reason to attack Ivan. We need to work together now to make the necessary budgetary cuts in each department without losing any productivity or morale."

This statement acknowledges Ellen's feelings, but also opens the door for a cooperative solution to their common problem as it invites all present to communicate their ideas.

It is also time to step back if we find ourselves internalizing another person's defensiveness. This occurs when we perceive ourselves as the cause of someone else's defensiveness.

Finally, there are times when others are threatened by who we are, so they lash out at us. They may only see the differences between us, not the things we share. A number of emotions may account for this behavior: anger, jealousy, and resentment are common reactions to such circumstances as our position at work, our perceived wealth, our attractiveness, or our popularity among our peers. If we realize that insecurities often motivate these individuals to communicate defensively, then it will be easier for us to detach ourselves from their defensiveness. By stepping back and analyzing their behavior, we reduce our chances of becoming defensive in return. This is the first step toward creating a supportive communication climate.

SKILL BUILDING   **Stepping Back from Defensiveness**

In this chapter we have discussed how and why defensiveness occurs in our communication. With a partner or on your own, explore the following issues:

1. What is the first step in creating a positive communication climate?

2. How does valuing others' views, opinions, and ideas help to alleviate defensiveness?

3. How might you change your own communication behavior in order to ensure a supportive communication climate?

SELF-ASSESSMENT   **Understanding Our Own Defensive Communication**

1. Describe a significant interpersonal relationship. Include in your description the length of the relationship, the type of relationship, and some general background about the two of you.

2. Describe the communication climate that exists in this relationship.

3. Identify the defensive and supportive communication mechanisms that occur.

Summary

Defensiveness is our response to a threatening situation, one that makes us feel anxious, uncomfortable, or fearful. Defensive communication acts as a shield that protects us from others, yet it creates barriers to effective communication.

We use a variety of defense mechanisms when we feel threatened by a situation or by another person. These include avoidance, psychological withdrawal, distancing, reaction formation, sarcasm, outdoing others, overly critical communication, and formula communication.

Since all of us use defensive communication and encounter its use by others, it is only natural that we should be interested in learning how to cope with defensiveness. Jack Gibb suggests that creating a supportive communication climate helps alleviate much of the tension and inhibitions that

exist between people. In his work, he identifies six pairings of behaviors that contribute to either a defensive or supportive communication climate: evaluation versus description, control versus problem orientation, strategy versus spontaneity, neutrality versus empathy, superiority versus equality, and certainty versus provisionalism.

In addition to Gibb's techniques for establishing a supportive communication climate, another way to cope with defensiveness is to step back from the other person's defensive communication. In order to do this, we must first realize that it is the other person's insecurities that trigger the undesirable communication. Our ability to avoid internalizing the defensiveness of others allows us to analyze their communication and minimizes our chances of becoming defensive in return.

Review **Q**uestions

1. Why do people behave defensively?
2. List eight defense mechanisms that emerge in social situations. Write a short example of each one.
3. Why is reaction formation a difficult behavior to change?
4. Differentiate between avoidance and psychological withdrawal.
5. What are the benefits of alleviating a defensive climate?

6. Briefly explain six ways to create a supportive climate.
7. Create or describe a situation in which empathy is used to establish a supportive climate.
8. How does internalizing another person's defensiveness stifle effective communication?

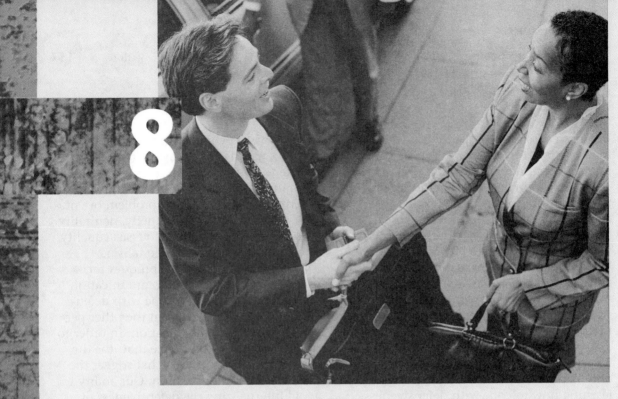

8

Interviewing

At the conclusion of this chapter, you should be able to:

- Define and differentiate between *open* and *closed*, *primary* and *secondary*, and *neutral* and *leading* questions.
- Explain the function of each of the following interview parts: the introduction, the body, and the conclusion.

- Construct and conduct an informational interview.
- Prepare a resume and cover letter for an employment interview.
- Apply techniques to improve your communication in an employment interview.

George is very excited. He is about to become the first member of his family to earn a college degree. It has taken him several years of night classes to graduate and now he is going to have his first job interview for a management position at a local engineering firm. He and his family have sacrificed their time together as well as the family savings for George to get his degree, but now it will all be worth it. This new job promises a large increase in pay and excellent benefits.

As he waits in the "holding" room with the other interviewees, George is confident that he and the recruiter will hit it off. George rehearses his opening comments about the score of the last Chicago Bulls game and how great the Michael Jordan years were for the city. He knows the interviewer will be impressed by his knowledge of sports—a very popular topic at the office. George knows he will fit in with the other guys.

A young African-American woman calls George's name and motions for him to follow her. When they reach the interviewing room, Gloria offers her hand for George to shake and invites him to sit down at one of the chairs in the room. George shakes her hand asks, "When will the recruiter arrive? I am awfully anxious about this interview and hope it will begin soon."

George's jaw drops when Gloria hands him her business card that reads, "Gloria McFerson, Senior Recruiter." She says, "The recruiter is right here and I'd like to begin the interview right now. I know you must be nervous, but try not to be. I just want to spend a few minutes getting to know you and discussing your qualifications for the position."

159

In this chapter, we'll see how the concepts of perception, listening, self-concept, self-disclosure, and communication climate affect the interviewing process. In addition, we will learn about interview organization, questions, and types of interviews.

Like George, we all feel uneasy when we interview for a job. When we think about being interviewed, one word may come to mind: *fear.* What are some factors that contribute to our anxiety? First, there is the risk of participating in an interview. We are not certain about whether or not we will get the job, and if we do not, can we handle the rejection? Second, it is difficult to interact with someone we have just met, especially when we realize this person will be judging our responses. And third, many of us are unsure about how to conduct ourselves during an interview. This chapter attempts to alleviate some of our anxieties about interviewing by explaining what an interview is and how we can improve our part within the interaction.

An **interview** is a planned and purposeful interaction between two parties in which questions are asked and answers are given. The party who asks the questions is the **interviewer;** the responding party is the **interviewee.** The "interviewer" can be more than one person, such as a group of board members, department personnel, or panel members. When we think of interviews, the first kind that comes to mind is the employment interview. There are, however, several other types of interviews: physicians gather information from their patients; mortgage loan officers gather information from prospective homeowners; contractors ask customers about the special features to be included in their kitchen, bathroom, or sunroom; and reference librarians ask patrons about the kind of information they need to answer their questions. A wide variety of careers and jobs require you to understand the dynamics of an interview.

The interview builds on several of the concepts discussed earlier in this book. For instance, *listening* plays a crucial role in the interviewing process, since both participants must actively listen carefully to each other's responses. Questions need to be worded with precision and clarity so that they communicate the intent of the sender, so *language* is important. *Nonverbal communication* is also crucial to the process. Participants need to observe both deliberate and accidental responses. Both parties need to be sensitive to their own interactions in order to respond appropriately to the other party's communication. A *supportive climate* set by the interviewer will allow for more *self-disclosure.* Most importantly, like all communication interactions, a successful interview hinges on both participants understanding and appreciating the other's diverse approach to the situation. The interviewer and the interviewee come to the interview with their own past experiences, culture, and social roles.

Interview Questions

Interviews contain a wide range of questions. While interviewers must formulate appropriate questions, interviewees should try to anticipate the types of questions that will be asked. On a job interview, for example, we expect to be asked about former positions we have held or why we think we are qualified for the job. Anticipating such questions can help us feel more comfortable with the interviewing process and, in turn, increase our ability to respond to questions. Several kinds of questions emerge during an interview, including the following pairings: open and closed, primary and secondary, and neutral and leading.

Open and Closed Questions

Open questions are nonrestrictive questions designed to give the respondent maximum latitude in formulating an answer. They provide an opportunity for interviewees to reveal more information about themselves: their feelings, philosophies, and biases. A question such as "What are your feelings about the proposed federal tax cut?" allows us to voice our opinion about the issue. At the same time, open questions are often successful in establishing an atmosphere of give and take between the interviewer and interviewee.

Open questions can be problematic, however. Consider the fact that our response to an open question, both in terms of the subject matter covered and the amount of time used, is beyond the interviewer's control. In fact, much of the information we yield in response to an open question can be far removed from the interviewer's purpose. For example, if our response to the question about the federal tax cut digressed into a discussion of deficit government spending, the interviewer would be getting more than he or she bargained for (in this case, the interviewer was simply looking for some indication of the degree of public support for the tax cut). Consider, too, that inexperienced interviewees or those with a low self-esteem might feel particularly anxious about responding to open questions because they are afraid to disclose personal information or they are afraid that their responses might be too off-base.

Closed questions are designed to elicit specific feedback from the respondent. They are especially useful in conducting surveys or polls in which the interviewer plans to statistically compare the responses. The interviewee's responses to closed questions should be brief.

The following series of closed questions could be used in a public opinion poll:

1. Do you support the proposed federal tax cut?

Most polls include closed questions because the answers can easily be compared.

2. How much will your taxes decrease with the tax cut?
3. Do you believe the tax cut will effect social programs like Medicare?
4. Who will receive the highest tax relief under the president's plan?
5. Which is more preferable: a small tax cut for you or increased spending on the environment ?

These questions, and several more like them, are necessary in order to gauge the public's attitude and knowledge of the proposed tax cut plan. It might take dozens of closed questions to determine the attitudes expressed in response to just one open question. Closed questions, however, are not meant to probe or explore another person's feelings or values; rather, their intent is to simply gather facts or discern what is already suspected by the interviewer.

Primary and Secondary Questions

Primary questions are those questions that introduce a major area of discussion to be guided by the interviewer. Whenever the interviewer summarizes one area of discussion and then moves in a new direction, the initial question he or she asks is known as a primary question. For example, a sportscaster might kick off each new area of an interview by asking the following questions of a baseball manager whose team just clinched the American League Pennant: "What did you say to your players before the start of today's game?" "What was the turning point in this deciding game?" "Did you ever lose confidence in your team?" "Who do you plan to start in game one of the World Series?" The sportscaster is able to introduce several key issues, each with a separate primary question. Interviewers generally prepare primary questions ahead of time. By the same token, interviewees can usually anticipate that some of these questions will be asked during the interview.

Secondary questions are designed to gain additional information from the interviewee. The interviewer is asking that we clarify or expand our response to the primary question. General questions such as "What do you mean?" "I don't think I fully understand your point," or "Why do you say that?" can be used, or the secondary questions can be more specific. For instance, as a follow-up to the primary question, "Who do you plan to start in game one of the World Series?" the sportscaster might ask: "Will his arm have enough rest with only three days off" "Are you worried about the number of walks he gave up during the two games he pitched in the Championship Series?" Certain nonverbal behaviors also can function as secondary questions. A raised eyebrow or a searching look might indicate that the interviewee needs to clarify or expand on his or her response to the last question.

Secondary questions also provide an opportunity for both parties to clear up any misunderstandings about statements made earlier in the interview because they allow us to check our perceptions. In addition, they allow the interviewee to give more detailed answers. Ultimately, this may affect how the interviewer interprets information, or reaches a decision, in the case of job interviews.

Neutral and Leading Questions

Neutral questions are those questions that reveal nothing of the interviewer's biases, preferences, or expectations. There is no "right" or "wrong" response to such questions as "Are accounting courses better at night or in the day?" "How do you like to spend your leisure time?" **Leading questions** are designed to move the interview in a specific direction. "Don't you agree that part-time students who work are more serious about their courses?" "Television coverage can make or break a politician's career, wouldn't you agree?" In the preceding questions, the interviewee is being led to a specific response. Leading questions can create problems, however. People can become extremely defensive when they feel forced to give responses that do not truly represent their views. This can increase the level of tension within the interview.

SKILL BUILDING · Recognizing Types of Questions

After reading each question, determine whether it is: (a) open or closed, (b) primary or secondary, or (c) neutral or leading.

1. What experience do you have with Microsoft Word?
2. When you say you have great people skills, what do you mean?
3. Why did you choose to major in political science?
4. You are looking for a challenging career, aren't you?
5. Don't you wish all days were as beautiful as today?
6. Which college course helped you to develop your writing skills?
7. What do you think about censorship?
8. Could you explain why you are applying for this position?
9. What questions do you have about the position?
10. Having a strong policy against sexual harassment is great for the company, isn't it?

Organizing the Interview

How do we incorporate the different types of questions discussed in the preceding section into the interview itself? To answer this question, we need to explore the issue of organizing the interview. While the following discussion is presented from the perspective of the interviewer, it should be of equal value to the interviewee. An awareness of the interview's structure can help the interviewee anticipate the types of questions he or she will be asked.

In many ways, the structure of an interview follows the pattern of a speech, which we will discuss is Chapter 13. Consequently, there are three parts to the interview: the introduction, the body, and the conclusion.

The Introduction

The **introduction** opens the interview. Its general function is to establish rapport between the two parties and to clarify the interview's purpose and scope. What the interviewer says during the introduction generally sets the tone for the rest of the interview. His or her ability to create a positive communication climate (see Chapter 7) depends, in part, on how interpersonally skilled he or she is. One way to create a positive climate is to create common ground with the interviewee. Common ground means that the interviewer and the interviewee share an interest, value, and past experience. Because the interviewer and interviewee are coming to the situation from different perspectives and with different and diverse approaches, it is important for the interviewer to find something he or she shares in common with the interviewee.

The introduction is an appropriate place to ask some general questions in order to relax the interviewee. These warm-up questions, often open in nature, give the interviewee an opportunity to express himself or herself in general terms: "Did you have any trouble finding the office?" "Have you been enjoying this unseasonably warm weather?" This process often reduces the tension for both interviewer and interviewee alike. The sequence should remain brief, however, lest the interviewee become nervous about supplying "correct" answers to these questions.

The Body

The next segment of the interview is the **body.** This is where the major part of the interview occurs. In developing the body, we must first determine the degree of flexibility we feel is appropriate for the interview. We might characterize the body in one of three ways: highly structured, moderately structured, or loosely structured (Stewart and Cash, 1997, pp. 42–45).

Highly Structured Body

A **highly structured body** includes all the questions that the interviewer plans to ask. Most of these questions are closed, leaving little opportunity for secondary questions to arise. Marketing surveys and public opinion polls follow a highly structured body. In employment interviews, the highly structured body generally works best for the inexperienced or untrained interviewer. The security of having a prepared list of questions in advance simplifies the process, especially for the novice. For instance, a newly promoted store manager may have little or no experience interviewing others for a position in sales. For her first interviewing experience, an already prepared list of questions might be a wise choice. She can move from one question to the next, taking time to listen to the response given after each question. What a highly structured body does not invite, however, is a spontaneous exchange between interviewer and interviewee. This is generally achieved during a moderately or loosely structured interview, where the interviewer is more experienced.

Moderately Structured Body

In a **moderately structured body,** the interviewer determines the primary questions ahead of time. These serve only as a foundation for the rest of the interview, however. The interviewer proceeds on the premise that the interviewee's responses will trigger secondary, related questions. In other words, the interview is open to give and take between the two parties. The moderately structured interview offers flexibility and a sense of naturalness. It is an excellent format for someone who has experience as an interviewer.

For example, the interviews conducted by Ted Koppel on ABC's "Nightline" follow a moderately structured format regardless of the evening's topic or invited guests. Mr. Koppel determines the ground he wants to cover prior to airtime. Once the initial questions are asked, however, he allows the interviewee's responses to dictate some of his follow-up questions. Of course, as a highly skilled interviewer, Mr. Koppel is always able to bring the topic back into sharp focus if the conversation goes too far afield.

Loosely Structured Body

The **loosely structured body** provides maximum flexibility for both interviewer and interviewee. The interviewer works from a list of possible questions or a list of possible topics and subtopics. These questions tend to be open ended, which allows the interviewer to observe the interviewee more closely. The loosely structured interview works best when the interviewer has no time constraints and has considerable experience. For example:

> Harvey owns four children's clothing stores. Over the years, he has interviewed and hired dozens of people; at present, he is seeking a new manager for one of his stores. In order to find the right person for the job, he decides to ask the applicants a few open-ended questions and then pay close attention to their responses. Harvey's experience as a business owner allows him to conduct a loosely structured interview. If the candidate's responses are too unfocused, Harvey can easily redirect his or her attention.

The Conclusion

In some respects, an interview's conclusion is similar to the introduction. One of its purposes is to end on a positive note, reinforcing the positive climate created in the introduction. To end an interview abruptly could destroy an otherwise positive climate. In "winding down" the interview, the interviewer might say, "I would be pleased to answer any questions you might have." This invitation provides the interviewee with an opportunity to ask a few final questions in order to clarify any uncertain factors: "Do the four store managers meet on a regular basis to discuss sales and advertising strategies?" "Do you encourage your managers to submit their suggestions for the company's advertising campaign?" After the interviewee's questions are addressed, the interviewer thanks him or her for participating in the session: "I'm glad you and I had this opportunity to talk. Thanks for coming in today."

Organizing an Interview

CRITICAL THINKING

Observe how a seasoned television interviewer (Ted Koppel, Oprah Winfrey, David Letterman, Chris Matthews, Dan Rather, Judy Woodruff, Barbara Walters, Jay Leno) conducts an interview. Then, answer the following questions:

1. What type of interview took place?
2. What was the primary goal of the interview?
3. How did the interviewer set the tone or climate for the interview?
4. What type of body does this interviewer use?
5. What types of questions did he or she ask?
6. How was the interview concluded?
7. Based on your observation, did the interviewer achieve the goal?

Jay Leno, seen here with former New York City Mayor Rudolf Giuliani, is a skilled interviewer.

Ethics in Communication

The Employment Interview

In the beginning of the chapter, we see an example of ethical and effective communication in Gloria McFerson and an example of unethical and ineffective communication in George. An examination of both communicators can give us some insight into how to succeed in an interview situation.

Gloria McFerson's communication with George is clearly effective and ethical. She ignores his preconceived notions of her and continues the interview as a professional. She tries to create a supportive communication climate, as interviewers should, and to put George at ease despite his serious blunder. She could have responded to George defensively by using one of several defense mechanisms, such as sarcasm or distancing. Instead, she effectively opens the interview and proceeds to gather information from George about his qualifications for the position.

George may have lost any chance at this position because of his ineffective and unethical communication. He obviously made several incorrect assumptions about the company he wants to work for and the recruiter conducting the interview. For example, he assumed that all engineers are men and like sports. Also, he assumed that an African-American woman couldn't be

the recruiter, but a secretary or administrative assistant.

What could have George done to increase his chances of success in this interview? First, and most importantly, George must realize and put aside his preconceived notions and stereotypes about men, women, ethnicity, professions, and so forth. As we learned in Chapters 1 and 2, these notions can only hinder the communication process and lead us to become defensive. He must realize that we all approach communication from diverse and unique positions and that this diversity is valuable and necessary. Second, George needs to thoroughly research each company before he goes to the interview. Thorough research would help George understand the products, services, and personnel of the company. If possible, he should visit the company to get a feel for the atmosphere and work environment. Lastly, George needs to practice his interviewing skills in mock interviews. Preparing for an interview should include constructing possible answers to popular interview questions, practicing listening skills, and paying close attention to nonverbal behavior. If George had done these things, he might well have succeeded in the interview and been offered a position with the company.

Types of Interviews

We have many opportunities to participate in interviews, including those related to job hiring, parent-teacher conferences, and questioning sales-people about particular consumer products, among others. There are many different types of interviews. These include the information-giving interview, such as a job orientation; the information-gathering interview, such as a survey or research interview; the selection or employment interview; the problem-solving interview; and the persuasive interview, such as that used in cars sales or fundraising (Stewart and Cash, 1997, p. 2). In addition, the counseling interview takes place between a therapist and a patient, and an exit interview is often required when we leave a job. Of the numerous interviews conducted daily, two are especially significant: the informational interview and the employment interview. The informational interview is presented from the interviewer's perspective; in it we discuss how to conduct this type of interview. In the section on the employment interview, the focus shifts from interviewer to interviewee. Preinterview preparations are explained, followed by a discussion of communication skills designed to improve our performance during an employment interview.

The Informational Interview

The purpose of an **informational interview** is to acquire facts about a specific topic. Perhaps our purpose is to gain an understanding of a company procedure or policy, to elicit an octogenarian's oral history, to determine the strategies used by the local high school football coach, or to learn about the successful techniques of a prominent business executive. Most importantly, you may use an informational interview to solicit support material for your speeches (see Chapter 12). In all these cases, we must interview someone knowledgeable in a specific area. There are several steps to consider when conducting an informational interview. These include (1) developing the objective, (2) adequately researching the subject, and (3) carefully planning the interview questions.

Developing the Objective

A clearly defined interview objective serves several purposes; namely, (1) it communicates the intent of the interview, (2) it helps the interviewer develop appropriate questions, and (3) it establishes a time frame for the interview. By having a clear picture of the interview's intent, both parties better understand the purpose of the interaction and the importance of each of their roles. Having a good idea of where the interview is headed allows the interviewer to outline meaningful questions that remain focused on the stated purpose. Finally, a clearly established objective helps determine a reasonable time frame for the interview. This forces the interviewer to take into consideration the interviewee's time. For example:

Ineffective objective: To learn about your business.

Effective objective: To learn the procedure that your company uses for hiring accountants.

Ineffective objective: To learn about the newspaper business.

Effective objective: To learn about the typesetting and printing stages in publishing the late edition of the paper.

The first statements in the preceding list are vague, while the second statements clearly establish the parameters of each interview. The interviewer can then proceed to develop concrete questions, while the interviewee has a strong sense of the direction of the interview.

Researching the Topic

If the purpose of the interview is to gain information, it is advisable to research the topic ahead of time. Researching the topic helps the interviewer determine what he or she needs to find out during the interview, it prepares the interviewer to ask pertinent questions, and it enhances the interviewer's credibility with the interviewee. Furthermore, researching the topic avoids wasting interview time asking questions that could already have been answered by doing some groundwork. A basic understanding of the interview topic allows the interviewer to respond to the interviewee's comments by asking spontaneous follow-up questions. This task becomes difficult if the interviewer is generally unprepared for the interaction.

Planning the Interview Questions

Once the interview objective is determined, the interviewer is ready to develop interview questions. In part, the purpose of the interview dictates the types of questions used; an oral history, for example, tends toward open questions because its purpose is to learn about the individual's experiences. As discussed earlier in this chapter, open questions encourage the interviewee to reveal personal thoughts or attitudes concerning a particular topic. Open-ended primary questions should be formulated prior to the interview, as should some anticipated follow-up questions. Other secondary questions are interjected during the interview, since they grow out of the interviewee's responses. Whatever questions are used in the interview, they should conform to the structure (high, moderate, or loose) deemed most suitable by the interviewer.

Example: Informational Interview

The purpose of this interview is to gather information about obtaining financial aid for college from the Director of Financial Aid Services (see Chapter 15 for the actual speech). It might cover the following three points:

I. Objective: To discover the background and history of financial aid
   A. What is financial aid?
   B. When did financial aid begin?
   C. Why did financial aid become necessary?
   D. Who started financial aid?
   E . Where did financial aid originate?

II. Objective: To find out about the different types of financial aid
   A. What are the types of financial aid available?
   B. What are the requirements to receive financial aid?
   C. What are the eligibility requirements for each type of financial aid?
   D. Why should I apply for financial aid?
   E. How will financial aid benefit me and my family?

III. Objective: To find out how to get financial aid
   A. How do I start the financial aid application process?
   B. Who do I speak to about getting financial aid?
   C. Where I should I apply?
   D. When should I begin seeking financial aid?

The Informational Interview

SKILL BUILDING

As a way to practice your interview skills, conduct an informational interview with a family member about a particular event in recent history (for example, the Great Depression, World War II, the assassination of John F. Kennedy, the Vietnam War, the Challenger Disaster, the end of communism in Europe and the fall of the Berlin Wall, the Gulf War, the Oklahoma City Bombing and the execution of Timothy McVeigh, and the September 11, 2001, terrorist attacks).

1. Develop a set of questions for each of the following categories:

   a. Description of the event

   b. Event's impact on the family

   c. Event's impact on the community or country

   d. Event's impact on the person

2. After conducting the interview, how does the information you gathered affect your perception of the event?

The Employment Interview

For an employer, the purpose of an employment interview is to uncover information about potential employees and to use that information to hire a new employee; for an applicant, the purpose is to find out more information about a position and to persuade the employer to hire him or her. Such factors as experience, educational background, interpersonal skills, and appearance enter into the employer's decision-making process. In the past, some employers selected applicants on factors not related to job performance, such as gender, race, or religion; today, guidelines prohibit this practice. The Equal Employment Opportunity Commission (EEOC) has developed strict guidelines for interviewing and testing potential employees. Both employers and employees should be aware of these guidelines, in addition to state laws that govern hiring. In this section we will focus on two aspects of the employment interview: preinterview preparations and communication skills during the interview.

Preparing for an Interview

There are several ways for an applicant to prepare for an employment interview. Take the time to assess your employment potential, to compile a clearly structured resume, to write a solid cover letter, to research the company or organization, and to evaluate the interviewer's perspective in the interviewing process. Each of the steps described in this section has the potential to make you a better prepared, more confident employment candidate.

Self-Assessment

In assessing your employment potential, you want to evaluate your suitability for a particular career. To do this, you must appraise your capabilities and talents in order to determine how well you might fit a particular position. Self-assessment involves asking yourself such questions as (1) Why am I interested in this position? (2) How important is my work to me?

Before going to an interview, be sure to do a thorough self-assessment.

(3) Do I have the necessary background for this job? (4) Could I grow into the position?

Many people look to their job to fulfill personal interests. For instance, a person who enjoyed doing research as a history major in college also might enjoy being a research assistant for an advertising firm. It is equally important to take stock of such personal qualities as motivation, intelligence, and sensitivity, because these directly affect your work behavior.

Do any of your personal accomplishments make you a viable candidate for a particular position? For instance, during your term as president of your son's school's Parent-Teacher Association, you probably demonstrated supervisory abilities that are applicable to a management position. Likewise, if you were responsible for financing your college education, you certainly demonstrated your ability to manage a budget.

Self-assessment forces you to realistically examine and evaluate your strengths and weaknesses. This internal review helps you to get a better sense of yourself and at the same time helps you to decide whether or not you are a good candidate for a particular job.

Preparing for Employment
SELF-ASSESSMENT

As you prepare to write your resume and then to interview for jobs, take a few moments to write down your skills, work experience, accomplishments and honors, goals, and strengths and weaknesses.

1. Work experience: jobs, length of employment, skills used
2. Special skills: computer, languages, artistic (music, design)
3. Accomplishments and honors: work, school, community
4. Career goals
5. Strengths and weaknesses: oral and written communication, leadership, small-group work, motivation, dealing with stress, conflict resolution

---

The Resume

A resume is a short account of one's qualifications for a particular position. The purpose of a resume is to present one's educational and experiential backgrounds, emphasizing his or her relation to the job under consideration. The resume requires thoughtful preparation and organization, because it is often a key factor in determining which applicants get interviews.

A carefully prepared resume should include the following information: (1) the applicant's name and current address, (2) current place of employment, (3) prior employment and related experience, (4) education/training, and (5) awards, honors, and professional recognition. In addition, the resume may include (1) activities and experiences that highlight leadership potential, (2) career goals, and (3) references. Figure 8.1 presents a sample resume.

The Cover Letter

The cover letter is a short letter that introduces you to a prospective employer. Its overall intent is to express your interest in the job and to create a positive first impression. To achieve this goal, the letter must be free of grammatical errors. Additionally, the cover letter should be tailored to the particular job vacancy. You want the organization or company to believe your letter is written expressly for them.

The first paragraph states your reasons for writing to the company. This is the place to indicate the specific position you are applying for and why you are applying for that position.

In the second and third paragraphs, explain your interest in the position and, more important, what you can do for the employer. Refer to specific professional or academic experiences, as well as job experiences, that contribute to your qualifications for the position. For instance, college courses in public relations and an internship at the county welfare department are details worth mentioning in a cover letter for a public relations position at the community hospital. This information gets the attention of those individuals who screen applications.

Next, refer to the enclosed resume, which summarizes your training and experience. Also mention where the employer can check your credentials.

In the final paragraph, indicate your desire for a personal interview. You can suggest possible dates or simply indicate your flexibility. Remember, do what you can to encourage further communication. You may wish to call on a certain date to arrange an interview or to find out when a company representative plans to be in the area (such as on your college campus) so you can set up an interview then. Figures 8.2 presents an example of a cover letter.

In recent years, more and more companies are accepting applications (resumes and cover letters) over the Internet via email. In addition, several web sites allow you to post your resume for companies and recruiters to see and evaluate.

Company Research

Finding out all you can about a particular company or organization will help you be better informed at the time of the interview. What kinds of things should you research? If the position is with a manufacturing company, learn about its products, the location of its plants, and the company's history, financial status, and growth potential. For service organizations, such as hospitals, libraries, and social service agencies, comparable information is important: the type of service provided to the public, the number

MARTIN GABRIEL SENDEJAS

6941 VAN BUREN AVE., WHARTON, OH 45863 • 419-321-0742 • CELL: 419-731-6931 • E-MAIL: mgsditto@hotmail.com

OBJECTIVE Electrical Engineering Technician

PROFESSIONAL PROFILE
- Enthusiastic, rising electrical engineering technology professional with relevant experience and expertise in use of high-tech equipment for analysis, documentation, and presentation; NC programming; computer hardware interface; and circuit design/PCB construction.
- Honest, reliable, punctual team player who exceeds expectations.
- Motivated achiever and problem-solver who will do what it takes to get the job done.
- Solid communicator who can explain technology in easy-to-understand terms; fluent in Spanish; studied nine years in a Spanish-speaking country.
- Computer-proficient in Windows, DOS, Linux/Unix, Microsoft Office (Word, PowerPoint, Excel), OrCAD, AutoCAD, Mathlab, Masm, D, C++, Visual Basic.

EDUCATION and TRAINING
- Bachelor of Science in Electrical Engineering Technology, Purdue University, Hammond, IN, May 2002; GPA: 3.43
  - Semester Honors for four consecutive semesters
  - Clare and Lucy Osterle Scholar
  - Harold C. Morgan Scholarship
- A+ Computer Service Technician, Computing Technology Industry Association

PROFESSIONAL EXPERIENCE

Sales Representative, Radio Shack, Lansing, IL, 08/2001–present
- Serve as electronics replacement and connectivity specialist.
- Assess customers in enhancing their in-home electronic devices.
- Increased sales by tailoring service to customers' needs and reducing amount of returned merchandise.

Maintenance Engineer, Holiday Inn, West Lafayette, IN, 08/1998–12/1999
- Juggled multiple responsibilities while maintaining hotel facility.
- Replaced and repaired electrical systems.
- Reorganized facility.
- Earned Worker of the Month Award, Sept. 1999.

Student, Purdue University, Hammond, IN, 08/2001–12/2001
- Organized, planned, and built a Computer Numerical Control (CNC) machine that exceeded expectations and was considered one of the best projects of the semester.
- Conducted research to design, build, and test machine that drilled holes and could rout and engrave.

PROFESSIONAL AFFILIATIONS
- Member, IEEE

FIGURE 8.1 **Sample Resume**

6941 Van Buren Ave.
Wharton, OH 45863

January 15, 2003

Mr. Robert Gray, Staffing Specialist
Northern Electronics, Inc.
1605 Revere Street
Morton Grove, IL 60053

Dear Mr. Gray:
I am seeking a cooperative education or internship position in electrical engineering
technology. Purdue University Calumet's Career Development Office informed me
that Northern Electronics has several positions open for the Fall 2003 semester.

As you can see from my enclosed resume, I have extensive experience in electrical
engineering technology from my studies at Purdue University Calumet and my work
experience. I am fluent in Spanish and am computer-proficient in several software
programs including AutoCAD, Masm, Windows, and Visual Basic. In my studies, I
have earned a 3.43 grade point average while working part-time. I have received several scholarships and have earned semester honors for four consecutive semesters.

As an electronics replacement and connectivity specialist, I have experience with
many different types of home and office electronics. I also have extensive experience
with customer service. I am a member of IEEE.

I am available for employment beginning August 2003. I hope to complete an internship by June 2003 when I will earn my Bachelor of Science Degree in Electrical Engineering Technology. Please contact me at (419) 321-0742 or (419) 731-6931. My e-mail address mgsditto@hotmail.com. I look forward to hearing from you soon.

Sincerely,

Martin G. Sendejas

enc.

FIGURE 8.2   **Sample Cover Letter**

of employees, and its reputation in the community, annual budget, and organizational structure. Collegegrad.com suggests that the best place to find information about a company is from its annual report. They state, "The letter catalogues not only the history of the past year, but even more important, the company vision for the future" (The Very Best Source of Employment Information, 2001). The annual report sometimes can be obtained from the company's own web site or certainly from the Shareholder Services Department. Other sources include web sites such as Monster.com, Dice.com, and others that have already done the research for you.

Another sound practice is to conduct research in your field or discipline. Find out about such things as average starting salaries, trends, current and future problems, and what the work is like on a day-to-day basis.

The Interviewer

Ideally, a prospective employer comes to an interview prepared to ask pertinent questions of the applicant and to supply information about the company. In many instances, the interviewer alone determines whether or not the interviewee will be considered for the position. In a well-structured interview, the interviewer has a clear set of primary questions that constitute the body of the interview. Typical questions might include "What prompted you to apply for a job with our company?" "On your application you state that you have work-related experience. Would you please elaborate?" "What are your career goals?" "What qualities do you possess that would convince me to hire you over applicants with similar training for this position?" The interviewee's responses to these questions can be revealing; from them the employer assesses the applicant's general knowledge, ability to communicate, prior achievements, ambitions for the future, and suitability for the job. Table 8.1 lists some of the most popular questions interviewers ask in an employment interview.

TABLE 8.1   Possible Employment Interview Questions

1. Tell me about yourself.
2. Describe your work experience at _____.
3. Why did you decide on _____ field of study?
4. Why do you want to work in this industry?
5. How do you describe success?
6. What motivates you to do your best work?
7. What are your short-term goals?
8. What are your long-term goals?
9. What is your greatest strength?
10. Provide an example of how you used this strength to succeed.
11. What is your greatest weakness?
12. How has this weakness hindered your success?
13. How has your education at _____ prepared you for this position?
14. What about this position excites you the most?
15. Why did you apply to this company?

COMMUNICATION and TECHNOLOGY

The Internet and the Job Hunt

The Internet is a wonderful tool for finding a job. Whether you are looking to change jobs or for your first job, the Internet can provide many kinds of information. For example, with a few clicks of the mouse, you can find information on resume writing (via regular mail or via email), company research, and job postings. Some web sites offer forums and chatrooms for job seekers to network and share stories and advice. Here are a few helpful general sites:

1. Monster.com. This site offers information on every aspect of the job search. It can even match your qualifications with jobs posted by employers. It is useful for all types of careers and majors.

2. Collegegrad.com. This site is similar to Monster.com in that it offers general information of the job search. Collegegrad.com, however, is geared toward entry-level jobs. First-time job seekers will find specific information on how to prepare for the first job.

3. Job-search-engine.com. This site is not an information site, but a search engine. It will search over 300 U.S. and Canadian job boards. You can search by keywords or by location of the job.

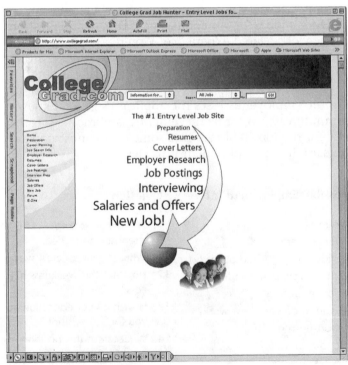

Used with permission of Collegegrad.com.

There are also sites dedicated to specific fields or careers. Some of these include:

1. Healthcarejobsite.com is for nursing, medical professions, and pharmaceuticals.
2. Fincareer.com posts positions in accounting, banking, and other finance jobs.
3. Dice.com specializes in high-tech and information technology positions.
4. Teacheroffice.com/employ.html contains information on teacher certification by state and also job postings for elementary and secondary school teachers.
5. Elabrat.com posts jobs in science and chemistry and offers information about resume writing and interviewing for science-related jobs.
6. Roundtable.org/search.html offers advice to professionals and first-time job seekers in communication, public relations, marketing, and advertising.
7. Hospitalityonline.com specializes in jobs with hotels, resorts, and restaurants.
8. Salesjobs.com is dedicated to sales professionals.
9. Imdiversity.com offers information and job postings for minorities and women. It posts only jobs by employers dedicated to workplace diversity.

Improving Your Interviewing Skills

Anxiety and nervousness are common reactions to an impending employment interview. To a degree, relief is possible by immersing ourselves in the process, that is, by concentrating on the questions generated by the interviewer and by applying specific communication skills to our responses. These skills include effective listening, ethics, language, effective nonverbal communication, and asking questions. Although these topics are treated in previous chapters, their specific application to the employment interview is discussed in the following subsections.

Listening

Without question, listening is an important aspect of the interview. Effective listening requires that we do two things: (1) listen closely to detect the exact nature of the interview questions, and (2) listen to the interviewer's responses to our answers in order to gauge how well we are doing in the session, to learn more about what is important to the interviewer, and to be able to keep conversing intelligently. Be sure to use the listening skills we described in Chapter 3: paraphrasing, interpreting, and questioning. These skills will help you check your perceptions of the interviewer and the questions he or she is asking.

One of our chief concerns in an interview is to be able to provide intelligent answers to interview questions. In order to do so, we must first understand the question. Listening closely to the interviewer is essential; however, a second step is sometimes warranted—asking for clarification when we do not fully understand what the interviewer wants. For example, to make sure that we are on target, we might paraphrase an interviewer's question this way: "Am I interpreting your question correctly? You want me to explain what steps I would take to correct an employee's chronic tardiness?" When the interviewer confirms that we have understood the question correctly, we feel comfortable offering our response.

Following our answer, the interviewer may make some comments before moving on to the next question. Listening to this feedback is just as important as listening to the questions themselves, because it provides us with clues concerning our performance. For instance, if the interviewer clearly misunderstands our reply, we need to clarify our position in order to eliminate the misunderstanding. This problem can be rectified only if we are listening closely to the feedback being given.

Finally, by listening carefully to the interviewer's questions and feedback, we can avoid asking questions or making comments about something that has already been mentioned in the interview. When we are nervous, this happens more frequently. The key here is to shift the focus away from ourselves (that is, our preoccupation about how stressful this interview is) to the other party, to pay close attention to the interviewer's message.

Ethics

One of our objectives during an interview is to present an honest picture of ourselves. This requires that we represent our skills accurately and that we take responsibility for any difficulties that we may have had in previous jobs. Misrepresentation of skills or experiences threatens both the likelihood that we will be selected for the position and, if we are selected, the chances of maintaining our employment. Consider the following:

> Sean has just graduated with a degree in public relations. He has done several internships and feels well qualified to write press releases and create brochures and other print promotional materials. He tells a prospective employer at the local finance company that he has web page design experience in order to appear better qualified for the job; despite his misrepresentation of the facts, Sean lands the position. Two months later he is asked to create a new web page for the personnel department. It becomes immediately apparent to Sean's boss that Sean misrepresented his abilities during the job interview. Sean may even have jeopardized his employment with the firm.

During the interview, questions may be raised about our reasons for leaving a previous job. It is best to offer straightforward responses to such questions: "I saw no place to advance within the company's structure. After four years I grew tired of doing the same job day after day. I needed a change to feel self-motivated again." "I found myself increasingly frustrated by the unresolved problems and tension between my supervisor and myself. Because I saw no sign of improvement for the future, I decided to find another job." Avoid placing the blame on other parties; it suggests a weakness on your part, an inability to adequately work through difficulties with others.

Language

Answering interview questions with direct, precise language communicates both a knowledge of the subject and a confidence in our own abilities. Precise language, especially terminology related to a specific occupation or profession, demonstrates our familiarity with the field: "I've worked with children at two preschools during the past seven years. In my opinion, a preschool curriculum should stress the development of gross motor skills, socialization skills, and reading readiness skills." Furthermore, being able to provide direct, concrete explanations communicates our self-assurance: "Reading readiness includes teaching such concepts as letter recognition and sounds, numbers, left and right, and sequencing (first, second, third)." Conversely, vague or general responses indicate a lack of knowledge or expertise and an apparently weaker job candidate. The lesson here is to know the subject and to show the interviewer that we know the subject by expressing ourselves with appropriate language.

Nonverbal Communication

Nonverbal communication can indicate our level of confidence within the interviewing situation. When we are nervous, for example, we communicate our discomfort not only through our verbal responses, but also through our nonverbal behavior. Signs of discomfort include averting our eyes each time the interviewer looks directly at us, repeated shifting in our seat, wringing our hands, and forced smiles.

In an employment interview, we want our nonverbal communication to support our other efforts to appear confident in the interaction. In other words, our effort to listen carefully to the interviewer's questions and comments can be accompanied by our effort to maintain direct eye contact. If we look away when the interviewer speaks to us, we will seem nervous and uninvolved. Likewise, our verbal replies to interview questions can benefit from appropriate gestures and paralanguage. For example, when we talk enthusiastically about our career goals, we can add to that positive image by using hand gestures, by increasing the rate of our speech, and by raising the pitch of our voice. (Chapter 5 has an in-depth discussion of these and other nonverbal communication behaviors.)

TABLE 8.2   **Questions to Ask the Recruiter**

1. What qualities do you want this employee to have?
2. How are employees evaluated and how often?
3. Why do you like working here?
4. What are the most positive aspects of working for _____?
5. What types of orientation or training do new employees receive?
6. Are there any opportunities for me to continue my education?
7. Based on my research, I noticed that this company did over $20 million in sales last year. How do you think the downturn in the economy will effect sales this year?
8. What are the opportunities for growth and advancement in this department?
9. How is the company responding to growing competition from _____?
10. Would you tell me what specific responsibilities I would have in this position?

Ask Questions

At the end of the interview, you will probably be asked if you have any questions for the recruiter. It is essential that you ask at least two questions to show you are prepared and interested in the position. These questions can illustrate that you have thoroughly researched the company and that you are motivated to know more about the interviewer and the position. Table 8.2 lists some possible questions you might ask during or at the close of an employment interview.

CHECKLIST   **Improving Your Interviewing Skills in an Employment Interview**

- Listen closely to detect the exact nature of the interview questions.
- Listen to the interviewer's feedback to gauge your performance.
- Use your responsive listening skills.
- Present an accurate picture of yourself.
- Answer questions honestly.
- Answer questions with precise language and concrete explanations.
- Maintain eye contact with the interviewer.
- Have communication-appropriate gestures accompany your verbal responses.
- When given the opportunity, ask questions of the interviewer to show you are prepared and motivated.

Summary

An interview is a planned interaction between two parties in which questions are asked by an interviewer and answers are provided by an interviewee. The interview consists of a variety of questions. Generally, each question can be classified as open or closed, primary or secondary, and neutral or leading. Open questions are designed to give the interviewee maximum latitude in formulating an answer, whereas the purpose of closed questions is to elicit specific feedback. Primary questions focus on the major concerns of the interviewer; secondary questions serve as a follow-up and are designed to gain additional information from the interviewee. Neutral questions reveal nothing of the interviewer's biases, preferences, or expectations; leading questions are designed to move the interview in a specific direction.

The basic structure of an interview is similar to that of a speech: both have an introduction, a body, and a conclusion. The introduction opens the interview and sets the tone for the interaction. The body is the heart of the interview; it is where the questions are asked and the responses are given. In the conclusion, the interviewer draws the session to an end, hopefully on a positive note.

Two types of interviews are especially significant: the informational interview and the employment interview. The purpose of an informational interview is to acquire facts about a specific subject. Generally, the most effective way to prepare for this type of interview is to develop an objective, research the topic, and plan the interview questions.

In an employment interview, the interviewer's goal is to uncover pertinent information about potential employees in order to select a qualified candidate; the interviewee's goal is to find out more about the position and to persuade the employer to hire him or her. The employer should be ready to supply information about the vacancy and the company offering the position. Before the interview, applicants should take the time to assess their employment potential, compile a well-structured resume, write a solid cover letter, research the company, and evaluate the interviewer's perspective on the process. There are specific ways to reduce anxiety and at the same time improve our communication in employment interviews. These skills include active listening, honesty, using direct language, using effective nonverbal communication, and asking questions.

Review Questions

1. What is the difference between a primary and secondary question? Open and closed? Leading and neutral?
2. Explain the three ways to structure the body of an interview.
3. What steps are involved in preparing for an informational interview?

4. Why is it necessary to do a self-assessment?
5. What is the primary goal of a cover letter?
6. What specific communication skills can you use to improve your interviewing effectiveness?

9

Communicating in Small Groups

At the conclusion of this chapter, you should be able to:

- Define small-group communication.
- Define the different types of groups.
- Explain the importance of norms, roles, cohesiveness, commitment, and arrangement to small-group communication.
- Explain the four phases a small group goes through to reach a decision.
- Explain the four decision-making methods.
- Apply three communication techniques to improve your participation within a small group.

ost groups are formed to solve problems. At Sheldon Advertising, Brenda Sheldon has assembled a group of her employees to create a strategic plan for improving work performance for the coming year. The members of this special group have been selected by Brenda and reflect the different units within the company. The participants include the following:

Hannah, who represents the marketing unit, is an Irish American whose parents where born in Ireland, but she was born in the United States. Her ethnic background has greatly influenced the way she sees the world. She earned her college degree in Communication and has worked for Sheldon Advertising for six years. Hannah is excited about being in this group. She has several ideas about how the marketing unit can expand and grow.

Mark, who represents the creative unit, is relatively new to the company. He is African American and earned his degree in Art and Design just two years ago. He feels somewhat uncomfortable being a part of this group. He hopes he can learn more about the advertising business by listening to his colleagues.

Raquel, who represents the accounting unit, has been at Sheldon Advertising for twelve years, since Brenda opened its doors. Raquel has a masters degree in Accounting and heads the accounting unit. She would rather not be part of this group because she is uncomfortable working with others. She would rather work alone at her computer. Raquel has a hearing impairment and has difficulty hearing when she is in small groups.

Darren, who represents the sales unit, loves to work in groups, and Brenda has asked him to lead the group in its initial discussions. He is usually the leader of any group he belongs to and believes he will be able to guide this group to create a brilliant strategic plan. His outgoing personality and overall confidence allow him to communicate with ease interpersonally and in groups.

At their first meeting, Darren asks each of the members to develop her or his own personal goals for next year. He then asks each member, one by one, to read aloud their goals. He actively listens to every participant and lets all members have an equal voice in the discussion, thus creating a positive communication climate. Hannah, Mark, and Raquel feel as if they are a vital and important part of the group because of Darren's communication.

185

Clearly, despite their different approaches to group communication and their perceptions of themselves and their co-workers, they are able to function very well as a group. This chapter discusses small-group communication and how our diverse approaches to it influence the overall effectiveness of the small-group process.

In the previous chapters, we discussed intrapersonal and interpersonal communication. We now turn to a discussion of small-group communication. Everything we have learned up to now is relevant to small-group discussion. Specifically, understanding the differences among people will help us function effectively in a group setting.

The complexities of small-group communication make it a fascinating area to study. Because so much of our time is spent in small groups, acquiring skills in this area will help increase our confidence and self-esteem. By participating in small groups, we have an opportunity to learn a great deal about ourselves, especially from the feedback other group members provide. At the same time, our participation increases both our understanding of how others communicate and our general knowledge of various issues and topics.

An Overview of Small-Group Communication

Our lives are filled with group activities: business meetings, dinners with friends, bowling teams, study groups that review for midterms and finals, bridge games, and planning committee meetings. Communicating in small groups requires special understanding and skill.

The dynamics of small-group communication are vastly different from those of either *dyadic* communication (two parties) or public communication (speaker and audience). Although small-group communication retains some of the spontaneity of interpersonal communication, it has the added pressure associated with interacting in public.

Small-group communication involves a small number of people who share a common goal or objective and interact face to face. Most small groups are composed of three to eight members, with five being the optimum number. Face-to-face communication means that people interact with each other on a personal level, either verbally or nonverbally; it is not enough to simply be designated a "member" of a group. A common goal or purpose binds the group together. Consider the shared purpose of individuals charged with raising money for the youth soccer league. This shared goal contributes to an overall feeling of belonging to the group. Finally, efforts to meet a goal or reach a decision demand that members work cooperatively. At various times during a group's interactions, individuals voice their suggestions or ideas; their comments or actions end up influencing the group as a whole.

In this chapter we shall discuss several aspects of small-group communication, ranging from types of small groups, to variables of the group process, to decision-making methods, to our verbal and nonverbal participation in small groups. The concepts covered in preceding chapters—perception, listening, verbal communication, nonverbal communication, understanding relationships, and building a positive communication climate—determine to a large degree how successfully we communicate in small groups. The relationship between these factors and small-group communication will become more apparent as you read this chapter.

Types of Small Groups

Small-group communication occurs in a variety of situations, ranging from loosely structured social gatherings to highly structured public presentations. You may participate in groups in this class or other classes, at work, or socially. All groups are formed to meet a specific goal or objective. There are four types of groups: knowledge-gaining, personal growth, social, and problem-solving.

Knowledge-gaining groups come together to learn or experience new things. The members may even come together to gain or improve a skill. For example, a painting class, the Young Republicans, soccer teams, and book clubs are formed to help the members share knowledge and learn. **Personal growth groups** focus on the individual and his or her personal well-being. The members come together to support one another as each person struggles with personal challenges. Counseling or therapy groups could be considered personal growth groups. Yoga classes, Alcoholics Anonymous, and health support groups such as Y-Me (for breast cancer survivors) are examples of personal growth groups. The purpose of **social groups** is not to solve problems or accomplish specific tasks, but to interact with others on an informal basis and to maintain interpersonal relationships. Members may meet once a week to play softball, watch and discuss a film, or meet for a drink after work. Finally, **problem-solving groups,** also called **task-oriented groups,** come together to answer a question or provide a solution to a problem. Most groups formed at the workplace are considered problem-solving groups. Your group may have to manage a budget, hire a new employee, or create new rules for workplace behavior. We will discuss problem-solving groups in more detail in Chapter 10.

One important note: groups can fit into one or more of these categories. For example:

> Bonita has always been an active person. She loved to play sports such as volleyball and soccer. Last year she had an automobile accident that left her unable to do many of the things she once loved to do. Her doctor

Personal growth groups, like this yoga class, focus on each person's well-being.

suggested she enroll in a water aerobics class in order to exercise her muscles. During the first few classes, Bonita met two other women who were also in automobile accidents. The three women became close friends and now go out for coffee after each class.

In Bonita's case, her water aerobics class could be categorized as a knowledge-gaining group (coming together to learn new things), a personal growth group (each member dealing with personal struggles), and a social group (maintain interpersonal relationships).

SELF-ASSESSMENT   **Belonging to Groups**

Take a few minutes to create a list of all the groups you belong to right now.

1. Which of the groups on your list do you consider knowledge-gaining groups?
2. Which of the groups on your list do you consider personal growth groups?
3. Which of the groups on your list do you consider social groups?
4. Which of the groups on your list do you consider problem-solving groups?
5. Why do you belong to these groups?

Variables in Small-Group Communication

What factors contribute to the communication that takes place in a small group? This section explores a number of variables affecting group communication, namely, norms, roles, cohesiveness, commitment, and arrangement.

Norms

In part, the communication behavior of small groups centers around **norms,** rules that dictate how group members ought to behave. Whether these norms are implied or openly expressed, they often provide a basis for predicting the behavior of group members. Consider the following:

> During the first few class meetings, Chris noticed that his sociology instructor, Dr. Vasquez, ignored students who asked questions without raising their hands. As Chris actively listened to Dr. Vasquez's lecture on racism and the economy during the third week of class, he had several questions about the membership of labor unions and the unions' ability to speak for minority issues. Chris shouts out questions in his other classes, but he knows Dr. Vasquez will not answer his questions if he does not raise his hand.

Chris understands that a norm for his sociology class is to raise his hand in order to have a question answered by his instructor.

Roles

Roles are a set of expected behaviors each member of the group must follow. Think about the roles you may play in your life today. Are you a friend? Parent? Supervisor? If you are reading this book, you have probably taken on the role of a student. As a student, you are expected to study, attend class, participate in class discussion, and so on. Members of every group also play a role or roles. Specifically, there are three types of roles we can play. These are task, maintenance, and dysfunctional or negative roles.

We play **task roles** when we are concerned about meeting the group's goal or objective. We are focused primarily on getting the job done or the task completed. Beebe and Masterson summarized the types of roles we can play (1997, p. 75):

Initiator/contributor: Proposes new ideas or approaches to group problem solving; may suggest a different approach to procedure or organizing the problem-solving task

Information seeker: Asks for clarification of suggestions; also asks for facts or other information that may help the group deal with the issues at hand

Opinion seeker:	Asks for clarification of the values and opinions expressed by other group members
Information giver:	Provides facts, examples, statistics, and other evidence that pertains to the problem the group is attempting to solve
Opinion giver:	Offers beliefs or opinions about the ideas under discussion
Elaborator/clarifier:	Provides examples based on his or her experience or the experience of others that help to show how an idea or suggestion would work if the group accepted a particular course of action
Coordinator:	Tries to clarify and note relationships among the ideas and suggestions that have been provided by others
Orienter/summarizer:	Attempts to summarize what has occurred and tries to keep the group focused on the task at hand
Evaluator/critic:	Makes an effort to judge the evidence and conclusions that the group suggests
Energizer:	Tries to spur the group to action and attempts to motivate and stimulate the group to greater productivity
Procedural technician:	Helps the group achieve its goal by performing tasks such as distributing papers, rearranging the seating, or running errands for the group
Recorder:	Writes down suggestions and ideas of others; makes a record of the group's progress

Maintenance roles deal with the relationships within the group. When we play a maintenance role, we are concerned about other people's feelings, creating a positive communication climate, and solving or mediating conflicts (Beebe and Masterson, 1997, p. 76).

Encourager:	Offers praise, understanding, and acceptance of others' ideas and suggestions
Harmonizer:	Mediates disagreements among group members
Compromiser:	Attempts to resolve conflicts by trying to find an acceptable solution to disagreements among group members

Gatekeeper and expediter:	Encourages less talkative group members to participate and tries to limit lengthy contributions of other group members
Standard setter:	Helps to set standards and goals for the group
Group observer:	Keeps records of the group's process and uses the information that is gathered to evaluate the group's procedures
Follower:	Basically goes along with the suggestions and ideas of other group members; serves as an audience in group discussions and decision making

Dysfunctional or negative roles hinder the group's ability to meet its goal or objective. Negative roles interfere with the task and maintenance roles.

Aggressor :	Destroys or deflates the status of other group members; may try to take credit for someone else's contributions
Blocker:	Is generally negative, stubborn, and disagreeable without apparent reason
Recognition seeker:	Seeks the spotlight by boasting and reporting on his or her personal achievements
Self-confessor:	Uses the group as an audience to report personal feelings, insights, and observations
Dominator:	Makes an effort to assert authority by manipulating group members or attempting to take over the entire group; may use flattery or assertive behaviors to dominate the discussion
Help seeker:	Tries to evoke a sympathetic response from others; often expresses insecurity or feelings of low self-worth
Special interest pleader:	Works to serve an individual need; speaks for a special group or organization that best fits his or her own biases (Beebe and Masterson, 1997, p. 76)
Joker/clown:	Makes little effort to participate in the task; uses inappropriate humor, sarcasm, or other distracting communication

Ethics in Communication

Understanding Group Roles

Within a small group, each member will play several roles at any given time. We may play a task, maintenance, or dysfunctional role throughout the group process. If we take a look at the Sheldon Advertising group described at the beginning of the chapter, we can see that each member will have a significant impact on the group and the group's ability to create a strategic plan for improving work performance.

Hannah likes to work in groups and is eager to offer her ideas. She may play the task roles of the initiator/contributor (proposing new ideas), opinion giver (offering her beliefs or opinions), or energizer (trying to motivate the group by sharing her enthusiasm). Hannah also may serve as a gatekeeper and expediter (encouraging less talkative members) or encourager (praising and accepting others' ideas). She may even play several dysfunctional roles, such as self-confessor (reporting personal feelings) or special interest pleader (serving her own needs or the needs of the marketing unit).

Mark, unlike Hannah, is shy and a bit unsure of himself. He is energetic and eager to learn new things. He may play the task roles of information seeker (asking for clarification), elaborator (providing examples based on his experience), or after some time with the group, energizer (trying to motivate the group by sharing his excitement). Concerning the relationships in the group, Mark may play the maintenance role of follower (going along with the ideas and suggestions of the group). Mark's shyness may play a dysfunctional role. If his uncertainty becomes an issue, he may play

the role of help seeker (trying to get sympathy from the others or expressing his feelings of insecurity).

Raquel is uncomfortable working in a group and would much rather work alone. She does not want to be in this group and states it clearly. Based on Raquel's experience as the head of accounting, she may play the task roles of recorder (making a record of the group's progress), procedural technician (distributing papers and other performance tasks), or elaborator (providing examples based on her extensive experience). Raquel may play the maintenance roles of group observer (keeping records of the group's progress for later evaluation) and follower (going along with the ideas and suggestions of the group). Her negative feelings about being in the group may cause problems for the group. Raquel may play the dysfunctional role of blocker (being generally negative and disagreeable).

Darren, the appointed leader of the group, loves working in groups and is enthusiastic and energetic. The success and failure of the group will rest on his ability to motivate and guide the group (see Chapter 10). As the leader, he will have to play the task roles of initiator/contributor (proposing new ideas and suggestions), coordinator (clarifying and relating ideas of others), and opinion seeker (asking for clarification). Within the relationships of the group members, Darren must play the encourager (offering praise and understanding and accepting others), standard setter (setting standards and goals for the group), and compromiser (resolving conflicts by finding solutions for all members). Darren could also serve a dysfunctional role. He may play the role of the aggressor (destroying others' status) or dominator (asserting his authority as leader by manipulating the group).

Each group member will play roles throughout the group process. Each member will be more effective and would help the group reach its goal by understanding the roles each plays within the group. Understanding and accepting each member of the group will also help minimize the dysfunctional roles.

Cohesiveness

Cohesiveness is a demonstrated sense of purpose within a group. A cohesive group works together as a unit to solve problems, reach goals, or accomplish a specified task. Cohesiveness develops as individuals in the group become more committed to a project, as they get to know one another better, and as trust between them grows. For example, individuals serving together on a committee for the first time are likely to be reserved with one another. If, however, during their subsequent interactions they recognize the shared purpose among themselves, they will likely proceed

A breakdown in group cohesiveness can lead to conflict.

with renewed enthusiasm. Decisions can be reached more easily this way. The importance of cohesiveness is evident in a group's accomplishments; generally speaking, the achievements are greater in a group that demonstrates this quality. Without cohesiveness, the task may take longer and more conflicts may occur during discussions.

Commitment

Commitment, the motivation of members to meet the goals of the group, also plays a significant role in the outcome of small-group interactions. Are the members genuinely committed to the stated goals of the group? Do they identify with the values expounded by the group? If the answer to these questions is yes, then the members are likely to be more productive and work as a cohesive unit. For example:

> Seven elementary school teachers are charged with studying a plan to implement a computer curriculum in grades one through three. Five of the seven teachers (Jan, Maria, Cara, Eli, Doug) are enthusiastic about the idea; as a result, they devote considerable energy to writing their recommendations to the school administration. They engage in thoughtful discussion and actively listen to each other's ideas and suggestions. The remaining two members (Rose and Cecilia) have little interest in the project, which is apparent by their minimal participation during meetings. Rose and Cecilia do not hinder the others from completing the task, but they do not help either.

Commitment, then, can energize or renew a group's interest in achieving a goal.

There are some potential drawbacks to commitment. First, we are often blind to others' viewpoints because we are convinced that ours is the best (and only) way. Second, when we are committed to a project, there is a tendency to try to persuade others to see things as we do. At times the pressure we apply is overbearing.

Arrangement

Another variable that affects group participation is the communication **arrangement,** the physical placement of the individuals within the group. Is everyone sitting in rows, around a conference table, or on the floors and couches in someone's living room?

Often the placement of individuals in the group determines the amount of interaction that takes place. For example, if a group is arranged in a row, direct eye contact is limited, especially for those who are seated at either end of the row. Dialogue is generally limited to those sitting next to one another. Interaction is increased when members are able to see each

TABLE 9.1	Variables in Small-Group Communication
Norms	Rules that dictate how group members ought to behave
Roles	Set of expected behaviors each member of the group must follow
Cohesiveness	Demonstrated sense of purpose within a group
Commitment	Motivation of the members to meet the goals of the group
Arrangement	Physical placement of the individuals within the group

other better. When we have a better view of those we are talking to, it is easier for us to detect the feedback others send and alter our message, if necessary. Having group members seated in a half wheel or circle facilitates direct eye contact and greater participation among everyone.

Participating in Small-Group Discussions

Thousands of groups meet each day to discuss issues and make decisions. Asking a small group of individuals to solve a problem or come up with a strategic plan suggests a belief that collectively a better decision can be reached than by asking an individual to do the same thing. Of course, this is not true for all types of decisions. Some decisions are highly personal, such as the brand of toothpaste we choose or the kind of car seat we purchase for our child. However, participating in small-group decision making can be more effective if we understand that every group decision is reached as a result of going through specific phases.

Phases of a Discussion

Every small-group decision is a process that goes through several phases. In order to become better participants in the process, it is helpful to recognize that decision making is frequently a slow, frustrating exercise that requires considerable patience and tolerance. In the subsections that follow we shall explore four phases of the decision-making process of a small group: orientation, conflict, emergence, and reinforcement (for a detailed discussion, see Brilhart, Galanes, and Adams, 2001). Although groups may go through each of the phases, they may not do so in a linear fashion. In other words, groups often regress back to earlier stages before moving through all stages. Furthermore, a basic understanding of these phases provides a framework for the skills discussed in the final section of this chapter.

Orientation Phase

During the **orientation phase,** or the beginning of a group discussion, members are chiefly concerned about establishing a comfortable social climate. Dialogue is apt to be guarded and superficial as members pay particular attention to "getting along" with everyone. This is also a time for individuals to become acquainted with the subject about to be discussed. For example:

> The library administration appoints a five-person committee to decide how to spend an additional $68,000 on library materials during the remaining two months of the fiscal year. At the initial meeting the committee members discuss the circumstances surrounding the acquired funds and voice their pleasure at being involved in this assignment. Everyone is in agreement that they can work out an equitable way to spend the allotted money. One member says, "I feel like we've hit the Powerball lottery! I can't wait to spend this money."

Conflict Phase

As ideas begin to surface regarding the decision making, it is natural for disagreement and tension to surface as well. This stage is known as the **conflict phase.** It would be unrealistic to expect a group to reach a decision without first experiencing conflict. The degree of conflict, however, varies from one group to the next and influences how much time is spent in this particular phase of the process. Our tolerance during this phase is particularly important (more on this in the final section of this chapter).

As individuals become passionate about their ideas and coalitions (subgroups) start to develop, the interaction becomes less inhibited. When individuals align themselves for or against a particular proposal, tension frequently results from any differences of opinion.

> The library committee is now splintered into two coalitions, each having a vastly different idea about what kinds of materials and equipment to purchase. One group proposes that the majority of the money be used to purchase print materials: "The library should maintain its image as an institution that provides books on all subjects." The other group favors audiovisual materials: "We disagree. The patrons who use the library today want to check out compact discs, DVDs, computer software, and videos."

How will they be able to resolve this problem?

Emergence Phase

As discussion continues, most groups grow anxious to reach a decision. This stage is called the **emergence phase.** In an effort to reach a consensus, there is a tendency among those members who expressed dissent during the conflict phase to now take a more ambiguous stand. These individuals attempt to disengage themselves from the passionate stands taken just a short time ago, but at the same time they avoid embracing the opposing position wholeheartedly. Ambiguity replaces passion as a modified form of dissent. As coalitions break up and dissent weakens, there is a gradual shift toward an apparent decision. Let us look once again at our library committee:

> A decision to purchase more audio-visual material is gaining favor. Those who voiced strong opposition during the conflict phase now make ambiguous comments about the same proposal. These comments reflect a shift in attitude from dissent to resigned acceptance: "The public would probably react enthusiastically to a larger collection of feature-film video-cassettes and DVDs."

Reinforcement Phase

In the final phase of the decision-making process, consensus is achieved; this is called the **reinforcement phase.** Members typically reinforce their positive feelings concerning the decision and also show their support of one another. Dissent all but vanishes.

> The members of the library committee applaud their efforts and state that they acted on behalf of the public which they serve: "Our patrons will be thrilled with all the new materials we've agreed to purchase. Everyone on the committee did a terrific job."

The example of the library committee used throughout this discussion of orientation, conflict, emergence, and reinforcement phases is idealistic; few group discussions go so smoothly. Even the most heated, emotionally tense discussions, however, proceed through these phases. In the final section of this chapter we will learn skills to help us cope with the frustrations of small-group discussions and to help us successfully participate in the process.

TABLE 9.2	**Phases of a Discussion**
Orientation phase	A time for establishing a comfortable communication climate and becoming familiar with the topic
Conflict phase	Disagreements surface; tension is a natural by-product
Emergence phase	There is a gradual shift toward an apparent decision
Reinforcement phase	Consensus is achieved; dissent all but vanishes

Decision-Making Methods

As we have said, most groups find it difficult to reach a decision, especially one that every member agrees is the best decision. According to Brilhart, Galanes, and Adams, the three most used methods are (1) decision by leader, (2) decision by majority vote, and (3) decision by consensus. Let's look at the different options your group has for reaching a final decision.

Decision by the leader of the group is quick and simple. This may be appropriate when time is of the essence or for routine decisions. There are several disadvantages, however. This method may cause resentment, lowered cohesiveness, half-hearted support for the decision, and an unwillingness to contribute to future group decisions (Brilhart, Galanes, and Adams, 2001, pp. 283–284).

Decision by majority vote is democracy in action. Every member of the group gets a chance to vote for a decision, and the decision with the most votes is chosen as the group's final decision. This method is quick because only a simple raising of hands or saying of "yea" or "nay" is required. The disadvantage is that there will be members of the group who will lose. They may feel their ideas were not given a fair hearing. This may cause cohesiveness and commitment to suffer and may hurt the overall productivity of the group.

Decision by consensus is the genuine agreement among members that an appropriate decision has been made; it is not the result of pressure applied by others in the group. If, for instance, members of a group, as a result of peer pressure, feel they must agree with a decision, then a true consensus has not been achieved. A consensus allows the group to reach closure on an issue or to complete the group's task. A group should be careful to avoid at least the following two things when engaged in the decision-making process: (1) making premature decisions and (2) succumbing to pressures to conform. A premature decision often indicates a lack of analysis by the group. Many sides of an issue or decision need to be explored before a consensus is reached. Sometimes individuals feel pressured to comply with a stand taken by other members who are in positions of power (see Chapter 6). We have all experienced instances when we have felt it is wiser to agree with a supervisor, parent, teacher, or some other person in authority than to subject ourselves to their displeasure. Our agreement does not constitute a true consensus.

One other concern when trying to achieve consensus is groupthink. **Groupthink** is the illusion of consensus among the group members (Beebe and Materson, 1997; Cline, 1990). When there is too much consensus, groups may stop critically analyzing ideas, suggestions, and decisions. Members begin to believe that the group is "invincible" and that any decision made by the group will be a good one. We can avoid groupthink by

NON SEQUITUR © Wiley Miller. Dist. by UNIVERSAL PRESS SYNDICATE. Reprinted with permission. All rights reserved.

critically analyzing all ideas and by using our responsive listening skills, such as paraphrasing, interpreting, and especially, questioning.

Communication Skills within Small Groups

Small-group communication challenges our ability to communicate effectively with others. It requires that we make constant adjustments to the various personalities within the group, that we exert a special effort to make our message understood by others, and that we, in turn, strive to understand the views held by other individuals in the group. Furthermore, the potential for conflict and communication breakdowns is substantially higher in small groups than it is in one-to-one encounters. This is particularly true for task-oriented or problem-solving groups, where ideas are apt to clash. Fortunately, we can overcome these obstacles by applying specific skills in the areas of verbal and nonverbal participation and by maintaining a positive communication climate.

Verbal Participation

As a member of a small group, each of us has an obligation to let others know our ideas or positions regarding a specific topic. While the degree of participation varies with each member, it is important to remember that a lack of participation fails to serve the best interests of the group. Sometimes groups are dominated by one person who tries to monopolize the conversation. What can be done to remedy this situation? To steer the attention away from this person, one can ask someone else in the group a pointed question, such as "What course of action would you suggest?" or "How will the proposed schedule affect people who work in your department?"

Questions serve many purposes: (1) they maintain your involvement in the group discussion, (2) they can refocus the group's attention or provide direction for a discussion that has strayed from the main points, and (3) they can be used to draw other members of the group into the discussion, especially quiet members. Any group member can use the technique of asking questions to improve the quality of the interaction.

SKILL BUILDING   **Communication Skills within Small Groups**

1. Begin by forming an even number of small groups (one group should be designated A and another B), each with five members. Have each group select one of the following topics to discuss:

   a. Should a city's public funds be used to purchase and display a Nativity scene?

   b. Should smoking be prohibited on campus?

   c. Should we allow government law enforcement agencies to lessen our free speech in order to stop terrorism?

   d. Do television commercials that advocate the use of condoms for "safe sex" erode the morality of our nation?

2. Group A discusses its selected topic for twenty minutes. Members should concentrate on practicing the communication skills discussed in the previous section: verbal participation, nonverbal participation, and maintaining a positive communication climate. During this discussion, each member of group B observes one member of group A. (Note: These pairings should be decided prior to the discussion.)

3. At the end of twenty minutes, members of group B begin discussing their topic. Group A observes their communication skills.

4. At the conclusion of the second discussion, each set of partners from group A and group B meets to give each other feedback on their participation within the group. Use empathy and descriptive language when communicating with your partner.

Nonverbal Participation

Another way to communicate our feelings is through nonverbal participation. Perhaps the most effective nonverbal behavior is that which communicates our agreement with or support of an idea. The simple act of nodding our head or smiling when someone makes a humorous comment offers encouragement to the person who is speaking. When we perceive another group member's nonverbal signals as negative (that is, a head shaking no, a glaring look, or eyes directed away from the person talking), there are specific actions we can take. One method is to ask the person why he or she disagrees with what is being said or proposed to the group. Another similar method is to confront the person about his or her negative nonverbal communication by saying something along these lines: "I noticed you shaking your head a moment ago. Are you having a difficult time understanding or accepting my proposal? I'll try to clarify my position if you want." The person's response to our comments and questions will indicate whether we have perceived this person accurately; then we can proceed accordingly.

Maintain a Positive Communication Climate

A positive communication climate, discussed at length in Chapter 7, encourages discussion among group members. During the orientation phase of a group discussion, the climate is likely to remain positive; however, this is not always the case during the conflict phase. As individuals

As this woman is doing now, by 2010 you will spend much of your work time in virtual groups.

COMMUNICATION and TECHNOLOGY

The Nature of Virtual Teams

According to Lipnack and Stamps, "People rarely work only by themselves" (2000, p. 6). In fact, most workers are part of a group or more specifically, a team. One study shows that in 2000, an employee's time was organized as follows (Soloman, 2001, pp. 60–61):

40% working alone
15% working with others in the same time zone and in the same place
15% working with others in the same time zone, but in a different place
30% working with others who are at a different place and different time

By the year 2010, an employee's time can be expected to change as follows (Soloman, 2001, pp. 60–61):

30% working alone
5% working with others in the same place and time
25% working with others in a different place and the same time
40% working with others in a different place and different time

Clearly, more organizations are using "virtual" teams to complete tasks (Lipnack and Stamps, 2001). According to a recent Gartner report, by 2004, "60 percent of the professional and management tasks at Global 2000 companies will be done via virtual teams" (Biggs, 2000, p. 100).

A virtual team is "a group of people who work interdependently with a shared purpose across space, time, and organizational boundaries using technology" (Lipnack and Stamps, 2000, p. 18). Some teams may meet face to face, while others may never see the other members of their team. The virtual team's primary focus is completing a task or solving a problem. Team members use email, message boards or chatrooms, fax, and sometimes video conferencing to communicate with one another. Many workers telecommute from their own homes.

In contrast to traditional groups that are composed of three to eight members, "there is not right size for virtual teams. Size depends first on the task at hand and second on the unique constraints and opportunities of the situation" (Lipnack and Stamps, 2000). So, a virtual team could have ten members, all in different states, in different time zones, and never meet face to face.

In Chapter 10, we will explore the roles of leadership and trust in virtual teams.

---

begin to take sides on an issue or proposal, the climate can quickly change. Our efforts to reduce defensiveness can restore a positive climate and at the same time improve the overall interaction.

The group process is disrupted when one or two people dominate the discussion and others begin to withdraw from it. How do we combat this? When a group discussion deteriorates to the point where individuals resort to name calling or threaten to walk out, we can remind everyone involved to avoid personal attacks on others. Instead, the discussion should be brought back to the issue at hand. We also can remind group members to allow others to voice their opinions without being interrupted. This forces us to listen attentively. If we have any questions, we can ask them after the person stops speaking. Finally, our comments, including the feedback we give to others, should be descriptive (not judgmental) and reflect our empathy for the positions taken by these individuals. Group discussion will progress more smoothly when these steps for maintaining a positive climate are taken.

Communication Skills within Small Groups   **CHECKLIST**

- Let others know our ideas or positions; ask questions to maintain involvement of ourselves and others.
- Communicate our support nonverbally; respond to nonverbal feedback of others.
- Reduce defensiveness by avoiding personal attacks and interruptions; provide descriptive feedback to others.

Summary

Small-group communication is communication involving three to eight individuals who share a common purpose, feel a sense of belonging, and usually meet face to face. Small-group discussion occurs in knowledge-gaining groups, personal growth groups, social groups, and problem-solving groups.

Several variables affect small-group communication, including norms, rules that dictate how group members ought to behave; roles, a set of expected behaviors; cohesiveness, the demonstrated sense of purpose within a group; commitment, the motivation of members to meet the goals of the group; and arrangement, the physical placement of the individuals within the group.

Effective small-group participation is based on two facts: (1) that every group decision is reached as a result of moving through specific phases, and (2) that the use of special communication skills improves our communication. The four phases of the decision-making process include the orientation phase, where the climate is established and the members acquaint themselves with the topic; the conflict phase, in which disagreements surface; the emergence phase, in which the desire for the group to reach a decision takes hold; and the reinforcement phase, where members voice their support for the decision that has been reached and for one another. Groups use one of three decision-making methods: decision by a leader, decision by majority vote, and consensus. When trying to achieve consensus, groups should avoid groupthink, the illusion of a small-group consensus.

Finally, our effectiveness within groups depends on how skillfully we communicate in the following areas: verbal participation, nonverbal participation, and maintaining a positive communication climate.

Review Questions

1. Define small-group communication.
2. How is small-group communication similar and different from the other forms of communication?
3. What are the four types of groups?
4. Briefly describe the following variables that affect small-group communication:
   a. norms
   b. roles
   c. cohesiveness
   d. commitment
   e. arrangement
5. What are the four phases of small-group decision making?
6. What are the strengths and weaknesses of each of the decision-making methods?
7. List and describe three communication skills that can improve our participation in small groups.

10

Solving Problems Using Small Groups

At the conclusion of this chapter, you should be able to:

- Understand why to use small groups to solve problems.
- Describe the five types of problem-solving formats.
- Identify small-group discussion questions of fact, questions of value, and questions of policy.
- List the steps involved in formulating a discussion question.
- Understand the importance of an agenda.

- Understand how to establish criteria, generate possible solutions, and choose the best solution.
- Define leadership.
- Identify and describe three perspectives of leadership.
- Compare and contrast democratic, autocratic, and laissez-faire styles of leadership.

We learned in Chapter 9 about the Sheldon Advertising problem-solving group and its goal to create a strategic plan for improving overall work performance throughout the company. Each member of the group represents a unit within the company. Hannah represents the marketing department, Mark is part of the creative team, Raquel is an accountant, and Darren represents outside sales. Darren has emerged as the leader of the group and is trying to develop and maintain a positive and supportive communication climate. But, as in every small group, conflict has occurred and the members are beginning to use defensive communication in and out of their meetings.

Before the last meeting, for example, Raquel had taken it upon herself to generate a list of possible solutions or ways to increase work performance. She presented the list to the group and asked the group to choose one, "so we can get this experience over with and go back to our real jobs." Darren thanked Raquel for taking the initiative to do the extra work outside of the group, but stressed that the group was several meetings away from finding a solution. "Why don't we hold on to your list and use it as a basis for our discussion then? Are we all agreed?" The members nod in agreement. "OK then," said Darren, "what did our attempt at gathering research turn up? Who would like to share their information first?"

Working in groups can be very frustrating, but it can also be an efficient way to solve problems. This chapter discusses small-group communication and how our diverse approaches to working in groups influence the overall ability of the small group and its leader to complete tasks and solve problems.

Solving Problems as a Group

As we discussed in Chapter 9, groups are used at work, school, and home. We rely on groups when there is a problem to be solved because small groups can be more effective than having a single person work on the problem. Specifically, small groups arrive at better solutions and have more resources, and a decision made by a group is more likely to be accepted by the whole group. Small groups arrive at better solutions because members "check on" one another. There is always someone to ask another question or offer a competing idea. Poor ideas are more readily pointed out and discarded. More resources are also available to small groups. As an individual, you are limited by your past experience, knowledge, and special talents. But, imagine the combined resources of five individuals. The differences each member brings to the group are truly an asset. Lastly, groups are more effective because decisions made by a group are more accepted by the whole. Of course, if members of the group are part of the decision-making process, they will "own" the final decision and want it to be successful. In addition, a decision reached by a group instead of an individual will take into account more views, ideas, and suggestions. These decisions are more acceptable to the group than decisions made by a person in authority. For example:

> Lisa Morrow, the current State Senator, has decided to run for reelection. In order to win, she knows she must campaign vigorously on many different issues in several diverse areas of her district. As she puts together her reelection team, Senator Morrow asks Joe Koch to be her advisor on regional transportation because of his experience in mass transit. She also asks Dee Williams to serve as her advisor on farm and agricultural issues. Dee has been a farmer for twenty years as well as a lobbyist for the local farmers association. Lastly, Senator Morrow enlists the help of Sydney Wells, a political communication specialist. Each of the members of her reelection team brings his or her special talents, knowledge, and expertise.

In this chapter, we look at small groups and how they solve problems. We begin with a discussion of problem-solving formats and then discuss the process of solving problems and the role that leadership plays in the overall process.

Types of Problem-Solving Formats

All groups use a format or structure when they meet to solve problems and complete tasks. The format chosen by the group is a reflection of the kind of problem the members are facing. Some formats require privacy to ensure frank discussion, while other groups operate in public and may even engage the audience in the process of solving the problem.

A **committee** is a small group of people assigned a task by a larger group. Although the group has a specific function, "business" tends to be conducted rather informally. For example, a campus club committee charged with planning programs for the year is likely to conduct its business in a member's home, with the discussion taking place while refreshments are served. A faculty textbook-selection committee meeting is slightly more structured—group members take minutes and cast votes over competing texts.

A number of small-group discussions take place publicly. These group presentations range from the less structured forum, to the panel discussion, to the highly structured symposium. Generally speaking, in a **forum,** a group presents its ideas to an audience, which is then invited to join the discussion. A town meeting is typical of a forum. A second type of public

Audience members play an important role in forums, such as this town meeting.

small-group discussion occurs when a **panel** of individuals attempts to solve problems or inform an audience about a topic. In many cases, a chairperson is selected to act as a moderator. (Although the audience may ask panel members questions, the role of the audience is diminished.) The more structured **symposium** includes a small group of speakers who share a topic, but who discuss it individually, often focusing on a specific aspect of the topic. A symposium on the September 11, 2001, terrorist attack on the World Trade Center and the Pentagon, for example, might include separate presentations on the hijacking, the role of New York City firefighters and police, and the victims. The presenters listen, along with the audience, to the comments of their fellow participants. Interaction among the speakers and between the audience and speakers is minimal.

Focus groups are used to discover what people are thinking and feeling and are primarily used by advertisers and marketers. Advertisers, for example, want to know what you think about the new sandwich at McDonald's or the new clothing line at the Gap in order to advertise these products more effectively. Members of a focus group offer information, but do not make decisions. Their opinions and thoughts are used as supporting material when others make the final decisions. A facilitator or leader encourages and guides the group through a series of questions, probing the members for specific feedback on the product or idea.

The Process of Problem Solving

As we have said, frequently the task of a small group is to discuss a question or resolve a problem. As participants, we feel more comfortable if we adequately prepare for the discussion in advance. Just as we feel ready to take an exam when we have read the assigned texts and studied our class notes, the same applies to our participation in a group discussion. Necessary preparation includes assessing the question, gathering material, developing an agenda, establishing criteria for the solution, and generating solutions before choosing the best solution. The first step is assessing the question.

Assessing the Question

One of the preliminary steps of small-group discussions is to assess the question before the group. Knowing this will help you decide how to proceed. To help focus the discussion, one useful exercise it to first determine whether the question is one of fact, value, or policy. A second step involves formulating the question. Both of these steps help shape the discussion that follows later.

Types of Questions

When dealing with a **question of fact,** the group argues whether a statement is true or false. Its purpose is to explore a "fact" and draw some conclusions based on its accuracy. A group of jurors, for example, must weigh the statements of various witnesses in order to judge whether these statements are true or false.

A second type of question centers around **value.** The group in such a situation must determine the morality of an issue, that is, whether something is good or bad, right or wrong. For instance, our jury must decide whether a defendant's actions are unlawful and, therefore, punishable by law, or whether the actions do not violate present laws.

Finally, with a **question of policy,** the group must decide if any specific action is in order. Such a decision often rests on taking another look at questions of fact and value that help shape policy. For example, if our jury decides in favor of the defendant (based on weighing earlier questions of fact and value), it might have to tackle the sticky issue of how much to award the defendant in damages—should the defendant be entitled to damages, and if so, how much?

CRITICAL THINKING   **Assessing Discussion Questions**

Identify the following as questions of fact, value, or policy:

1. Does lowering your blood cholesterol level reduce your risk of developing heart disease?
2. How can the laws be changed to reduce the number of gun-related deaths?
3. Is it important to have an ideologically balanced Supreme Court?
4. Should parents receive a tax credit if their children attend private schools?
5. Many psychologists agree that viewing violence on television can lead to acts of violence by individuals. Is their stand on this issue useful?
6. Should cloning be allowed for infertile couples?

Formulating the Question

Once the group determines whether the question is one of fact, value, or policy, the next stage is to formulate the question. Is the question stated clearly? Is the question neutral? Does it promote discussion? These three factors should be considered when constructing the question.

Is the question clear? "Do you feel that music videos are eroding traditional values?" Each member of the group may have a different interpretation of "traditional values" in the preceding question. To ensure that each member understands the topic, it is best to use concrete language, as discussed in Chapter 4. Additionally, it is useful to construct a question that contains only one idea; the more complicated the question, the greater is the confusion among group members.

Now consider this question: "Do the sexual themes portrayed in rock videos harm adolescents by influencing their attitudes toward sexual relationships?" In this second question the language is concrete, providing the group with a greater sense of direction than the first question allowed.

Is the question neutral? In constructing the question, care should be taken to avoid alienating group members. "Should the racist practice of the school board be stopped?" This question would undoubtedly provoke some individuals and might lead to an unproductive conflict within the group. A question can be **neutral,** that is, one that does not "take sides," yet still promote natural conflict and discussion among group members. For example, "What steps should the school board take to celebrate diversity in the schools?" Because the second question neither condones nor attacks the present policies of the school board, it is unlikely to alienate group members before the discussion starts. Its neutrality can lead to a more fruitful discussion.

Does the question promote discussion? The question should be one that generates a meaningful, engaging discussion. Controversy frequently stimulates members to participate in a discussion. A question that is controversial, then, should successfully accomplish this task. "Are the welfare agencies and juvenile courts justified in returning abused children to their homes?" This question does not suggest that there is a simple answer. The issue is obviously a complex one and can certainly lead to a lengthy debate. Table 10.1 provides a checklist for formulating the question.

TABLE 10.1 Formulating the Question

Is the question clear?	Use concrete language. Construct a question that contains one idea.
Is the question neutral?	The question should avoid "taking sides."
Does the question promote discussion?	Controversy may stimulate discussion.

Gathering Material

Once the discussion question is decided, the next step is to gather research material. This process is discussed at length in Chapter 12; however, a brief review is included here as well. To support our position or contentions, we need to gather reliable information that is culled from either **primary sources,** documents such as letters, manuscripts, and taped interviews, or **secondary sources,** interpretations of primary material. For example, to prepare for a discussion on President Bush's reaction to the terrorist attacks,

Primary and secondary sources help groups make decisions.

we would want to examine his personal copy of his address to the nation. This primary source, however, is unavailable to the general public. What is available in its place is a wide range of secondary sources: newspaper accounts, reports by television journalists, and analyses in magazines and journals. Of course, sources that include a transcript of the president's message, such as the *New York Times* or *Vital Speeches of the Day,* are considered to be more accurate than interpretations of his message that appear in other periodicals. Furthermore, assessments of the meaning and impact of Bush's message are offered by many, but those of noted authorities are better secondary sources than those of lesser known individuals. And remember, whenever you use another person's information, be sure to give the source credit (see Chapter 12 for more on this).

The Agenda

Our preparation for a discussion should include an **agenda,** an outline of the points to be discussed. One member of the group may be asked to prepare the agenda (this individual may assume a position of leadership within the group), an agenda subcommittee may be assigned this task, or all members can suggest points to be discussed. Although the group is likely to shift back and forth as the members discuss the topic, an agenda will help them stay focused. The agenda should allow for adequate time both to discuss the problem and to explore several solutions.

It is important to let all group members have an opportunity to share their ideas. This process guarantees that several different approaches to the problem will be explored and adequately discussed before moving on to a solution. Even after a tentative solution is reached, the group is likely to debate the positive and negative aspects. The agenda should take this fact into account.

Preparing for a Discussion

SKILL BUILDING

1. Given the topic, the campus parking problem, formulate a discussion question.
2. What kinds of resources would you use to gather information about the subject?
3. Develop an agenda for the discussion. Take into account the various arguments, both pro and con, surrounding this subject. Consider how much time to allow for each point discussed.
4. Share your agenda with a small group to elicit feedback.
5. Use this feedback to improve your agenda.

Establishing Criteria for the Solution

Before finding a solution, the group must first decide on the criteria for a good solution. **Criteria** are the minimum requirements a solution must have to be acceptable. For example, if a group of student leaders from several student organizations is planning a homecoming celebration, the group members would need to know what specific events need to be scheduled and when. Specifically, the solution—or in this case, the schedule of events—must include a parade and a dance, and these events must be scheduled in conjunction with the football game on Saturday morning. The more specific the criteria, the easier it will be for the group to make its final decision.

Developing Possible Solutions

Now that the group has established its criteria, it is time to develop possible solutions. This is the time for members to be creative and to generate as many possible solutions as they can. It is not the time to be evaluative or critical. The group hopefully has established a positive and supportive climate (see Chapter 7) and will allow members to voice even the wildest of ideas and possible solutions. If the group is stalled, it may use brainstorming. **Brainstorming** encourages creativity and the free flow of ideas. Members throw out ideas while other members write them down. This generates a long list of possible solutions. For brainstorming to be effective, the members should refrain from evaluating ideas or offering negative feedback. In addition, members should "piggyback" on one another's ideas, thus combining two or three people's ideas to generate a new solution (Beebe and Masterson, 1997, p. 227).

Choosing the Best Solution

Through brainstorming, research, and discussion, the group has developed a list of possible solutions. The group must know how to choose the best solution to solve the problem. The first step is to evaluate each idea according to the criteria set. Any idea that does not meet the minimum criteria must not be considered further. Second, the members must decide which ideas best meet the criteria. As we discussed in Chapter 9, consensus is the best way to come to a decision, and the group members should strive for a true consensus among all the members.

Leadership

Regardless of a group's purpose, whether it is planning a class reunion or deciding which computer to purchase for the office, the group's success depends, in part, on its leadership. **Leadership** is the ability to exert influ-

DILBERT © UFS. Reprinted by Permission.

ence on a group by providing a sense of direction or vision. This influence can come from an individual designated as the leader or can be shared by several members of the group. Leaders can also empower the members of the group. When members are **empowered,** they have the power to make decisions, be creative, and explore their own potential (see Chapter 6). An effective leader can create opportunities for the members and thus empower them. Obviously, group leaders possess one or more types of power (expert, legitimate, referent, coercive, and reward, as discussed in Chapter 6), and their power can effect the overall group's decision-making process.

In this section we shall discuss a variety of leadership perspectives, ranging from the trait perspective with its "born leaders," to the situational perspective with its democratic, autocratic, and laissez-faire styles, to the functional perspective with its shared leadership by means of task-related and process-related behaviors. Knowing about these perspectives can help us to recognize the leadership roles played by others and assist us in developing our own leadership capabilities.

Trait Perspective

The **trait perspective** of leadership suggests that certain individuals are born leaders because they possess such qualities as a forceful personality, marked intelligence, and dynamic communication skills. While we can think of individuals who have these characteristics, they are not necessarily effective leaders when placed in small groups. Why? This perspective has some serious flaws. The chief flaw with the trait perspective is that its outlook is too narrow: it does not take into account the other individuals in the group. The leadership qualities just described do not guarantee that an individual will be a successful leader. So what if Angela is aggressive, intelligent, and a skillful communicator? If she has no interest in a group's intended purpose or function, she may prove to be an ineffective leader.

Situational Perspective

In most groups the type of leadership required depends on two chief ingredients: (1) the reason for the group's existence (that is, to set a preliminary budget or to plan a surprise birthday party) and (2) the composition of the group, including how these individuals interact. In other words, each group creates a new situation, and this situation dictates which style of leadership is most appropriate. This is called the **situational perspective.** We frequently label a leader's style as democratic, autocratic, or laissez-faire. Let us take a look at what each of these means.

A **democratic leader** demonstrates his or her confidence in the group by involving group members in decision-making matters. Rather than dominate the group, the democratic leader allows the group to decide who will tackle specific tasks or jobs. Such involvement generally increases both the group's cohesiveness and the overall satisfaction with the group process. We take pleasure in knowing that we have contributed to the group's efforts, that we have been personally involved.

The **autocratic leader** is a more domineering presence. This individual usually decides what direction the group will take; he or she assigns tasks to members, dictates the nature of all activities, and makes policy statements. The separation between "leader" and "group member" inhibits input from the group; the lack of involvement often leads to dissatisfaction on the part of group members. Because the process is more expedient under an autocratic leader, group members are frequently more productive. However, the satisfaction of participating in the decision-making process is absent.

A **laissez-faire leader** gives minimal direction or instruction to group members; rather, members have complete freedom to make decisions. The laissez-faire leader offers advice only when directly asked by the group or one of its members. Practically speaking, this style of leadership is the least effective of the three. The group often fails to make progress because it is unsure about where it is headed.

From the descriptions just given, we might easily conclude that the democratic style of leadership is the best approach. While this is true in many cases, there are instances when either an autocratic leader or a laissez-faire leader is wanted. Consider, for example, two groups who are given the same assignment in their public administration class: to write a job description for a town manager serving a population of 18,000. Group A has three members with no work experience and a fourth member who served for five years as a clerk in a mayor's office. Because of her experience, Julia "takes charge" of the group, especially after fifteen minutes of floundering and indecision by the other members. Her role as an autocratic leader succeeds in mobilizing the group.

The four members of group B, however, all have work experience. Suggestions for the town manager's job description seem to come easily, and there is agreement among the group members about the necessary qualifications. For this group, a laissez-faire style of leadership is appropriate. There is no need to have a controlling presence when the individual members already function as a cohesive group.

Functional Perspective

A **functional perspective** of leadership focuses on the kinds of leadership behaviors that any member of the group can exhibit that collectively result in the group's making progress. This perspective differs from the other leadership perspectives discussed so far because it does not promote the role of a single leader. Two primary types of behavior associated with functional leadership are task-related leadership behavior and process-related leadership behavior.

Task-related leadership behaviors include those actions whose purpose is to keep the group focused on the problem or question. Groups frequently get sidetracked from their intended function; to rescue them there are such task-related behaviors as initiating ideas, elaborating on the ideas of others, raising questions, and summarizing thoughts.

An individual who offers new or fresh ideas helps the group move closer to solving a problem. This is especially true if the group seems stuck on a particular point. When an idea generates enthusiasm, someone can take that idea a step further by elaborating on the subject. For example:

> Monica's idea is to make the theme of their twenty-year high school reunion "Time for Me to Fly," a popular song by REO Speedwagon in 1983. The planning committee likes her idea, and Jim responds by suggesting that this theme be carried out in the invitations and music. He thinks the invitations should request that all guests dress as they did during their senior year and that the band play songs popular during the early 1980s.

Another behavior that moves the group forward is asking questions. Even a simple question such as, "Where do we go from here?" refocuses the group's attention to the task at hand. Finally, summarizing a discussion accomplishes two things: (1) it clarifies the various points by restating them, and (2) it brings into sharp focus what has already transpired and, by doing so, points out what remains to be done. This gives the group an opportunity to hear the ideas or arguments again and to ask for clarification if necessary.

The task-related behaviors just described go hand in hand with **process-related leadership behaviors**—those behaviors concerned with maintaining a positive climate within the group. These include such things as relieving tension, gatekeeping, and offering encouragement to other group members.

When the interaction within a group becomes tense, it is a relief to have someone say, "Let's take a break for a few minutes," or to interject a little humor to ease the tension. An equally important function is carried out by a **gatekeeper,** one who attempts to regulate the flow of communication within the group. This role requires that the individual draw quiet members into the discussion (perhaps by asking a direct question) and, at times, take the center stage away from a group member who is dominating the discussion. The person who acts as a gatekeeper believes that each member has something to contribute to the group. Praising an individual's ideas, for example, can lead to increased self-esteem and satisfaction as a group member. When members feel better about themselves, the overall quality of the group process is enhanced.

CRITICAL THINKING Leadership

The Chief of Medicine at Parkline General appoints a five-member committee to recommend changes in the hospital's present emergency room procedures. The committee consists of the two senior ranking emergency room nurses, two emergency room physicians, and the physician in charge of the emergency room.

1. The emergency room chief is the appointed leader of this committee. Describe how he or she would operate:

   a. as a democratic leader

   b. as an autocratic leader

   c. as a laissez-faire leader

2. Describe two task-related and two process-related behaviors that members of this committee might demonstrate in a functional approach to the assignment.

Leaders, such as Senator Barbara Boxer (D-CA), shown here, must possess effective communication skills.

COMMUNICATION and TECHNOLOGY

Leadership in Virtual Teams

As we learned in Chapter 9, most workers spend much of their time in groups or teams. Very few workers spend their entire day working alone. Virtual teams, groups that work independently using technology, are fast becoming an essential part of business life. But, more than 50% of virtual teams fail to meet their goals or objectives (Biggs, 2000). Ineffective leadership contributes to the failure of most virtual teams.

A new kind of leader is needed in a virtual team. Like other groups, an authoritarian leader may hinder the communication within the group, but in virtual teams, it is even more important that the leader allow members to communicate freely. Phil Carroll, Chairman and Chief Executive Officer at Fluor Corporation, states, "In a networked organization leaders have to use influence and powers of persuasion, which is more complex and much more challenging than giving orders. Young leaders have the ability to operate in this new environment. They recognize that they're not working on the authoritarian model" (Lipnack and Stamps, 2000, p. 11). The nature of the virtual team also requires a new leadership style. According to Charlene Solomon, "The complexities and subtleties of dealing with widely different personalities, cultures, and languages make communication far more difficult among virtual team members. These new challenges require diverse management skills, such as the ability to determine the best technology to facilitate communication, and the ability to engender trust and productivity among team members even when there is no direct supervision" (2001, p. 64).

The following is a list of suggestions for leaders of virtual teams:

1. Share the leadership tasks. Use a democratic style of leadership.
2. Facilitate a positive communicate climate by building trust early.
3. Encourage cooperation among the team members.
4. Encourage frequent contact among team members. Have members meet face to face, if possible.
5. Have a clear understanding of the technology necessary for the team to complete its task (email, chatrooms, video conferencing, etc.).
6. Create a shared (cyber) space for team members to talk about things other than work. Solomon calls this a virtual water cooler (2001).

Effective Leadership Communication

Being a leader of a group is a large responsibility. Ultimately, the success or failure of the group may rest on the leader's shoulders. To help ensure a positive outcome, leaders can take several steps. First, create and maintain a positive communication climate. Try to minimize defensive communication by including every member in the discussion and decision-making

Ethics in Communication

Effective Leadership

At Sheldon Advertising, Darren has been appointed the leader of a problem-solving group made up of employees from different units. The group's task is to develop a strategic plan to increase the work performance of all employees. Although Darren was appointed the leader, he has also become the emergent leader. All the members of the group (Hannah, Mark, and Raquel) look to Darren for direction and advice. He knows that the group's success rests on his shoulders.

Darren uses his communication to effectively guide the group through all the phases of the group process. Specifically, Darren:

1. Creates a positive climate and tries to minimize the defensive communication in the group. He is sure to actively listen to all members and has created a feeling of mutual trust and respect among the members. In addition, Darren has empowered Hannah, Mark, and Raquel to make choices for themselves as they gather materials and formulate questions to help the group complete its task.

2. Recognizes the strengths and weaknesses of each member (including himself) and tries to encourage each member to use his or her skills to take an active role in the group. He clearly communicates to the members that he appreciates and respects their diverse points of view and encourages them to share their views with the group.

3. Addresses conflicts. As problems arise between group members, Darren tries to help the members resolve their conflicts. In addition, he strives for consensus or compromise with each decision that needs to be made.

4. Keeps the group on task. After the group has been together for a while, meetings tend to begin with discussions about personal things such as families, vacations, or holiday plans. Darren makes sure the group does not waste too much of its time and stays focused on the day's task.

Darren may be a born leader, but it is his communication skills that allow him to serve as an effective and motivating leader.

process. Second, recognize that each member brings diverse strengths and weaknesses to the group. One member may be an excellent researcher, but shy and hesitant during discussions. Effective leaders encourage members to use their strengths to help the group complete the task. Third, tolerate and use conflicts as a means to further the group's progress. Conflicts can "clear the air" and can also bring to the surface underlying problems within the group that must be addressed. Finally, attempt to keep the group on task. Without an effective leader, groups can flounder and drift for a long time and never meet the goal or objective.

Effective Leadership CHECKLIST

- Create and maintain a positive communication climate.
- Recognize that each member brings diverse strengths and weaknesses to the group.
- Tolerate and use conflicts as a means to further the group's progress.

Summary

Small groups are effective in solving problems because they arrive at better solutions and have more resources, and because the decision is more likely to be accepted by the larger whole. Small-group formats include committees, forums, panels, and symposiums. Focus groups help advertisers discover our views on ideas, products, and issues.

Several steps help the group solve a problem: (1) assessing the question, which includes determining whether the question is one of fact, value, or policy, and formulating the question, which means deciding whether the question is clear, whether it is neutral, and whether it promotes discussion; (2) gathering material, either from primary or secondary sources; (3) having an agenda or outline of the points to be discussed; (4) creating criteria for the solution; (5) generating possible solutions; and finally, (6) choosing the best solution.

Leadership is the ability to exert influence on a group by providing a sense of direction or vision. It is defined by a variety of perspectives, ranging from the trait perspective, with its notion that certain individuals are born leaders, to the situational perspective, in which the group situation dictates the most appropriate leadership style (democratic, autocratic, or laissez-faire), to the functional perspective, which focuses on the kinds of leadership behaviors any group member can exhibit that result in the group's making progress. Effective leaders try to create and maintain a positive communication climate, acknowledge the diverse strengths and weaknesses of each group member, use conflicts in a positive way to further the group's objective, and keep the group members on task.

Review Questions

1. Why are small groups an effective way to solve problems?
2. Differentiate between a question of fact,

a question of value, and a question of policy. Give examples of each.
3. List three factors a group should consider

when formulating its discussion question.

4. Why is an agenda necessary for small-group discussion?

5. How can a group develop possible solutions?

6. Define leadership.

7. Compare and contrast the situational and functional perspectives of leadership.

8. What are the communication strategies of an effective leader?

11

Selecting a Speech Topic and Adapting to the Audience

At the conclusion of this chapter, you should be able to:

- Describe four ways to use yourself as a source for topics.
- Describe the three aspects of the situation you need to analyze before choosing a topic.
- Describe the demographic factors of an audience.
- Describe six other audience characteristics.

- Develop three types of questionnaires to gather information from an audience.
- Describe how a topic can be adapted to audience needs.
- Differentiate between individual and group brainstorming.
- Develop a specific purpose statement.
- Develop a thesis statement.

Rolanda is trying to choose a topic for her first speech. Her speech must inform the audience about a topic that is important and interesting and must be three to five minutes in length. Rolanda loves all kinds of music and would like to talk about that, but knows that music is too broad a topic. She must narrow it down to something she can talk about in the time limit, and that will be interesting to the audience.

On the advice of her instructor, Rolanda distributes a survey to her classmates asking them about their tastes in music and what they would like to know about music history, famous musicians, or types of music. Her survey shows that the audience's taste in music is varied, and there seems to be no agreement on what her audience would like to know. One thing everyone has in common, however, is an interest in advertising jingles. One student wrote on the survey, "Who writes the songs for commercials that always stick in your head, like 'Hold the pickle, hold the lettuce, special orders don't upset us?'" This, Rolanda decides, is a great speech topic: advertising jingles. But in order to further narrow her topic, she will have to do some research.

In this chapter, we will look at the process we go through to choose a topic when we engage in public communication. Specifically, we will discuss the need to analyze yourself, the situation, and the audience. Understanding the unique interests, knowledge, and enthusiasm you possess, and understanding the diversity of your audience can help you to develop an interesting and thorough public presentation.

Selecting a Topic

Throughout our lives we are asked to deliver speeches, whether it is a presentation at work, a toast at our friend's wedding, a campaign speech, a victory or concession speech following an election, an after-dinner speech, a eulogy for a departed friend, or an assignment for a public-speaking class. Like Rolanda, a question speakers often ask is "What can I talk about that will interest my audience?" Frequently, the very nature of the occasion dictates the topic we select. For example, your supervisor may ask you to discuss the strengths and weaknesses of the new software program your department just adopted. Some speaking situations (for instance, the public-speaking classroom) require more imagination on our part, however. For such occasions, we can look to ourselves, the situation, and our audience, or try brainstorming to come up with an interesting topic.

Yourself

Sometimes the best place to look for a speech topic is yourself. It is logical to assume that you will deliver a more interesting and effective speech if you are comfortable with the topic. By looking inward, you can draw from your own concerns, experiences, knowledge, and curiosity to select a topic. You are a unique person with much to share with your audience.

Concerns

One of the most important factors that can assist you in selecting a topic is to choose something that is important to you. By doing so, you communicate sincerity to your audience, which, in turn, enhances the quality of your delivery by communicating your enthusiasm. In addition, when you pick a topic that you care about, it is easier for you to concentrate on it during the delivery. You both look and feel more confident before your audience. This positive feeling may inspire you to want to share your concerns with the audience. Consider the following:

> Jovan, who is thirty years old, has recently moved back to his parents' home so that he can afford to go to college full time. He has an assignment to speak to his class for eight minutes. His instructor suggests that

It is easy to communicate your enthusiasm when you choose a topic you feel strongly about.

students choose topics that they feel committed to. Jovan knows that he wants to speak about chemical warfare, primarily because his brother, a Gulf War veteran, has experienced health problems since the war with Iraq during Operation Desert Storm. Jovan's brother Tom also lives at home because he is too ill to take care of himself. Jovan's speech will focus on the likelihood that chemical warfare in the Gulf caused his brother's numerous illnesses. He also wants to discuss how the Veteran's Administration has failed to help Gulf War veterans such as Tom because administrators will not recognize the group of illnesses called Gulf War syndrome as legitimate.

Jovan is so involved in this subject, he forgets that he is in front of the class. His speech is very successful.

SELF-ASSESSMENT   **What Are Your Concerns?**

1. At any point in your life has there been a cause, issue, belief, or concern about which you felt passionately?

2. Did you take any action? What was it? If not, would you act now? What would you do?

3. What aspect about this concern might make an effective topic?

Experience

Your own experiences also can help you to select a speech topic. Since you are a unique person, you have something special to bring to your audience. Drawing from your own experiences can provide a rich source of topics for you. Furthermore, when speaking from your own experiences, it is easier to visualize what you are talking about, which makes the entire public-speaking experience easier. The following example illustrates this:

> Jeanine contracted cerebral palsy at the age of one. During her childhood she underwent several operations to alter the fixed stiffness in some of her limbs, and as a result, she is now leading a rather normal life. She wanted her audience to realize how important it is to not stereotype people with disabilities. When discussing cerebral palsy, Jeanine described her own experiences and emphasized how she was able to overcome many of the disease's crippling effects. As she spoke, she could help the audience visualize the different stages of recovery she went through with the disease, and as a result, her speech was very convincing.

While Jeanine's topic is a dramatic one, other personal experiences can be the basis for equally compelling speeches. Consider, for example, renting your first apartment, the thrill of hang gliding, or the birth of your first child or grandchild.

Your past experiences can often be used as a speech topic.

Knowledge

Your knowledge about a given topic serves as a reservoir of information you can share with your audience. You know intuitively which points are important to include in your speech and which to omit. This is a distinct advantage over having to research a totally unfamiliar topic and then having to sift through the information to decide what to include or leave out. Consider this example:

> Jeff is employed by the A. E. Public Relations Corporation and has a bachelor's degree in public relations. His company is committed to public service, so his supervisors graciously donated Jeff's time to the local women's shelter, the Haven House. The director of the Haven House asked Jeff to prepare a forty-minute presentation to the staff on techniques of fund raising, including creating a new brochure. Since Jeff's specialty is graphic arts, he decides to prepare several different types and designs of brochures so that the staff can have a foundation to work from. His presentation, then, will focus on how the staff can use his designs to help attract more contributors and to increase the awareness of the shelter's mission in their new brochures.

Jeff's knowledge of graphic arts allowed him to capably present a speech on the related topic of brochures. Picking a topic that you are familiar with also will help increase your confidence before a group, because you will be comfortable with the fact that you have a certain level of expertise concerning your topic.

SELF-ASSESSMENT   **Are You an Expert?**

1. Is there any area in which you consider yourself to be an "expert" or knowledgeable (hobby, work-related, sport)?
2. Could your knowledge be used as an effective speech topic?

Curiosity

The process of learning is lifelong. An idea, an event, or a well-known personality may have piqued your curiosity at some point, and now you want to learn more about it in order to share your knowledge with others. Your enthusiasm for the subject will likely contribute to a dynamic presentation. For example:

> Mariaha has always been a history buff. At forty-five years old, she has vivid memories of her parents being deeply saddened by the death of John F. Kennedy. They had told her about his alleged assassin, Lee Harvey Oswald, and about the Warren Commission Reports, which analyzed the assassination. She was curious about the assassination and especially

wanted to find out why some people did not believe that Lee Harvey Oswald had acted alone in assassinating President Kennedy. In her research she discovered information about the "dancing bullet" theory and wanted to share this with the class. Her curiosity proved to be the foundation of an exciting presentation.

What Are You Curious About? SELF-ASSESSMENT

1. Think of three topics that have piqued your curiosity over time.
2. What triggered your interest in each one?
3. Which of these would make an effective speech topic?

The Situation

The second step in choosing an appropriate topic is to analyze the situation in which you will be speaking. Specifically, you want to consider the size of your audience, the time limit, and the size and shape of the room.

The size of the audience or the number of people in the audience is very important. Some obvious adjustments need to be made in developing your presentation based on the audience's size. For example, with a larger audience, you may find it necessary to be more formal in your presentation, right down to the way you deliver the speech. With a large audience you are less likely to interact directly with members of the audience. In addition, it is more difficult to respond to feedback because it is so difficult to establish direct eye contact with members of the audience. Conversely, you will probably find that with a smaller audience you can present a speech with abstract ideas, because it is easier for you to detect any nonverbal feedback the audience generates and act on it. Consider the following:

> Professor Gerard's lecture was on the subject of how the media create pseudo-events. As he was explaining the concept of a pseudo-event, he noticed a look of confusion on Andrea's face. Because of the relatively small size of the group, he was able to detect her nonverbal cue and respond to it. To further illustrate his point, he used the story of Elian Gonzalas, the little boy from Cuba who was found floating in the ocean after his mother and other passengers drowned in their attempt to enter the United States. Dr. Gerard pointed out that many people believe that the media inflamed the feelings of Cuban Americans living in Miami by depicting Attorney General Janet Reno and other government officials as bureaucrats whose only intention was to return Elian to Cuba with little concern for his well-being. The media reports helped create and provoke several days of protesting by the Cuban-American community, which resulted in nonstop media coverage of the boy's return to Cuba. Andrea's

nod communicated that she now understood the concept. In a larger group, a response to Andrea's cue would have been less likely.

Another fact to consider concerning the situation is time limit. For your speaking assignment in this class, you will have a relatively short amount of time. Outside the classroom, however, you may have to speak for 30 minutes or longer. The time limit will greatly impact the amount of information you can effectively convey. You may want to pick a very specific topic and cover it in-depth. Another option may be to choose a broader topic and only cover the major ideas. Either way, you must consider the length of time you have to present your material. For example, Debbie, a single mom of three children, was asked by her daughter's fourth grade teacher to teach the students how to make a kite. She was given one hour to talk about kites and to have the children actually build and fly a kite. Debbie decided that it would be more effective to spend her time demonstrating how to construct a kite instead of discussing the different types of kites or the physics behind how a kite flies. She brought materials for each child to build his or her own kite. Debbie's talk will be more successful because she took into account the amount of time she was given for her presentation.

The third consideration concerning the situation is the size and shape of the room. Specifically, you will want to know how the seats are arranged, what the lighting is like, and how much space there will be for you to move around the room. Knowing the size and shape of the room will help you to choose appropriate visual or audio aids and will also help you to adjust your delivery style so that everyone in the room can see and hear you. Xavier was selected by his local electricians' union to discuss his experiences as a contract negotiator. All the members were invited to attend the presentation, so the event would have to take place in the very large union hall. The hall holds five hundred people, has very poor lighting, but is equipped with a sound system and a computer system capable of projecting images so all can see. Xavier decides to adjust his topic and focus on the actual contract because he can use the projection system to show how the specific negotiations progressed using several charts and graphs.

It is important to consider the size of the audience, the time limit, and the size and shape of the room when choosing your topic. Each of these elements can have a great impact on what your topic is and how you present your material.

CHECKLIST   **Understanding the Situation**

- How many people will be in the audience? How will this affect your choice of a topic?

- How much time do you have to present your material? Can your topic be fully explained in the time allotted? How may you have to adjust your topic to fit the time limit?
- How large is the room in which you will be speaking? Is it long and narrow or small and wide? How will the room size and shape affect your topic selection?

Finding an Appropriate Speech Topic SELF-ASSESSMENT

To help in the process of finding a topic for your first speech, do some self-analysis.

1. What do you do in your free time?
2. What are your favorite subjects in school?
3. Is there a cause, issue, or concern you feel passionately about? If so, describe it.
4. What unique experiences have you had?
5. What do you consider yourself knowledgeable about?

How can you use the answers to these questions to find a topic for your speech? Make a list of four possible topics.

The Audience

Audience analysis goes hand in hand with selecting and developing the speech topic. For instance, preparing for a speech on "safe sex" depends, in part, on the audience. Consider the different approach you would take when talking to 150 ninth grade students from the approach you would take when talking to 15 administrators of social service agencies. Many factors such as audience attitudes, needs, age, sex, and knowledge must be taken into account.

Before developing any speech, consider the audience; your efforts to develop an effective speech will be wasted if you fail to consider who you are talking to. For example, your speech is headed for failure if your audience has no interest in your topic, if the information you are providing is beyond the audience's level of comprehension, or if your message runs counter to beliefs firmly held by the audience.

What criteria do you use to assess your audience? This section will explore the areas of demographics, characteristics of an audience, appropriate methods for gathering audience information, and adapting to the audience.

Demographic Factors

Segments of the population are routinely analyzed according to **demographics,** that is, easily identifiable characteristics such as age, sex, and ethnic/cultural/religious background. Demographic analysis of an audience should be considered for the purpose of preparing a public speech because it can assist you in tailoring the topic to a specific audience.

Age

The composite age of the audience often plays a role in the selection of a speech topic, because some topics are better suited to one age group than another. These topics are based on the unique frame of reference of a particular audience. Topics based on the Vietnam War, for example, will have a different impact on those Americans who "lived the war" via the front line or who worked for the war effort "stateside" than on those Americans too young to have anything but secondhand experience.

The age of the audience also can affect how you develop the topic. It may even be a primary factor in determining how you will discuss a topic that you consider highly sensitive. In such cases, your choice of words might change with the audience's age in an effort to not alienate them. The age of the audience suggests a general frame of reference that may or may not be in tune with the topic. Consider the following:

> Antonio has recently been elected a member of the local public school board. In recent months, the board has been discussing the issue of sex education in the classroom. Antonio is the only board member under the age of forty-five. Many of the other board members have children who were teenagers during the rebellious 1960s and early 1970s. Since Antonio is speaking in favor of sex education in the classroom, he is cautious as he puts his words together. He knows his audience is sensitive to the issue, so he avoids language that might remind them of rebellious times.

As you become more sensitive to the age of your audience, you should find yourself feeling better able to communicate with them.

Sex

As our society changes, so do the attitudes we hold concerning sex roles. Consequently, there are very few topics that are regarded as strictly "male" or "female." More men are spending time participating in child-rearing responsibilities, while more women are spending a significant amount of time expanding their careers. It would be dangerous, then, to cling to outdated stereotypes that categorize people's interests according to sex roles. In fact, men and women often have similar responses to a topic.

We cannot, however, avoid the fact that many people are raised in an environment filled with sexual stereotypes, and it would be impossible for those individuals not to be influenced by those stereotypes. An all-female audience, for example, may have a high level of knowledge concerning childcare; likewise, an all-male audience may be familiar with the standings of the hometown football team. Still, it is important to remember that not all members of a gender group will possess knowledge about a particular subject. The authors of this text are a great example of this. For example, Dan often is the primary caregiver for his daughter, while Lisa is a sports enthusiast. A speaker who does not know us might incorrectly assume that Dan knows little about childcare and Lisa little about basketball, baseball, or football. Can you see a problem here?

Ethnic, Cultural, and Religious Background

The United States has been aptly labeled as a beautiful patchwork quilt of racial, ethnic, and cultural groups, as well as of diverse religions. Although we are bound together in our society, we also retain all the unique qualities of our heritage. This is as true today as it was during the great wave of immigration during the 1800s and early 1900s. It is important to keep these differences in mind when you prepare your speech so as to not alienate a particular segment of the audience. On the other hand, discovering that the audience's background is similar to your own, or that because of its cultural or ethnic background it is sympathetic to your topic, makes it easier for you to prepare your speech.

During his 1984 bid for the presidency, Jesse Jackson made some denigrating remarks about Jews that created quite a stir. Hostility developed between the Jewish and black communities because of these anti-Semitic remarks and the coverage of this incident by the newspaper and television media. At the Democratic National Convention, Jackson attempted to heal those wounds:

> If in my high moments, I have done some good, offered some service, shed some light, healed some wounds, rekindled some hope . . . or in any way . . . helped somebody, then this campaign has not been in vain. . . . If in my low moments, in word, deed or attitude, through some error of temper, taste or tone, I have caused anyone discomfort, created pain or revived someone's fears, that was not my truest self. . . . Please forgive me. Charge it to my head . . . so limited in its finitude; [not to] my heart, which is boundless in its love for the entire human family. I am not a perfect servant. I am a public servant. . . . Be patient. God is not finished with me yet (Magnuson et al., 1984, p. 26).

Jackson, aware of the tension his remarks had caused, made an effort to reach out to those he had offended and unite the black and Jewish communities. Whether or not he succeeded, at least some of the audience may acknowledge his efforts. Students can certainly learn from Jesse Jackson's experience.

Audience Characteristics

In addition to the demographic factors just discussed, it is possible to assess an audience based on such criteria as knowledge, attitude, needs, societal roles, occupation, and economic status. Knowledge of these characteristics can help you adapt or adjust the speech to fit the audience. This applies to both the structure of the speech and the style of delivery you choose.

Knowledge

The amount of information the audience possesses about your topic may give you some insight concerning the way you want to approach the speech. If your audience is unfamiliar with your topic, you may need to take an elementary approach; on the other hand, if your audience is familiar with the topic, you can take a more detailed approach. Suppose you select the subject of identical twins as your topic. For a group of expectant parents whose knowledge of the subject is limited, a successful speech would likely focus on raising twins, with perhaps a brief biological explanation of how twins are created. If, however, your speech is directed at a group of biology majors, the genetic factor would likely be the focal point of your talk. With this group, the level of detailed information would be much greater.

Attitude

Generally speaking, at the outset of a speech, the audience has formulated an attitude toward both the topic and the speaker. Knowledge of the audience's attitude toward the topic can help you adapt what you say to the group. Consider this example:

> Elizabeth Jones, the Assistant Superintendent, plans to speak to a group of disgruntled parents about the school board's recommendation to close Taft Elementary School at the end of the year. Realizing that her audience strongly opposes this action because their children would have to ride a bus to school instead of walking, she begins by stating that the board gave serious attention to this issue and regretted having to make this difficult decision. Her opening remarks are meant to reduce some of the audience's hostility, so she can proceed to explain the reasons for the board's decision.

In the situation described here, it is reasonable to presume that the sentiment toward Elizabeth was probably negative prior to her speech. Her remarks were intended to diffuse some of the natural resentment both toward an unpopular board decision and toward herself as president of the school board. Had Elizabeth not taken the audience's resentment into account, her speech would not have been as sensitively prepared.

Needs

According to Abraham Maslow, people have the same basic needs, which are best understood when explained in terms of a hierarchy. These needs are classified as physiological, safety, belonging, esteem, and self-actualization (1970, pp. 35–58).

As a speaker who is familiar with Maslow's hierarchy, you have the advantage of being able to develop your topic according to the appropriate audience need. What does this mean? First, it means examining the topic you have selected (this time from the audience's perspective) and asking yourself, "What is the connection between my topic and people's needs as identified by Maslow?" What, for example, is the relationship between the threat of nuclear disaster (your topic) and Maslow's hierarchy of needs? Answer: This topic appeals to the audience's need for safety. Second, once you have established the link between your topic and the audience, you can begin the process of adapting your speech to appeal to these needs. Need identification is simply one more way of analyzing the audience.

Physiological needs are the lowest level needs on Maslow's hierarchy; food, water, and air are examples. A speech on the starvation of African children relates to physiological needs on Maslow's hierarchy; such a speech appeals to the physiological needs of the members of the audience and therefore most likely evokes their sympathy and interest. You might, for example, develop a speech that informs the assembled clergy about two U.S. programs aimed at alleviating hunger in African countries.

Safety needs, the second level on Maslow's hierarchy, refer to our desire to feel secure. They function on two levels: (1) physical security and (2) personal security in social situations. The example given earlier about the threat of nuclear disaster deals with physical security. A speech that focuses on the difficulties of social interactions also may relate to an audience's need for safety. For example, a possible speech topic could inform the audience about three techniques to increase their confidence during their first day at a new job.

The **need to belong** refers to the desire to be part of a group. The group, of course, may vary in composition. Some individuals join Los Latinos (a Hispanic organization) because of their desire to be part of a group that is popular on a college campus and want to be with people who share a common culture. Other individuals participate regularly in religious

FIGURE 11.1   **Maslow's Hierarchy of Needs**

organizations because they enjoy being with people who hold convictions similar to their own. If your audience happens to be twenty-five students taking a course entitled "Introduction to News Writing and Editing," you may want to persuade the members of this class that joining the student newspaper staff can help them feel more involved in campus activities.

Esteem needs, the desire for influence or status within the social structure, are next on Maslow's hierarchy. Everyone wants to feel important and needed in their lives. Consider the following situation:

> Tyler Laufer is raising two sons on his own. For support, he joined Parents Without Partners and is now the Executive Director. Tyler has been asked to speak to the members of a new chapter. He plans to speak about the importance of the organization, but he refines his topic to persuade the members that they can shape the future of their chapter by serving as officers during the coming year.

Self-actualization is perceiving that you are at the highest level of what you believe to be your potential. Maslow emphasizes the importance of reaching your full potential as you grow toward self-actualization. On the day before a co-ed volleyball league championship, you attempt to persuade your teammates that you can win the match because you have practiced hard and are well prepared. Your pep talk helps to build the team's self-confidence and inspires them to play their best.

Targeting the Needs of the Audience **CRITICAL THINKING**

For each of the following topics, use Maslow's Hierarchy of Needs to relate it to your classmates (audience). For example, the topic "AIDS" could relate to the physiological and safety needs, as anyone in the audience could theoretically contract the disease.

1. Stress
2. Hang gliding
3. Social security
4. Home-roasting coffee beans

Societal Roles

We wear several "hats" during the day. Right now, as you read this text-book, you are playing the role of college student. At home, you may also be a mother or father, brother or sister, aunt or uncle, spouse or partner, grandmother or grandfather. At work, you may be a cashier, server, super-visor, manager, or intern. A **role** is a group of expected behaviors placed on us by our society or culture (see Chapter 9). The roles that we play each day shape our experiences and knowledge about many topics. For example, a grandmother may know many home remedies for a common bee sting, or a woman who has been a supervisor for twenty years knows much about employee training. It is important to understand and appreciate all the roles your audience plays in their lives outside of the university. This will help you choose an appropriate topic and be able to adapt it to the audience.

Occupation

Unlike the college classroom, which includes students with a variety of majors, roles, and backgrounds, many public-speaking situations have an audience with a similar occupation. For example, you may be asked as the supervisor of technical support to inform the nursing staff on how to use the new computer software to track patient care, or as the head server, you may be required to persuade the kitchen staff to be more precise in com-municating to the servers about daily specials. In each of these examples, the audience shares a body of knowledge or interest because they have the same occupation. This kind of audience will understand technical language or jargon, and this can help you relate your topic to them more easily.

An audience's occupation may influence your topic selection.

Economic Status

Economic status or income level is another characteristic you will want to know about your audience. Mick wanted to persuade his audience to spend their spring break in a tropical location such as Cancun or the Virgin Islands. After doing some audience analysis, Mick realized that almost all of his fellow students work full time so that they can afford their college tuition. It is unlikely that Mick's audience would be able to afford such an elaborate vacation. Instead, Mick chooses to persuade his fellow students to visit one of the local art museums during the spring break. Knowing the economic status of your audience can be important in finding an appropriate topic and a means of adapting the topic to it.

Gathering Information

How do you determine the demographics and characteristics of your audience described in the above section? Basically, there are three methods for gathering information: observation, interviews, and questionnaires (see Chapter 12 for a more detailed discussion). Whether you have an opportunity to observe your audience ahead of time, whether you manage to interview some of the members individually, or whether you prepare a questionnaire for each member to complete, you will undoubtedly draw some inferences based on your observations and the responses you receive from members of the audience. In turn, these will be used to develop and adapt your speech to the audience.

Observation

A great deal can be learned about an audience by simple observation. It is not difficult to determine such demographic factors as sex, age, and race. You also can note how a group reacts to what others say; in particular, how they react to other speakers. For example, if you are scheduled to conduct a workshop on bathroom plumbing repair at the local hardware store, you may want to attend a couple of workshops prior to your speech. This gives you a chance to observe how the class reacts to the different speakers' styles, content, and so on. Use this information as you work on developing your speech. Are there any special appeals you can make because of the group's composition, attitudes, and needs? In a communication class you have a perfect opportunity to practice this method.

Interviews

A more time-consuming method of gathering information is the interview. In an interview, your purpose is to gain background information about the audience by asking another party specific questions. This approach is especially useful in situations in which you have been asked to speak to an audience about whom you know nothing. To avoid speaking to the group "blindly," you would want to ask one of the members (probably the person who invited you to speak) about the audience's interests, age, knowledge about the topic, and so on. His or her response to your questions will help you prepare a more appropriate speech. Further information on constructing interview questions and conducting an information interview can be found in Chapter 8.

Questionnaires

Questionnaires can pose a variety of general questions, such as number of years of education, marital status, age, and income bracket, and they can ask questions that relate to a specific topic, such as "Are you an organ donor?", "Was President Clinton treated fairly by the Senate during his impeachment trial?", or "What is your favorite type of exercise?" Such specific questions can help you to analyze an audience's knowledge, attitudes, and needs concerning your selected topic. You can choose from three types of questionnaires: closed, open, and graduated scale.

In a **closed questionnaire,** the respondent must select an answer from two or more choices:

Did you vote in the last presidential election?

Yes _____   No _____   Don't remember _____

While a questionnaire composed of questions such as the preceding does not provide much detail, it does offer additional information in a limited way. Because responses are clear-cut, you can generally detect whether or not there is a consensus of opinion among the members of the audience. If there is, you will have a better idea of how to develop your presentation.

An **open questionnaire** gives respondents the opportunity to fully express their feelings:

Why don't the majority of Americans vote?

Responses to such questions, which tend to be more detailed, often provide insight about people's reasons for feeling strongly about a topic. Despite the sense of "knowing" the audience better, there is the drawback of having to sift through a great deal of extraneous information in an open questionnaire.

The **graduated scale,** also known as the **Likert scale,** gives individuals the opportunity to rank their feelings on a continuum:

For the following statement, circle the number that most accurately represents your feelings:

The majority of the American public does not vote because elections are held on a workday instead of the weekend.

1	2	3	4	5
Strongly agree	Agree	Undecided	Disagree	Strongly disagree

The responses can indicate the intensity of audience feelings toward a particular topic. This information is valuable to a speaker.

SKILL BUILDING   **Writing Questionnaires**

You would like to do your informative speech on the environment. In order to further narrow your topic and be able to adapt it to your specific audience, you need to develop a questionnaire. In groups or on your own, write the following:

1. Three closed questions to determine the audience's interest in or knowledge of the environment
2. Three open questions to determine the audience's feelings or attitudes about the environment
3. Three graduated scale questions to determine the strength of the feelings or attitudes held by the audience about the environment

---

Observations, interviews, and questionnaires are tools to assist you in choosing an appropriate topic. Rolanda, in the beginning of the chapter, began with "music" as her topic. After distributing a questionnaire to her audience, she was able to determine that "advertising jingles" was a topic that interested everyone. Thus, a thorough audience analysis made topic selection easier for Rolanda.

SKILL BUILDING

Understanding Audience Analysis

Analyzing your audience can help you select an appropriate topic for your speech and will also help you adapt the topic to the audience. Answer the following questions about your audience:

1. What are the ages of your audience members?
2. How many men and women will be in attendance?
3. What are the ethnic/cultural/religious backgrounds of the audience?
4. Describe the general characteristics of the audience, such as knowledge, attitudes, needs, societal roles, occupations, and income levels.

How can you use the answers to these questions to help you choose a topic? After choosing a topic, how can these answers assist you in adapting the topic to this particular audience?

Brainstorming

If, after you have considered yourself, the situation, and the audience, you find that you still have a difficult time deciding on a suitable topic, try brainstorming. **Brainstorming,** a spontaneous method for generating ideas, also can help you to select a speech topic. This process involves listing as many ideas as you can within a given amount of time, either by yourself or with a group. Alex Osborn, noted authority on the subject, maintained that in brainstorming two basic principles must always be followed: (1) defer judgment on all ideas and (2) strive for quantity (1979, p. 141).

Perhaps the best way to individually brainstorm is to write down as many topics as you can within five to ten minutes (five minutes if you think fast). Do not discard or reject any ideas that come to mind; that can be done later on. What is important here is to get as many ideas on paper as you can. As you do this activity, you may find that one idea triggers another; this free association often produces several good topics. What happens, for example, when you begin with the word *food*? Manuel ended up with the following list:

food

hamburgers

hot dogs

baseball

World Series

television

happy

Manuel's first thought upon hearing the word *food* was *hamburgers*. *Hot dogs* came next because he always associates one with the other. *Hot dogs* reminded him of baseball; Manuel loves to eat hot dogs at baseball games. From *baseball* he jumped to *World Series*. He looks forward to watching the World Series on *television*. Finally, Manuel remembered being *happy* when he watched the Arizona Diamondbacks beat the New York Yankees in the 2001 World Series. From this list he decided on a speech topic: the creation of the Arizona Diamondbacks franchise. Now you try it! Using the same starting point, see where food takes you. Give yourself three to four minutes.

Group brainstorming, an extension of individual brainstorming, maintains the two principles just discussed, that is, defer judgment and strive for quantity. There are advantages, however, to having a small group toss out ideas: (1) the number of possible topics increases dramatically, (2) one member's suggestion often triggers a chain reaction among the rest of the group, (3) a healthy competition often develops between members (each member tries a little harder to express an idea that captures everyone's attention), and (4) good ideas receive reinforcement from others.

CRITICAL THINKING   **Group Brainstorming**

Form a group of four or five members. Using *food* as a starting point, spend ten minutes brainstorming for a speech topic. Apply the method of free association described above. At the end of the ten minutes (and with a speech topic decided by the group), answer the following questions:

1. How many possible topics did your group generate?

2. What was the final topic selected? How is it similar to Manuel's topic of the Arizona Diamondbacks and the World Series? How is it different?

3. Did the group adhere to the basic principle of "no criticism of ideas"? If criticism did surface, what effect did it have on the group's output?

4. Did members reinforce each other's ideas? How did this behavior affect the group's progress in selecting a speech topic?

Adapting to the Audience

Once you have chosen a topic based on your analysis of self, situation, and audience or through brainstorming, you are now ready to adapt your topic. Specifically, analyzing an audience takes considerable time and effort; however, this generally translates into a better understanding of your audience. How do you use the information you have gathered (through observation, interviews, and questionnaires) about an audience's demographics and such related characteristics as knowledge, attitudes, needs, societal roles, occupation, and economic status? Simply stated, you must use these data to adapt your topic to your audience. Adapting your topic means that you create a relationship between you, the topic, and the audience. Specifically, there are four strategies you can use to adapt to the audience:

1. *Make a personal connection to the audience.* In other words, show the audience how you relate to the topic or why you are concerned or interested in the topic. The audience wants to know why the topic is important and worthy of their attention. You may indicate why you chose the topic, or explain your past experiences with the topic. Audiences are more apt to listen to a speaker who is like them in some way. Showing your relationship to the topic will also create a connection between you and the audience.

2. *Be sure to define all your terms.* From your thorough analysis, you have a pretty good idea what the audience may or may not already know about the topic. One way to adapt to the audience is to clearly and precisely communicate your ideas. This means that as you develop your speech, be sure to explain and define all the terms or concepts about which the audience may have little knowledge.

3. *Address the audience's needs, concerns, and interests.* Indicate to the audience that your topic is relevant to their experiences, desires, or curiosity. Audiences will listen to speeches that have a direct connection to their lives. Make your topic relevant to them and they will want to listen.

4. *Use vivid example or stories to make your topic come alive.* Since childhood, we all love to listen to stories. Your audience will more easily relate to your topic if you get them involved in a story about you or a compelling character. As you begin to develop your speech, keep in mind all the things you have learned about your audience and use them to find or create a story that the audience can relate to.

For example, perhaps you realize that your audience, 80 percent female between the ages of twenty and forty-five, has a very positive attitude about preschool education. Obviously, a speech that advocates additional state funds for preschool education should be well received. Your next step, then, is to develop your topic with this in mind. You decide that you can tell your own story (of finding an affordable preschool for your three-year-old daughter, Sydney) as a means of creating a relationship between you, the topic, and the audience. Furthermore, you realize you will need to find source material that shows how quality preschool education positively affects not only the child, but also the whole community (of which your audience is a member).

You will be a better public speaker if you can take what you have learned about your audience and temporarily become one of its members as you begin to develop your speech. Your efforts to empathize with your audience, a skill so essential to successful interpersonal communication, will lead you to a successful public presentation. The next two chapters will take you through the process of preparing your speech; gathering information about your topic is treated in Chapter 12, while organizing your speech is the subject of Chapter 13.

Ethics in Communication

Adapting to the Audience

Rolanda, at the beginning of the chapter, struggles to find and appropriate topic for her first speech. She begins by reflecting on her interests and knowledge. She also surveys her audience. After thorough analysis of self, situation, and audience, Rolanda finally decides on a topic.

Rolanda is acting ethically and effectively in this stage of her presentation's development. First, she found a topic that was not insensitive to anyone in the audience. She took into account and understood the differences of her audience. She is clearly meeting their needs. Second, she also met her own needs as the speaker. Because she has a genuine interest in and cares about her topic, Rolanda will be able to communicate her enthusiasm through her delivery. Obviously, Rolanda has worked hard to accomplish these goals.

On the other hand, it is relatively easy to act unethically or ineffectively when choosing a topic. As a speaker, you could simply ignore the audience altogether. You could choose a topic that you care about, but the audience has no interest in. You risk offending them, however. Or, you could choose a topic that you know meets the needs of the audience, but not your own. As a speaker, your lack of interest will be easily seen through your delivery by your lack of enthusiasm and sincerity (see Chapter 14). More importantly, you are not being honest with the audience. Each of these scenarios is unethical and will not lead to a successful public presentation.

Successful public presentations begin with a topic selection that understands and celebrates the diversity of the audience and reflects your interests and enthusiasm.

The Speech Purpose

After choosing a topic and determining the best way to adapt it to your audience, you must establish the purpose of your presentation. If your stated purpose is in line with the expectations of the audience, you will likely feel more comfortable about presenting your ideas. The development of your speech purpose usually follows three steps: (1) determining the general purpose, (2) determining the specific purpose, and (3) creating a thesis statement.

General Purpose

Establishing the **general purpose** of your presentation means deciding whether your overriding goal is to inform, to persuade, or to entertain. In most instances, your purpose is to inform or to persuade, although these frequently overlap. When your purpose is to inform, your chief concern rests with presenting information as clearly and accurately as possible. For example, as personnel director, you set a time and date to explain each of the three medical plans now available to company employees. As you try to increase the audience's understanding of your topic and to broaden their knowledge, clear, descriptive language is essential.

When your purpose is to persuade, you want to go beyond simply presenting information. With this type of speech, your primary goal is to induce change in the audience; that is, you want to move them to action. Your goal as a speaker is to get the audience to empathize with your position, to feel the concern that you feel. If you are successful, the audience will be motivated to change. You are scheduled to speak to ten employees about XYZ health maintenance organization, one of three health plans to be voted on by the group. As a representative of this health insurance company, your aim is to convince (persuade) the group that XYZ is the best plan on the market. While you are concerned about presenting the information clearly, your speech goes one step further—it asks the audience to respond in some way.

When your purpose is to entertain, you strive to make others happy. This is usually accomplished by interjecting humor into your speech. Craig Kilborn and David Letterman make entertaining presentations on their nightly television shows. Although their monologues sometimes fail to draw laughter, their overriding purpose is to entertain.

Specific Purpose

In order to make your speech more manageable, both for you to develop and for your audience to understand, you must determine its specific purpose. Stated in a single sentence, your **specific purpose** takes into account the following factors: (1) what you hope to accomplish, (2) which aspect of the topic you will cover, by narrowing your topic, and (3) your intended audience. This process moves you from your general purpose (to inform, to persuade, or to entertain) to a more focused speech topic. Consider the following:

> Amy, a first year speech student, must give a four-minute informative speech. She was advised to describe something to her audience and to base her speech on a personal experience. This meant choosing a topic she was familiar with. Amy knew she would be more convincing if she discussed a topic she cared about. She wrestled with several topics before finally deciding on the topic of parenting. Amy just had her first child three months ago and is very concerned about raising a self-confident and happy daughter. Because parenting is a broad topic, she knew she would have to narrow its focus. After some additional thought, she decided to focus on disciplining children.

When Amy began developing her speech, she started with the general purpose "to inform." Now she has to determine which aspect of parenting she wants to talk about. Her first attempt to narrow her topic produced the following results:

Specific purpose 1—to talk about parenting. Would an audience have a strong sense of the speech purpose after hearing this statement? Probably not. Amy still needs to decide exactly what she wishes to tell her audience. She tries it again, this time with better results.

Specific purpose 2—to inform the audience about the importance of parental discipline. Amy is now offering more information, but she still is not telling us anything specific. Amy needs to be more specific. For example, she may want to determine the different ways to discipline a preschool child. By doing so, she will have a better idea of what to share with her audience. Upon further reflection, Amy comes up with the following.

Specific purpose 3—to inform the audience about three ways to effectively discipline a preschool child. This shows some improvement, but Amy still has not identified the group to whom she wishes to deliver the speech. This seemingly minor point is important, because it helps her to keep her audience in mind as she delivers her speech. Here is Amy's final effort.

Specific purpose 4—to inform my class about the three ways to effectively discipline a preschool child. Do you see what Amy has accomplished? She has moved from a very general treatment to a more specific treatment of the topic. As a result, Amy should have an easier job constructing an effective speech because she has created specific guidelines for herself.

What process can you use to develop your specific-purpose statement? Let us analyze the preceding example. Amy's final statement, "To inform my class about the three ways to effectively discipline a preschool child," clearly states her specific purpose. Note that it is written in the form of a statement, not a question, that it contains only one idea, and that the language is concrete. Also note that Amy needed to revise her statement several times before constructing an effective one. The message is clear: you must refine your statement until it includes all the components just mentioned.

Developing a Specific-Purpose Statement   SKILL BUILDING

Develop a specific-purpose statement for the following topics.

1. Television dramas
2. Dealing with supervisors at work
3. Popular music

Keep the following in mind:

1. What do you want to accomplish with the speech?
2. What specific aspect do you wish to cover?
3. Who is your intended audience?

Thesis Statement

Once you have constructed an effective specific-purpose statement, the next logical step is to develop your thesis statement. A **thesis statement** includes the major ideas of your speech; at the same time, it refines your specific purpose.

Whereas the specific-purpose statement lays the groundwork for constructing your speech, the thesis statement reflects the outcome of your research (see Chapter 12). In fact, your research may cause you to construct a thesis statement that is different from the one you initially envisioned. For example, prior to conducting any research on your topic, "leading causes of death for women," you develop the following specific-purpose statement and thesis statement:

Specific purpose—to inform my classmates about the two leading causes of women's death.

Thesis statement—The two leading causes of women's deaths in the United States are automobile accidents and cancer.

COMMUNICATION and TECHNOLOGY

Marketing, Audience Analysis, and the Computer

Advertisers and marketers understand the importance of doing a thorough audience analysis. Before they advertise or market any product or service, experts attempt to find everything they can about the target market, or who they want to buy their service or product. Two of the most sought after target market groups are leading companies to rethink and redefine how they use and market technology. Generation X and Generation Y have dictated to marketers that computers and technology are essential to gaining their money.

Generation X is composed of consumers born between 1961 and 1981, or who are between the ages of 20 and 40 years. In order to reach these potential buyers, banks and other financial institutions, for example, are providing "technology based delivery mechanisms and credit cards" (Merrifield, 1997, p. 46). Because so many members of this age group grew up with computers and own computers and subscribe to online services themselves, Generation X values the ability to have access to their accounts and the ability to pay bills electronically (Merrifield, 1997). According to Diane Merrifield, in her article "The X Files," she argues, "What is obvious to nearly everyone is the importance to younger financial services customers of convenient distribution channels, such as ATMs, phone banking with interactive response systems, and PC banking. While there are members of every generation who prefer the personal touch of conducting business at a branch, members of Generation X are more likely to be comfortable with high-tech delivery channels and appreciate the

convenience such channels offer" (1997, p. 46). Through audience analysis, banks and other financial institutions determined that the best way to attract younger customers was to provide technology-based services.

Another example of marketing and the importance of technology is Generation Y. Generation Y consumers range in age from 5 to 20 years. Individuals between the ages 12 and 19 years are the "fastest growing demographic group in the United States under age 65 with estimates of annual spending of $275 billion" (Nucifora, 2000, p. 16). This group is similar to Generation X in that its members are also tied heavily to the computer. "Because they spend so much of their time attached to their computers, online marketing and the web will be dominant strategies for developing a marketing relationship with the Ys. Communicating through email is essential to this group," according to Alf Nucifora in the *Business Journal* (2000, p. 16). Companies like Tommy Hilfiger, Old Navy, and Abercrombie and Fitch have tried to define "cool" for this group, and the Internet has been one important tool, according to Nucifora (2000).

Banks and clothing stores are just two examples of companies that have come to understand the importance of thorough audience analysis and the importance of technology. Their sales increase when they have established common ground with their target market. In the cases of Generation X and Generation Y consumers, technology has become an essential marketing tool.

Your research, however, turns up different evidence; you must now change your thesis statement to reflect your findings:

> *Amended thesis statement*—The two leading causes of women's deaths in the United States are heart disease and cancer (Center for Disease Control, 2000).

In constructing your thesis statement, there are a few guidelines to follow: (1) put your thesis statement in a complete sentence, (2) avoid general or vague language, and (3) preview the main ideas. By taking these factors into account, your thesis statement will provide a good basis for developing the major ideas in your speech.

The previous section included this example of a specific-purpose statement: "To inform my class about the three ways to effectively discipline a preschool child." Fine-tuning resulted in the following thesis statement: "Three ways to discipline a preschool child are time-outs, scolding, and praise. While this thesis statement refines Amy's specific-purpose statement, it also reflects what she wants her audience to remember after her presentation.

Developing the Thesis Statement   SKILL BUILDING

Select one of the three specific-purpose statements you developed in the preceding skill-building activity.

1. Identify the possible major points in the speech.
2. Write a thesis statement incorporating the major points.
3. Share your thesis statement with a classmate.
4. Using the feedback you received, refine your thesis statement.

Summary

Selecting a topic is the first order of business in preparing a public speech. A key variable in the selection process is you—your concerns, experiences, knowledge, and curiosity often provide excellent speech topics. Another key element is the situation. Knowing about the size of your audience, the time limit, and the shape and size of the room will help you determine an appropriate topic.

You can increase your understanding of the audience by assessing such things as audience demographics, including age, sex, and ethnic/cultural/religious background, and the additional characteristics of knowledge, attitudes, needs, societal roles, occupation, and economic status. What you learn from your assessment can help you to choose a topic and to adapt it to fit your particular audience. How do you gather these data? Basically, there are three methods: observation, interviews, and questionnaires. Questionnaires can include closed questions, open questions, or those on a graduated scale (or combinations of all three). If after careful examination of yourself, the situation, and the audience you still do not have a topic, consider brainstorming. Brainstorming, either by yourself or with your peers, is an alternative method for exploring additional topics.

Your observations, interviews, and questionnaires provide a great deal of information about your audience, which you must now use to adapt the topic selected at the beginning of this process to the audience you have come to better understand as a result of the assessment process.

Once you have selected your topic, you must determine the purpose of your presentation. The development of your speech purpose usually follows three steps: (1) determining the general purpose (to inform, persuade, or entertain), (2) determining the specific purpose, and (3) creating a thesis statement. The move from general purpose to specific purpose helps you focus your topic by taking into account such factors as (1) what you hope to accomplish, (2) which aspect of the topic you will cover, and (3) your intended audience. With some fine-tuning you develop your thesis statement, which includes the major points of your speech.

Review Questions

1. What factors in your background can assist you in choosing a topic?
2. How can the elements of a situation affect your topic selection and how you develop the topic?
3. Why is knowing the demographics and other characteristics of your audience so important in choosing and developing a speech topic?
4. How can you incorporate an audience's need for esteem in a speech on corporate advancement?

5. Describe three types of questions you might ask your audience before choosing your topic.
6. How can you adapt your speech topic to a specific audience?
7. What factors should be included in your specific purpose statement?
8. What factors should be included in your thesis statement?

12

Researching and Using Supporting Material for Your Speech

At the conclusion of this chapter, you should be able to:

- Identify at least six potential sources of information for your speech.
- Locate reference and periodical sources at the library or on the Internet to use in your speech.
- Properly footnote sources used in your speech.

- Briefly describe the forms of supporting material that may be used in your speech.
- Briefly describe the different types of presentational aids.
- Explain the special problems associated with the use of presentational aids.

Rolanda is on her way to the campus library to do the research necessary to write her speech. She knows that her topic, advertising jingles, is interesting to her audience because of her thorough audience analysis, which included a survey. Her task now is to find as much information on advertising jingles as possible.

After several hours in the library, Rolanda found:

- two quotes from the creative director at Sheldon Advertising about the importance of jingles in advertising campaigns in an article published in a periodical dedicated to the business of advertising.

- five articles in a national newspaper about composing jingles. Two of these articles are interviews with composers.

- two audio records of famous advertising jingles.

- a documentary on the history of television advertising, which includes many commercials she could use as examples.

- three books on television advertising. Each book contained a chapter on advertising jingles.

- web sites for two advertising agencies that welcomed questions about advertising. Rolanda sent both agencies an email requesting information on how they create jingles.

Obviously, Rolanda has found plenty of information for her speech. She must now read through it and determine the best way to organize it so she can clearly communicate it to her audience. In this chapter, we discuss how to find material, both in and out of the library, to support your topic. A diversity of source material will add to the fullness of your speech and strengthen your overall arguments. It will also help you to feel more confidant about presenting the speech because you will know your research is credible and interesting.

Regardless of your topic, integrating evidence into your presentation helps you to construct and develop your ideas more logically. In your presentation, you will be making a claim (the thesis statement described in Chapter 11). Your claim must be supported with various forms of evidence. Furthermore, the added documentation helps you to inform your audience more accurately and thoroughly and increases the credibility of your arguments. Rolanda has already done a great job of collecting and organizing her supportive material. In this chapter we shall take a look at the types of information available to you, where to look for these sources, how to cite them in a speech, and the kinds of supporting material you can use as a speaker.

Sources of Information

When contemplating supporting material for a speech, it is important to know the kinds of materials available and where they can be found. In this section we shall discuss such important sources as personal experiences, interviews, and in the subsequent two sections, information that can be found in the library and on the Internet.

Personal Experiences

Speeches that relay personal experiences add a special dimension to public presentations. Whether the speech topic is a personal experience—hiking through Yellowstone National Park, your first day on a new job, delivering a child at home, being robbed—or whether personal experiences are included to augment an aspect of the topic (that is, interjecting a brief story about your effort to stop smoking as a way to reduce hypertension), the overall effect is one of adding "life" to the talk. No one knows better than you the significance of a particular experience, and the public speech provides you with an opportunity to successfully communicate these personal feelings.

The speech that focuses on personal experiences is ideal for the novice speaker. Being intimately acquainted with the subject, the individual can avoid some of the anxiety associated with public speaking; in its place is the feeling of confidence that comes from knowing the subject. In addition, using your diverse experiences encourages the audience to appreciate you as a speaker and helps increase your credibility.

Interviews

While searching for sources of information for your speech, remember that the experiences and knowledge of other people can enhance almost any topic. These people may range from professionals, to researchers, to practitioners. Look for someone who has something special to bring to your topic—an individual who possesses some unique knowledge that can be used to enhance the quality of your presentation (see Chapter 8 for a detailed discussion about interviewing).

How do you decide who would make a good interviewee? First, take a serious look at your topic. What are some of the individual ideas you want to explore? Are there experts or individuals with experience you can contact for an interview? For example, if you have selected diabetes as your topic, you may wish to interview a physician who specializes in the treatment of the disease, someone who is conducting research on a new method of treatment (if such a person is available), or a person who has had diabetes since childhood. Naturally, different questions would be asked of each individual; in turn, their responses would help refine your topic, perhaps changing its focus. The information provided by the physician, for instance, might include both widely practiced treatments of the past and treatments used today. After sorting through your notes, you might decide that you want to focus your talk on current treatments and those treatments that look promising for the future.

There are several steps to keep in mind if you decide to interview someone: (1) come to the interview with prepared questions, (2) use concrete language to phrase your questions, and (3) listen carefully.

Come to the Interview with Prepared Questions

Before you go to the interview, think about the purpose of your speech and the kind of information you want to obtain from the interview. Do you want statistics? Do you want facts or opinions? Do you want stories or examples? Prepare and write down specific questions in advance that will help you to get the information you need (see Chapter 8 for a detailed discussion of the kinds of questions).

Use Concrete Language to Phrase Your Questions

Your questions should be phrased using language that is concrete (that is, specific enough to be easily understood, see Chapter 4). Try to keep in mind the interpersonal skills discussed earlier in this book. Questions that place interviewees on the defensive may cause them to become hostile or, worse, leave the interview. Instead, word your questions so that they promote trust and openness. Why risk losing out on valuable information if you can take the necessary steps to avoid this situation? Consider the following:

> Kelly, a Women's Studies major, must do a presentation for her "Human Resources and Personnel" course on the efforts of local companies to recruit women for management positions. She arranges an interview with the chief of personnel at the leading packaging and shipping business in her city. After the initial social dialogue, she asks this loaded question: "Why don't you have any women working here?" The personnel director becomes defensive and announces that the interview is over.

While **penetrating questions** can provide interesting information, you need to display some sensitivity when formulating your queries. For example:

> James, a former police officer and Criminal Justice major was granted an interview with the chief of police after a shooting at the local shopping center in which a white police officer killed the African-American robbery suspect. Realizing that the chief was likely to be sensitive (and possibly defensive) about the issue, James very wisely avoided leading questions that might be construed as an attack against the department's handling of the situation. Instead, he tried to keep his questions focused on the impact the shooting had on the community. First, he asked the police chief to relay the sequence of events, thereby giving the chief an opportunity to describe the situation in detail. He followed up by asking the chief what steps were being taken to prevent any similar incidences in the future.

In this example James was able to gain valuable information without placing the interviewee on the defensive.

Listen Carefully

The main purpose of the interview is to gain information from the interviewee. Consequently, it is important to practice effective listening skills. Try to stay focused on the statements of the interviewee rather than concentrating on your own role in the interaction. Use the listening skills we discussed in Chapter 3. These include paraphrasing, interpreting, and questioning. Use these to check your perception of the message given. Specifically, if you are unclear about something that has been stated, make sure that you ask for clarification. If necessary, paraphrase the interviewee's statement so that he or she can confirm that you understood the point. Consider the following:

> Fidel was interested in finding out about the new fall TV programs. He wanted an expert's opinion and decided to interview Ross McKenney, a local television critic, about his attitude toward primetime sitcoms. In his

discussion, McKenney alluded to the "puerile nature" of many of the new programs on the air. Fidel was not certain about the meaning of the word *puerile*. Although somewhat intimidated by the critic, Fidel's over-riding concern for accuracy motivated him to ask McKenney to elaborate on this particular point. He then paraphrased the critic's words to ensure his own understanding of the term's meaning. "What you're saying, basically, is that many of today's programs are childish." Fidel was able to clarify the critic's position by actively listening to McKenney's comments and responses to questions.

Finding Sources: The Library

In addition to using yourself and interviewing others, the academic or public library is usually the next best place to search for supporting materials. Several areas of the library can help you research your topic in order to prepare a more thorough speech. These include the Library of Congress Classification system, the online catalog, indexes and databases, and the Internet.

Library of Congress Classification

The first step in doing research in the library is finding out how your topic has been classified by the library. All source material is cataloged and shelved by their keywords. These keywords are based on a system developed by the Library of Congress (LOC). The LOC Classification outline is available at the reference desk. Ask a librarian for help in determining what keywords you should use in your search. For example:

> Megan grew up in a family that loves cars. Her parents even turned their garage into a body shop so they could restore old Mustangs. Megan shares her parents' love for old cars. Specifically, she wants to do her informative speech on the history of the Corvette. She begins her research by using the word *cars* to find any books held in the library. The search results in "no holdings found." After checking with the LOC classification outline, she learns that her topic is found under *automobile*, not *cars*. Her search will be much more successful now that she knows what keywords to use.

Online Catalog: Library Holdings

In the past, library catalogs were organized by title, subject, and author on card catalogs, drawer after drawer of index cards. Today, all this information can be accessed from a computer terminal. From the online catalog, you can find out what books, periodicals, newspapers, encyclopedias, biographical sources, government publications, and other media your library holds.

Books

Because of the amount of space books provide, treatment of a topic is frequently more in-depth than that found in newspaper, magazine, or journal articles. Rarely, however, does a speaker have time to read an entire book to get information about a topic; more commonly, a section or chapter of a book is used for that purpose.

Specialists in a field often write books. Because books take longer to publish, however, the information they contain may be more dated than what can be found in either periodicals or newspapers. When timeliness is not an important factor, books often make excellent sources of information.

Finding Books

CRITICAL THINKING

Using your campus library online catalog, find three books for each of the following topics.

1. The creators of jazz
2. The presidential election of 1960
3. How to prevent heart disease

Which of the books you found would be an appropriate source for an informative speech?

Newspapers

An excellent source of supporting material for current topics is the newspaper. Articles tend to be brief, but focused. Daily newspapers routinely include detailed accounts of events and reactions to those events, as well as factual and statistical information. For example, in the November 9, 2000, issue of the *New York Times* there are dozens of articles on the 2000 presidential election, ranging from popular vote counts, to the process of the Florida recount, to editorials on the Florida recount and the electoral college, to the statements made by Vice President Gore and Governor Bush, to the legal and public relations strategies of both campaigns.

Because most major news stories require a second source to verify the position taken in the article, there is a great deal of pressure to describe the situation accurately. Even so, newspapers often have a bias, a fact that public speakers should understand.

Periodicals

Periodicals, written sources published at regular intervals (that is, weekly, monthly, quarterly, or semiannually), provide a wealth of factual and interpretive information on hundreds of topics. Speakers can rely on these sources to add substance to their presentations.

Magazines have a longer interval between issues than daily newspapers, which allows the writers to devote more time to researching the topic and to put into perspective the circumstances surrounding a particular event. Generally, magazine articles are more in-depth than newspaper articles because of the additional time provided for research and because of the greater amount of space allotted to these stories.

As you consult magazines for information, keep in mind that many magazines (like newspapers) have a particular bias. For instance, to get varying perspectives on the subject of mothers who work outside the home, you might read articles in *McCall's,* a traditional women's magazine; *Newsweek,* where the approach is likely to be neutral and matter-of-fact; and *Ms.,* which provides a feminist perspective. Using all of these types of magazines allows a more thorough examination of your subject.

Journals contain research findings carried out in a particular field, such as medicine, social welfare, electrical engineering, or communication. They are also valuable resources for supporting material to enhance your speech. You might look at journal articles for several reasons: to get data and statistics provided by research studies, to get commentary on a subject by specialists, or to get more in-depth coverage of a topic. To continue the example from above, you might want to look in *Signs,* a journal of women's studies or *Management Communication Quarterly,* a journal of business management. Each of these journals will provide you with more specialized information concerning working mothers.

Encyclopedias

Nearly everyone has had an occasion to look up information in a general encyclopedia, such as *World Book* or *Encyclopaedia Britannica.* However, most libraries also own specialized encyclopedias published for numerous disciplines. Titles often found in the reference collection include *International Encyclopedia of the Social Sciences, McGraw-Hill Encyclopedia of Science and Technology, Encyclopedia of Women's History in America,* and *Encyclopedia and Dictionary of Medicine and Nursing.* These sources include signed articles written by scholars in the field and are often accompanied by bibliographies or references to related works.

Biographical Sources

If your topic focuses on the accomplishments or fame achieved by a well-known individual, there are many biographical reference sources that await you. For example, *Biography Index,* published since 1949, contains citations to both periodical articles and books written about well-known people.

Current Biography is a monthly publication with an annual accumulation called *Current Biography Yearbook.* This source includes biographical sketches of many living persons. The articles usually conclude with a brief list of additional references. Finally, there are several *Who's Who* biographical dictionaries that contain background information on thousands of individuals. Those considered standard reference sources include *Who's Who, Who's Who in America, Who's Who of American Women,* and *Who's Who in American Politics.*

Government Publications

Perhaps your speech topic necessitates that you have current statistics to report to your audience. For example, are more men or women involved in fatal automobile accidents? How many Americans died of AIDS in 2000? *Statistical Abstract of the United States* would be an excellent place to check for these figures. A few others worth mentioning include *Business Statistics,* published annually by the U.S. Department of Commerce; *Uniform Crime Reports,* an annual publication of the Federal Bureau of Investigation, U.S. Department of Justice; and *Congressional Record,* the proceedings of the daily sessions of both houses of Congress. This source is particularly useful when researching how an issue was debated on the floor of the House of Representatives or the Senate. Which members of Congress spoke in favor of a proposed piece of legislation? Who opposed it?

To track down the thousands of government documents printed each year, check *Monthly Catalog of United States Government Publications.* Each monthly issue includes title, author, and subject indexes, and these are cumulated into semiannual and annual indexes.

Other Media

Audiovisual sources, including radio and television broadcasts, films, sound recordings, and videos, have both advantages and disadvantages for the public speech. First, we shall consider radio and television broadcasts. As information sources, the chief advantage of radio and television news broadcasts is their immediacy. When news stories receive considerable attention via television and radio (which is especially true for such crises as the shooting at Columbine High School; natural disasters such as floods, earthquakes, and volcanoes; the attack on September 11, 2001; and important political events such as the 2000 presidential election and inauguration in 2001), vast audiences are reached. Therefore, when you incorporate information from the broadcast in your speech, several members of your audience will likely instantly recognize what you are saying. You and your audience share a common ground, which increases the audience's understanding of your message. Another advantage of these sources is their dramatic nature. For example, coverage of the same issue in such print media as newspapers and magazines cannot compete with the drama of a live broadcast.

Films and sound recordings are good sources for reflecting the moods and attitudes of a particular time. Consider, for example, the way popular/ rock music, motion pictures, and television comedies and dramas all reflect what our society is like during a specific period. A song, a film clip, or a clip from a television program can portray a "slice of life" to your audience.

Finally, videos, especially commercially produced educational videos, also can provide useful background information, particularly for an informative speech in which your purpose is to educate your audience. Excerpts included in your presentation can effectively complement your verbal explanations.

This brings us to the disadvantages or drawbacks of using audiovisual sources. Incorporating material you gather from the types of media just discussed poses two problems: (1) having adequate time in your speech to "set up" or introduce the material, and (2) operating the necessary machinery (film projector, CD or tape player, or VCR). You must consider these special conditions when contemplating the use of audiovisual materials in your presentation.

Indexes and Databases

Computers have made doing thorough research much simpler. Instead of having to check each journal, magazine, or newspaper that may have information relevant to your topic, you can now check them all at once using an index or database. Virtually every library owns either *Readers' Guide to Periodical Literature* or *Magazine Index,* or both. *Magazine Index* indexes over 400 popular periodicals. *Reader's Guide to Periodical Literature* indexes over 180 magazines with an alphabetical, topical arrangement. Also published by the H. W. Wilson Company are specialized periodical indexes, such as *Business Periodicals Index, Education Index, Social Sciences Index,* and *Humanities Index,* to name a few.

Large libraries also have newspaper indexes on hand, most notably the *New York Times Index, Wall Street Journal Index, Washington Post Index,* or *National Newspaper Index.* At many libraries you can expect to find copies of these newspapers on microfilm. Furthermore, all the indexes mentioned here are available online.

Large databases of information can also be accessed from your library's computer. ERIC has thousands of research reports collected from over 700 educational journals by the United States Department of Education. MEDLINE indexes articles from 3,600 journals on topics such as biomedicine, health sciences, and medicine. PSYCLIT has articles from 1,400 journals dealing with education, psychology, and sociology. SOCIOFILE can help with topics such as communication, criminal justice, geography, sociology, political science, and speech. MLA International Bibliography has over a million records dealing with literature, language, linguistics, and folklore. PAIS International indexes over 1,600 journals on topics such as economics, business, law, international trade, government, and politics. AGRI-COLA has over two million records dealing with agriculture, agronomy, animal science, biology, chemistry, ecology, forestry, nutrition, pollution, and zoology. All of these databases can be used to obtain abstracts of articles and bibliographic information, and some offer full articles for you to print. A reference librarian can help you determine which of these databases is most appropriate for your topic.

Finding and Evaluating Periodicals   **CRITICAL THINKING**

Using several of the indexes listed above, find at least three articles about the following topics:

1. women's professional sports
2. the Challenger shuttle accident
3. laser eye surgery

Which of these articles would be appropriate for use in an informative speech?

Using the Internet: World Wide Web

Most colleges and universities are connected to the information superhighway or the Internet. The Internet is a network of computers from around the United States and the world. From your computer terminal, you can access information from millions of web sites. To begin your search, you must first choose a search engine. A search engine will provide you with a list of possible web sites that may be helpful. Use several different search engines because each uses different criteria in selecting and organizing relevant web sites. Yahoo!, Excite, Lycos, and Google are just a few available. For example, with the Yahoo! search engine, you use the keywords *vegetarian* and *cooking*. Yahoo! will provide you with over 100 "hits." You then must choose a subcategory and begin sorting through the list to find credible sources. In this example, you can choose sites concerning recipes, cookbooks, restaurants, festivals, and medical information.

It is important to understand that just because information is on the Internet does not mean it is credible or true. When accessing information from the World Wide Web, you need to ask four specific questions. First,

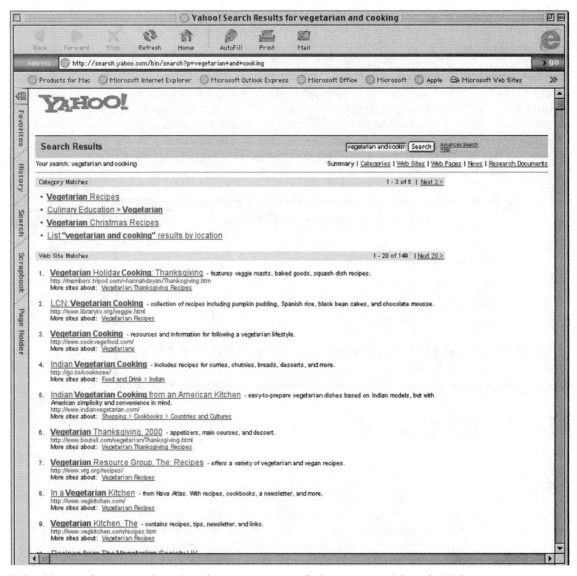

Yahoo! is one of many search engines that you can use to find source material on the Web.

who is the source of the information? Is the source biased? Does he or she have a vested interest in the information? Is the source an expert? Second, how old is the information? When was the last time the site was updated? Third, is the information verifiable elsewhere? In other words, can you cross-check the information from other sources? Finally, is an email or

TABLE 12.1   **Four Questions to Ask about Web Sites**

1. Who is the source?
2. How old is the information?
3. Is the information verifiable elsewhere?
4. Is an email or other contact information provided?

other contact information provided? You may need to clarify or verify information on the site. Web sites that do not provide other contact information should be regarded very carefully.

Another way to determine if a site is credible is to look at the Uniform Resource Locator, or URL. The URL indicates where the web site originated. Each web address is also called a URL. For example, our web address is www.purdue.calumet.edu. The edu indicates that our web site is located at a university or other educational institution, Purdue University Calumet. Other addresses might include .org for nonprofit organizations such as the Public Broadcast System (pbs.org), National Organization for Women (now.org), and American Civil Liberties Union (aclu.org) ; .gov for government agencies such as the White House (whitehouse.gov) or United States Senate (senate.gov); .mil for military such as the Army (army.mil), Navy's Blue Angels flying team (blueangels.navy.mil), and United States Air Force (af.mil); and .com for commercial sites such as Amazon Books (amazon. com), Cable News Network (cnn.com), and the *New York Times* (nytimes. com).

Using Electronic Mail

If you are using your college or university's online resources, you may also have an electronic mail address. Your email account allows you to send and receive messages from anyone online. Email is a valuable tool when doing research for your speech. Specifically, you can request information from experts in the field or others who have experience with your topic. In the beginning of this chapter, Rolanda sent two emails to advertising agencies requesting information on how they create jingles. When sending emails, be sure to identify yourself, what specific information you are seeking, and why you want the information.

Using the Library   SKILL BUILDING

Now that you have decided on a topic for your first speech, it is time to do some research. Go to your library and check the following reference sources for possible supporting material:

1. Your library's online card catalog for books
2. *Reader's Guide to Periodical Literature*
3. *New York Times* or other newspaper index
4. Database appropriate for your topic, such as ERIC, MEDLINE, MLA or others
5. Internet for any web sites

List the possible source material you found. Which of these is the most useful? Why? Which of these is not useful? Why?

Citing Sources

An important part of constructing your speech is to indicate your sources of information. This process should enhance your credibility, especially if you are planning to present a controversial argument. More important, it is unethical to omit mentioning whose ideas you are borrowing for your speech. When you use the ideas of another and do not indicate where those ideas come from, you are plagiarizing.

COMMUNICATION and TECHNOLOGY

Limiting Your Web Frustration

In a recent survey, college students reported that they "surf" the World Wide Web an average of sixteen to seventeen hours per week (Garcia, 2000). The accessibility of information and the speed at which it can be found were the primary reasons students gave for their use of the Internet. The Internet provides us with access to limitless information and we don't even have to leave our homes. With a few clicks of the mouse, we can find information, for example, about environmental topics such as the diminishing rain forest and global warming, or the latest scores for our favorite sports teams, and we can even find the full text of the President's last national address. But, the Internet can be frustrating to navigate and even dangerous to our speech purpose or goal. In order to limit your frustration and to successfully find the information you need to support your main ideas in your speech, consider the following:

1. *Search engines limit the information you can find.* Yahoo!, students' favorite search engine, only indexes about 7 percent of the information available on the World Wide Web (Goss, 2000). That means, for example, when you search for information on the history of Affirmative Action in the United States, Yahoo! will leave out 93 percent of the information available. Always

use more than one search engine. Others include www.altavista.com, www.excite.com, www.infoseek.com, www.lycos.com, and www.metacrawler.com. Any of these search engines can help you access information on your topic.

2. *Define your topic carefully.* There are several things to consider before doing a search. First, try several different terms for your topic in order to find relevant information. For example, to find information about the history of the Internet, you might use these key words: *Internet, World Wide Web,* and *information superhighway.* Second, if your topic is too broad, you may find yourself overwhelmed with "hits" or web sites that apply to your topic. Doing a search on "baseball," for example, will provide you with over 50,000 sites. You could not possibly check all of these sites. Narrow your topic to the World Series of 2000 or the invention of baseball. These topics are more manageable. Third, some topics are difficult to search on the Internet because of the nature of the words used to do the search. Specifically, searches on topics such as breast cancer, self-breast examinations, and sexual harassment will turn up pornographic sites.

3. *Use the links provided.* Many web sites will lead you to other sites that are similar in content via a hyperlink. Use these links to find sites that your search engine may not know about. Be careful, however, to keep track of your path. Jeffery Schantz states, "They [students] forget a hyperlink can, and often does, take them to an entirely new source. That's a problem when they try to document sources. They may inaccurately attribute sources and may have

trouble retracing the steps that led them to a specific source" (1999, p. 4).

4. *Check the credibility of the source.* Users of the Web often believe that if something is online, it must be true (Goss, 2000). Anyone can develop, design, and maintain a web site, and just about any information can be included on that web site. It is your job and ethical responsibility to provide your audience accurate and reliable information. Earlier in this chapter, we discussed the questions you should ask about any information you find on the Internet. In addition, according to Goett and Foote, "web pages are created for advertising, sales, advocacy, education, reference and entertainment. Students need to recognize that these goals may bias the presentation of factual information. Recognizing such bias does not mean that a source be discarded, since we sometimes wish to examine all sides of controversial issues, but it does caution about accepting facts and figures gathered from Web pages at face value" (2000, p. 92).

5. *Avoid plagiarism.* Plagiarism is using someone else's words or ideas without crediting that person at the time of use. Any time you take information from a web site, you must credit the source by providing a citation. Even if you paraphrase or summarize information, a citation must be provided. Because information can be downloaded right from the web to your computer, don't be tempted to "cut and paste." Don't take ideas that belong to someone else and pass them off to the audience as yours.

Using the internet to find supporting material can be easy and fun if you follow these guidelines.

In written material, you must provide a citation for any source material. Its purpose is to indicate where someone else could find the data you used. A citation should indicate whose idea is being used and the source from which it was obtained. In order to give proper credit to others, you should include a citation after every direct quote, as well as for those times when you paraphrase someone else's ideas. Several stylebooks describe the proper format for citations. Your instructor may require that you use a specific style manual for citing sources in your speech outline (see Chapter 13).

It is possible (and acceptable) to give credit orally to a source you have used. This is known simply as the **oral citation.** For example,

> Bradley and his wife Jill have a seven-year-old son named Jacob. Jacob was born prematurely and has many special needs. Bradley has been asked by a local support group for parents with special needs children to discuss how his family has tried to help Jacob. Several years ago, Jacob began taking classes in the martial arts. In addition to sharing Jacob's experiences, Bradley wants to support his ideas with testimony from experts. In his speech about the benefits of karate for special-needs children, Bradley included the following oral citation: "Dr. Meryl Lipton, a pediatric behavioral neurologist, said in a recent *Chicago Tribune* interview, 'Karate can be excellent for some special-needs children in terms of their motor development and more important, their self-esteem'" (*Marcus,* 2000, p. 4). This statement lets Bradley's audience know that the idea originated with someone else.

As you gather information for your speech, you may wish to prepare a bibliography of all your sources. The bibliography should include all the sources you use, even if they are not directly cited in the text of the speech. The style manuals used for citations also should be used for these bibliographic citations. Whenever questions arise about the information you have presented in your speech, you can refer to your bibliography to direct the questioner to particular magazines, books, films, and online sources. A thorough bibliography, appended to your speech outline, usually indicates a well-researched speech.

Forms of Support for Your Speech

In an effort to present your ideas clearly and convincingly, it is important to include evidence to support those ideas. The purpose of using supportive material is to supplement your major ideas, and this, in turn, adds credibility to your position. A diversity of source material will make your argument stronger. An added benefit is increased self-confidence, because you know that the argument you are presenting is thorough and well documented. Several different types of supporting material are discussed in the following subsections.

Examples

One of the strongest types of support is the use of examples. **Examples** are statements that attempt to illuminate the facts. They can be very effective in your effort to involve the audience in your presentation. Moreover, they help to clarify your presentation by reinforcing the points in your arguments. This assists the audience in following the progression of your ideas. A properly used example is one that is relevant and relates to the major ideas of your presentation. Let's take a look at three types of examples.

Factual Example

A **factual example** is something that you have observed. It grows out of your own experience, and as with any good example, it helps to reinforce a point. When the example is believable, it keeps the audience involved in your presentation and can lead to greater interest on their part. Consider the following:

> Dave is a psychology major and his topic for his first speech, "emotional pain," needed the focus of a specific example to illustrate one type of emotional pain. He recalled attending the funeral of a friend's teenage daughter who was killed in an automobile accident and the pain he witnessed there. The language Dave used to describe the situation—people sobbing uncontrollably, the parents needing to be supported by other family members, and so on—captured the emotional pain this family was experiencing and earned the attention of the audience as well.

Hypothetical Example

A **hypothetical example** is one that invites the audience to imagine a situation created expressly for the speech they are listening to. It is an effective way to capture the audience's interest, because it involves them directly in the process. Consider the following:

> Denise, a member of the Highland election board, was addressing a local women's group. Her purpose was to inform the audience of the procedure for registering voters. She believed her speech was crucial to increasing voter turnout in the upcoming off-year election. To emphasize her point, she created a hypothetical situation—she asked the audience to imagine that they were living in Afghanistan in the 1990s. She spoke of Rebecca, a young woman who is not allowed to leave her home without a male escort or to attend school. Of course, like all women in Afghanistan, she cannot vote. While not an actual case, Denise's example dramatically expressed her feelings that our freedom should not be taken lightly. She then moved back to her original theme: we need to be aware of the registration process and exercise our right to vote.

This example works because it kept the audience involved in the presentation and served to reinforce the central purpose of the speech.

Examples, then, can play an important role in your presentation because they can help clarify and reinforce your ideas. In addition, they add a personal touch to your presentation by providing a safe way to relay your personal feelings to your audience.

Anecdotes and Stories

Anecdotes, brief narratives, and stories help to personalize your ideas. They can help you make abstract ideas come alive for your audience. In other words, anecdotes and stories put a human face on an issue. President Clinton used these often in his speeches. For example, in his 2000 State of the Union Address, he said:

> Now, we have all seen what happens when guns fall into the wrong hands. Daniel Mauser was only 15 years old when he was gunned down at Columbine. He was an amazing kid—a straight A student, a good skier.

Former President Bill Clinton used many anecdotes and stories in his speeches.

> Like all parents who lose their children, his father, Tom, has borne unimaginable grief. Somehow he has found the strength to honor his son by transforming his grief into action. Earlier this month, he took a leave of absence from his job to fight for tougher gun safety laws. I pray that his courage and wisdom will at long last move this Congress to make common sense gun legislation the very next order of business. Tom Mauser, stand up. We thank you for being here tonight (2000).

President Clinton told the story of Tom Mauser as a way to put a human face on the issue of gun control. Like examples, stories and anecdotes should reinforce or clarify your overall argument.

Statistics

Why use **statistics** in a public speech? The reasons are clear. First, people have an easier time conceptualizing ideas that are presented in numerical terms; somehow things seem real when you quantify them. Take the issue of poverty: you see the epidemic in a more serious light when you are told that 12.7% of the population lives in poverty (U.S. Census Bureau, 1995). Second, statistics add credibility to your arguments because they document the points you are advancing. For example, a speech that proposes a law requiring trigger locks on all handguns to lower the number of accidental fatalities in the United States is made more effective if it includes statistics to back up these claims. Possible statistics to support your claim could be: (1) 40% of all homes in the United States have guns available; (2) 13.8% of all deaths by gunshot were children under the age of 19; and (3) each year 1,225 to 2,000 accidental deaths are caused by firearms (Teret et al., 1998).

SIGNE
PHILADELPHIA DAILY NEWS
Philadelphia
USA

CARTOONISTS & WRITERS SYNDICATE http://CartoonWeb.com

SIGNE WILKINSON, CARTOONIST & WRITERS SYNDICATE/cartoonweb.com

Despite the support statistics offer, caution should be exercised regarding their use. The discussion that follows focuses on understanding statistics and using statistics.

Understanding Statistics

In order to assess the value and limitations of statistics, a basic understanding of the methods used to compile statistics is desirable. Statistics are calculated in one of three ways: according to the median, according to the mean, or according to the mode.

The **median** is the middle point of a set of numbers, which means that half the numbers are above the midpoint and half the numbers are below the midpoint. In this set of numbers—6, 8, 9, 32, 37—9 is the median, because half the numbers are above 9 and half are below 9.

The **mean** is sometimes referred to as the "average." To calculate the mean, add all the values and divide the total sum by the number of numerals in the set. If one number is significantly higher or lower than the rest of the numbers, it can greatly affect the outcome of the mean. For instance, in the following set of numbers—3, 6, 9, 12, 15, 64—the number 64 would greatly raise the average of the combined scores.

The **mode** is the number that occurs most frequently in a set of numbers. In this set of numbers—1, 4, 7, 9, 9, 15—9 represents the mode because it occurs more frequently than any other number. Consider the difference in the median, mean, and mode for this set of numbers: 1, 12, 13, 37, 75, 75, 130.

Median: # 37
Mean: # 49
Mode: # 75

Using Statistics

As a speaker, it is important to be sensitive to the way you use numbers when developing your arguments. In fact, before deciding to use statistics in your talk, you should consider the following: (1) Is the statistical sample representative? (2) Do the statistics mislead your audience? (3) Are the statistics confusing to your audience?

It is your responsibility to make sure the statistics you use are based on a representative sample. Is the sample large enough? For example, in her speech about parking conditions at the university, Juanita reports that "nine out of ten students feel that there is a campus parking problem." While it appears that 90 percent of the students concur with Juanita's belief that there is a parking problem, there is something wrong with the data she used. Her sample of only ten students is not large enough to draw any conclusions.

A second problem arises from the data. Are these ten students representative of the total student body? After some questioning, Juanita reveals that the ten students she interviewed were all late for their eleven o'clock classes, the busiest time of day on campus. Many were angry because they could not find a parking spot. In addition, the day she conducted her survey the university was hosting a statewide journalism symposium, which meant that there were more visitors on campus than normal. Both of these circumstances would render Juanita's findings invalid.

Another point to consider is whether or not the statistics might mislead your audience. Statistics can vary dramatically, depending on the particular numerical representation used, namely, median, mean, or mode. All three are ways of explaining numbers, yet each represents a different measure for the same data. Consider the following:

> At a national conference of real estate agents, speakers cited various statistics to advance their own positions. For example, Angela, an agency owner, claimed that "with the average [mean] selling price of a home at $125,000, real estate commissions were providing a good income for brokers." Luke, a part-time sales representative and full-time college student, however, used $89,000 [the mode] as an argument for raising the commission percentage. With the median at $105,000, both groups chose to use related statistics to support their stand on the issue of real estate commissions.

This case illustrates that statistics are often selected because they support a position; it is this very selectivity that can mislead an audience.

While statistics can help you quantify a point you are trying to make, and thereby enhance your argument, you should be careful not to clutter your speech with too many statistics that may confuse or overwhelm the audience.

Working with Statistics   **CRITICAL THINKING**

1. The following is a set of test scores from an industrial psychology class:

   94 92 83 83 75 74 71 70 69 64 51 42

2. Please calculate the mean, mode, and median.

3. What is the potential problem with using this information?

Authoritative Opinion

Authoritative opinion, the words or ideas of individuals knowledgeable about a topic, can add credibility to your presentation. Use of authoritative opinion also indicates that you are not alone in your thinking. When using an authoritative opinion, you should (1) verify that the testimony comes from a qualified source, (2) verify that the source is unbiased, and (3) accurately quote or paraphrase your source.

Two types of testimony include the comments of recognized authorities and the comments of persons uniquely qualified on a given subject. Comments made by the President of the American Bar Association concerning the legal qualifications of a Supreme Court nominee would be regarded as expert testimony by a recognized authority. Likewise, Joe Torre's (Manager of the World Champion New York Yankees) comments about the qualities of a successful major league baseball manager also fall into this category. On the other hand, if you are giving a speech on how to do your own picture framing, you might decide to include Ms. Sutter's suggestions for matting art prints and needlework because of her fifteen years of experience in the custom framing business. Ms. Sutter is not a "recognized" authority, yet she is uniquely qualified on the subject of picture framing.

Comparisons

One way to make your arguments stronger is to compare to similar or different ideas, facts, or concepts. Analogies and similes can help you to clarify you message.

Analogy

An **analogy** compares the similar features in two seemingly different objects or situations. For example, "what racquetball does for Barb, needlepoint does for Chris." Two totally different activities reduce stress for these two women. If your speech topic is "ways to reduce stress," this analogy breaks down the topic into subpoints that are more easily understood, in part because the comparison drawn between the two activities is valid.

When you use an analogy, develop it completely so that the audience can follow the logic of your thinking, as in this example:

Barbara, President of her local chapter of PETA (People for the Ethical Treatment of Animals) was asked to speak to a group of high school students about the lack of humanity in hunting and trapping animals. She spoke of the different methods of slaughtering to demonstrate her point. In order for the audience to visualize what she was saying about the suffering of trapped animals, she compared it to the brutal treatment of prisoners of war incarcerated in Third World countries. She asked the students to imagine the torture experienced by some of our prisoners of war and then compared it to the brutal slaughter of innocent animals for recreational purposes. This analogy was compelling and drew the audience into the presentation.

Similes

Similes, like analogies, compare two things. But, unlike analogies, similes compare similar objects or situations using the words *like* or *as*. For example, you may argue that "giving a speech is as easy as riding a bike" or "learning CPR is like buying an insurance policy." The use of a simile not only helps you to clarify your message, but also makes your message more vivid and creative.

Definition

When your speech includes **jargon** (terminology of a specialized group or activity) or technical terms that the average audience has difficulty understanding, you should define those terms using language that is more appropriate. For example, if the members of your audience have no experience with computers, you would need to provide definitions for such terms as *byte, laser, high-density disks, MS-DOS,* and *disk drive*. Where do you turn for these definitions? Because specialized terms are often not defined in *Webster's,* you may need to consult one of the dozens of dictionaries that exist for specific disciplines (for example, art, construction, psychology, data processing, and biology).

Identifying Problems with Supporting Material **SELF-ASSESSMENT**

Several different uses of supporting materials follow. Can you identify the problem with each?

1. In a random poll of Detroit, Michigan, citizens, 87 percent felt that Americans should only buy and drive cars made in the United States.

2. The relationship between the music of Bruce Springsteen and the music of Bob Dylan is comparable with the relationship between the television programs "Masterpiece Theater" and "Dawson's Creek."

3. According to several people in my class, parking on campus is horrible.

4. According to basketball star Michael Jordan, McDonald's has the best hamburgers.

Presentational Aids

One of the most effective ways to clarify a concept or point is to include presentational aids in your presentation. **Presentational aids** are visual or audio support for your verbal message. A speech on arteriosclerosis (hardening of the arteries), for example, would be enhanced by an illustration showing what a clogged artery looks like. Your message is more likely to be understood if you include such visual aids as graphs, drawings, slides and movies, photographs, your body, or computer-generated presentational aids.

Graphs

Graphs are helpful when you wish to present statistics. Used appropriately, they can add clarity to your presentation and increase your audience's level of comprehension. There are three different types of graphs: (1) line graphs, (2) pie graphs, and (3) bar graphs.

The **line graph** is especially useful in demonstrating change over a period of time. For example, you want to communicate to your audience that the births to teenage mothers has been decreasing over the past few years. After checking the *Statistical Abstract of the United States: 1999,* you find that in 1995 the rate was 13.1, in 1996 the rate was 12.9, and in 1997 the rate was 12.8. A line graph can help show your audience the decrease in births over the past three years.

The **pie graph** (a pie shape divided into wedges) is helpful in demonstrating to an audience the way something whole is divided into parts or

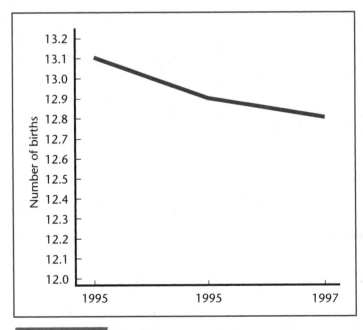

FIGURE 12.1 **Line Graph** (*Source:* U.S. Census Bureau.)

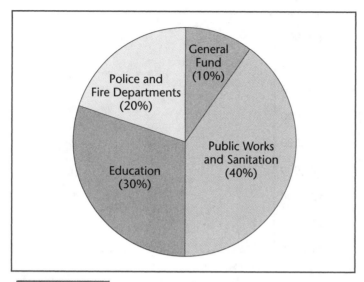

FIGURE 12.2 **Pie Graph** (*Source:* U.S. Census Bureau.)

the way one part of a whole relates proportionately to the other parts. For instance, a pie graph of a municipal budget would show the relationship between public works spending and funds appropriated for education. The audience gains a visual sense of the way their tax dollars are spent.

A third type of graph is known as a **bar graph.** A bar graph is primarily used to show the way different items compare and relate to one another. For example, you want to persuade your audience to finish their college degrees because they could increase their yearly income. You create a bar graph that shows: (1) men with a high school diploma earn on average only $26,542, and women only $13,786; (2) men with an associate's degree earn $35,962, and women earn $21,290; and (3) men with a bachelor's degree earn $45,749, and women earn $27,415 (U.S. Census Bureau, 1998).

Drawings

A drawing that is easy to produce can help the audience to better understand your topic. Your drawing need not be complicated, nor do you have to be an artist to use one. Consider the following:

> Evelyn, a volunteer at the Caring Place, a shelter for battered women and their children, wanted to inform her audience of single mothers about how easy it is to change the oil in their cars with little effort and at a great monetary savings. She obviously cannot bring a car into the center to demonstrate the process. Instead, she drew two diagrams, each illustrating the process of removing and replacing the oil and oil filter.

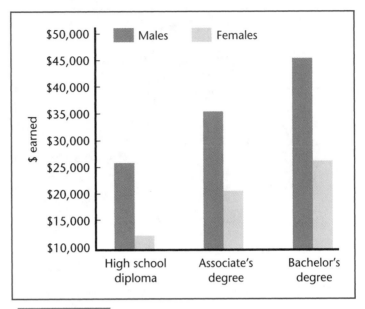

FIGURE 12.3   **Bar Graph** (*Source:* U.S. Census Bureau.)

These drawings helped complement Evelyn's oral presentation by simplifying the message, which increased the audience's understanding of this aspect of a car tune-up.

Slides and Movies

Slides or movies can be especially useful when you wish to stir the emotions of your audience. At times, a speaker might find it advantageous to show a movie clip to illustrate a point, as demonstrated by the following:

> Dagmar, a widow with three small children, belongs to a self-awareness group from her church. Currently, members of the group are discussing the importance of family communication. Each member is reading Judith Guest's novel *Ordinary People*. In addition, Dagmar has been asked to speak before the group on some aspect of family dynamics. She decides to talk about the importance of female family members expressing their feelings. She recalls how stirring and powerful the movie *Ordinary People* was and decides to show a scene between the mother and son. It brings several members of her audience to tears.

Slides and movies present a special kind of difficulty, however, because of the mechanics involved in operating the necessary equipment. If you choose to include slides or a movie, make sure you understand how to operate the DVD player, VCR, or other equipment. Take some extra time to practice before your actual presentation.

Photographs

Well-chosen photographs can capture an emotion, an attitude, or a special image. Furthermore, photographs that are directly related to your topic can have a powerful impact on your audience. Imagine, for example, the impact of a set of before-and-after pictures, the first depicting a child on the verge of starvation, the second showing the same child three months after having received food and medical attention. One drawback to photographs, however, is their size. Be sure that your photographs are large enough for everyone in the audience to see. For example, a 4 x 6 photograph of the Grand Canyon will not be large enough to communicate its beauty, complexity, and size. It may be better to have the photograph made into a transparency or slide.

Your body can make a very effective presentational aid.

Your Body

You may wish to demonstrate or explain an important point in your speech by using your body. The movement of your body also can have an additional benefit—it helps reduce excess tension. Consider the following:

> Michael has been studying dance since he was twelve. He has been asked by the campus committee on cultural awareness to discuss the relationship between dance and culture. Specifically, he wants to demonstrate how the twist, disco dancing, and break dancing grew out of the cultures of particular time periods. In order to make sure that the audience is familiar with these dances, Michael briefly demonstrates each one. Michael's "performance" adds a special quality to the presentation and assists him in advancing his theme.

Computer-Generated Presentational Aids

Computers can make it easier for you to prepare and use presentational aids. Charts, graphs, maps, diagrams, pictures, and many other aids can be produced using computer software. These aids are professional in appearance and enhance your overall presentation. PowerPoint or other presentation software may be available on your campus. Check with your computer lab instructor for help. One drawback to using presentation software is that it is easy to get carried away and prepare too many aids. Remember, presentational aids should not substitute for your arguments, but enhance the audience's understanding of them.

SKILL BUILDING   Presentational Aids

There are several possible types of presentational aids you can use to clarify and illustrate your ideas.

1. What information have you gathered that might need a presentational aid?
2. What type of presentational aid would work best to convey this information?
3. List and describe at least four ideas you have for presentational aids. Be sure to describe how you might create these presentational aids and how they might fit into your overall presentation.

Using Presentational Aids

It is important that your visual aids enhance your presentation, but that they do not become the center of your presentation. On the contrary, they should support the points you wish to make. If, for example, your audience becomes preoccupied with a presentational aid (for example, a graphic picture or a breathtaking photograph), your message may get lost.

Too often speakers pay so much attention to a presentational aid that they forget to talk to the audience. It is crucial that you not speak directly to your presentational aid; instead, glance at it and then establish direct eye contact with the audience. By focusing exclusively on the presentational aid, you risk losing contact with the audience.

For your presentational aid to complement and enhance your presentation, all members of your audience need to be able to see it. Avoid making the audience squint or strain their eyes in an effort to see your aid. Also,

Ethics in Communication

Using Support Material

In the beginning of the chapter, we read about Rolanda and her search for supporting materials. She chose to inform her classmates about advertising jingles. Now that she has collected relevant information from a variety of sources, Rolanda must use this material to organize and support her main ideas.

How will she communicate her supporting material to her audience in an effective and ethical way? As a speaker, it is her job to communicate her ideas as clearly as possible and to provide thorough support for each of her ideas. She has gathered several different types of supporting material that will enhance her effectiveness. She must also be concerned about communicating the information honestly. Rolanda (and all speakers) should apply the following guidelines:

1. Be sure to provide an oral citation for the supporting material during the delivery of the speech. Also, you will need to document the source in a bibliography or works cited page. Documenting your support material will ensure that you have not engaged in plagiarism. Lastly, this will give your audience the opportunity to judge the validity of the information and the credibility of the source.

2. Rely on a diversity of source material to support your ideas. This will provide the audience with an understanding of the topic and will also make your speech richer.

3. Avoid biased sources and make every attempt to provide more than one point of view.

4. Be sure your material is up to date and current.

5. Avoid manipulating data and statistics. Be sure that the sample is representative and that your statistics don't mislead your audience.

6. Don't ever fabricate or make up evidence, quotes, or other supporting material.

Following these guidelines will ensure that your use of supporting material will be effective and ethical.

when selecting your presentational aid, keep the size of the room in mind. What is the length of the room? How are the seats arranged? Ask yourself these questions to help you determine the appropriate size for your visual aids. If you have difficulty seeing the presentational aid when standing in the back of the room, chances are the audience will, too. Here are three additional pointers for use of poster board: (1) use extra-wide markers in preparing graphs or drawings; (2) use dark colors, which show up better from a distance; and (3) make the characters large enough to see from a distance.

CHECKLIST

Using Presentational Aids

- Be sure the aid supports your main ideas.
- Speak directly to the audience, not the presentational aid.
- The entire audience needs to be able to see your aids.
- Keep the size and shape of the room in mind when choosing your aids.

Summary

An arsenal of supporting materials will help to make your speech clearer, more credible, and more accurate. In this chapter we identified several sources of information for your speech, including personal experiences, interviews, books, newspapers, periodicals, other media such as radio and television broadcasts, and the Internet.

In order to use these various sources, you must know how to find them in the library or online. The reference collection includes such helpful sources as encyclopedias, biographical materials, and government documents. Magazine, journal, and newspaper articles are accessible with the use of indexes such as *Readers' Guide to Periodical Literature, Magazine Index,* and the *New York Times Index,* or databases such as ERIC, MLA, or MEDLINE. You can also use a search engine from your computer to find

web sites that contain useful information. Lastly, you may want to send an email requesting information from an expert or someone with personal experience with your topic.

After locating supportive material and deciding what to incorporate in your speech, you begin the process of developing the ideas in your speech. You are responsible for giving credit to others for any ideas of theirs that you use. This is done through oral footnotes during the delivery and in your bibliography.

Your efforts to find supporting materials for a speech generally produce a number of possibilities. Depending on your topic, you will want to include one or more of these types of supporting material: examples, both factual and hypothetical; anecdotes and stories, and statistics; authoritative opinions; comparisons like analogies and similes; definitions; and visual aids, including graphs, drawings, slides and movies, photographs, your body, and computer-generated aids. Knowing how to incorporate appropriate forms of support increases your confidence during your speech. Furthermore, using a diversity of support material such as examples, statistics, stories, and other materials assists you in developing your ideas more completely, which is the purpose of using supporting materials.

Review Questions

1. List six sources of information that provide supporting material for your speech.
2. What three steps are important to remember when interviewing someone?
3. List three resources you can find on your library's online catalog.
4. Explain how you can use the Internet to gather support material.
5. What four questions should you ask about information found on a web site?
6. Why is it important to cite your sources?
7. Explain the benefit of using examples in a speech.
8. Explain the difference between median, mean, and mode.
9. What guidelines should you keep in mind when you plan to use statistics in your presentation?
10. Under what circumstances would you incorporate these presentational aids in your speech:
    a. Line graph
    b. Pie graph
    c. Bar graph

13

Organizing Your Speech

At the conclusion of this chapter, you should be able to:

- Name and describe the three major parts of a speech.
- Describe five patterns that are useful for organizing the body of your speech.
- Develop the body of your speech.
- Construct the introduction of your speech.
- Construct the conclusion of your speech.

- Compose transitions, including transitional previews and summaries, and signposts for your speech.
- Compose a full-sentence outline for your speech.
- Develop a key-phrase outline for your speech.

dam had always been active in his community. He has volunteered at the local homeless shelter, served as a mentor in the Big Brothers and Big Sisters program, and tutored at-risk students at his children's elementary school. Adam believes strongly that individuals can make significant changes in their community, schools, and places of worship by helping one another.

As a student at Kenwood Community College, Adam is majoring in sociology and hopes to be a social worker. For his Introduction to Sociology course, he must present the class with information about social services or agencies in the Kenwood community that help people in need. Because of his extensive experience, Adam decides to discuss the importance of mentoring and the need that many nonprofit agencies have for volunteers.

After doing extensive research, including looking at several web sites, interviewing agency managers, and reading several journal articles, Adam must decide how to organize his ideas. He knows that as the speaker, it is his responsibility to make his presentation easy to listen to and understand.

First, he tries to organize his ideas around the process of mentoring. This includes making contact with the agency, going through training, establishing a relationship with the mentee, and maintaining the relationship. Adam decides this is too complicated to explain in five minutes. Second, Adam tries to organize his ideas around one agency, Big Brothers and Big Sisters. He could discuss the history of the organization and how it helps children in his neighborhood. As he outlines his speech, Adam realizes he has too much information. Lastly, Adam narrows his topic down and decides that his three main points will be: (1) a description of mentoring; (2) the effects of mentoring on the mentor and mentee; and (3) opportunities for mentoring in the local community. This organization seems to work best for Adam, his audience, and the speaking situation.

283

As Adam discovered, there are multiple ways to organize ideas. Depending on your topic, the speaking situation, your audience, and yourself, you must decide which approach will help you to effectively communicate your information. You can then be confident that the audience will listen to and understand your speech.

In this chapter, we will discuss the format of a speech. Specifically, a speech has an introduction, body, and conclusion. Chapter 11 concentrated on selecting a speech topic, determining the purpose of your speech, and analyzing the audience. Chapter 12 focused on gathering supporting materials for your topic. This chapter builds on the discussions of the previous two chapters.

As a speaker, you want your audience to find your speech not only informative and interesting, but easy to follow. You are responsible for ensuring that members of the audience understand your speech. Remember from Chapter 3 that listening is very difficult, and as the speaker you need to make it as easy as possible for the audience to listen to your presentation. To do this, your presentation must be well organized. A well-organized speech will take your audience from a position of unfamiliarity with your treatment of a topic to a position of enlightenment.

Traditionally, a speech has three major parts: a beginning, a middle, and an end. These parts are known, respectively, as the introduction, the body, and the conclusion of a speech. Transitions between the major parts of the speech further clarify your presentation.

The Body

The **body** is the main part of your speech; as such, you begin your work here. Those ideas expressed in your thesis statement are fully developed in the body. For example, a speech on situation comedies might include the development of factors that contribute to a successful show: good scripts, appealing characters, and a degree of social commentary. Furthermore, it is in the body of your speech that you incorporate the supporting material gathered from personal experiences, interviews, sources of information found at the library, and the Internet. The ideas you wish to express in your speech can be shaped into logical, observable patterns. In fact, logically developed ideas contribute to a speaker's confidence and at the same time make it easier for the audience to follow the presentation. Two helpful steps in preparing the body include organizing your ideas and outlining.

Organizing Your Ideas

An element that helps create a logical flow of ideas is **sequence,** or order. Ideas that are organized in a definite pattern or progression help your audience follow the development of your talk. Generally speaking, certain topics are better suited for a particular organizational pattern, although there are no ironclad rules for selecting one over another. Ultimately, you must decide which pattern seems most appropriate for the development of your topic and the audience you will be speaking to. Five organizational patterns may be used are causal order, problem/solution, spatial order, time order, and topic order.

Causal Order

Causal order establishes the fact that certain events are linked to other events that have precipitated them. When using a cause-and-effect format, first define the cause and then follow up by discussing effects. For example:

> Rashelle is a nursing student and works as a nurse's aide at State Hospital. She has been asked by her son's teacher to discuss the importance of hand washing to prevent getting colds and flu because many of the students have missed school due to illness. Her son and his classmates are in the fourth grade, so Rashelle knows she must organize her main ideas so that her presentation will make sense to them. She decides to organize her main ideas in a causal order. First, she will discuss how people don't wash their hands as often as they should after sneezing, blowing their noses, and using the bathroom. Second, she will discuss how cold and flu germs are transmitted to others and the resulting effects of fever, sore throat, nausea, and headache.

Problem/Solution

The **problem/solution** approach to organizing a speech involves identifying a conflict and then offering a potential course of action that will correct the problem. In most instances, the first part of the speech is reserved for discussing the problem; in the second part of the speech the speaker offers a solution to that problem. In most cases, the speaker is attempting to persuade the audience to follow the solution offered in the speech. This organizational pattern would be appropriate for the following topic: "Thousands of Americans suffer from hypertension [problem], but there are proven ways to reduce this condition, namely, controlling your diet, exercise, and medication [solution]."

Spatial Order

Spatial order refers to organizing the parts of a topic according to the relationship of their positions. This relationship can be geographic (the different wine-producing regions of France), rank ordered (the degrees of proficiency in karate), or directional (the exterior, then interior features of a house, car, boat). In the case of karate, the body of your speech might be organized around describing the specific techniques required for each rank from beginners (white belt) to experts (black belt).

Time Order

Time order arranges ideas in a chronological framework. This pattern of organization is best suited to topics that present a step-by-step explanation (how to wallpaper a kitchen, how to cook a turkey) or a historical development. For example, Shelly is doing her speech on the history of the women's movement. Her three main ideas will corresond to the three "waves" of feminism. Within each main point, Shelly will discuss how women tried (and most times succeeded) in changing their lives for the better.

CRITICAL THINKING   Identifying Organizational Patterns of a Speech

Name the organizational pattern illustrated in each of the following descriptions:

1. There are several Hollywood celebrities who have gone into public office:
   a. George Murphy served as a U.S. Senator during the 1960s.
   b. In 1986, Clint Eastwood was elected mayor of Carmel, California.
   c. Ronald Reagan has served as both Governor of California and President of the United States.
   d. Sonny Bono was a United States Representative from California.

2. Society is putting fewer resources into our large urban cities. If this trend continues, these cities will continue to decay.

3. The following steps are helpful when buying a new car:
   a. Research the different models available.
   b. Select the model that best suits you.
   c. Go to several dealerships that sell the car.
   d. Purchase the car at the dealership where you feel you received the best treatment.

Topic Order

Topic order involves breaking down your main topic into smaller points that are pertinent to the main idea. For example, if the purpose of your speech is to define what a teacher is, you might discuss each of the following subtopics: (1) a teacher is someone who educates others, (2) a teacher is a role model, and (3) a teacher is someone who instills a love of learning.

The order of the discussion may be unimportant, or you may view one subtopic as more important and want to address it first. That is something you must determine.

Outlining the Body

Why should you outline the body of your speech next? Is not selection of an organizational pattern enough to develop your speech? The answer is no. Your decision to adhere to a particular organizational structure is based on the way you view your total topic, including both its general and specific purposes. Outlining the body of your speech helps you to develop fully the points made in your thesis statement. Outlining is simply another step in the process of preparing a speech. To summarize what has happened so far, consider the following:

General purpose: to inform

Specific purpose: to inform my classroom audience about the role of mentoring children in our community

Thesis statement: To understand the role mentoring children plays in our community, we will discuss the definition, benefits, and local opportunities for mentoring.

Organizational structure: topic order

The next step is the outline:

I. Definition of mentoring
II. Benefits of mentoring
III. Opportunities for mentoring

In other words, the task that awaits you is to construct an outline that develops the three ideas mentioned in your thesis sentence.

The main purpose of outlining is to help both the speaker and the audience follow the development of ideas in the speech. When constructing an outline for the body of your speech, it is sometimes helpful to use full sentences. Specific outlining rules follow, and each is related to the body of the speech.

An Outline Consists of Coordinate and Subordinate Points

Coordinate points are the major ideas in a speech that grow out of the thesis statement. It is essential for the speaker to clearly identify the major points, because this helps clarify the direction of the talk for the audience.

Subordinate points are minor points that grow out of the major ideas. It is equally important to realize that your subordinate points should at all times support your major ideas. When analyzing and developing your

COMMUNICATION and TECHNOLOGY

Computer Software and Organization

Outlining and organizing your ideas for presentation can be frustrating. It is sometimes difficult to see how all the ideas fit together. You could put your ideas on note cards, spread them out on the floor, and begin organizing them until you have a complete outline. Today, however, computer software can help in this process.

Inspiration (www.inspiration.com), a computer software program, can help us organize, diagram, map, and outline ideas. Students can type in their ideas and then see how the ideas look using the "Diagram View" button. Then, using the "Outline" button, your ideas will appear in a hierarchical outline. Topics and ideas can be dragged into different places within the outline. The final outline can be converted into handouts, speaker's notes, and even presentational aids.

If you don't have access to Inspiration, Microsoft Word can also help with organizing and outlining your ideas. Using the drop-down menu from "View," you can click on "Outline" or "Document Map." Each of these features will show you how your ideas (as typed into the document) are organized. The "Outline" function, however, will not include Roman numerals, letters, and the like. You will have to add them to the outline.

Organizing and outlining software is an excellent tool for creating your presentation. Be aware: the software only works well when it has good ideas to organize and outline. Make sure your research is thorough and well documented.

presentation, be sure that a clear connection exists between your major and minor points. Furthermore, make sure you include at least two subordinate points for each coordinate point.

In the following example, the coordinate points (Roman numerals) represent the major ideas of the talk, while the subordinate points (letters) are minor points whose function is to support the major ideas.

I. The definition of mentoring includes the mentors and mentees.
   A. According to the Office of Mentoring Programs of Maryland, mentoring is "a supportive, trusting one-to-one relationship between a caring adult or youth and a school-aged child" (2001, p. 1).
   B. A mentor has the following characteristics: dependable, patient and caring, good listener, self-confident, and conscientious (Office of Mentoring Programs). According to R. Gilligan, a Senior Lecturer in Social Work, the mentor, "involves encouraging talents and interests in the young person which help build confidence, self-esteem and social skills" (1999, p. 190)
   C. Over fifteen million children are "at risk" in the United States today, according to Colin Powell, Secretary of State (1997, p. 484).

II. There are several benefits for the mentees and mentors.
  A. The most important benefit for the mentee is the validation of self. According to Gilligan, "mentors may be important in validating, in the young person's eyes, the young person's effort, ability and personal qualities" (1999, p. 191). The increased self-confidence of the mentee lowers his or her risk of dropping out of school, participating in risk-taking behavior, and suicide.
  B. The benefits for the mentor include self-satisfaction and increased learning about children and youth. According to Kathryn Taaffe McLearn et al. in an article entitled, "Child Health: Mentoring Makes a Difference," mentors find the relationship with youth highly satisfying and rewarding, and say they would do it again (2001, p. 3).
III. There are several opportunities to become a mentor in our community.
  A. According to our local United Way, several organizations need mentors. The United Way can be reached at (219) 923-2302.
  B. Some of these include:
    1. LACASA (Latin American Community Alliance for Support and Assistance) can be reached at (219) 884-0095.
    2. The Boys and Girls Clubs of Northwest Indiana provides a variety of educational, social, and recreational programs for boys and girls ages seven to seventeen. They can be reached at (219) 887-2020.

Each Idea in an Outline Is Discrete

Discreteness is the quality of being separate. Your ideas are said to be discrete if they have the ability to stand on their own. For your outline, this means making sure that only one idea is contained in each sentence. The two subordinate points in the following example are discrete, separate ideas. Each one achieves its goal of supporting the coordinate point. Look at the above outline. Each of the three main ideas is discrete and different from the other ideas.

Limit the Number of Major Ideas

It is wise to limit the number of major points you choose to include in a classroom speech. Your speech will be too lengthy or cumbersome if you include more than five major points; with too many main ideas, you run the risk of treating your topic superficially.

Outlining the Body of Your Speech   **CHECKLIST**

- Coordinate points should represent your main ideas.
- Subordinate points support your coordinate points.

- Make each idea discrete.
- Limit the number of major ideas.

SKILL BUILDING   **Developing a Speech Body**

1. Choose one of the following topics:
   a. Making your favorite dinner
   b. The triumph and tragedy of Bill Clinton's presidency
   c. Parking at your campus
   d. Last year's Super Bowl or other sport's championship
2. Create a speech body that contains three coordinate points and two subordinate points under each coordinate point.
3. Use full sentences in completing this task.

The Introduction

The introduction is the place where you strive to create a "need to know" for the audience. What motivates an audience to listen to the development of your ideas during the body of your speech? Hopefully, your introduction gains their attention. An effectively constructed introduction can elicit support from your audience and ensure their attention. As a speaker, it is both exciting and encouraging to see an audience show signs of interest and involvement in the first minute of your presentation. The objectives of your introduction are threefold: (1) to capture the audience's attention, (2) to establish your credibility, (3) to communicate the nature of your topic to the audience.

Drawing the Audience's Attention

Drawing the attention of your audience in the introduction is crucial if you expect to maintain their interest during the body of your speech. There are a number of ways to achieve this goal, including the use of one of the following: a narrative, a startling statement, a rhetorical question, or a quotation.

Determining a suitable format for your introduction requires that you analyze both your topic and what you consider to be the needs of your audience. In Chapter 11 we addressed the subject of topic selection and

Begin each presentation by gaining the attention of the audience.

adapting to the needs of the audience. At this time you may find it helpful to review that discussion. Remember, that your audience will approach their interaction with you and your topic from diverse points of view. The more you know about their frames of reference, the easier it will be for you to create the "need to know" for them. Each of the following introductions could be used with the speech outline we prepared earlier in this chapter on mentoring children.

Narrative

An effective way to introduce a speech is to use a **narrative,** or story. It can enable the speaker to create a feeling of understanding with the audience. Because narratives are often based on personal experiences that the audience can easily identify with, they can capture the audience's interest right away. A narrative can be either factual or hypothetical as long as it relates to the central theme of the talk. Consider the following:

Rose was sixteen years old when I first met her. Her parents were separated, and since her father had moved out to be with a younger woman,

> Rose was associating with "the wrong crowd." Her grades had dropped drastically; she was ditching school and drinking. Her mother was depressed and seemed helpless in the face of her daughter's burgeoning gang activity. She became alarmed when she found a will that Rose wrote. The will bequeathed her belongings to her gang if she were shot and stated, "if I am brain damaged, pull the plug" (Leader, 1994, p. 120).

This story, told by a mentor, puts an actual face on the need for mentors and how many children are at risk.

Startling Statement

A **startling statement,** one that shocks, arouses, or surprises an audience, will certainly capture their attention. Remember, however, that this statement must relate to the topic. If not, you may gain the audience's attention, but for the wrong reasons, making it difficult to bring the audience back to the topic later on. This is particularly true if you incorporate something gimmicky or humorous and then attempt to speak on a serious topic. The startling statement can be very effective if it is used properly. Consider this opening statement: "A *USA Today* survey ranked our nation's capital as one of the deadliest places for children to live in the country. In D.C., this year city officials estimate 2,500 children will be abused" (McCarthy, 1994, pp. 9–10). The speaker's attempt to startle the audience was done for the express purpose of gaining interest in the topic of mentoring and what mentors can do to help children.

Rhetorical Question

Try asking a rhetorical question to introduce your speech. A **rhetorical question** is one that is posed to the audience and later developed or answered in the talk. The speaker does not expect the audience to answer a rhetorical question; its purpose is to motivate the audience to think about the topic. If the speaker is successful, the audience will want to hear more. Consider the following:

> As a child, did you ever feel alone or isolated? Think back to your childhood . . . do you remember an adult who helped you ease your loneliness or isolation by listening to you or helping with your homework, or just "hanging out" with you? The adults who helped you are called mentors and play a significant role in our society.

In this example, the speaker asks the audience to think about their own childhood and the mentors they may have had in their lives. This is accomplished by including a question that the audience can easily relate to and understand.

Quotation

Using a **quotation** to introduce a speech involves taking someone else's exact words to support the ideas covered in your speech. Quotations are often dramatic in nature and can therefore elicit the audience's interest. After stating the quote, follow up by drawing a connection between the quote and the topic for the audience. Occasionally you may be forced to take excerpts from a lengthy quotation. When this occurs, be sure you are capturing the essence of the quote. The following quotation by Colin Powell, Secretary of State, at a National Volunteer Summit on April 28, 1997, could be used to grab the attention of the audience concerning mentoring:

> Up to fifteen million Americans today are at risk. They are at risk of growing up unskilled, unlearned or even worse, unloved. They are at risk of growing up physically or psychologically abused. They are at risk of growing up addicted to the pathologies and poisons of the street. They

Using quotations, like the one above by Colin Powell, can enhance your presentation.

are at risk of bringing up children into the world before they, themselves have grown up. They are at risk of never growing up at all. Fifteen million young lives are at risk, may not make it unless we care enough to do something about it (1997, p. 484).

In this example, the speaker uses a quote as a springboard for the speech, and it is successful because it is directly related to the topic. Note the brevity of the quote; with a lengthy quote you risk losing the audience's attention. Also, it is more difficult to deliver a quote because you are stating someone else's words and the speech patterns are likely to be unnatural to you. Because of these factors, a quote that is short and to the point will work better for most circumstances.

Establishing Your Credibility

After capturing your audience's attention, you must still address two remaining goals before moving to the body of your speech: (1) to establish your credibility and concern and (2) to communicate the nature of your topic. Establishing your credibility as a speaker for a particular topic involves conveying your knowledge about the topic (for example, mentioning personal experiences or recently conducted research), as well as your concern. For our speech on mentoring, it would be important to tell the audience about any experience you have had as a mentor or as a mentee. You could relay a narrative about your own experiences, for example. This would communicate to the audience that you have hands-on experience, as well as knowledge found during your research. Specifically, Dominick has decided to do his informative speech on mentoring. As part of his introduction and attempt to establish his credibility, he states:

> Twenty years ago, I was not the same person I am today. I was only eight years old and was wild! I didn't listen to my mother or grandmother, who lived with us, nor did I listen to my teachers at school. I was a pretty troubled kid. Out of desperation, my mother signed me up at the local community center for a mentoring program. My mentor, Archie, became my best friend and saved my life. Today, Archie and I are still very close and I have become a mentor to a young man named Simon. In my presentation, I will share my experiences as a mentee and as a mentor. In addition, I will share the information I found about the role of mentoring in our society.

When constructing your introduction, you want to communicate that your topic is important and that you are committed to sharing it. Ask yourself a few questions, such as "How does this topic relate to my needs?" and "Why do I want to share my views with this audience?" The answers to these questions will help you to communicate your involvement in the topic.

Establishing Your Credibility SELF-ASSESSMENT

Establishing your credibility is one of the most important aspects of the introduction.

1. How do you plan to do this in your speech?

2. How will you communicate your experience and interest with your topic?

3. How will you communicate that you've done research on your topic?

Providing Information about Your Topic

In the last phase of your introduction, indicate what the body of your speech will include, stopping short of actually developing your ideas. Save that discussion for the body. What you should reveal to your audience is the purpose of your speech. For example, you would want to preview your main ideas of your speech on mentoring: the definition, benefits, and local opportunities for mentoring. Your actual discussion of these subjects would follow in the body.

Gaining the Attention of the Audience SKILL BUILDING

1. Earlier in this chapter you developed a speech body. Using the same topic, write four different types of introductions:

   a. Narrative

   b. Startling statement

   c. Rhetorical question

   d. Quotation

2. As you write these introductions, ask yourself how you can capture the audience's attention.

3. How could you demonstrate your credibility as a speaker on this subject?

4. Share your introductions by forming small groups.

5. Elicit the feedback of your peers on how involved they become in your talk.

The Conclusion

The functions of the **conclusion** are (1) to draw your speech to an end, (2) to reiterate the central theme of your presentation (especially in an informative speech), and (3) to indicate to the members of your audience what you would like them to do (especially in a persuasive speech).

As you begin your conclusion, give your audience a cue so that they can refocus their attention. Phrases such as "in conclusion" or "in closing" generally work. Now use your remaining time to reinforce your speech's purpose or to ask something of your audience—either that they change the way they look at an issue or that they take some action. There are different techniques to achieve this goal, including the summation, the challenge, and the call for action.

The Summation

One way you can conclude your talk is with the **summation,** which reinforces the main points in your speech. For example, the following statement could be a meaningful close for a talk that centers on mentoring:

> Today, I have discussed some of the major points concerning mentoring in our society: the children at risk, the adults who serve as mentors, the benefits for everyone involved, and finally, opportunities for you to get involved as a mentor in our community.

The Challenge

Another way to end your speech is by **challenging the audience.** This occurs when the speaker calls on the audience to think further about the topic. After speaking about his experiences as a mentee and mentor, Dominick concludes with the following:

> We all need help at some time or another. Children in our society are now at risk more than any time before. As citizens, it is our responsibility to ensure their safety. I challenge you today to think about the children in your family, place of worship, or community and how you might help them.

The Call for Action

There are times when you want to persuade your audience to act. This is known as a **call for action.** Such a call necessitates going a step further than presenting information. Although the conclusion still grows out of the presentation's central purpose, you make an effort to inspire, motivate, or move the members of your audience to take a stand, change their behavior, or act on their beliefs. Consider the following:

In closing, I want you to remember the words of Colin Powell. There are millions of children at risk today in our communities. We all must care enough to make a difference in these children's lives. If we don't do it, who will? So today, I want each of you to pledge to become a mentor to just one child. It could be a child in your family, from your place of worship, or from your community. If you don't know how to become a mentor or want more information, contact one of the organizations I discussed in my third main point. Again, if not us, then who?

The speaker calls the audience to act—to become involved as a mentor. What makes this call to action so effective is that the speaker has provided specific information on how to become involved. Audiences are more likely to follow through and take action if they are given specific instructions. In this case, the speaker provided the names and phone numbers of organizations that need mentors.

Writing Conclusions   **SKILL BUILDING**

1. Use the same topic from the last two skill-building activities to create two conclusions.
   a. Make sure each conclusion summarizes your thesis statement.
   b. Have one conclusion challenge the audience.
   c. Have the second conclusion call the audience to action.
2. Share your conclusions with other members of the class.
3. Use the feedback you receive to revise your conclusions.

Transitions

A **transition** provides a link between the main parts of your speech. There are three specific types of transitions: the transitional preview, the transitional summary, and the signpost. It helps to have a **transitional preview** after the introduction (to give your audience an idea of what is to come), to have transitions between the coordinate points in the body of your speech ("Now that I've explained the definition of mentoring, I'll move next to the effects of mentoring"), and to have a **transitional summary** before the conclusion (to recap all the coordinate points). Transitions show the relationships between the ideas in your speech, while transitional previews and summaries allow the audience to hear the main ideas several times. Because the audience can miss a point during your presentation, previews and summaries provide an additional chance for them to follow and understand your speech. **Signposts** help the audience know where you are in the speech. Phrases such as "My first main point" or

"In closing" help the audience follow along as you proceed through your presentation.

Preparing the Speech Outline

For help in preparing and delivering your speech, use a speech outline. There are two types of speech outlines: the full-sentence outline helps you construct or develop your topic (see the earlier section on "Outlining the Body" for more discussion); the key-phrase outline helps prepare you for your presentation to the audience.

Full-Sentence Outline

The first step in constructing your speech is to prepare a full-sentence outline—one that uses full sentences to list the major and minor points, as well as the different forms of support in your talk. This process helps you to clearly delineate the different parts of your speech. An added benefit of this exercise is that you will feel more confident that you are presenting a well thought-out speech. As you develop your full-sentence speech outline, keep these techniques in mind: (1) label the different parts of the speech, (2) use a consistent symbol system, and (3) attach a bibliography.

Your outline will be more effective if you take the time to label the different parts of your speech (introduction, transitional preview, body, transitional summary, conclusion). Make these labels in boldface print so that the different parts stand out. You can write these headings in the center of the page or place them off to the side.

As you construct your speech outline, it also is helpful to use a symbol system that follows standard outlining procedures. Those ideas of greater importance are placed farther to the left in the outline than ideas of lesser importance. The symbol system used in the following example shows the relationship between ideas. Major points are indicated by Roman numerals, subordinate points are designated by capital letters, followed by Arabic numerals for sub-subpoints.

When you develop a talk for a classroom presentation, you may be required to show the instructor the sources you used in gathering your information. These sources, including books, magazines, journals, newspapers, interviews, Internet sites, or audiovisual materials, should be listed in a bibliography that is attached to your full-sentence outline. Several style manuals exist that describe acceptable bibliography formats. Check with your instructor to see if there is a preferred one for your class. (See Chapter 12 for a more detailed treatment of this topic.)

We are ready to put together our speech on mentoring. First, we will write a full-sentence outline.

Introduction

I. According to Colin Powell, Secretary of State, "Up to fifteen million Americans today are at risk. They are at risk of growing up unskilled, unlearned or even worse, unloved. They are at risk of growing up physically or psychologically abused. They are at risk of growing up addicted to the pathologies and poisons of the street. They are at risk of bringing up children into the world before they, themselves have grown up. They are at risk of never growing up at all. Fifteen million young lives are at risk, may not make it unless we care enough to do something about it (1997, p. 484)." Powell and others believe mentoring is the way to save these children.

II. To understand the role that mentoring children plays in our community, we will discuss the definition, benefits, and local opportunities for mentoring.

III. Twenty years ago, I was not the same person I am today. I was only eight years old and was wild! I didn't listen to my mother or grandmother, who lived with us, nor did I listen to my teachers at school. I was a pretty troubled kid. Out of desperation, my mother signed me up at the local community center for a mentoring program. My mentor, Archie, became my best friend and saved my life. Today, Archie and I are still very close and I have become a mentor to a young man named Simon. In my presentation, I will share my experiences as a mentee and as a mentor. In addition, I will share the information I found about the role of mentoring in our society.

Signpost

IV. My first main idea is the definition of mentoring. Any definition of mentoring must include a discussion of who are the mentors and mentees.

Body

I. The definition of mentoring includes the mentors and mentees.
   A. According to the Office of Mentoring Programs of Maryland, mentoring is "a supportive, trusting one-to-one relationship between a caring adult or youth and a school-aged child" (2001, p. 1).
   B. A mentor has the following characteristics: dependable, patient and caring, good listener, self-confident, and conscientious (Office of Mentoring Programs, 2001). According to R. Gilligan, a Senior Lecturer in Social Work, the mentor, "involves encouraging talents and interests in the young person which help build confidence, self-esteem and social skills" (1999, p. 190).
   C. Over fifteen million children are "at risk" in the United States today, according to Colin Powell, Secretary of State (1997, p. 484).

Transition

Let's now turn to a discussion of the benefits of mentoring.

II. There are several benefits for the mentees and mentors.
   A. The most important benefit for the mentee is the validation of self. According to Gilligan, "mentors may be important in validating, in the young person's eyes, the young person's effort, ability and personal qualities" (1999, p. 191).
      1. The increase in self-esteem helps students to stay in school.
      2. The increase in self-esteem and confidence helps students do better in school.
      3. Validation by a mentor helps students to avoid risk-taking behavior such as engaging in sexual intercourse, using drugs, and joining gangs.
   B. The benefits for the mentor include self-satisfaction and increased learning about children and youth. According to Kathryn Taaffe McLearn et al. in an article entitled, "Child Health: Mentoring Makes a Difference," mentors find the relationship with youth highly satisfying and rewarding, and say they would do it again (2001, p. 3).

Transitional Summary

Having defined mentoring and discussed the benefits of mentoring, I'd like to inform you about opportunities for mentoring in our community.

III. There are several opportunities to become a mentor in our community.
   A. According to our local United Way, several organizations need mentors. The United Way can be reached at (219) 923-2302.
   B. Some of these include:
      1. LACASA (Latin American Community Alliance for Support and Assistance) can be reached at (219) 884-0095.
      2. The Boys and Girls Clubs of Northwest Indiana provides a variety of educational, social, and recreational programs for boys and girls, ages seven to seventeen. They can be reached at (219) 887-2020.

Signpost

In closing, I would like to summarize my main ideas.

Conclusion

I. We have discussed the children who need mentoring and the adults who serve as mentors. We have also discussed the benefits of mentoring for both the mentee and the mentor. Finally, I have provided you with some places you might want to contact to become a mentor in our community.

II. I want you to remember the words of Colin Powell. There are millions of children at risk today in our communities. We all must care enough to make a difference in these children's lives. If we don't do it, who will? So today, I want each of you to pledge to become a mentor to just one child. It could be a child in your family, from your place of worship, or from your community. If you don't know how to become a mentor or want more information, contact one of the organizations I discussed in my third main point. Again, if not us, then who?

Developing a Full-Sentence Outline   **CRITICAL THINKING**

1. Using the principles of effective outlining, create a full-sentence outline for one of the following topics:

   a. Human rights

   b. Balancing work and school

   c. Olympic Games

   d. Budgeting home expenses

   e. Finding adequate child care

2. Be sure to include sections for the introduction, body, conclusion, and transitions.

Key-Phrase Outline

While the intent of a full-sentence outline is to help you develop the ideas in your speech, the purpose of a key-phrase outline is to help you to prepare your delivery. The **key-phrase outline** is an abbreviated version of the full-sentence outline that is intended as a cue to each point in your presentation. Use it to practice your delivery.

Consider the following points as you develop this outline. First, convert the major points in your full-sentence outline from full sentences to key phrases. You may still need to include complete word-for-word quotes in your outline to ensure you communicate someone else's words accurately. Second, use standard outlining procedures: Roman numerals, capital letters, Arabic numbers. Third, space generously between the lines (key phrases) in your outline so that you can easily follow along during the delivery of your speech. It is easy to lose your place during the delivery when the outline is crowded or cluttered. Finally, insert directions or cues regarding delivery, such as *pause, slow down,* and *eye contact.* The necessity for these notes will become apparent as you practice your delivery.

Let's convert our full-sentence outline on mentoring into a key-phrase outline we could use to practice our delivery.

Introduction

I. According to Colin Powell, Secretary of State, "Up to fifteen million Americans today are at risk. They are at risk of growing up unskilled, unlearned or even worse, unloved. They are at risk of growing up physically or psychologically abused. They are at risk of growing up addicted to the pathologies and poisons of the street. They are at risk of bringing up children into the world before they, themselves have grown up. They are at risk of never growing up at all. Fifteen million young lives are at risk, may not make it unless we care enough to do something about it" (1997, p. 484). *(Calm down)*

II. Mentoring in our community
   A. Who are the mentees and mentors
   B. Benefits
   C. Local opportunities

III. My experiences as mentee and mentor

Signpost

IV. First main point

(Pause)

Body

I. Definition
   A. According to the Office of Mentoring Programs of Maryland, mentoring is "a supportive, trusting one-to-one relationship between a caring adult or youth and a school-aged child" (2001, p. 1).

(Eye contact with entire audience)

   B. Mentors
      1. Dependable
      2. Patient and caring
      3. Good listener
      4. Self-confident
      5. According to R. Gilligan, a Senior Lecturer in Social Work, the mentor, "involves encouraging talents and interests in the young person which help build confidence, self-esteem and social skills" (1999, p. 190).
   C. Fifteen million children at risk, Colin Powell

Transition

Turn to next point

II. Benefits of mentoring

A. Validation of self for mentee.
B. According to Gilligan, "mentors may be important in validating, in the young person's eyes, the young person's effort, ability and personal qualities" (1999, p. 191).
   1. Helps student stay in school
   2. Helps student do better in school
   3. Avoid risk-taking behavior
      a. Sexual intercourse
      b. Using drugs
      c. Joining gangs
C. Mentors satisfied.
D. Mentors would do it again.
E. According to Kathryn Taaffe McLearn et al. in an article entitled, "Child Health: Mentoring Makes a Difference," mentors find the relationship with youth highly satisfying and rewarding, and say they would do it again (2001, p. 3).

Transitional Summary

Definition and benefits discussed

(Pause)

III. Local Opportunities
   A. LACASA (219) 884-0095
   B. Boys and Girls Clubs (219) 887-2020

(Remember eye contact)

Signpost

In closing

Conclusion

  I. Discussed definition, benefits, local opportunities for mentoring

(Pause)

  II. Remember Powell's words, who will help the children?

Developing a Key-Phrase Outline   **CRITICAL THINKING**

1. Use the same topic you selected from the critical-thinking activity on page 301. Convert it from full sentences to key phrases.
2. Use the key phrases to practice delivering this speech.
3. Insert notes to yourself at appropriate points to make your delivery more effective.

Ethics in Communication

Organizing Your Speech

In the beginning of this chapter, we read about Adam and his informative speech to his classmates in their Introduction to Sociology course. Like all speakers, it is Adam's responsibility to make his presentation as easy as possible for his classmates to listen to, and he must communicate his ideas clearly so they can be understood by the audience. The way to ensure that his presentation is effective and ethical is for Adam to present a well-organized speech. Specifically, Adam's speech must:

1. be logically organized. His ideas need to be in some sequence or order. Using one of the patterns (causal, problem/solution, spatial, time, and topical) we have discussed can easily organize his ideas.
2. have discrete main ideas that can stand alone. Each of his main ideas should be fully developed.
3. have a limited number of main ideas. Too many ideas can clutter the speech and not allow Adam to fully develop his most important ideas.
4. gain the attention of the audience in the introduction. Adam must create interest in his topic for the audience. This will ensure that his audience listens to his ideas as he progresses through the presentation.
5. establish Adam's credibility. As the speaker, Adam must inform the audience about why he is credible to speak on the topic of mentoring. He should discuss his past experience as a mentor and the extensive research he has done to prepare his ideas.
6. conclude by reiterating his thesis statement or main ideas. Adam must remind the audience of his main ideas to ensure they remember the information.
7. link together the main ideas using transitions throughout the presentation. Adam will make it easier for his audience to listen to his speech if he joins his three main ideas together into one speech. Using transitions will make it easier for his audience to listen to his presentation.
8. be delivered using a key-word or key-phrase outline. This will allow Adam to cue himself to the main ideas he has developed as he speaks before his classmates.

Adam's responsibility to ethically and effectively develop and deliver his speech can be met by following these guidelines.

Summary

This chapter provided discussions on the major parts of your speech and how to prepare a speech outline. The body is the main part of your speech. The ideas in that body often form patterns that provide a framework for arranging your speech more effectively; these patterns include causal order, problem/solution, spatial order, time order, and topic order.

The chapter also promoted outlining the body to help with your speech's development. Among the outlining principles discussed were the following: (1) an outline consists of coordinate and subordinate points, (2) each idea in an outline is discrete, and (3) the number of major ideas should be limited.

The introduction serves three purposes: to draw the audience's attention, to establish your credibility as a speaker, and to provide information about the topic. You can use a narrative, a startling statement, a rhetorical question, or a quotation to introduce your speech.

The conclusion signals the end of your speech. It also reinforces the central ideas in the speech and indicates what you would like the audience to do after the speech has ended. The conclusion can take various forms, including the summation, the challenge, and the call for action.

Transitions provide a link between the main parts of your speech. By previewing and summarizing ideas, they provide an additional opportunity for the audience to follow the speech. Signposts allow your audience to follow along with you as you proceed through the presentation.

Ideally, as a speaker you should use two outlines to prepare your speech. The first, a full-sentence outline, is meant to assist you in developing the ideas you wish to include in your speech. In preparing this outline, such principles as coordination and subordination, discreteness, labeling the parts of the speech, and a consistent symbol system are followed. The second outline, consisting of key phrases drawn from the full-sentence outline, is intended as an aid for the speech delivery (more about this in Chapter 14).

Review Questions

1. Briefly describe the major parts of a speech.
2. Describe five ways to organize the ideas in the body of your speech.
3. What is the difference between coordinate and subordinate points?
4. Explain the three purposes of an introduction.
5. Identify the four different ways to introduce your speech.
6. Differentiate between a challenge and a call for action in the conclusion.
7. What is the primary purpose of a transition?
8. What are the benefits of preparing a full-sentence outline?
9. Why would you use a key-phrase outline?

14

Delivering Your Speech

At the conclusion of this chapter, you should be able to:

- Explain the differences between oral and written communication.
- Identify four factors that help control speech anxiety.
- Recognize the four types of delivery.
- Understand the importance of spontaneity and sincerity in speech delivery.

- Discuss six ways to use your body to enhance your delivery.
- Identify five ways that your voice can improve your delivery.

Professor Nancy Webber, Director of the Women's Studies Department, has been invited to speak to the City Economic Council on job training for women. She is excited about the opportunity to talk about this topic because she has written several books about training women to rejoin the workforce.

She has lectured about this topic many times in her classes. But, preparing for this speech, she realizes that she will be speaking in a different situation and to a different kind of audience. For example, she won't know the members of the audience as she does when she lectures to her students. Also, the group will be larger than she is used to and the setting will be much more formal. Her lecture notes will not work in this speaking situation.

For the speech before the City Economic Council, Professor Webber decides to write her comments out word for word and to create several charts and graphs to use as presentational aids. Although the content may be the same as what she discusses with her students in class, Professor Webber's delivery will not.

There is not one right way to deliver a speech. Multiple types of delivery are possible depending on the audience, situation, and your own talents. It is best to find your own voice and the best approach for you and that situation, as Professor Webber has done. In this chapter, we will discuss the options you have for effectively delivering your speech. Effective speakers appreciate the different approaches to communication an audience brings to the interaction. Through thorough self- and audience analysis and practice, you can decide what is the best option for you.

Delivery is usually the most dreaded aspect of the speaking situation. Understandably, people feel self-conscious when they are standing in front of an audience. Fear of rejection is an overwhelming factor in public speaking; however, learning what to do in order to feel comfortable during speech delivery can lead to improved self-confidence. An audience views a composed public speaker as a confident communicator with a message worth listening to. Furthermore, the positive feedback received from the audience reinforces your self-confidence.

We are all afraid that we aren't "doing it right" and that the audience will reject us. It is essential that your delivery style be appropriate for your audience and the situation. Thorough analysis of your talents and skills and of the audience will help you to understand the diverse frames of reference you need to consider when delivering your speech. We begin this chapter with a discussion of the differences between oral and written communication. Many of us mistakenly believe that the speech is just an essay read aloud. To deliver your ideas effectively, you must understand the nature of oral and written communication.

Oral and Written Communication

There are several aspects of oral communication that make it very different from written communication. Public communication is not just a message read aloud to an audience. First, the speech is a cooperative act between the speaker and the audience. Remember from Chapter 1 that all communication is an interdependent process. Your audience will be right with you and will provide immediate feedback to you. An effective speaker will adjust to the audience's feedback. Written communication does not allow for immediate feedback and does not allow the sender the opportunity to adjust to the audience's diverse approaches to the communication situation.

Second, the speaker's priority is to make it easy for the audience to hear the message. Remember in Chapter 3, we discussed how difficult it is to listen. You can help your audience listen by making your message simple, informal, personal, and vivid. In a written message, the writer has the luxury of using complex, formal messages, as the receiver can reread and review the message. Your audience will only listen to your message once. There is no opportunity to replay your speech.

TABLE 14.1 Oral Communication

- Is a cooperative act between speaker and a diverse audience.
- Provides immediate feedback to the sender.
- Must be simple, informal, personal, and vivid.
- Contains both intentional and unintentional nonverbal messages.

Lastly, you must be concerned about all the intentional and unintentional nonverbal messages you send as well as the nonverbal feedback your audience will be giving you. In written communication, nonverbal messages are of little or no concern to the writer or the reader.

In the rest of this chapter, we will discuss specific ways to improve your delivery and to understand the interactive process of public communication. To that end, we will focus on the different types of delivery, sharing ideas, bodily action, and voice quality and control. Incorporating the techniques that are natural to you will help you to deliver your speech more effectively and, in turn, lead to greater confidence when you are giving a speech.

Oral and Written Communication SKILL BUILDING

Find an essay you have written for another class. Read it aloud.

1. How does it sound? Do you think an audience could easily listen to it?
2. How could you change the essay so that it could be delivered orally?
3. How might the diversity of the audience affect your delivery?

Understanding Speech Anxiety

Although most people like to talk in informal settings, many have a genuine fear of delivering a public speech. Personal concerns about how others perceive us are intensified when we speak in public. The internal tension is understandable; no one likes being rejected—the greatest fear associated with public speaking. Unlike writing in a diary or turning in a project to an instructor, our public speeches are visible to an entire audience.

While there is no magic formula to dispel your fear of public speaking, you can take comfort in knowing that your nervousness can be significantly reduced by following a plan. This plan requires that you follow several of the points mentioned in Chapters 11, 12, and 13: select an appropriate topic, analyze your audience, find supporting materials to incorporate in your speech, and organize your ideas and support into a logical presentation. As a result of doing this extensive preparation, you will know where your speech is going and what you are about. You will have become the expert on your topic and know how to relate your ideas to your diverse audience. All your hard work will pay off by translating into a feeling of confidence that you are well prepared and that you will not be caught off guard.

A few additional pointers can help you deliver your speech with less apprehension: control excess tension, focus on the topic, remember that you are not alone, and develop a positive attitude.

Control Excess Tension

When told that they must deliver a speech, most people generally feel nervous. It's as if the word *speech* triggers an alarm. Nervousness often manifests itself in tension; it is possible, however, to use your body in a way that allows you to reduce the excess energy caused by tension. Merely taking a deep breath or a few steps away from the lectern may help free your body of extra energy. These small efforts will help you feel more relaxed when delivering your speech.

Focus on the Topic and Audience Feedback

Concentrating on what you are talking about, rather than thinking about the fact that you are standing in front of an audience, is an important step in reducing speech apprehension. Concentrating on your message helps reduce your anxiety because you stop focusing on your role and instead direct your energy toward the treatment of your topic. It is also important to remember that the audience is a vital part of the speech process and their feedback can help you succeed. If you have done thorough audience analysis, you know what diverse approaches the audience has brought to your speech and you know how to adjust accordingly. Once you take the focus off yourself, you will be able to share your ideas with the audience. These ideas and the audience need to be the center of attention, not you! A second important factor, then, is to select a topic in which you are genuinely interested (see Chapter 11 for a more complete discussion of selecting a topic). Consider the following:

> Gale is a single mother of three young daughters and is working on a degree in social work at night. At least once a month, Gale volunteers as a "Big Sister" at the local YWCA. She strongly believes in giving back to her community and has seen how the children in her neighborhood have been changed positively by the Big Brothers/Big Sisters program. She decides to persuade her fellow classmates to volunteer their time. Gale feels passionately about her topic and becomes very involved in the

process of persuading her audience. Her audience gets caught up in Gale's enthusiasm and provides her with overwhelmingly positive nonverbal feedback by shaking their heads and smiling. As a result, Gale forgets about being nervous in front of her audience.

Remember That You Are Not Alone

Try to place the speech experience in its proper perspective. It is likely that several members of your audience have been in your shoes before, so they can empathize with your nervousness over speaking in public. People are basically kind. They do not want to see you fail. Perhaps this example will demonstrate our point: Have you ever been backstage in a theater when an actor forgot his or her lines? The audience did not laugh or ridicule the actor; instead, they remained quiet and probably empathized with the performer.

Develop a Positive Attitude

When you get up in front of your audience, it helps to remember that you have prepared something worthwhile to say to them. Since you are the person who has researched, developed, and organized your subject, no one will know your topic as well as you. In addition, the way you have decided to handle your topic probably depends on your values, attitudes, and past experiences. Even a simple assignment gives you an opportunity to bring your own rich background to the speaking experience. Condition yourself to think, "I have something interesting to share with others."

This positive attitude can carry over to your audience. Being involved in your presentation communicates a feeling of confidence to the audience. In turn, you should feel more comfortable because you will be able to observe the audience's involvement in your presentation. Remember that you are a unique individual who has something special to share with

FoxTrot   by Bill Amend

FOXTROT © Bill Amend. Reprinted with permission of UNIVERSAL PRESS SYNDICATE. All rights reserved.

the audience. There is no one "right" way to deliver a speech. An understanding of your individual approach to the speaking situation and your appreciation for your audience's approaches to the topic can only increase your confidence. Believe in your ability to share ideas. You do it all the time with your friends, work associates, and family.

CRITICAL THINKING   Speech Anxiety

Jackie is a student in your Communication class. The thought of having to deliver a speech is so threatening to her that she is seriously thinking about dropping the class. In a small group, discuss the following:

1. In what ways can Jackie control some of the anxiety she feels?
2. How can Jackie use her unique approach to communication to alleviate her anxiety?
3. What role does the audience play in helping Jackie feel more at ease?
4. What can you suggest from your own experiences to help Jackie cope with her fear?

CHECKLIST   Understanding Speech Anxiety

- Control excess tension by taking a deep breath and taking a few small steps away from the lectern.
- Focus on the topic and audience by thinking about what you are sharing with the audience.
- Remember that you are not alone and others can understand your nervousness.
- Develop a positive attitude by remembering you have something unique and interesting to share.

SELF-ASSESSMENT   Understanding Your Speech Anxiety

Everyone who gives a speech is afraid or nervous. Speech anxiety is normal. In an essay, discuss the following:

1. When you think about giving your first speech, what frightens you the most?

2. What strategies can you use to combat your fears?
3. How can you use your anxiety to your advantage?

Types of Delivery

Four methods of delivery can be used to share information in public. Each, of course, has its own place in a communication situation. However, certain methods appear to be more advantageous than others. Depending on your talents, the speaking situation, the topic, and your audience, one of these methods will be more effective. Described below are the different methods of delivery.

The Impromptu Speech

What is the usual response when someone is asked to deliver an impromptu speech? Panic comes to mind! An impromptu speech is delivered without advance preparation or practice. Although difficult for the student, the impromptu speech has its benefits. An instructor may want to give his or her students an opportunity to "think on their feet" and at the same time expose them to being in front of the class. The typical introductory speech on the first day of class helps fulfill this goal. In this context, the impromptu delivery represents a useful tool. On a more practical level, business seminars or meetings frequently give rise to impromptu speeches.

For example, the assistant director of the botanical garden asks Jerry to summarize his findings on the viability of instituting a continuing education program for the community. Although Jerry has no advance notice, he talks about the program to the staff members at the meeting. In this situation, the impromptu speech came about as a natural part of the meeting. Despite Jerry's success in the preceding example, the impromptu speech generally does little to bolster a speaker's confidence. After just a few minutes, the presentation commonly becomes repetitive, which causes the speaker to become self-conscious and nervous.

To give an impromptu speech simply because you have failed to prepare comments ahead of time communicates to your audience that you really did not care about your responsibility enough to adequately prepare for your talk. An ill-prepared speaker does not gain the respect of the audience. As a speaker, your credibility and confidence will be diminished if the audience perceives you as either unprepared or uncaring.

The Manuscript Speech

If you were in a position of authority, like the President of the United States, it would be appropriate for you to use a manuscript speech, one delivered from a prepared script. Consider President Bush's delicate position after the September 11, 2001, attacks. When he spoke to the nation, the public was looking to the President for reassurances that everything was being done to catch the attackers and that the government was keeping our country safe. In addition, the world was watching to see what the United States' response would be to the attacks. The gravity of the situation required that Bush use a manuscript in which each word was painstakingly selected.

It is unlikely that you would find yourself in a situation of such magnitude; however, there are circumstances where a manuscript speech is appropriate, even desirable. If, for example, you are asked to explain new company procedures or describe the steps used in cardiopulmonary resuscitation (CPR), where accuracy is essential, a prepared manuscript is beneficial. The purpose of the manuscript is to keep you focused on your speech.

There are drawbacks, however. Because the manuscript speech is extremely precise, it is apt to be mechanical, lack spontaneity, and stifle interaction with the audience. It does not allow you to respond to the feedback you will receive from the audience. Some speakers even plan their gestures in advance. Indeed, it is a rare individual who can appear fresh when such minute details are orchestrated beforehand. If you must use a manuscript, make every effort to appear to be talking to your audience instead of reading lines to them. Remember from the beginning of this chapter, a speech is not the same as an essay. Consider the following:

> Myra Crandall is the newly elected president of the Southridge Elementary School Parent-Teacher Organization and a stepmother to two boys in first and third grades. As an administrative assistant to the plant manager at Rey Manufacturing, she does very little public speaking. Myra is nervous about the acceptance address she must deliver at her installation because she doubts her ability to speak in public. She writes out her entire speech ahead of time and essentially reads it to the group. When she looks at the audience, she sees people gazing around the room in a sure sign of boredom.

Manuscript delivery is undoubtedly difficult to master. Obviously, Myra's delivery was lacking in the preceding illustration. Successful delivery takes considerable time, practice, and familiarity with the types of situations that necessitate its use.

The Memorized Speech

The type of delivery that requires the greatest investment of time is the memorized speech. The speaker not only develops the complete manuscript, but he or she also spends additional time memorizing it word for word. When would a speaker choose to memorize a speech? Perhaps in these cases: when delivering a eulogy, making a sales pitch (especially if it has proven to be successful in the past), or toasting the bride and groom at a wedding. In each of these situations, considerable effort has gone into preparing the message and selecting appropriate words; the speaker wants to communicate his or her thoughts exactly as planned.

Delivering a memorized speech has its drawbacks, most notably the difficulty in maintaining spontaneity. As with the manuscript speech, it does not allow you to adjust to the audience feedback. There is an additional pitfall to the memorized presentation, one that most experienced instructors have seen snare the inexperienced speaker: countless students forget a word or a phrase midway through their speech, lose their composure, and out of desperation return to the beginning of the speech to start again.

If you practice a speech sufficiently before giving it to your audience, a certain degree of familiarity results. Because you are now familiar with the ideas in your speech, you probably will not be shaken if a particular word or phrase escapes you during the pressure of the speaking situation. Unless your instructor asks you to memorize a speech for a specific assignment, try to avoid doing so.

Let us say that you need to memorize a phone number as part of a message you will later relay to a friend. Since you do not have a pencil and paper, you recite the numbers until they are committed to memory. While engaged in this task, you try your best to visualize the numbers. This seemingly simple task requires a great deal of concentration. When considered on these terms, the business of memorizing a speech suddenly becomes enormous. Nearly all the speaker's energy in this type of delivery is focused on remembering words, rather than on sharing ideas with an audience. The process of memorizing leaves little or no time for concentrating on how you deliver the speech to your audience.

The Extemporaneous Speech

The type of delivery that combines the best features of the preceding methods is the extemporaneous delivery. An extemporaneous speech is thoroughly prepared and practiced, but it is delivered in a conversational style. In an extemporaneous delivery, the emphasis is placed on sharing ideas that have been researched and analyzed. The speaker often uses note cards or an outline while delivering the talk and can enjoy some flexibility with the audience because he or she has prepared, organized, and practiced his or her thoughts in advance. This allows the speaker to respond to the feedback he or she receives from the audience.

Extemporaneous delivery implies that the speaker has a thorough knowledge and understanding of the topic and an intelligent plan to present it. It avoids the stilted, formal presentation inherent in the manuscript speech or memorized speech. In addition, it suggests to the audience that

Ethics in Communication

Delivering Your Presentation

Professor Nancy Webber has been invited to speak to the City Economic Council on job training for women in their community, a topic that Professor Webber knows much about. Thus, much of what she will present to the Council is the same as the material she would present in one of her classes. But the audience is different, and the situation is certainly different. How can she ensure that her delivery will be both effective and ethical when she speaks to the Council?

First, Professor Webber must consider the diverse audience and their approaches to communication. The men and women of the Economic Council have many different types of experiences, knowledge, and perception than her students might have. This audience will have a different motivation for listening to her (they need her information to help formulate a plan), and they have different types of expectations for the interaction (they do not wish to be lectured to and want the opportunity to ask questions). If Professor Webber does not take all of this into account when planning her delivery, her audience may not listen to her, and she will be speaking ineffectively and unethically.

Second, the situation must be considered when determining the type of delivery to use. How formal should she be in her dress and voice quality? A more formal dress will help her establish her credibility and a formal voice quality will project confidence and expertness, qualities that are essential to create a favorable first impression. What is the size of the audience? This

has a direct bearing on her use of presentational aids, eye contact, and voice quality. Her classroom only holds twenty-five students, but in this speech, she will be speaking in a much larger room. Effective and ethical delivery demands that she consider the situation in which she will be speaking.

Third, as she delivers her presentation, Professor Webber must pay close attention to audience feedback. In order to effectively get her message across, she must be able to adjust her delivery to audience feedback. She cannot ignore the nonverbal messages being sent by her audience. In this sense, her delivery will be similar to her classroom lecture. Every speaker must take into account audience feedback.

Fourth, in order to create immediacy with her audience and to ensure that they feel a part of the interaction, Professor Webber must be sincere and spontaneous. She must be natural in her delivery and needs to show the audience she cares about the topic, its presentation, and the audience.

Lastly, it is imperative that Professor Webber be herself. She must use her own style and voice in her delivery. In other words, pretending to be someone or something she is not would be ineffective (not sincere or spontaneous) and certainly not ethical.

Should Professor Webber ignore her audience and their diverse approaches to communication, the situation constraints, and audience feedback, her delivery would clearly be ineffective. She would be speaking *at* her audience, not engaging them in the communication process. Communication is, above all, an interdependent process, and it is the speaker's responsibility to ensure that the audience is included in the process. Only then will the speaker's delivery be both effective and ethical.

the speaker is trying to interact with them, because the speaker's language is more spontaneous and the response to audience feedback is more immediate. This feeling helps keep the audience involved because their diverse perspectives can be acknowledged.

Perhaps one of the most successful moments in speechmaking in recent history occurred when Martin Luther King, Jr., spoke extemporaneously at the Lincoln Memorial in 1963. His ringing words proclaimed "I have a dream." The moment is captured by Reverend Ralph Abernathy:

> It is the usual custom of a preacher as he finishes a prepared text to say some other words. Here he establishes eye contact with his audience. On this day, Martin Luther King's speech really began when he left his text. He said, "I have a dream," in a very musical voice, and he lifted his hands in oration. As he lifted his hands, the people lifted theirs, and he went on. "I have a dream that one day on the red hills of Georgia, the sons of former slaves and the sons of former slave owners will be able to sit down together at the table of brotherhood . . . I have a dream that my four little children will one day live in a nation where they will not be judged by the color of their skin, but by the content of their character." People were standing on their seats, yelling, "Amen!" and those who were not standing began to applaud. He was calling for integration at its best, for the tearing down of walls of an unjust system. He was expressing the longings, hopes, and dreams of every person in that assembly of 250,000 people. He took the audience higher and higher, and as he left, the entire group rose to its feet. It was one of the greatest moments in the history of our nation (1977, p. 94).

In Abernathy's words, the key moment in King's speech was the point where he began to extemporize. His attempts at audience involvement were an immediate success. On a lesser scale, King's skills as a public speaker can be compared with others you may know. Consider the following:

> Harriet Gaynor teaches Economics 200, a required course for all liberal arts and sciences students at Western University. Over the years, Gaynor has developed a reputation on campus as a superior lecturer. She teaches multiple sections of this course. Much of her success is a result of the tremendous amount of time she spends preparing her material. She practices each lecture to become familiar with the ideas she wishes to present. Although she brings the same outline to each section of Economics 200,

Rev. Dr. Martin Luther King delivers his "I Have a Dream" speech.

the words she delivers to each class differ. Her choice of words grows out of her relationship with each class. The humor, pace, and movement in each lecture depends on the feedback she receives from her class. Specifically, Gaynor's morning class includes mostly traditional students, eighteen to twenty-two years of age, while her night class consists of nontraditional students who work full time during the day and attend college classes at night. Her delivery during her night class is more flamboyant, loud, and energetic. She does this in an attempt to maintain their attention. She also varies her examples, depending on the makeup of the class.

Professor Gaynor's ability to rely on the extemporaneous delivery has contributed to her success as a speaker and teacher. She is able to adapt to the

TABLE 14.2 Types of Delivery

Impromptu	No advance preparation or practice
Manuscript	Delivered from a prepared script
Memorized	Manuscript committed to memory
Extemporaneous	Prepared, practiced, but conversational in style

different attributes, attitudes, and interests of her students. The flexibility and adaptability inherent in the extemporaneous delivery allow for a degree of give and take between speaker and audience.

Sharing Ideas

Every speech delivery is enhanced by the speaker's ability to share ideas. The more a speaker can concentrate on the ideas in the speech rather than on himself or herself or the speaking situation, the more likely the receiver also will concentrate on those ideas. In other words, the speaker's goal is to get his or her audience just as involved in the subject as he or she is. This objective is possible only if the speaker is genuinely interested in the topic. A lukewarm attitude will not get the audience's attention. The individual who is able to concentrate on sharing his or her ideas will develop into a more confident, effective speaker. Several factors discussed in this section will aid the speaker in confidently communicating with the audience.

Developing an Awareness of the Qualities of Effective Speech Delivery   **CRITICAL THINKING**

1. Name a speaker you most admire
2. List several of his or her positive communication behaviors when delivering a speech.
3. How does this person adjust to the diversity of the audience?
4. How does this person use his or her own unique talents to enhance speaking effectiveness?

Spontaneity

Just as involvement leads to greater sharing of ideas, so too does a feeling of spontaneity with the audience. Spontaneity refers to a speaker's apparent natural behavior at the time of delivery. As a speaker's involvement with the topic increases and his or her concentration becomes focused on ideas and audience, he or she sends signals of spontaneity and immediacy that are absent from memorized and manuscript deliveries. Words chosen spontaneously convey to an audience that the sender both is interested in the topic and wants to share his or her ideas. Not only are the words more appropriate to the specific audience, but the accompanying vocal inflections add to the interest, further capturing the attention of the audience.

The same is true of movements and gestures (see Chapter 5). The speaker may not be aware of facial expressions, gestures, or bodily movements, but when spontaneous, these reiterate the desire to share. For example, a preplanned gesture, such as mechanically pointing a finger when a certain word is said, can communicate an aura of superficiality. However, the same gesture made spontaneously will help draw the audience more completely into the talk.

Sincerity

Another key component to sharing ideas is the incorporation of sincerity into the presentation; that is, a speaker wants to show the audience that he or she cares about the topic, its presentation, and the audience. By doing so, the speaker may capture the audience's interest in the topic. The speaker wants to start a chain reaction from speaker to audience. In turn, the positive feedback he or she gets from the audience will help the speaker feel more confident during the speech and in subsequent speeches as well. Audience support builds confidence.

Using Your Body

Effective use of your body is another way to enhance your speech. Your nonverbal communication can convey as much to the audience as the words in your speech. In fact, your bodily actions can reinforce the major ideas in the presentation. Becoming aware of some of the ways to use your body to increase audience involvement and understanding is highly desirable. Many components contribute to the role your body plays in delivering a speech, including gestures, facial expressions, walking transitions, appearance, posture, and eye contact (see Chapter 5 for a detailed discussion of nonverbal behavior).

Gestures

Hand movement in a speech delivery should be spontaneous; in other words, it should naturally stem from the speaker's involvement with the subject. Your hands can be used to emphasize or clarify your ideas.

Gestures are useful only as long as they remain natural. Adding gestures for the sake of incorporating movement into the delivery will detract from, not enhance, your presentation. President Bill Clinton, for example, would point his finger aggressively in an effort to drive home his points. This was no more apparent than during the Monica Lewinsky scandal. When confronted with allegations of a sexual affair, Clinton definitely pointed his finger at the press and said, "I did not have sexual relations with that woman, Monica Lewinsky" (January 26, 1998). His nonverbal message enhanced his verbal message and further emphasized his denial. The gesture appeared spontaneous and real.

Facial Expressions

Your face usually communicates your feelings, so use it to help communicate your message to the audience. As with gestures, your facial expressions should be spontaneous, arising naturally from your involvement with your topic. Allowing the audience to see your commitment to your topic also may elicit their interest; knowing that you have the audience's attention gives your confidence as a public speaker a welcome boost. Good technique obviously has its rewards.

We can look to the 2000 presidential primary race for an example of inappropriate use of facial expression. George W. Bush was often criticized

A speaker's facial expressions can enhance or detract from his or her credibility.

for his "smirk." Bush's facial expressions often gave the impression he was not serious or sincere. This hindered his ability to convey his credibility to the voters. In contrast, consider the following example, in which a natural expression of emotion is displayed to the audience:

> For her informative speech, Susan decides to draw from her experience as an aide at the Bollingstone Nursing Home as the basis for her speech. Specifically, she focuses on the relationship she had developed with one of her patients. Over the course of a few months, Susan had come to know Mrs. Steele. This bright woman had been in the nursing home for two years, and she deeply resented what her life had become. In their frequent conversations Susan was successful in getting Mrs. Steele to let her guard down. What this woman feared most was slipping into senility, as so many of the other nursing home residents had already done. For both women, this admission was charged with emotion. Susan's insight into the elderly was deepened by this experience, and she focuses her speech on this important event. While describing the situation to her audience, Susan's tear-filled eyes clearly expressed her emotions. This natural expression captured the attention and support of the class.

Walking Transitions

Foot movement can also be used to enhance your talk. More important, foot movement can help the speaker decrease the amount of physical distance between himself or herself and the audience. Foot movement has the benefit of reducing the speaker's dependency on the lectern. It also allows the speaker to divert some of his or her excess energy, thereby relieving the mental anxiety associated with talking before an audience. Taking a step or two forward to emphasize a point or turning slightly during a transition captures the group's attention and shows your involvement with the presentation.

When incorporating walking transitions, make sure that they grow out of your involvement with the presentation. They should not detract from your speech. If you have a reason to move about, you will avoid overuse. When you appear relaxed enough to move about in front of your audience, your efforts will contribute to a greater sense of confidence on your part.

Appearance

The speaker's appearance also communicates a message to the audience. The members of the audience see you before they hear you speak; consequently, their first impression of you can be shaped by your appearance. In formal settings we see political speakers paying particular attention to their appearance. Al Gore, for example, changed his appearance during the 2000 primary elections. Gore, trailing in some polls behind Bill Bradley, traded the traditional navy blue suit and red tie for an earth tone suit and blue

Democratic presidential candidate Al Gore changed his appearance several times during the 2000 campaign.

shirt. This shift in appearance was intended to help Gore attract female voters. This example reflects the need for speakers to understand the diversity of their audiences and to adjust their style accordingly.

Although personal attire does not play a significant role in classroom speeches, you should make sure that your appearance does not draw the audience away from your intended message. For example, a wild hairdo will surely distract the audience. You do not want the audience to pay more attention to what you are wearing than to what you are saying to them. In fact, if your audience's attention is focused on your appearance, it is probably safe to say that your appearance is doing you a disservice. In deciding what to wear, consider both the audience and the nature of the speaking situation. For example, a talk with high school students about drug abuse would call for casual attire (no suits), while a presentation to a group of business managers would call for a suit (no jeans with sweaters). Both audiences would likely be uncomfortable if the speakers dressed differently. You should use your appearance to enhance your credibility, if possible. For example, if you were giving a speech on the importance of yearly veterinarian visits for pets, you might wear the uniform you wear as a veterinary assistant. Your uniform will communicate your expertise and will also help you feel more confident.

Posture

Good posture is one aspect of bodily action that commands the attention of your audience. When speaking in front of a group, avoid slouching or bending your knees; keep your spine straight, your shoulders back, and your feet a comfortable distance apart. You do not, however, want to look like a soldier standing at attention. Avoid a rigid stance because it communicates that you are tense and inhibits any other natural movement. Avoid, too, appearing so loose and casual that you find yourself leaning against the blackboard or sprawling over the lectern. Finally, avoid shifting your weight from foot to foot as you speak. Good posture can enhance your presentation because you will appear more confident and involved in the topic and the audience. You want the audience to concentrate on what you are sharing; proper posture will not detract from this goal. Instead, it will reinforce your image as a well-prepared, confident public speaker.

Eye Contact

Perhaps one of the most difficult skills for the public speaker to master is direct eye contact. As mentioned earlier, your eyes are one of your most revealing features; therefore, a conscious effort to establish direct eye contact acknowledges that you wish to draw the audience in. Understandably, many speakers feel anxious about this task. However, the rewards are gratifying: your audience will feel more involved in your presentation, and you will be able to see it on their faces and in their eyes.

For many it is easier to establish direct eye contact with a small audience, because the size of the group is less threatening. Even with a small group, however, it is difficult to establish direct eye contact with every member of the audience; an attempt to do so will result in little more than scanning the audience. This is not direct eye contact; rather, it is a mechanical back-and-forth motion. Some speakers tend to look above the heads of those in the audience in an effort to appear to be looking at everyone. Still others simply stare out a window or keep their eyes glued to their notes. These techniques prohibit the speaker from responding to any feedback the audience sends.

What the speaker needs to do is establish direct eye contact with certain members of the audience. We suggest picking individuals who are scattered in different parts of the room. For your first speeches, try to include people with whom you feel comfortable or those who you believe will be supportive. Doing so will make it easier for you to practice this technique and to respond to any feedback they might give you. As you gain experience and confidence, you will be able to gradually include members of the audience whom you do not know, as well as those who give negative feedback. You need to respond to both positive and negative feedback in order to make your speech more effective.

In our culture, direct eye contact is extremely important because it communicates confidence and the appearance of a strong self-concept. In addition, it shows concern about communicating with others. An audience can sense when a speaker is in control and usually reacts favorably as a result. Naturally, a boost to one's self-image will provide greater confidence for subsequent speeches. This "snowball" effect leads to growth and maturity for the public speaker.

Learning to use direct eye contact is like learning any other skill: practice is the key ingredient. At first, your attempts may seem mechanical. You may feel uncomfortable because you are self-conscious about your behavior. With time and practice, however, direct eye contact can become a natural part of your communication behavior. Know in advance that many people in the audience will be unable to establish direct eye contact with you; this does not mean that they are rejecting you.

Learning to Incorporate Movement in Your Speech   **SKILL BUILDING**

1. Develop a list of topics you could discuss in an impromptu one-minute speech.

2. As you deliver your one-minute speech, use your body to communicate your ideas. Specifically, try to incorporate:
   - Gestures
   - Facial expressions
   - Walking transitions
   - Posture
   - Eye contact

3. Afterward, discuss the diverse approaches to bodily movement. How did you and your classmates use your bodies to communicate ideas?

Using Your Voice

Your voice gives meaning to the words in your speech. As you may remember from Chapter 5, this is called **paralanguage.** Your voice can reflect the way you feel about your topic; therefore, you can use it to emphasize points. For example, a voice that quivers during the eulogy at a friend's funeral expresses the speaker's sorrow and pain. Likewise, a voice that grows louder reflects anger or passion about some issue, for example, a speaker's outrage over the number of homeless people in the United States and the lack of assistance governmental agencies provide. It is equally important that you pronounce words clearly and precisely so that the audience will understand your message. Several vocal aspects of delivery are discussed below, including volume, rate, inflection, pause, and pronunciation and articulation.

Volume

Volume refers to the loudness of a speaker's voice. Before the use of electronic devices, it was essential for an individual to speak in a loud and powerful voice. This holds true in the classroom as well, since it is not likely that you will have the opportunity to use a microphone. Consequently, you will find it necessary to adjust your voice so that all members of the audience will be able to hear your message. If your audience must strain to hear you, they will probably miss a large part of your message. In fact, you run the risk of losing them altogether as responsive members. Additionally, if you speak very softly, you may appear to lack confidence.

By the same token, you do not want to shout or scream at your audience in order to capture their attention. Shouting can be construed as over-dramatization and may communicate to your audience that you are not sincere about the ideas you are sharing with them. Instead, it appears that you are acting a part in a play.

The level of your voice should correspond to the way you treat your topic. There will be times when you will want to raise or lower your voice based on your feelings about the subject. Let the volume of your voice change as a result of your enthusiasm for the topic. If possible, practice your speech in the same room you will be presenting it. Have classmates or friends sit in the back of the room during your practice session. Adjust your volume according to their feedback. You will then know how loudly to deliver your message when the time comes.

Rate

The rate of your speech is dependent on the number of words you deliver in a given amount of time. Most Americans deliver between 120 and 150 words per minute. Your rate should vary, depending on the speaking situation. The appropriate rate will grow out of the relationship among the audience, the message, and the speaker. Furthermore, the rate will fluctuate throughout the speech; there will be moments when you find it necessary to pick up the pace and other times when you find it more appropriate to slow down.

Although some beginning speakers talk too slowly, most novices experience the opposite problem: they tend to speak too rapidly. Anxiety usually causes this condition. When we get nervous, we tend to speak more rapidly owing to excess tension. The difficulty of the situation is compounded when the audience is unable to comprehend the message.

Special efforts are necessary first to identify and then to correct this problem. For instance, it is helpful to listen to your voice on a tape recorder. This gives you an opportunity to hear the speed at which you speak, thereby increasing your awareness of the problem. A friend or family member also can help by listening to you practice your speech. Ask that person to listen specifically to whether you deliver your speech too rapidly. Finally, indicate in italic print in your notes to slow down at particular points. Such reminders will keep you aware of your speaking rate during your delivery. For example:

> As part of his job as a sales representative, Patrick must do a lot of public speaking. In order to increase his presentational skills, he joined the local chapter of Toastmasters. Each month, members gather to give speeches and offer feedback to one another. In his first speech, the other members indicated that he spoke much too fast and that some of his important points were lost to them. In preparation for his second speech, Patrick has written *SLOW DOWN* at the top of his notecards to remind himself to speak at a normal pace.

Inflection

Think of how boring it is to listen to a speech delivered in a monotone voice. Inflection is the tone of your voice. Lack of variety in vocal inflection has been known to put more than one audience to sleep. The inflection of your voice can and should change as you move to different points in the speech. As you try to stir your audience, for example, the pitch of your voice should rise.

Pause

It is virtually impossible to deliver a speech without inserting some pauses. There are a few places in a speech where pauses can be very effective. First, a pause is helpful as you shift from one idea to the next. This gives your audience a sense that you are about to move on to another point. Furthermore, it allows your audience time to assimilate new or complex ideas. Second, pauses are used effectively when you are striving for emphasis.

The technique of using well-placed pauses is developed with practice. As you become more adept at using pauses, you will achieve your goal of sustaining the audience's interest. An audience often responds to a pause by looking up at the speaker. They are waiting to hear more. You have got their attention—now proceed.

Vocalized or verbal pauses such as *ah, um, like,* and *you know* should not be confused with well-placed silent pauses. In fact, these interjections can be interpreted as signs of nervousness or lack of adequate preparation and will detract from your effectiveness and credibility as a speaker.

Pronunciation and Articulation

If your audience is to understand the words in your speech, you must say them correctly (pronunciation) and clearly (articulation). A common occurrence in speech is the mispronunciation of words. We have all done it at one time or another and have probably suffered a degree of embarrassment when the error was pointed out. For example, the following table illustrates four words that are frequently mispronounced:

Word	Common Pronunciation	Correct Pronunciation
February	Feb-u-ary	Feb-ru-ary
disastrous	di-sas-ter-ous	di-sas-trous
burglar	bur-ga-lar	bur-glar
athlete	ath-a-lete	ath-lete

To ensure that your delivery is free of mispronunciations, consult a dictionary for those words you have any doubt about. Also, practicing your delivery in front of a friend or family member may help catch errors.

Articulation refers to the clear or distinct pronunciation of words. It is not identical to pronunciation, for you can say a word crisply but still mispronounce it (for example, saying the *w* in *sword* or the *1* in *salmon* is a mistake in pronunciation). A few general pointers may give you more confidence over the question of articulation. Avoid the following when delivering your speech: (1) running words together, such as "wanna" for *want to* or "didja" for *did you*; (2) omitting word endings, such as "havin" for *having* or "runnin" for *running*.

SELF-ASSESSMENT Practicing Using Your Voice

Using the topics you developed in the activity concerning movement, deliver another impromptu one-minute speech. As you deliver your speech, use your voice to communicate your ideas. Try to incorporate emotion into your speech using your voice. Pay close attention to:

- volume
- rate
- inflection
- pauses
- pronunciation and articulation

Afterward, discuss the diverse approaches to the use of voice. How did you and your classmates use voice to communicate ideas and emotions?

Practicing Your Speech

We have discussed several steps that are designed to help you feel more confident when you are required to speak in public. It is important to remember that there is no one right way to deliver a speech. The appropriate delivery style will depend on you, your topic, the situation, and the audience. Implementing the skills in this chapter will help you feel more self-assured and in control. The finishing touches for your presentation are achieved through practice. The following are several steps that will help you to prepare to speak in front of an audience:

1. Begin to practice the speech aloud. There are several techniques you can use to become comfortable with your material. Try to become familiar with your ideas. This necessitates going through the speech completely several times. Even if you make a mistake, continue to go through the speech until you reach its conclusion. This will help you to grasp the ideas and keep you focused on the ideas when you actually deliver the speech. You should know your message thoroughly so that you do not need your note cards—but have them handy just in case.

2. Once you become comfortable with the ideas, you need to refine your delivery. Begin to practice your delivery in front of a mirror. Take note of your movement, and keep in mind that any movement should reflect your involvement with the ideas. If you notice any annoying mannerisms, try to refrain from repeating them. You also may choose to use a tape recorder to check the quality of your voice. This can be especially helpful if you are having a difficult time with pronunciation. Finally, if a video camera and recorder are available to you, consider taping your delivery. Video equipment has the advantage of combining the techniques just mentioned in a single operation—you can both see and hear your delivery.

3. Once you have practiced your speech in front of the mirror or have taped your delivery, you may wish to elicit feedback from friends and family. While you are delivering your speech to the audience at home, practice establishing direct eye contact with them. This will help you to incorporate direct eye contact with members of your actual audience and help you practice adjusting your message to audience feedback.

4. Once you feel comfortable with your presentation at home, you also may wish to practice the speech in an empty classroom. Do so before the day that the speech is scheduled. This will give you an opportunity to become familiar with the setting of the speech. Also, practice with your presentational aids. It will take several practice runs for you to feel comfortable handling and presenting your presentational aids.

Keep in mind that each individual's background brings a uniqueness to any topic he or she chooses to share with an audience. Believing that

COMMUNICATION and TECHNOLOGY

Effective Delivery and PowerPoint

PowerPoint is very rare at CEO conferences. Like Supreme Court justices, captains of industry like to see a speaker think, not watch him read (Stewart, 2000, p. 210).

The essence of any public presentation is the interaction between the speaker and the audience. The speaker must be able to continually adapt and adjust to audience feedback in order to effectively get his or her message across. For example, the speaker must be able to adjust voice quality and use walking transitions or other bodily movements to help the audience stay focused on the message.

With the advent of presentational software, such as PowerPoint by Microsoft, many speakers have forgotten the all-important relationship between speaker and audience. According to H. Dennis Beaver, a lawyer and college instructor, "Most public speaking still takes place with just a speaker and an audience. That's why they are there, to hear a speaker. To be moved, persuaded, entertained, challenged, and motivated. Speakers do this. Overheads do not" (2000, p. 80). PowerPoint and other presentational software have become a substitute for a "real" speaker.

Presentational software has become so prevalent in business and the military, for example, that middle managers would not dare do a presentation without several slides for fear it might hurt their credibility (Zuckerman, 1999). According to *USA Today*, "In 1995, the average PowerPoint user created 4.5 presentations a month, Microsoft says. In 1998, the number has doubled" (Maney, 1999, p. 3B). Despite its millions of users, many businesses, conferences, and the mili-

tary are beginning to ban the use of PowerPoint because it is interfering with, not helping, speakers communicate their messages clearly and effectively.

PowerPoint can help speakers organize their ideas and can help visual learners understand the message. The *New York Times* reports, "PowerPoint has elevated the general level of discourse by forcing otherwise befuddled speakers to organize their thoughts and by giving audiences a visual source of information that is a much more efficient way for humans to learn than by simply listening" (Zuckerman, 1999, p. B11). PowerPoint can be a helpful tool for both speaker and listener if it is used properly.

Many times, however, speakers overuse or misuse presentational software. Specifically, PowerPoint limits the speaker's ability to creatively communicate ideas. "Many people believe that the ubiquity of prepackaged computer software that helps users prepare such presentations has not only taken much of the life out of public speaking by homogenizing it at a low level, but has also led to a kind of ersatz thought that is devoid of original ideas" (Zuckerman, 1999, p. B9). In addition, Cliff Nass, Associate Professor of Communication, states, "Any technology that organizes and standardizes tends to homogenize" (Zuckerman, 1999, p. B11). In other words, all presentations look and sound the same. The speaker cannot be as creative within a predetermined and prepackaged software program.

Second, and most importantly, PowerPoint detracts from the interaction between the speaker and the audience. According to Thomas Stewart, PowerPoint discourages questioning by the audience (2001). The speaker does not have a lot of freedom to pause, for example, in the middle of a slide presentation, to engage the audience's questions. Everyone, including the speaker, stares at the screen. Geoffrey Nunberg states, "What's troubling is the way that slides have begun to take on a life of their own, as if they no longer needed a talking head to speak for them" (1999, p. 330). And Jaffe reports one Army official as saying, "People are not listening to us, because they are spending so much time trying to understand these incredibly complex slides" (2000, p. A1). The speaker's responsibility is to engage the audience, and it seems that PowerPoint can hinder the interaction between the speaker and his or her audience.

If you decide to use PowerPoint or some other presentational software, there are some guidelines you can follow to ensure that you creatively present your ideas and that you engage your audience. First, remember that more is less. Keep your slides simple and to the point. Don't put too much information on a single slide and don't have too many slides. Second, slides should be used to clarify ideas or help the audience visualize our main points. Charts, graphs, and photos, for example, are excellent tools that can be enhanced with the use of PowerPoint. Third, as you deliver your presentation, remember all the important aspects to effective delivery, such as eye contact (avoid reading your slides, talk to the audience), conversational quality, and spontaneity. Most of all, don't forget that the audience is there and maintain constant contact with them through your delivery style. Lastly, "your speech should be deliverable even if every visual aid you had planned to use simply wouldn't work" (Beaver, 2000, p. 80). You need to be flexible because sometimes technology fails. Be prepared for this to happen.

PowerPoint can be a useful tool if it is used properly. Just remember that the essence of any public presentation is the relationship and interaction between the speaker and the audience.

you have something special to share will give you a tremendous boost in confidence. The speech is an interactive process between you and the audience. As a speaker, it is your goal to communicate your ideas in a way your audience can understand and appreciate them. Appreciating their different approaches to your message can go a long way in ensuring a successful speech.

Summary

This chapter provided information to help you deliver a more effective speech. There are distinct differences between oral and written communication. Oral communication is a cooperative act that includes immediate feedback from the audience. It requires the speaker to create a message that is easy for the audience to listen to.

Unlike written communication, the sender must be concerned about the nonverbal messages of both the speaker and the audience. Stage fright is a fear common to many people, but there are ways to cope with it. These include reducing excess tension, focusing on the topic, realizing that you are not alone, and developing a positive attitude. If you can remember to keep public speaking in its proper perspective, you will be less fearful of speaking in front of an audience.

There are four different types of speech delivery: impromptu, manuscript, memorized, and extemporaneous. Of these, the extemporaneous delivery has a major advantage: the speaker prepares the topic in advance, but the delivery is still flexible enough to allow the speaker to adapt to the audience.

There are several techniques you can learn to improve your ability to share ideas with an audience. Spontaneity and sincerity are two important aspects of delivery. In addition, you can use your body to its best advantage by incorporating the following into the delivery: natural gestures, facial expression, walking transitions, appropriate appearance, good posture, and direct eye contact. Still another way to enhance delivery involves the use of your voice. Volume, rate, inflection, appropriately placed pauses, and pronunciation and articulation are factors to consider when delivering your speech. Your confidence as a speaker will increase as you learn to effectively incorporate these techniques into your delivery.

Finally, the following suggestions may help when practicing your delivery. Once you feel comfortable with the material, begin practicing the speech aloud. Whether you do this in front of a mirror, a video camera, or your family, remember that you have something of value to share with the audience. Practicing your delivery should increase your confidence, because you will know that you have adequately prepared for your presentation.

Review Questions

1. What are the differences between oral and written communication?
2. What steps can you take to help control speech anxiety?
3. Name the four methods of speech delivery and briefly describe each one.
4. Why is it important for your bodily movements to be spontaneous?
5. Why is it helpful for a speaker to establish direct eye contact with an audience?
6. What are the different ways in which you can use your voice to improve your delivery?
7. What steps can you use to practice your delivery?

The Informative Speech

At the conclusion of this chapter, you should be able to:

- Explain the purpose of an informative speech.
- Describe three ways to make a topic relevant to the audience.
- List several appropriate informative speech topics.

- Structure an effective informative speech.
- Use the methods of narration, description, definition, and demonstration to present an informative speech.

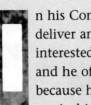

n his Communication course, Melvin must research, write, and deliver an informative speech. One topic that he has always been interested in is illiteracy. Melvin's grandfather never learned to read, and he often told Mel about his struggles at work and at home because he could not read. Melvin decided to find out about illiteracy in his community.

After interviewing several volunteers who teach adults to read at the high school, Melvin searches the library and the Internet for source material. He discovers that illiteracy is a problem that effects all ages and ethnic groups. In his community alone, over 12 percent of all adults cannot read at the eighth-grade level. Several factors contribute to illiteracy. These include family income, educational opportunities in the community, local crime rate, educational level of the family, and family support.

Melvin must decide how best to inform his audience about illiteracy. He could tell the story of his grandfather and describe all the struggles he went through because he could not read. Or he could use his speech to define illiteracy. But Melvin chooses to describe how illiteracy affects his community and what can be done to help those who are illiterate.

In this chapter, we will see that there are different types of informative speeches, and for each topic, there are several approaches. Before we begin our discussion about the special qualities of this type of speech, it might be helpful to review how we got to this point. You will soon discover that all the necessary tools for preparing and delivering an informative speech were provided in the previous four chapters on public speaking.

Chapter 11 provided you with the foundation for public speaking and gave you direction; armed with a topic, a purpose, and a sense of your audience, you were ready for the next step in preparing a public speech—gathering materials. In Chapter 12 you discovered that your credibility as a speaker, and your topic itself, could be enhanced by supporting materials gathered from such sources as interviews, newspapers, periodicals, the Internet, and books. What did you do with this additional information? You incorporated it into the development of your speech. Chapter 13 showed you how, by ordering the ideas related to your topic, you could develop a logical, fluent speech. Outlining these ideas proved to be a systematic way to further develop your speech. At last you were ready for the delivery. Chapter 14 provided you with techniques for translating your written ideas into an effective oral presentation. Now let us put into practice all that you have learned, beginning with the informative speech.

The Nature of the Informative Speech

The purpose of an informative speech is to educate an audience. "About what?" we might ask. Today we live in an information age that bombards us with new facts and ideas each day, yet we cannot possibly digest all this information, nor do we desire to. Rather, we make decisions about what interests us and our audiences, and then we focus our attention on those issues and ideas. This becomes a key consideration when we select a topic for an informative speech and when we develop that topic.

Unlike the **persuasive speech,** whose purpose is to change an attitude or motivate to act, the overriding concern of the **informative speech** is to impart knowledge. Your appeal as a speaker is directed at the audience's desire for information that matters. In other words, you must operate on the premise that the members of your audience are eager to learn something new and that part of your function is to make the information relevant to them. How do you accomplish this?

Your first objective is to *engage* your audience. Ask yourself such questions as, "What do I know about the demographics of this audience?" and "What do I know about this group's attitudes and interests?" In other words, "What do you know about the frames of references of the audience members?" Remember, the audience brings diverse approaches to the communication process, and as the speaker, it is your responsibility to acknowledge and value these approaches, even if they are different from your own. You will likely be successful at drawing the audience's attention and establishing the relevance of your topic if you keep this in mind. For example:

> Artie is 33 years old and married, and he and his wife have three children. After receiving his bachelor's degree in Finance, he went to work as a stockbroker. After several miserable years, Artie decided to go back to college and earn his teaching certificate, as he always wanted to be a high school social studies teacher. One requirement for his certificate is the completion of a basic communication course. When given his first speech assignment, to inform the audience, Artie struggles with what to teach the audience. His instructor suggests that he talk about his prior experience as a stockbroker, as he would have instant credibility. "That's boring and this audience of students who are twenty-five to thrity-five years old don't have any money to invest," said Artie. Artie's instructor suggests he focus on individual retirement accounts (IRAs) and the notion that the Social Security system will likely be bankrupt when his audience retires and that they need to prepare for their retirement. Artie agrees this would be appropriate for his audience, and he certainly knows a lot about the topic.

In this example, Artie has taken into consideration his interests and expertise and his audience's needs and interests to develop his informative speech topic.

This leads us to a second important quality of the informative speech—simplicity. If your audience is unfamiliar with your topic, yet you have succeeded in capturing their interest, it is crucial that you present your information so that it is easily digested. A sure way to lose an audience is to present information that is too complex or sophisticated for them to comprehend as you are speaking. This is not to say that the development of your topic should be simplistic; it should, however, be easy enough to follow. Clear understanding is essential to an informative speech. If the members of your audience cannot understand a point, they are apt to stop listening. When that happens, the relevance of your speech vanishes.

An informative speech with clear, easily understood ideas is made even better by the use of appropriate language. To a large degree, whether or not ideas are understood depends on the words you use. Concrete, descriptive terms help any audience to understand new ideas. It is therefore wise to limit the use of abstract language (review Chapter 4 for a discussion of abstract and concrete language).

The remainder of this chapter is divided into three sections: (1) informative speech topics, (2) organizing the informative speech, and (3) methods for presenting an informative speech. At the end of the chapter you will find a sample informative speech, complete with commentary.

COMMUNICATION and TECHNOLOGY

Information Overload

This generation is more besieged by information than any that preceded it, and perhaps more so than all previous generations combined. We have more things competing for our time and attentions than any group in history.
—Jeff Davidson, Executive Director, Breathing Space Institute of Chapel Hill

Do you feel overwhelmed by all the information you are confronted with each day? If so, you may suffer from information overload. This phenomenon has also been called data clutter, info glut, and info pollution. According to Marsha White and Steve Dorman, information overload "refers to the vast quantities of information speedily disseminated to a large and growing number of people" (2000, p. 160).

We are exposed to more information today than any other generation. For example, according to White and Dorman:

- We see six times more advertisements today than 20 years ago.
- 3,000 ads come our way each day.
- Around the world, 1,000 to 2,000 books are published each day.
- More information has been produced in the past thirty years than in the previous 5,000.
- One weekday issue of the *New York Times* contains more information than the average seventeenth-century individual would have seen in a lifetime (2000, pp. 160–161).
- According to Jeff Davidson, "All told, more information is generated in a twenty-four-hour period than you could take in for the rest of your life" (2000, p. 496).

Information overload affects just about everyone. It can hinder learning and overall productivity. For example, it can cause higher blood pressure, digestive disorders, lack of concentration, tension, less time with family and friends, longer days, and shorter leisure time (White and Dorman, 2000, p. 160). Jeff Davidson puts it this way: "Here's what happens when you're besieged by information on a continual basis. You begin to feel overwhelmed, which leads to the feeling of over-work" (2000, p. 498).

What can we do? Here are a few tips from White and Dorman on how we can reduce our information overload:

1. Turn off the television. In the average U.S. household, the television is on for more than seven hours a day.
2. Turn off the cell phone and pager. These electronic devices tend to control us rather than the reverse.
3. Say no to junk mail. Have your name removed from mailing lists that contribute little to your development.
4. Restrict computer time. Excess time on the computer keeps you from living in "real time."
5. Learn efficient ways to search online. Adopt a search engine and learn its quirks so you develop expertise in using it.
6. Practice information triage. Determine the importance of each piece of information, and act on the decision.
7. Avoid info-littering. Avoid the urge to forward every email to all your acquaintances.
8. Follow netiquette guidelines.

Informative Speech Topics

As a speaker, you have the luxury of drawing from a vast body of potential topics for an informative speech. What you do with that topic determines whether or not your speech will be successful or unsuccessful. The key ingredient is discovering how to develop the topic to make it relevant to your audience. For example, a high school football team needs to listen to the coach's detailed strategy for Friday night's game, yet high school faculty interest would be limited. Similarly, an instructor would present different speeches about seeing eye dogs to an audience with a visual impairment and an audience with sight. For the first audience, the focus might be on instructing students how to use a guide dog; for the second audience, the focus might shift to working with students with visual impairments who use guide dogs. Whatever the topic, it must be adapted to the audience.

The bulk of informative speech topics fall into one of the following categories: recreation, concepts, places, objects, events, and people.

Recreation

One area that offers several topics for the informative speech is recreation. Activities such as sports, exercise, hobbies, and creative arts have a broad appeal. You can easily develop speeches that take a "how to" approach, such as how to play handball or croquet, how to carve a watermelon into a whale, or how to plan a cross-country biking trip. There are also all sorts of prospects for pointing out the benefits of recreational activities, as in this example:

> Cheryl works as a fitness instructor at the local YMCA. Her job is to develop and deliver workshops to the members about physical fitness, nutrition, and stress relief. Cheryl's supervisor has asked her to hold a workshop for the working mothers of the YMCA on how they can stay fit and relieve stress. After doing some research, Cheryl decides to focus her

DILBERT © UFS. Reprinted by Permission.

discussion on aerobic exercises and planning nutritious lunches that her audience can take to work with them.

Cheryl's effort to give her audience information that was related to their well-being helped reinforce the relevance of her speech.

Concepts

Topics for informative speeches can be drawn from concepts, that is, ideas, theories, or thoughts generally used to explain abstract subjects, such as democracy, supply-side economics, or bigotry. Because concepts are often abstract, your purpose will be in part to explain in more concrete language the ideas inherent in the topic. Your goal is to have the audience arrive at a better understanding of the concept by the speech's conclusion. Consider Juan's topic:

> Juan has come back to college after a two-year absence. He has been able to secure financial aid and can now complete his degree in political science. He hopes someday to go to law school and become a lawyer. One of Juan's passions has been to study the First Amendment to the United States Constitution and issues such as flag burning, freedom of the press, and the separation of church and state. For his informative speech, Juan decides to define and explain the concept of "free speech" to his class-

Free speech and other abstract subjects can make excellent speech topics.

> mates and to show how important this right is to democracy. To make the topic clear, Juan uses the case of a journalist who refused to reveal her sources in a story about a very important criminal case and was jailed.

Juan knows that for his speech to be effective, he must make the abstract topic of free speech concrete for his audience. He does this with the use of a true to life example.

Places

As the subject of informative speeches, places can include such things as institutions, historical sites, cities, geologic landforms, and buildings. Specific examples are Wrigley Field, the Lincoln Memorial, and Kilimanjaro. Consider the following:

> Nell and her family have recently relocated to Georgia because of her husband's job. She is taking a few classes at the local community college in order to complete her associate's degree in nursing. As part of one of her nursing classes, Nell must talk about some aspect of herself and her experiences. She wants to tell her class of about the excitement of Chicago, where she grew up and lived until last year. In order to give them a flavor of what Chicago has to offer, she decides to talk about the Museum Campus. She describes the Field Museum of Natural History with its huge dinosaur exhibits, the Shedd Aquarium with its new Ocean-aquarium, and the Adler Planetarium's extensive telescope, all located within walking distance of one another. By the time she has completed this description, her audience is more than a little intrigued by these interesting places in the Windy City.

When you give a speech about a place you have visited, you have the opportunity to bring some of your own experiences to the topic. Your efforts are likely to maintain the audience's interest.

Objects

Our environment is filled with thousands of unique and interesting objects; many make ideal subjects for an informative speech. When speaking about an object, you might explain how its use has a special significance for your audience. A few objects you might choose to discuss include computers, video cameras, or antique cars.

When you speak about an object, your purpose might be to explain its use, its appeal to a particular segment of the population, or its impact on society. For example:

> Terri is a market research analyst for General Motors and a recent graduate with a bachelor's degree in Marketing. She is scheduled to speak to a group of design engineers about the relationship between cars and cul-

Places like monuments and historical sites make interesting speech topics.

ture. Specifically, she plans to focus her comments on the vehicle-buying trends of baby boomers, those individuals born between 1946 and 1964, because they represent one of the largest groups of consumers in the United States and as they age, their tastes in vehicles have changed. She also makes some predictions about what features will appeal to this consumer group in the future and projects the average price they will be able to afford. Terri's information is invaluable to the engineers because it gives them ideas concerning additional features to include in the cars they produce over the next few years.

Terri's success in this example can be attributed to her efforts to tailor the information to the needs of her audience.

People

People represent a tremendous source for speech topics. You can easily develop a fascinating informative speech about an individual or a group of people, such as political leaders, steelworkers, or professional boxers. If you decide to speak about a person or group of people, try highlighting their unique qualities, contributions, or importance. For example, you might focus on the impact that Steven Spielberg has had on the motion picture industry, the contributions of Susan B. Anthony to the Women's Rights Movement, or the role played by Monica Lewinsky in the impeachment of President Bill Clinton.

Events

Exciting and important events take place in the world every day, and most would make interesting speech topics. For example, the relief effort in India after the 2001 earthquake included rescue teams from all over the world. The United States presidential election in 2000 included several interesting court cases and a vote recount in Florida, which could be easily adapted for your informative speech. Events you might talk about could be recent or historical. The Civil Rights movement during the 1960s and the Space Shuttle Challenger accident were important historical events in U.S. history. When speaking of an event, you might want to discuss the event in chronological or time order to ensure your audience can follow along as the event or events actually took place. Consider this example:

> Charles has been working as a computer programmer for ten years and has recently moved into management. His supervisor has asked him to present a short seminar on the impact that the *United States v. Microsoft Corporation* may have on his company's ability to continue to update

Ground Zero in New York City reveals the devastation of the September 11, 2001 attacks.

their current software. Charles decides to first discuss the judge's ruling to split Microsoft into two companies and then detail how Microsoft is planning to accommodate demands for updated further software design and distribution. Obviously, the Microsoft court case and the events after the case have a significant impact on Charles' company.

Table 15.1 provides a summary of informative speech topics.

Organizing the Informative Speech

It may be helpful to review the material in Chapter 13 as you begin to structure your informative speech. There you will find a discussion about organizational patterns for the ideas in your topic; suggestions for developing the body, introduction, conclusion, and transitions; and outlining principles. Because you are working on an informative speech, you must always bear in mind that your purpose is to fill an information need of your audience. Your speech should first engage the audience's interest and then strive to present ideas that can be easily understood, always with the intent to maintain the relevance of your topic.

In the body of the speech, where you will focus your attention first, make sure to use an organizational structure that best fits the purpose of your speech. For instance, if your purpose is to describe the women's movement, you may first want to discuss many of the important leaders of the movement, such as Elizabeth Cady Stanton, Soujourner Truth, or Gloria Steinem, in a topical order. Another approach may be to discuss the problems women faced and then discuss the long-term effects the movement had on women's lives with a cause-and-effect organizational pattern. Similarly, if you want to explain how the movement developed over time, you could discuss the "first wave" (1878–1920), the "second wave" (1959–

TABLE 15.1	**Informative Speech Topics**	
Recreation	*Concepts*	*Places*
Swing dancing	Volunteerism	Colonial Williamsburg
Herb gardening	History of communism	Rain forest
Sky diving	Autism	U.S. national parks
Objects	*People*	*Events*
DVD players	The Beatles	Assassination of Malcolm X
Shaker furniture	Colin Powell	Massacre at Columbine High School
Novels	Elizabeth Dole	Winter/Summer Olympics

1979), and finally, the current "third wave" (1985–present) using a chronological pattern. The key is to identify the organizational pattern that best relates to the purpose of your speech.

As mentioned in Chapter 13, it is advisable to limit the number of points you plan to present in the body of an information speech. The audience will have an easier time absorbing the information in a speech that has a well-developed theme rather than one that is overburdened with minute facts. While facts are essential to the development of a topic, it is counterproductive to overwhelm the audience with excessive details.

When you construct an introduction, remember that your intent is to trigger a need in the audience. You want to demonstrate why it is important for them to listen to your presentation. Try to do this by highlighting ways in which the information is relevant to them. For instance, if you plan to inform the audience about ways to improve relationships, you might point out how this information will benefit their relationships. It is critical to encourage the audience to listen to you as you develop your ideas.

In the conclusion, summarize your ideas and suggest to the audience what it is you want them to walk away with after listening to your speech. If you have explained a new procedure to the audience, you will want to encourage them to be patient as they attempt this new task. Furthermore, you might suggest sources where they can gain additional information on the process you have just explained.

Finally, transitions should be used as a bridge between the major parts of the speech and to reinforce the points you present in the body. These transitions help your audience to retain the information you impart.

Methods of Presenting an Informative Speech

The effectiveness of an informative speech depends on the development of the topic and on your ability to narrate, describe, define, and demonstrate the ideas in your speech. These skills are discussed in the following section.

Narration

One way to present material in an informative speech is with a narrative. A **narrative** is a story or an account of an event told orally. The speaker can use a narrative to introduce a speech or to illustrate or clarify a point within a speech. In order to be effective, a narrative should evoke a feeling of "being there." When the members of an audience are able to visualize a point the speaker is trying to make, they develop a better understanding of the topic.

Narratives should use vivid language, should be easy to follow, and should avoid being too lengthy. You can create your own narrative for an informative speech, or you can quote the written or oral narratives of others. In a narrative, the speaker can use personal experience as the basis for a story.

For example, to illustrate her point about perseverance and success, Janet Reno, Attorney General of the United States, said:

> First of all, be yourself and believe in yourself. I began to learn that lesson when I was eight years old. We lived in a little wooden house; we were outgrowing it. My father did not have enough money to hire a contractor to build a bigger house. My mother announced that she was going to build a house. And we said what do you know about building a house? And she said, I'm going to learn. And she went to the brick mason, the electrician and the plumber and asked how do you build a house? She then came home and over the next two years, she dug the foundation with her own hands with a pick and shovel, put in the electrical system and the plumbing. She and I lived in that house until she died, just before I came to Washington and it is still my home. Every time I have come down that driveway over these years with a knotty problem to solve or a crisis that seemed insurmountable, that house standing there has been a symbol to me that you can do anything you want to if it's the right thing to do and if you try hard enough (1999, p. 548).

The narrative here is effective because it successfully transports the audience to the house built by Reno's mother. An audience is often drawn to a

Former Attorney General Janet Reno effectively uses a narrative (above) to enhance her speech.

personalized account related to the speech topic, as illustrated in this example.

SKILL BUILDING   Narration

1. Think about the topics you are considering for your informative speech. Choose one of those topics.

2. First, write down a personal experience that helps communicate your feelings about this subject.

3. Next, gather outside resources to help illustrate your feelings about the topic. Write down the information as a narrative.

4. Share both narratives with a classmate.

5. Use the feedback from your classmate to improve one of the narratives for your speech.

Description

A **description** is an image that is created verbally. In an informative speech, a description can be used to effectively communicate a speaker's ideas. How effectively depends on the language used. Descriptions that use **concrete terms,** where the language is detailed and specific, are easier for an audience to visualize than descriptions that use **abstract terms,** where the language is general or vague. A speaker might describe an object by telling about its shape, size, color, or texture. He or she uses words to paint a picture that the audience can visualize. Adjectives generally work best for this purpose, since by definition they act as descriptors. The following is a very effective description of *The Greatest Generation,* according to Tom Brokaw:

> Here, the young men and women who had just been tested by the Great Depression were to be tested again—in the battlefields thousands of miles across the Atlantic or thousands of miles across the Pacific. In bitter European cold and the suffocating heat of the jungle. In the air and on the seas, they fought—often hand to hand—for more than three years, day in and day out. More than 12 million more at home on the assembly lines, converting the American economy into a war machine overnight. Women went to work where only men had prevailed—in cabs of trucks, in research labs, in ship yards (1999, p. 608).

The following description of the World War II generation pales by comparison: "A generation of men and women sacrificed at home and around the world to save our country." An audience, after hearing this description, would have little sense of how severely tested this generation was and how hard they fought. The vague language used here fails to promote understanding.

Description　　　**CRITICAL THINKING**

1. Pick one of the following topics:
   a. air travel
   b. hot tubs
   c. working overtime
   d. your favorite holiday
2. Using concrete language, describe the topic in as much detail as you can, making sure you define any terms the audience may not be familiar with.
3. With a partner, share your description and provide feedback on his or her description.

Definition

Definition is a valuable form of support in the informative speech (see Chapter 12). Terms that are generally unfamiliar to an audience, however, need to be defined in language that the audience can easily understand. There are a number of ways to accomplish this, including the use of synonyms, antonyms, comparisons, and etymology. Anita Taylor, Professor of Communication and Women's Studies at George Mason University, attempts to define the term *gender* for her audience as it relates to *Men Are from Mars and Women Are from Venus*. She states:

> We have concluded that it is the concept of gender, which is quite troublesome for many earthlings. Gender is the term that English speaking earthlings apply to the whole complex of behaviors, dispositions, attributes, values, etc. that are supposed to go along with either a male or a female. In a kind of shorthand gender is often described is being feminine or masculine. In this idea called gender, major changes have occurred in the past 10 years (1999, p. 271).

Taylor clearly defines the abstract concept of gender for her audience.

One way to define a term is by using synonyms. **Synonyms** are different words that have the same or nearly the same meaning. Substituting the word *customs* for *mores* or *drunkenness* for *insobriety* can help to clarify the definition of an idea in your speech.

A speaker also can use **antonyms,** words that have opposite meanings, to define a concept for the audience. *Despair* is an antonym for *hope*. For instance, a speaker might use the word *despair* as an antonym for hope and talk in terms of a "hopeful future in light of a despairing past."

It is sometimes desirable to define a concept or an idea by making **comparisons.** In his acceptance address at the 1984 Republican National Convention, Ronald Reagan attempted to illustrate the differences between the Democratic and Republican parties' views of America:

> The choices this year are not just between two different personalities, or between two political parties. They are between two different visions of the future, two fundamentally different ways of governing—their government of pessimism, fear, and limits, or ours of hope, confidence, and growth. Their government sees people only as members of groups. Ours serves all the people of America as individuals. Theirs lives in the past, seeking to apply the old and failed policies to an era that has passed them by. Ours learns from the past and strives to change by boldly charting a new course for the future (1984, p. 706).

SKILL BUILDING — Defining

1. Define the concept of freedom by:
   a. using synonyms
   b. using antonyms
   c. making a comparison
2. Use the preceding definitions to organize a speech on freedom.
3. How can the use of definitions help add clarity to your presentation?

In this statement, Reagan attempted to define the differences between the two parties by characterizing his party as one of the future and the Democratic Party as one plagued by the past. His proffered future of hope, confidence, and growth was contrasted with a past defined by pessimism, fear, and limits.

Still another way to define a term is to refer to its **etymology,** or origin. The etymology of a word is the history of its development or use in the language where it is found. For example, in a speech about three mayoral candidates, you might characterize one candidate as a liberal. To clarify what you mean by the term *liberal,* you refer to the word's etymology: *liberal* comes from the Latin *liber,* meaning "free, or liberated, befitting a freeman, generous" (Skeat, 1958, p. 293). One of the best reference sources for the etymology of words in the English language is the *Oxford English Dictionary.*

Demonstration

Demonstration is often an effective method for explaining a point or idea to an audience. In an effort to clearly explain a particular activity, such as cake decorating or operation of a video camera, you might show the audience the steps involved in the process. For example, Bill wants to explain the differences among various baseball pitches. To him the most logical and effective way to accomplish his goal is to demonstrate the different ways to grip the baseball for each type of pitch and to show the "follow through" motion for each pitch. His demonstration is accompanied by a verbal explanation.

Ethics in Communication

The Informative Speech

In the beginning of this chapter we met Melvin, who was preparing for his informative speech. Because of his grandfather's experiences, Melvin is interested in illiteracy. He decided to inform his audience about illiteracy and its effects on the community after surveying his audience as part of his audience analysis. After doing extensive research, including an interview with his grandfather, Melvin was ready to organize and deliver his presentation. In order to ensure that his speech is effective and ethical, Melvin should adhere to the following guidelines:

1. After doing extensive audience analysis, Melvin needed to adapt his topic of illiteracy to his particular audience. He needed to pay special attention to their needs, desires, and interests and find a way to relate his topic to them. This is why he chose to focus on the effect of illiteracy in their community. Ignoring the audience will certainly lead to an ineffective presentation and is unethical.

2. Melvin needs to use a variety of support material to make his ideas clear. Relying solely on his grandfather's experiences will not make his speech very informative and would certainly hurt his audience's perception of his credibility.

3. Melvin must prioritize his information and only discuss the most interesting and important. He cannot possibly discuss everything he knows about illiteracy. Using an organizational pattern discussed in Chapter 13 will allow him to clearly communicate his ideas to the audience and will ultimately make the information easier for the audience to hear, ensuring that his presentation is both effective and ethical.

4. Whenever possible, Melvin should use concrete language that the audience can understand. If he uses abstract terms, he needs to remember to define and explain anything the audience may not understand. For example, his first goal must be to clearly define illiteracy.

SELF-ASSESSMENT   Demonstration

1. Think about a special skill you have and one that you could demonstrate to an audience, such as origami, cooking, or karate.
2. Outline the necessary steps involved in teaching this skill to someone else.
3. Ask a classmate to watch your demonstration.
4. Ask your classmate to give you feedback concerning how well you presented your ideas. Were you thorough? Did your demonstration proceed logically? Did you go through the steps slowly enough?

CHECKLIST   Presenting Your Information

- Narratives educate with a story.
- Descriptions enlighten through concrete language.
- Definitions explain unfamiliar ideas.
- Demonstrations illustrate concepts or processes.

Summary

The purpose of an informative speech is to educate an audience. From the early stages of selecting a topic through the final stages of presenting that topic, the speaker must strive to make the information relevant to the audience. The speaker accomplishes this by engaging the audience's interest in the topic, by presenting ideas that can be easily digested, and by using appropriate language.

Informative speech topics generally fall into one of these categories: recreation, concepts, places, objects, or people. Whatever topic the speaker selects, it should be adapted to the audience in order to remain relevant. Determining what the audience

wants to know is a major consideration for the speaker.

Once the topic is selected, work begins on developing the major and minor points. All this planning and outlining is done with one thing in mind: every step of the way, give the audience information that will make a difference. The audience must come away from the speech having learned something worthwhile. Certain methods are especially effective in passing on new information. These include the narrative, education through a story or account; description, enlightenment through concrete, sharply focused language; definition, explanations of unfamiliar ideas by means of language that the audience already understands; and demonstration of a concept or process. All these parts add up to

the speaker being a teacher, and the members of the audience being eager listeners.

Review Questions

1. What is the primary concern when developing an informative speech objective?
2. List the six major categories for informative speech topics, and give an example of each.
3. When concluding an informative speech, what do you want to reinforce?
4. What are some resources you can use to create a narrative?
5. Why is it best to use concrete language when attempting to describe something in an informative speech?
6. Differentiate between the use of antonyms and the use of synonyms to define ideas in an informative speech.
7. When demonstrating something, why is it important to proceed slowly?

Sample Informative Student Speech

Graduating Debt-Free: Grants and Scholarships
for College Students

The speaker asks a rhetorical question to capture the audience's attention. She also cites her source with an oral footnote.

The speaker relates the topic to the audience.

The speaker establishes her credibility by discussing her research and past experience.

The speaker previews her main points in her thesis.

The speaker uses a signpost to indicate that she is moving to the body of the speech.

The speaker uses an oral footnote to cite her source.

The speaker uses a transition to her second main point.

Did you know that over half of all college students rely on financial aid to get through school, according to the Scholarship Resource Network? It is true! That means that over half of us sitting in this classroom right now are here because some form of financial aid is relieving the sometimes overpowering burden of tuition, books, and other school-related expenses.

I am one of the 50 percent who relies on financial aid. My family and I pay less than $500 per semester for a fifteen credit hour class load. In addition to being a financial aid recipient, I have done additional research for this speech. Therefore, I feel qualified to speak with you today about financial aid.

Obtaining financial aid seems like a daunting task. There are so many types and it seems like each type of financial aid has its own set of rules. It makes the whole process seem overwhelming. According to Purdue University Calumet's financial aid department, there are two types of financial aid: gift aid and self-help aid. Self-help aid includes student loans (which have to be paid back) and employment opportunities through work study programs. My speech will focus on gift aid, which is financial aid that does not have to be paid back. The essential elements of gift aid include its history and definition, types (grants and scholarships), and the application process. First, I will discuss the definition and history of financial aid.

According to the Scholarship Resource Network, financial aid is "designed to help individuals meet their educational expenses when their own resources are not sufficient." This idea is not new. They also say that the first financial aid occurred in 1643 when Lady Anne Moulson established the very first scholarship at Harvard College. Although this scholarship was awarded over three hundred and fifty years ago, financial aid distributed on a wide scale is a fairly new idea. Its history dates back only thirty years. That is when the Educational Amendment of 1972 was established to help students defray the costs of their education. As a direct result, explains the Scholarship Resource Network, financial aid "emerged as a vital force in financing American Higher Education." Now that I've explained the definition as well as a brief history of financial aid, let us now discuss grants, one of the two types of gift aid.

Salliemae, a financial planning service, explains that grants are available through federal and state governments as well as from employers, professional associations, and educational institutions. Purdue Calumet's financial aid department states that many grants require a student to show financial need, which according to the Scholarship Resource Network is the "difference between the student's educational expenses and the amount of money the family is expected to contribute." They provide an easy formula that will help you determine your own financial need. The formula is the cost of attendance minus your family's contribution minus any financial aid awarded to you. A popular grant that many of you may have heard of is the federally funded Pell Grant. The Pell Grant is awarded to needy students and makes up the basis of a student's financial aid package.

The other type of gift aid is scholarships. Scholarships do not have to be repaid. There are federal, school, and private sector scholarships. Each scholarship has its own requirements, but most of the federal and school scholarships are awarded on the basis of academic merit and financial need or a combination of both. There are a variety of private sector scholarships available according to Salliemae. Many of these are awarded based on academic achievement, need, religious affiliation, ethnicity, memberships, hobbies, or special interests.

Everyone, I'm sure, would love to have 100 percent of his or her tuition covered by gift aid. Because this is rarely possible, with some determination and a plan, you can considerably reduce the cost of your tuition. Take, for example, this success story listed on the Scholarship Resource Network's web site. A high school senior went after scholarships with a vengeance. He prepared a scholarship packet that included an essay describing his academic and career goals, a resume, letters of recommendation, his high school transcript, and SAT scores. He carried two backpacks with him to school, one held his books and the other held all his scholarship application information. Whenever he found a scholarship that he felt he was qualified for, he attached the completed application to his scholarship packet and mailed it to the sponsoring agency. His ingenuity paid off. He was awarded over $27,000 during his college career. It is success stories like this one that make the effort of applying for scholarships seem more worthwhile. I bet you wonder how you can be just as successful as the young man I just told you about. This brings me to my last point: how to get grants and scholarships to help defray the high costs of higher education.

The logical place to start is with our own university's financial aid department. Check out the web site at <u>esc.calumet.edu/finaid</u>. This site will help you get started and will familiarize you with the types of financial aid you are eligible for. Another helpful site that you can visit is the Scholarship Resource Network. Their web site is at <u>www.srnexpress.com</u> or use their link when visiting the Purdue Calumet's web site. Another source listed on the PUC web site is "FastWEB," a financial aid search through the web. It is the "largest and most complete scholarship search on the Internet." It lists 400,000 scholarships, grants, fellowships, and student loans. You may want to visit these sites to get an idea of what opportunities you may have.

Now you know where to go for financial aid information. Do you know when to start applying? According to the Scholarship Resource Network, it

---

Margin notes:

The speaker refers to a poster that shows the formula and a specific example of one student's expenses. The poster helps the speaker to clarify her ideas for the audience.

The speaker uses an example to illustrate how successful the application process can be.

The speaker uses a signpost to indicate she is beginning her final main idea.

The speaker shows a visual aid with the address clearly printed.

The speaker shows another visual aid with the address clearly printed.

The speaker uses expert testimony to support her main idea.

is imperative to start now. They state that, "the Federal and institutional aid process begins in January for the following academic year." Beth Richardson, Dean of Student Affairs at Indiana University, agrees. She explains, "Students tend to start the application process too late. They need to start six to twelve months ahead of time before the applications are due. And applications are usually due sometime in the fall or spring." Richardson also encourages us to start even earlier if an essay is required.

The speaker gives specific examples of scholarships.

Financial aid isn't just for the brainiacs or for overachievers. There are plenty of scholarship opportunities out there for "average" students. For example, did you know that a telecommunications student at Ball State University can apply for the David Letterman scholarship? If you lived in Muhlenberg County, Kentucky, you could apply for the Everly Brothers scholarship. Aspiring writers can apply to the "Let's Get Creative" scholarship. A person with a disability can apply to Nordstrom Awards College Scholarship. And at our university, we communication students can apply for the Com 114 scholarship simply by earning an A or B in this course. Simply put, there are scholarships out there for every kind of student in every kind of situation. It is just a matter of being organized and driven enough to find these opportunities.

The speaker uses a signpost to indicate to the audience that the speech is coming to an end.

In conclusion, in order to better understand how gift aid can benefit us all, I have discussed the definition and history, types, and ways to obtain gift aid. From personal experience, I know it can be an overwhelming task to find and apply for grants and scholarships. But, believe me, the time and energy is worth it when you graduate from college debt free. Thank you.

The speaker restates her main points.

Erin Okamoto Protsman
Purdue University Calumet
Spring 2001
Used by permission.

Works Cited

Department of Telecommunications Program, Ball State University. (n.d.). David Letterman Scholarship. Retrieved February 19, 2001, from www.+com.bsu.edu/program3.htm.#letterman.

Duvall, B., Duvall, T. (n.d.). The Everly Brothers Homecoming. Retrieved February 19, 2001, from on-the-square.com/muhlenberg_ky/evernts/everly.htm.

Scholarship Research Network. (n.d.). *A discussion on scholarships.* Retrieved January 31, 2001, from srnexpress.com/discuss.htm.

Scholarship Research Network. (n.d.). Federal programs. Retrieved January 31, 2001, from snexpress.com/federal.htm.

16

The Persuasive Speech

At the conclusion of this chapter, you should be able to:

- Write a clear persuasive speech objective.
- Organize an effective persuasive speech.
- Understand how to increase your credibility.

- Be aware of the importance of making ethical statements.
- Develop logical and emotional appeals in your speech.

Melvin's informative speech on illiteracy was very effective (see Chapter 15). Afterward, several students asked Melvin for more information on how they could help. He was more than happy to provide them with the information because after the process of researching and writing his speech, Melvin had become motivated to volunteer at the local high school literacy program. The program is in dire need of more people to help teach adults in the community to read.

Melvin's next speech assignment is to persuade his audience to take an action. He decides that he can use some of the same information from his first speech to persuade his audience to volunteer, like he does, at the local literacy program. Instead of focusing on describing the problem of illiteracy, Melvin will motivate his fellow students to help others.

He hopes to gain their attention by telling the story of his grandfather. He then will describe the extent of the problem of illiteracy in their community and the need for volunteers at the literacy program. Next, Melvin will explain to his audience how they can volunteer and that it will only takes a few hours a week. Lastly, he will describe how great they will feel, as he does, by helping others in their community. He will strongly urge his audience to take this action by signing a pledge to volunteer three hours of time.

In this chapter, we will discuss the process of persuasion. Specifically, we will describe how to organize and present a persuasive speech that will motivate your audience to take action or change a belief, attitude, or value.

Although many of us may never seek election to a political office, we all participate in the persuasive process. We may try to persuade our employer that we deserve a raise; or we try to persuade our children that we know what is best for them by turning off the television; or convince our spouse that the expensive sofa would be perfect in the living room. In addition, we also encounter persuasive appeals on a daily basis; we read newspaper articles, watch television commercials, surf the Internet, and listen to the appeals of salespeople and candidates running for office.

Persuasion is the act of convincing an audience, through verbal and nonverbal communication, to adopt or change an attitude, belief, or value or to take an action. For example, a minister may try to persuade her congregants that they should annually contribute a certain percentage of their income to the church; a salesperson may try to persuade a customer that the red Ford Explorer is the perfect SUV for her; or a sports celebrity may try to persuade junior high school students to stay in school. In each of these cases, the speaker hopes that audience members will experience a change in their thinking as a result of his or her message and ultimately will take an action they may not have normally taken. Persuasion is often a complex process because the speaker must appeal to a group of unique individuals who each possess a special frame of reference. As we discussed in all the previous chapters, it is essential that you, as the speaker, know and understand the diversity of your audience. Each audience member will bring his or her unique approach to the persuasive interaction. Ignoring your audience's diverse approaches will doom your presentation to failure. Thorough audience analysis is essential to persuading your audience.

Developing a Persuasive Speech Objective

When developing a persuasive speech, it is essential that you define your goal. What do you want the audience to do after listening to your speech? For example, do you want them to change their attitudes about allowing a tax credit to families whose children attend private schools, or do you want them to sign a petition to recall the mayor? In a persuasive speech, the speaker either calls for the audience to modify their beliefs or asks them to act on behalf of an issue or belief. As indicated in Chapter 11, developing a clear speech objective is essential in carrying out this process.

When calling on an audience to change a belief, use evidence to argue for or against a position. You are attempting to convince the members of your audience to alter their beliefs or behavior on a specific issue. To do this, you should use persuasive appeals (discussed later) to convince the audience of the value, morality, or advantage of your position.

Sometimes persuading your audience to alter an attitude is a question of degree. For example, if you wish to bring about a dramatic change in the audience's opinion, you might try to create a conflict for audience members to contemplate. After presenting your arguments, you hope the audience members will change their opinions. On the other hand, perhaps an audience is already sympathetic to a particular issue or policy; if so, you might try to reinforce or strengthen the audience's already positive feelings about the topic. For example:

Skye, an African American student, has very strong feelings about the policy of racial profiling. She and several of her friends have been stopped by police because they "fit the description" of suspected criminals in her community. She wants this police practice stopped in her city. Her church is holding a rally against racial profiling next week and she has been asked to speak. Skye knows that her audience is already in favor of proposal, so she wants to reinforce the audience's strong feelings against racial profiling. To make her points strong and clear, Skye will recount her encounters with local police and how she was a victim of racial profiling.

A second type of persuasive speech objective attempts to move the audience to immediate action. The speaker calls on audience members to adopt a specific behavior or to discontinue their present actions. For instance, you might call on audience members to fulfill their civic responsibility and vote in the next election, or you might call for a halt to the picketing of abortion clinics and harassment of those women who seek counseling there. In both of these cases you are calling on the audience to act. Ted's speech is one example:

Ted has returned to the local university to complete his degree in mechanical engineering. Ted has multiple sclerosis, a degenerative nerve disease, which forced him to leave his job as a construction worker. After a few weeks on campus, Ted has found it increasingly difficult to walk from one building to the next in the ten-minute time allotted. He is always late for his next class. As a member of student government, Ted proposed to his fellow senators that there should be more passing time between classes in order to make it easier for students with disabilities to get to their classes. His speech at the student government meeting urged his audience to take action by passing a resolution to increase the passing time and to begin discussions with the university's administrators.

Topics for a Persuasive Speech

How do you decide what would make a good topic for a persuasive speech? The first thing you need to think about is your speech objective, which, as indicated earlier, grows out of what you are trying to accomplish with the audience. Obviously, some topics lend themselves to a persuasive speech

TABLE 16.1 Persuasive Speech Topics

Change a Belief/Value/Attitude	Motivate to Act
Everyone should protect themselves from AIDS.	Use a condom.
Global warming is destroying the environment.	Use alternative energy sources.
Being overweight can kill you.	Exercise regularly.
Americans don't participate in the democratic process.	Vote in the next election.

better than others. Topics that are controversial or current are more appropriate for persuasive speeches than topics that are dated and no longer socially relevant. When choosing a topic, it is important to consider the things we discussed in Chapter 11: yourself, your audience, and the situation. Choose a topic that is important to you, relevant to the audience, and appropriate for the situation. Table 16.1 shows some examples of persuasive speech topics.

Developing Persuasive Speech Topics SKILL BUILDING

In a group, brainstorm topics for your persuasive speech.

1. Which of the topics attempts to change an attitude, value, or belief?
2. Which of the topics attempts to motivate the audience to act?
3. Pick one topic and discuss how you might relate the topic to your audience.

Organizing Your Persuasive Speech

In many ways, the organization of a persuasive speech follows the structure of an informative speech (see Chapter 13). First, you must engage the audience's attention; next, you attempt to appeal to a specific need or interest. The difference between persuasive and informative speeches, however, must be addressed at this point in the preparation process. As a speaker, you must decide whether you wish to educate your audience (the goal of an informative speech) or to do more, that is, change an attitude, belief, or value, or motivate them to action (the goal of a persuasive speech). If you choose the latter, the development of your speech body takes a slightly different focus. You must set out to "prove your case," or offer a solution to a problem. This section examines four organizational plans for doing just that: problem/solution, topical, comparative advantage, and Monroe's motivated sequence.

Problem/Solution

One way to organize your ideas is by using a problem/solution organizational pattern. The body of your speech first describes a problem that exists and then offers solutions to the problem. Many times, the solution you offer is the proposal you want the audience to believe or act on. For example, you could discuss the problems with parking at your school, and then offer solutions such as a parking garage or more parking lots. This organizational pattern helps the audience to see clearly the connections between the existing situation (problem) and the future possibilities (solution). For her presentation before the hospital board, Tami, the head nurse in pediatrics, used a problem/solution plan:

> Tami needed to show the hospital administrators that more registered nurses are needed on each shift to properly care for the children. During the first part of her presentation, Tami discussed the large patient/nurse ratio, the long amount of time children had to wait for their medication, and the number of times each child needed to have his or her vitals taken (temperature, blood pressure, and pulse) during an eight-hour shift. She then discussed how having just one more nurse on each shift would solve these problems and thus would provide better care for the children in the pediatrics ward.

Topical Sequence

An important part of successful persuasion is providing good reasons for the belief you want the audience to hold or the action you want them to take. In the body of your speech, you can provide a detailed description of each of the reasons the audience should adopt your proposal. Using strong evidence and support, each of the reasons leads the audience to the conclusion you want them to reach. It is best to either put your strongest idea first or put your strongest ideas last. Either way, the audience will more likely hear your reason clearly. Never put your strongest reason in the middle of your speech. It will likely not be heard or will be forgotten by the audience. Let's see how Tami could have used a topical sequence instead of a problem/ solution plan.

> Tami could begin the body of her presentation by discussing the reasons why another registered nurse is needed on each shift. Her strongest reason is an increase in the quality of patient care. With one more nurse, each patient could receive personalized attention from a nurse, thus ensuring that all doctors' orders are followed and the patient is comfort-

able. Another reason is that nurses could share the responsibility of answering and returning the calls from concerned parents, which is important in a pediatrics ward. Parents need to be more informed about their child's health and in a timely manner. Lastly, Tami could discuss the cost savings of having an additional nurse on each shift. Now, many nurses stay after their shift is over to care for especially sick children. When a nurse remains, she is paid time and a half for her overtime. An additional nurse would only have to be paid the normal rate per hour. Each of these ideas is a reason for adding an additional nurse to each shift.

Comparative Advantage

Often, the audience already understands the problem, but is looking for the best solution. In this case, you might want to use a comparative advantage plan. This plan allows you to compare your solution to others and to show how your plan or proposal is superior. The body of your presentation, then, consists of descriptions of your proposal and that of others. Each of the main ideas emphasizes how your proposal is the best and emphasizes the weaknesses of the others. In Tami's presentation, she could discuss the merits of her proposal, adding one additional registered nurse to each shift, while discussing why instituting longer shifts or adding non-nursing personnel would not increase patient care.

Motivated Sequence

The **motivated sequence** design, advanced by Alan H. Monroe, focuses on creating a sense of need and then explaining how that need can be satisfied. It this sounds familiar to you, there is a good reason—the basic organizational pattern is that of problem solution. There are five steps in this plan: (1) arousing attention, (2) showing a need, (3) satisfying the need, (4) visualizing the results, and (5) calling for action (see Table 16.2).

TABLE 16.2	**Monroe's Motivated Sequence**
1. Arousing attention	We attempt to capture the audience's attention with our opening remarks.
2. Showing a need	We determine the need or problem our topic suggests.
3. Satisfying the need	We argue how our proposal will meet the need or resolve the problem described earlier.
4. Visualizing the results	We create a visual image that projects what will happen if our proposal is embraced or rejected.
5. Calling for action	We urge the audience to demonstrate its support.

The first step in Monroe's motivated sequence—arousing the audience's interest in your subject—is basic to all types of public speeches, whether they are informative, entertaining, or persuasive. You cannot expect an audience to listen attentively if you have not captured its attention. The techniques for drawing the audience's attention discussed in Chapter 13—using a narrative, a startling statement, a rhetorical question, or a quotation—apply to the persuasive speech. For instance, this opening statement is aimed at capturing the audience's interest: "According to the Urban Institute, even in a booming economy, at least 2.3 million adults and children, or nearly 1 percent of the U.S. population, are likely to experience a spell of homelessness at least once during a year" (2000).

Step two, demonstrating a need, requires that you look closely at your topic in order to determine the need or problem that your topic suggests. For example, with the topic "homeless Americans," you might appeal to the audience's need for safety or shelter (refer to the discussion of Maslow's hierarchy of needs in Chapter 11) or establish the nature of the problem and its relevance to the audience. For example: "Our country is faced with a perplexing problem. A nation that takes pride in its high standard of living and considerable wealth must confront the mounting evidence that increasing numbers live without a roof over their heads and that the ranks of those who live in poverty are also on the rise."

In step three you begin to argue your case, to show how your proposal will either meet the need or solve the problem described earlier. This is the body of your speech, the place where you develop a well-reasoned logical appeal, a solid emotional appeal, or a combination of the two (discussed later in this chapter). You might propose, for instance, that "additional low-cost shelter must be made available for this growing segment of our population. In fact, this is in contrast to what is actually happening in our large cities, where low-cost housing is disappearing."

The purpose of the next step—visualizing the results—is to create a visual image that projects what will happen if your proposal is embraced or what will happen if it is rejected. It is also possible to show your audience both sides of the picture. In fact, by presenting the negative aspects first, followed by the positive, you can build a strong case for having your audience support the action you have proposed. In this part of your presentation, you want to increase your audience's identification with the problem. One of the most effective ways to do this is by describing the projected outcome in vivid language; the better your description, the better is the audience's conceptualization of the situation. If you choose to present a scenario that depicts the dangers the future holds should your proposal for increased low-cost housing be rejected, you might include this warning:

> Thousands of middle-class Americans are inching closer to joining the ranks of poor America. I've described what happens when unemployment becomes a way of life, when homes are repossessed by banks, when

dejected individuals give up all hope and "check out" of life as they've known it. Expect to see more of these people on the streets in the future. They won't be able to afford a place to live if low-cost housing is replaced by parking lots, high-rise office buildings, and high-rent housing meant to lure prosperous people back to our cities. It's not only their sad plight—it's all of ours.

If the intent of your speech is to alter the audience's attitude, you can end on this note. If, however, you want your audience to actually demonstrate its support for your proposal, you would go one step further.

The call for action is the final step of the motivated sequence. In it you want to capitalize on the support you have attempted to win during the visualization step. For example, you might ask everyone to write their U.S. senators and representatives to urge them to vote for additional funds for housing for the poor and homeless or to volunteer at the local homeless shelter or to help build homes for Habitat for Humanity.

Developing Persuasive Appeals

Throughout your presentation, it is essential that you use several persuasive appeals. There are three types of appeals: credibility, logical, and emotional. Presentation of an effective persuasive speech rests on your ability to establish or enhance your credibility, as a speaker, as well as on your ability to develop sound logical or emotional appeals. Consider this point: If a speaker is not perceived by the audience to be a credible source, then even a well-constructed appeal will have little impact. Conversely, a well-reasoned argument can increase a speaker's credibility. The importance of each of these factors is discussed in the following section.

Speaker Credibility Appeals

A variable that plays a significant role in the persuasion process is the credibility of the speaker; does the audience perceive the speaker as someone who is qualified to speak on a particular topic? For example, your experience as a swimming instructor would likely make you qualified to speak on the subject of water safety, yet it is unlikely that the same audience would perceive you as someone qualified to speak about the benefits of tax-deferred annuities. To a large degree, perception is a strong determinant in establishing your credibility as a speaker.

Some audiences may see you as more qualified than other audiences. For example, an audience of persons who possess little information about a subject may see you as a credible speaker, whereas an audience of people whose background or experience is extensive may see you as less qualified. In addition to audience reaction, several other variables contribute to a

TABLE 16.3	Speaker Credibility
Competence	A demonstrated ability, quality, or special knowledge
Dynamism	Degree of excitement, energy, involvement in topic
Trustworthiness and ethics	Character and integrity perceived by the audience

speaker's credibility, including competence, dynamism, trustworthiness, and ethics (see Table 16.3).

Competence

Competence is a demonstrated ability or quality. In persuasion, competence is often a measure of a speaker's knowledge concerning a topic. Speakers may possess a special ability that qualifies them as experts. For example:

> Annie is a sixth-grade teacher and the girls' basketball coach. She has played basketball since she was five years old and even received a full athletic college scholarship. During Women's History Month, Annie was asked by a Girl Scout troop to discuss her experience as a student athlete at the high school and college levels and how athletics helped her become a better student. The goal of the presentation is to entice the young girls to play organized sports. Because of Annie's past experiences and her natural athletic ability, the Girl Scouts found her to be a credible speaker.

Classroom speakers, too, can achieve a degree of expertness because of the knowledge gained from personal experience.

> Luanne is very committed to M.A.D.D. (Mothers Against Drunk Driving). She became involved in the organization six years ago when her son was killed by a drunk driver. That experience changed her life dramatically, but it gave her a special competence in mobilizing others to support the work of M.A.D.D. For her communication class, Luanne naturally wanted to address drunk driving, but more importantly, to persuade her classmates to join her as a volunteer for M.A.D.D. When she addressed her class about her experiences as a mother and volunteer, her fellow students listened attentively.

One of the best ways to demonstrate your knowledge or competence is to incorporate evidence in your speech. The use of supporting material can add substance to your ideas. For example, reference to a study by a leading cardiologist as reported in the *Journal of the American Medical Association*

Competence is an essential part of speaker credibility.

would add credibility to your speech's goal: "To persuade your audience that a high-fat diet can lead to heart disease." A thorough discussion of supporting materials can be found in Chapter 12. Being able to demonstrate your credibility increases the likelihood that your audience will listen to your presentation and support the position you are promoting.

Dynamism

Another dimension of credibility is dynamism. **Dynamism** is the degree of excitement that you bring to your presentation, often accomplished by demonstrating concern for and involvement in your topic. The dynamic speaker communicates that he or she is excited about the presentation, which in turn can elicit excitement on the part of the audience.

There are different levels of energy that can be demonstrated during a presentation. It is not necessary to scream and shout to show that you are a dynamic speaker; you can demonstrate involvement by being forceful, energetic, or sensitive—whatever is appropriate for your selected topic. How do you exhibit these qualities? By incorporating facial expressions, gestures, movement, and variety of vocal inflection into your speech. These behaviors were discussed in detail in Chapter 14.

Trustworthiness/Ethics

Trustworthiness refers to the kind of "character" you communicate to your audience. In other words, are you an ethical person? **Ethics,** the rules that govern moral behavior, must be considered as you develop your persuasive speech. The integrity you bring to your message affects both the way you interact with your audience and the way the audience assesses your credibility. People want to put their faith in someone of high moral character, someone whom they believe is honest and reliable. Political leaders, for example, attempt to use their character or trustworthiness as a way to gain your support. Many times they may even support their "trustworthiness" with examples of past promises kept or by discussing their background. Or, candidates for office may have others speak to their character or trustworthiness. For example, during the Democratic National Convention, vice-president nominee Joseph Lieberman said:

> I have known Al for fifteen years. I know his record and I know his heart. I know him as a public servant and I know what it is like to sit with him around the dining room table. We have discussed—sometimes even debated—policy issues, and we have shared private moments of prayer. I can tell you that Al Gore is a man of family and faith—a father, and now a grandfather. When my daughter was six, after spending time with Al, she looked at me and said, "He must be a daddy." Al Gore is a man of courage and conviction. He believes in service to America. He volunteered for Vietnam (2000, p. 680).

Many speakers have others describe their character and trustworthiness, as Joe Lieberman (here) did for Al Gore in the 2000 presidential campaign.

Al Gore can establish his character and trustworthiness without mentioning his own accomplishments because his running mate has done it for him.

How do you convey your trustworthiness to an audience? If you are already familiar to an audience, your past behavior may speak for itself.

Ethics in Communication

The Persuasive Speech

In the beginning of the chapter, we learned about Melvin and his attempt to persuade his classmates to volunteer their time to teach adults to read in their community. Melvin has done extensive audience analysis and understands the diversity of his audience. This will greatly improve his chances at persuading his audience because he can tailor his use of appeals to them. Melvin, and any persuasive speaker, needs to also consider the ethical dimensions of the persuasive presentation.

First and foremost, extreme care should be taken not to compromise your integrity in order to reach your speech goals. To ensure that this does not happen, practice the following principles:

1. *Be honest with your audience.* In Melvin's case, he must relate the story of his grandfather honestly. He cannot make up the story or exaggerate his grandfather's experiences. He must also be honest about his own volunteer work. He cannot say he volunteers for the local high school program if he doesn't. Speakers can be tempted to fabricate facts or even exaggerate experiences because they think it will make their speech more effective. Any argument you construct should be based on reliable and verifiable information (see Chapter 12). Part of your responsibility

as a speaker is to present accurate information to your audience. The use of evidence or supporting materials helps you to achieve this goal. Exaggerated claims, fabricated stories, and misuse of statistics all represent deliberate efforts to distort information.

2. *Do not engage in name calling.* It would be easy for Melvin to call his audience "lazy slugs" or "uncaring," "selfish" or "unconcerned." Name calling will only put his audience on the defensive and they will be less likely to listen to Melvin's arguments. The ideas in your speech should be strong enough to stand on their own merit. Verbal attacks directed at others are an inappropriate way to gain support for your cause. Besides, an audience is apt to question the ethics of a speaker who resorts to name calling.

3. *Give credit to outside source materials.* Melvin needs to be sure he uses oral footnotes throughout the speech. (See Chapter 12.) Bear in mind that quotations should be accurate and that the information you cite should not be taken out of context or fabricated. Not crediting the source at the time of use is plagiarism. Following these guidelines will ensure that your persuasive efforts will be both effective and ethical.

However, how do you establish trust with an audience who has never heard or seen you before? You might try revealing a bit of your background as a way of introducing yourself. Often, mentioning how you are directly involved in your speech topic leads your audience to perceive you as sincere or committed, that is, trustworthy. A perception of the audience that you lack ethics or are not trustworthy can greatly diminish your credibility and decrease the believability of your propositions.

Techniques for Enhancing Your Credibility

While the ability to persuade an audience depends on a speaker's competence, dynamism, and trustworthiness, you can employ specific techniques to enhance your credibility as a speaker.

Establish Common Ground with the Audience

One way to enhance your credibility is to establish common ground with the audience. Tell the audience how you are like them in some way. For example, you might try to share information about yourself that reflects a value system similar to the audience's. Another way to establish common ground is to include supporting material that your audience can identify with, preferably early in the speech. Consider the following:

> Pauline, a dietician, was invited to speak at a gathering of Weight Watchers, a group designed to help individuals to lose weight and eat healthier. At the beginning of her speech she related a story about herself and made reference to the fact she had once weighed 250 pounds and took the initiative to change her lifestyle by eating healthy and exercising regularly. After hearing this story, her audience was "with" her. Her effort to motivate the audience to begin an exercise program was successful, in part because of the shared experience she had with the audience.

Indicate Your Special Knowledge

Another technique that increases your credibility is to indicate that you have special credentials or knowledge that makes you uniquely qualified to speak on a topic. Without appearing to brag, tell the audience about your background and its special relationship to your topic. For example,

> The Parks and Recreation Department called a special meeting to respond to the community's outcry over the cancellation of a popular summer music camp for elementary school children. In an effort to justify the cancellation, the Parks and Recreation board members prefaced their remarks to the assembled parents by stating their qualifications as experts in recreation and child development. Dave, a concerned parent, was

angered by what he considered to be their inept handling of the issue. He offered his own credentials, a Ph.D. in Music Education, and then spoke about the dire need for affordable musical instruction and experiences for children in the community and the effect the cancellation will have on the children already involved in the program. The effectiveness of his insightful remarks was reinforced by the positive response he received from the audience.

The person who introduces you to an audience can help reinforce your expertise. For example, the emcee at an American Association of Retired Persons luncheon introduced the keynote speaker in the following way:

> It is my sincere pleasure to introduce Dr. Clarice Fernandez to you. She is a clinical psychologist with an extensive background in the area of human sexuality. She is the author of two books, one which deals with sex after sixty. Please join me in welcoming Dr. Fernandez, who will speak to you on improving intimate relationships after the age of sixty.

In this example, the introduction served to enhance the credibility of Dr. Fernandez. By highlighting her achievements, the emcee showed how Dr. Fernandez was uniquely qualified to speak on her topic. Clearly, it is essential to establish your credibility by discussing your qualifications to speak on the topics or to have someone else inform the audience of your qualifications.

Identifying Credibility

CRITICAL THINKING

1. Name a public speaker or speakers who possess each of the dimensions of credibility discussed above:

   a. Competence

   b. Dynamism

   c. Trustworthiness/ethics

2. Why does the speaker possess these dimensions of credibility, in your opinion?

3. What can you do to increase your own credibility based on the behavior of speaker(s)?

Logical Appeals

The heart of a persuasive speech lies in the argument that the speaker constructs. There are a few ways to approach this argument; choosing the best one depends on such factors as (1) your speech objective, (2) the topic that you have selected, (3) the audience to be addressed, and (4) how successfully you have established your credibility. Your assessment of these factors will help you to determine how you wish to build a logical argument.

COMMUNICATION and TECHNOLOGY

Persuasion and the Internet

A recent study indicates that 83 percent of college freshman use the Internet to do research or to complete homework (Browne, Freeman, and Williamson, 2001). The Internet is an easy and fast way to find information. Using any number of search engines, we can locate hundreds of sites for just about any topic. According to Browne et al., "Information found on the internet varies in its purpose: Web sites advocate causes, advertise products, entertain visitors and express opinions in addition to presenting scholarly research" (2001, p. 392). Thus, most of the "stuff" on the Web is persuasion.

It is necessary for us to carefully evaluate any information found on the Web. Before using any information as support in our speeches, we must determine whether it is academic or scholarly research, propaganda or commercially driven information. For example, when we do a search for *holocaust,* hundreds of sites appear. Among the legitimate scholarly sites, we also find sites that appear scholarly, but use unsubstantiated and false information. One such site is sponsored by the Institute for Historical Review, which claims to be "a non-ideological, non-political, non-profit" group that is dedicated to historical revisionism. This sounds pretty legitimate, doesn't it? A closer examination shows that

this site, with the use of nonsense support, tries to persuade the viewers that gas chambers were not used and only a few thousand people died. Other examples of bogus sites that look legitimate include a site "dedicated" to Martin Luther King sponsored by a white supremacist group; Melatonin.com, which claims to be a "leading consumer information site" while selling products; Halloween, which looks like a historical and factual account of the holiday, but is an argument against modern-day Pagan religions (Winter).

Remember that written material is usually reviewed by others and is edited before publication. Anyone can put anything on a web site. Thus, it is even more important that speakers check and double-check the information on the Internet. In Chapter 12, we discussed how to evaluate a web site. Review those four questions (Who is the source? How old is the information? Is the information verifiable elsewhere? Is an email or other contact information provided?) and ask them of any web site you find while researching and preparing your speech. The authors of the web site may just be selling you something, or worse yet, advocating racist, sexist, or homophobic ideals while looking quite legitimate.

A **logical argument** helps your audience understand your ideas, thereby increasing the likelihood that members will be persuaded by what you say. An argument means giving one or more "good" reasons for your plan or proposal. Two ways to develop logical appeals are through deductive reasoning and inductive reasoning.

Deductive reasoning follows a simple formula: It starts with a general premise, is followed by a minor premise, and ends by drawing a conclusion. In a persuasive speech, deductive reasoning can provide a clear development of your ideas and at the same time can assist the audience in following your thoughts. With deductive reasoning it is imperative that your premise, the proposition that serves as the basis for your argument, warrants the conclusion you are advocating. In the following example, your audience would probably accept the claims you are making because they are based on fact:

General premise: One cause of skin cancer is exposure to the sun's ultraviolet rays.

Minor premise: Those who sunbathe regularly expose themselves to ultraviolet rays.

Conclusion: As a group, sunbathers are at a higher than normal risk for getting skin cancer.

Before constructing a persuasive speech using the deductive reasoning just provided, you should establish the relationship between your argument and your speech objective. In this case your speech objective might be "to persuade the classroom audience that sunbathing poses a risk to everyone's health." Beginning with your general premise, ask yourself whether or not the audience is likely to accept your statement without questioning its truthfulness. If you are in doubt, offer supporting evidence.

As a speaker, you need to realize the importance of building your arguments on a sound foundation. Lack of a sound premise spells disaster for the persuasive speech. Consider the following:

General premise: All college students watch MTV.

Minor premise: Catherine is a college student.

Conclusion: Catherine watches MTV.

The general premise in this example is faulty. Not all college students watch MTV. As a matter of fact, the average age of college students is steadily rising and the average age of the MTV viewer is between twelve and eighteen. Consequently, the incorrect premise means the conclusion is faulty.

Another type of reasoning you can use when developing a persuasive speech is inductive reasoning, in which one moves from specific instances to generalizations. For example,

Murder rates have declined over the past eight years (CNN.com, 2000).

Robbery rates have declined over the past eight years (CNN.com, 2000).

Assault rates have declined over the past eight years (CNN.com, 2000).

Conclusion: Crime is on the decline.

Logical appeals are enhanced by strong supporting material.

Speakers who use inductive reasoning need to be sure about the soundness of their ideas before making a generalization. Faulty logic can trip you up if you are not careful, as in the following example:

Susan had mechanical problems with her Pontiac after 25,000 miles.

George had his Ford in for repairs at 23,000 miles.

Valerie's Toyota has not required repairs. It now has 45,000 miles.

Conclusion: Toyotas are superior cars.

In this example, the audience should be suspicious because the generalization is unwarranted. A larger and more representative sample is necessary to convince the careful listener of the validity of the generalization.

Supporting material in the form of statistics, research findings, or authoritative opinion can bring an added dimension to the logical appeal and can strengthen your argument, whether you have chosen to use deductive or inductive reasoning. For example, in the speech on crime, the citing of statistics (the number of reported cases of murder and assault for each of the last five years) or research findings would lend strength and credibility to the argument.

Fallacies

Fallacies are flawed arguments. The above example about cars clearly shows an overgeneralization, which is one type of argument fallacy. Such flaws as arguments ad hominem, assumptions of cause and effect, nonsequiturs, overgeneralizations, and faulty analogies can weaken persuasive speeches.

No doubt you have heard speakers attack the character of another person. This is called the fallacy of argument **ad hominem.** President George W. Bush, in his derogatory comments about al Qaeda leader Osama bin Laden, used an argument ad hominem. Instead of constructing a well-reasoned argument that protested bin Laden's terrorist policies, Bush resorted to name calling: "He's not in charge of Afghanistan anymore. He's not in charge of the—he's not the parasite that invaded the host, the Taliban" (2002, p. 2). Uppermost in Bush's mind was to present a negative image of bin Laden to his audience. However, in the process of name calling, little was said about the issue of terrorism.

A second kind of argument fallacy is the **faulty cause-and-effect argument.** For example, the speaker who blames children's poor test scores on the teachers' strike earlier in the school year invites a challenge to his or her argument. There is no proof offered to show that one event caused the other to happen.

In a **nonsequitur,** the minor points are not related to the major points, or the conclusion does not logically follow the points that precede it. Look at this persuasive argument:

We need to reverse the trend of teen gun violence in the United States.

Television programs depict too much violence.

Less violent television programs will help reduce the number of violent crimes annually.

The conclusion drawn by this speaker does not logically follow the earlier points.

Overgeneralizations add a dramatic effect to your speech, but are not logical. Be sure that your argument does not draw conclusions from a small sample or from just a few examples. Finally, a **faulty analogy** can hinder your persuasive efforts. In Chapter 12 *analogy* was defined as a form of support that compares the similar features in two seemingly different objects or situations. This definition implies that the comparison must be a valid one; when it is not, the analogy is flawed. The perceptive listener will be able to detect a faulty analogy, as in the following:

Hans, in presenting his arguments for overturning the *Roe v. Wade* decision, which legalized abortion, compared the abortion of unborn human embryos and fetuses to Hitler's annihilation of millions in the gas chambers during World War II.

"Your Honor, we're going to go with the prosecution's spin."

© The New Yorker Collection 1997 Mike Twohy from cartoonbank.com. All rights reserved.

SKILL BUILDING   **Creating Inductive and Deductive Arguments**

1. Choose one of the speech objective topics you developed earlier in this chapter.
2. Develop an outline for an inductive and deductive argument for that topic (refer to Chapter 13 for help with outlining skills).
3. Be sure to include supporting material for both arguments you construct.

Emotional Appeals

Emotional appeals are used to trigger the emotions or feelings of an audience: anger, fear, and pride. For instance, photographs of starving children in Third World countries can effectively stir our emotions. However, emotion should not be a substitute for reasoning; rather, the emotional appeal can serve as a supporter of a well-reasoned argument.

In constructing an emotional appeal, you can attempt to stir a wide variety of feelings. To a great extent your topic will dictate the type of emotional response you want your audience to exhibit. Do you want to anger them so they will be moved to take action? Do you want to appeal to their sense of pride or compassion? Or do you want to trigger their fears? Whatever your decision, there are specific ways to achieve the desired response.

One technique is to use emotionally charged language. This also serves as an indicator of your own involvement in the topic. The following examples help illustrate how language can play a significant role in generating an emotional appeal. This introductory statement is void of emotional language: "Statistics point to an alarming trend in this country. The rise in teenage suicides needs to be stopped." Now consider the treatment of the same topic using more powerful language:

> Your first reaction is to cry when you learn how this deadly disease is sweeping our society. It is like a cancer, spreading at a rapid pace, touching people from all walks of life. This cancer touches individuals in our rat-infested ghettos, as well as those in upper middle-class suburban ghettos. I am speaking about the epidemic of teenage suicides; the thousands of time bombs ticking away in today's adolescents.

In the second example note how much more of an impact the speaker's message would have on the audience. The language used by this speaker dramatically builds the case.

Another way to use the emotional appeal is to personalize your speech by telling a story. New York Governor Mario Cuomo shared part of his background in his Keynote Address at the 1984 Democratic National Convention. His words are intended to stir our national pride:

> That struggle to live with dignity is the real story of the shining city. It's a story I didn't read in a book, or learn in a classroom. I saw it, and lived it. Like many of you.
>
> I watched a small man with thick calluses on both hands work fifteen and sixteen hours a day. I saw him once literally bleed from the bottoms of his feet, a man who came here uneducated, alone, unable to speak the language, who taught me all I needed to know about faith and hard work by the simple eloquence of his example. I learned about our kind of democracy from my father; I learned about our obligation to each other from him and from my mother. They asked only for a chance to work and to make the world better for their children and to be protected in those moments when they would not be able to protect themselves. This nation and its government did that for them.
>
> And that they were able to build a family and live in dignity and see one of their children go from behind their little grocery store on the other side of the tracks in south Jamaica where he was born, to occupy the highest seat in the greatest state of the greatest nation in the only world we know, is an ineffably beautiful tribute to the democratic process (1984, p. 649).

The success of Cuomo's appeal rests on his ability to make the audience feel as much gratitude toward his parents and as much pride in this country as he feels.

Emotional appeals alone will not persuade an audience. Your persuasive effort will be much more successful if you use emotional appeals in conjunction with your well-reasoned argument.

CHECKLIST

Persuasive Speaking

- Choose a topic based on your analysis of self, audience, and situation.
- Arrange your ideas using one of the organizational patterns.
- Include logical appeals.
- Avoid argument fallacies.
- Include emotional appeals.
- Establish your credibility through your verbal and nonverbal behavior.

Summary

Persuasion is the act of convincing an audience to alter or change an attitude, belief, or value, or to take an action. In a persuasive speech your objective is either to modify a belief or ask your audience to act on behalf of an issue or belief. With the speech objective and audience in mind, you begin to consider what would make a suitable topic. We discussed the fact that certain topics lend themselves to persuasive speeches, namely, those that are controversial or current. Choose a topic based on your extensive analysis of self, audience, and situation.

Once you have decided on your topic, your next decision involves choosing an effective organizational design. Four patterns were described in this chapter: problem/solution, topical, comparative advantages, and Monroe's motivated sequence. With the motivated sequence, the focus is on creating a sense of need and then explaining how that need can be satisfied. Each of the five steps in the motivated sequence was described: (1) arousing attention, (2) showing a need, (3) satisfying a need, (4) visualizing the results, and (5) calling for action.

There are three types of persuasive appeals. These include credibility, logical, and emotional appeals. Credibility is the audience's perception of the speaker's competence, dynamism, and trustworthiness or ethics.

Also discussed were techniques for increasing your credibility, such as establishing common ground with the audience and demonstrating to the audience that you have special knowledge regarding your topic. Your efforts in both of these areas will help convince your audience—and yourself—that you are a credible speaker.

It is in the body of the speech that you develop your persuasive argument with the help of either a logical appeal or an emotional appeal. In this chapter we discussed how to develop a logical appeal by using either deductive or inductive reasoning. Deductive reasoning starts with a general premise, is followed by a minor premise, and ends by drawing a conclusion. Conversely, with inductive reasoning you move from specific instances to generalizations. While an argument should always be built on a strong logical base, it is sometimes appropriate to trigger the emotions of an audience. In an emotional appeal you can use emotionally charged language or attempt to personalize your speech in order to achieve the desired response from your audience. As your ability to develop convincing arguments increases, so too will your confidence as a public speaker.

Review Questions

1. Identify the two different types of persuasive speech objectives.
2. Discuss why audience analysis is so important in choosing your persuasive speech topic.
3. Describe each of the persuasive organizational patterns.
4. Briefly describe the five steps in Monroe's motivated sequence.
5. What steps can a speaker take to increase his or her credibility?
6. How does the issue of trustworthiness and ethics enter into the development of a persuasive speech?
7. Differentiate between inductive and deductive reasoning. How can you use both types of reasoning in a persuasive speech?
8. What are argument fallacies?
9. What role does language play in a speaker's attempt to trigger the emotions of the audience?

Sample Persuasive Speech

Eliminate Your Credit Card Debt

The speaker grabs the attention of the audience with the use of a rhetorical question.

The speaker tells her story, which functions to get the audience involved in her topic and presentation.

The speaker creates common ground with the audience by showing they share past experiences and emotions.

The speaker establishes her credibility.

The speaker previews her main ideas.

The speaker uses a transitional preview to connect to the body of the speech.

The speaker uses oral footnotes to cite her source material.

Would you ever pay $6,000 for a t-shirt? Of course you wouldn't! But I did during my first week of college when I signed up for my very first credit card. At a table near the student lounge, a very nice man handed me a cotton t-shirt and a promise that I would be "financially free" with my very own credit card. Who could argue with financial independence and a free t-shirt? I signed on the dotted line and less than a month later, I had a major credit card with a $2,000 credit line. Soon after, other credit card companies came calling and I signed up for their cards as well. I was starting to form bad credit habits. When shopping at the mall, instead of paying cash for items I needed, I'd apply for instant credit to get an additional 10 percent off on items that I merely wanted. Before I knew it, I had an amazing amount of open credit. For a while, I was in heaven. I was enjoying a lifestyle of the rich and famous. The unfortunate thing is that I'm not rich and I'm living well above my means. I now owe $6,000 to various credit card companies and it all started with a simple cotton t-shirt.

With a show of hands, how many of you have at least one credit card? Three? Five? Ten? Like you, I have many credit cards, and until recently, have enjoyed using them immensely. See? (Shows audience her credit cards displayed like an accordion.) Does what I'm saying sound familiar? Having credit card debt is a struggle, it's depressing, and it's time for all of us to make a change. Because of my desire to be debt free, I have done a lot of research about getting out of credit card debt, therefore, I am qualified to talk about this topic. Today, I am going to urge you to join me in eliminating our credit card debt. In doing so, we will discuss the problems that credit cards cause us and encourage you to take five easy steps toward getting out of credit card debt. First, I will explain just how problematic credit cards can be, especially for college students like us.

Our use of credit cards is taking too much of our hard-earned money and ruining our credit ratings. According to Nolo, a consumer rights law firm, American adults have over two billion credit cards. That's nine credit cards per adult. Even scarier, *Time* magazine reports that Americans owe an average of $5,800 on their credit cards, and that figure doesn't even take into account the yearly interest. Buying on credit is expensive. Nolo states that we pay an average of 18 percent on our credit card purchases and 20 percent on purchases made with gasoline and department store cards. That means that the average American owing $5,800 had to pay over $1,000 each year just in interest. Can you image what it would be like to invest $1,000 a year instead? It would feel really good, wouldn't it? Saving that amount of money makes sense, yet, the *Chicago Tribune* recently reported that personal savings rates have dropped to 2.4 percent. In the meantime,

Americans continue to sink into debt. Now that I have explained how Americans in general are affected by credit card debt, I would like to explain how credit card debt affects college students.

You may be interested to know that 60 percent of undergraduates and 90 percent of graduate students have at least one credit card, according to Nellie Mae, a national student loan provider. As you may already know, college students are prime targets for credit card companies. These companies come on campuses all across our nation and entice us to sign up for their credit cards, often with the offer of free gifts. Consolidated Credit Counseling Service states that 80 percent of college campuses permit on-campus credit card solicitation. Why would credit companies solicit students who often do not make much money? According to Consolidated Credit Counseling Service, three out of four college students will keep their first credit card for at least fifteen years. It pays to secure a student's loyalty early on. There are obvious problems with obtaining easy credit, which I will now explain.

Consolidated Credit Counseling Service reports that the average outstanding balance for a college student is $2,226. The Public Interest Research Group reports that students who get their credit from the campus tables have higher balances on their credit cards than those students who obtain credit elsewhere. These students are also less informed about the credit they are signing up for and as a result are more likely to go into debt than other students.

Obtaining easy credit before we are financially ready not only affects our pocketbooks, it also can affect our credit ratings, even our abilities to secure jobs. Howard Dvorkin, President of Consolidated Credit Counseling Service, warns that each time we apply for a credit card, an inquiry shows up on our credit report. He states, "The greater the number of inquires, the greater the number of red flags." Future creditors will see all those red flags, and as a result, may decline our credit. Gaining credit becomes a vicious cycle since many credit card companies offer credit even after we've been declined. Dvorkin explains that we should be extra careful with these offers, even if they seem enticing. Dvorkin says that these offers are from "bottom feeders, the secondary predatory lenders." These companies actually like us because they see us as desperate customers who need credit. Dvorkin warns that this means we will be charged higher interest rates, lower credit limits, and stiffer penalties if we make late payments. Obviously, credit card debt often can mean trouble for college students.

Although many of us have some credit card debt, 10 percent of all college students have outstanding credit card debts of over $7,000. Some students are in so deep that they are forced to quit school in search of a full-time job just to pay off their credit cards. A student with financial problems due to credit card debt may have problems finding employment, as many employers do background checks, according to an article by Knight-Ridder

The problems associated with credit card debt are clearly defined as part of showing the need. The speaker uses a transitional preview.

The speaker relates the topic to the audience by quoting a relevant statistic as support and uses an oral footnote to cite the source.

The speaker clearly describes the problem and is showing the need to act.

Newspapers. How responsible will we seem to future employers when we are not responsible with our finances? Now that I have explained the seemingly endless problems one incurs with credit card debt, I'm going to explain the warning signs of credit card debt and five easy steps toward being debt free. First, I'll discuss the warning signs.

According to the National Institute for Consumer Education, you are in credit trouble if you (show a chart): continually make late payments; reach the limits of your credit card; make the minimum payments on credit card balances; have difficulty saving; use savings to pay bills; use credit cards to get cash; are denied credit; and finally, use credit cards to pay off other credit cards. If any of these warning signs apply to you, join me today in taking action. This brings me to my next point: what we can do to rid ourselves of credit card debt.

The speaker uses a transitional preview to move to the next main idea.

There are many credible companies who offer ways to get out of credit card debt. However, Oxygen.com's suggestions, in my opinion, are the easiest to follow. They suggest taking five steps toward credit card freedom (shows another chart). First, stop incurring debt. It is important to cut out any unnecessary spending. I plan to do this by canceling all but one card. Second, keep track of cash. List everything you purchase. This will help you see where all your money is going. Third, plan for the future. Set attainable goals. I, for one, plan to eat out only once a month, and when I do, I'll pay cash. Once I pay off my debt, I plan to take the money I would normally use to pay bills and invest it. Fourth, don't expect miracles. Getting out of debt takes time, patience, and discipline. Lastly, seek professional help. If you are feeling overwhelmed and simply cannot achieve goals on your own, you can call credit counseling agencies such as Consolidated Credit Counseling Service.

The speaker lays out the action to be taken as a way to satisfy the need.

The National Institute for Consumer Education acknowledges that learning to control credit card use is not easy, but self-discipline is key. They suggest that you don't use a credit card for impulse shopping or take cash advances. Credit cards should be used only in an emergency. Also, if you have a variety of credit cards, keep the one with the lowest interest rate, that does not charge an annual fee, has a grace period, and does not charge nuisance fees. In addition, there are many companies who can help us tackle our credit card debt. For example, *Time* magazine cites SmartMoney.com and Money.com. Both companies will help you understand and manage your budget. Quicken.com has a debt reduction planner that can help you prioritize debt and puts you on a payment schedule. These steps are doable. Join me today in tackling debt.

The speaker lays out the action to be taken as a way to satisfy the need.

Visualize your life free from credit card debt. Think about how good it will feel to actually look forward to opening the mail. Wouldn't it feel great to take the money you would normally use to pay your creditors and put it into a savings account or to invest it for your future? These things I just mentioned can happen to you, simply by paying off your credit cards.

The speaker paints a picture of what the world would be like as a means of visualization.

In conclusion, I hope I have persuaded you to join me in eliminating our credit card debt. In doing so, I explained the problems credit cards cause us and encouraged you to take five easy steps toward getting out of credit card debt. I'm taking the first step now . . . I've stopped incurring debt. I am eliminating all but one of my credit cards, which I will put away and use only in emergencies (the speaker takes out scissors and cuts up two credit cards). In addition, I have written cancellation letters (shows letters) to all my credit card companies. I challenge you to join me in a better life free from credit card debt by following the five steps I have just outlined. When you get home, take your credit cards and cut them up. Pay for necessities in cash and look forward to a future of financial security. Thank you.

A signpost is used to indicate to the audience the speech is coming to a close.

The speaker calls the audience to action.

The speaker shows her appreciation for the audience's attention.

Erin Okamoto Protsman
Purdue University Calumet
Spring 2001
Used by permission.

Works Cited

Bergen, K. (2000, February 24). Debt load looms as danger for many families. *Chicago Tribune.* Retrieved March 4, 2001, from chicagotribune.com/ business/businessnews/article/0,2669,2-42494,FF.html.

Flynn, M. (n.d.). Credit card debt high among undergraduates. *The Post-Ohio University: Athens Campus U-Wire.* Retrieved March 4, 2001, from www. studentadvantage.com/article/print/0,4281,c6-i70-t0-a23768,00.htm.

Melia, M. K. (2001, January 16). The hole story of getting out of debt. *Chicago Tribune.* Retrieved March 4, 2001 from chicagotribune.com/business/ businessnews/article/0,2669,ART-49256,FF.html.

National Institute of Consumer Education. (n.d.). Getting out of debt. Eastern Michigan University. Retrieved March 4, 2001, from www.emich.edu/public/ coe/nice/Debtma1.html.

Nolo.com. (n.d.). Using credit and charge cards FAQ. Retrieved March 4, 2001 from www.nolo.com/Encyclopedia/faqs/dc/dc2.html#FAQ-38.

Oxygen Media. (2000). Five easy steps to get out of debt. Retrieved January 31, 2001 from wysiwyg://159/http://ka-ching.oxyg...ics/ym/ managing-orama01_steps.html.

Schneider, M. (n.d.). Credit card activation: The beginning of the end. *The Pitt News–University of Pittsburgh U-Wire.* Retrieved March 4, 2001 from www. studentadvantage.com/article/print/0,4281,c6-i69-+311-a15898,00.html.

Sowle, T. (2000, September 19). State legislators lobby for credit card policies for students. *Knight-Ridder Newspapers,* 2000. Retrieved January 31, 2001 from www.mankato.msus.edu.edu/Dept/reporter/reparchive/09_19_00/news5.html.

Stohr, K. (2000, November 7). Financial lifelines: drowning in debt? Or does it just feel that way? In either case, the Internet can help you get out of deep water. *Time Digital Magazine.* Retrieved March 4, 2001 from www.time.com/ time/digital/magazine/articles/0,4753,59303,00.html.

Taylor, N. (n.d.). Is your college student ready for a credit card? Consumer Affairs Department of the Institute of Certified Financial Planners. Retrieved January 31, 2001 from protectassets.com/news/art/1999/student2499.html.

Wuorio, J. (2001, March). Digging into debt. *Good Housekeeping,* pp. 55–57.

Glossary

A

Abdicrats　People who lack confidence and find it difficult to make decisions.

Abstract terms　Language that is general or vague.

Abstraction　The use of broad terms to explain ideas or concepts.

Active listening　Listening with a sense of purpose.

Ad hominem　An argument that attacks the speaker and does not address the issue.

Adaptors　Nonverbal behaviors individuals use to adjust to or cope with uncomfortable communication situations.

Affect displays　Nonverbal signs of our emotional state.

Agenda　An outline of the points to be discussed by a group.

Aggression　Hostility; forcing a solution advantageous to ourselves.

Allness stereotyping　We attribute a particular characteristic to a group of people for the purpose of this discussion.

Analogy　Compares the similar features in two seemingly different objects or situations.

Antonyms　Words that have opposite meanings.

Arrangement　The physical placement of the members of a group.

Attitude　A predetermined position regarding a person, event, concept, or object; affects the way we interpret data.

Attribution　Involves assigning causation to our behavior and the behavior of others.

Authoritative opinion　Words or ideas of individuals knowledgeable about a topic, similar or different ideas, facts, or concepts.

Autocratic leaders　People who dominate the communication process.

Avoidance　We retreat from a problem in a relationship.

Avoiding　The eighth stage of relational development; characterized by distancing.

B

Bar graph　Primarily used to show the way different items compare and relate to one another.

383

Blind quadrant   A window in the Johari window that represents the part of self that we either unconsciously reveal to others or are actually unaware of.

Body   Main part of a speech.

Bonding   The fifth stage of relational development; characterized by public expressions of commitment.

Brainstorming   Encourages creativity and the free flow of ideas.

C

Call for action   To inspire or motivate the audience to act.

Causal order   Establishes the fact that certain events are linked to other events that have precipitated them.

Certainty   The belief that others cannot possibly contribute new knowledge to the situation.

Challenging the audience   Occurs when the speaker calls on the audience to think further about the topic.

Channel   The vehicle by which the message is communicated from the source to the receiver.

Chronemics   The study of how we use time.

Circumscribing   The seventh stage of relational development; characterized by less communication and defense mechanisms.

Closed questionnaire   The respondent must select an answer from two or more choices.

Closed questions   Designed to elicit specific feedback from the respondent.

Closure   Filling in the gaps when parts are missing from stimuli.

Coercive power   Derived from one's perceived ability to control another's behavior through negative reinforcement.

Cohesiveness   Demonstrated sense of purpose within a group.

Commitment   Motivation of members to meet the goals of the group; also plays a significant role in the outcome of small-group interactions.

Committee   Small group of people assigned a task by a larger group.

Communication   The interdependent process of sending, receiving, and understanding messages.

Communication climate   State of mind brought to each communication situation.

Comparisons   Similarities and differences between ideas, facts, or concepts.

Competence   Demonstrated ability or quality.

Conclusion   The last section of a speech. It functions to draw the speech to an end, to reiterate the central theme of the presentation, and to indicate to the audience what you want them to do.

Concrete terms   Language that is detailed and specific.

Conflict phase   Ideas begin to surface regarding decision making, and disagreement and tension surface.

Connotative meaning   Meaning determined by someone's experiences, values, and culture.

Content message   The obvious message, words or language used.

Context   The conditions surrounding communication with others are referred to as the context of the interaction.

Control　Power or influence; a means of making the other party conform to our way of thinking.

Control needs　Desire for power or influence.

Coordinate points　Major ideas in a speech that grow out of the thesis statement.

Cost-benefit theory　People choose to maintain or exit relationships based on the rewards they receive within those relationships.

Cover letter　A short letter that introduces you to a prospective employer.

Criteria　The minimum requirements a solution must have to be acceptable.

Critical listening　Evaluating the speaker's message or intent.

Culturally bound　Meaning derived from one's culture.

Culture　The customary beliefs and attitudes of a racial, religious, or social group.

D

Dating　The use of a specific time reference to clarify a message.

Decision by consensus　Genuine agreement among members that an appropriate decision has been made.

Decision by leader　The leader makes all decisions for the group.

Decision by majority vote　Democracy in action.

Decoding　The process of interpreting or attaching meaning to symbols.

Deductive reasoning　Follows a simple formula: it starts with a general premise, is followed by a minor premise, and ends by drawing a conclusion.

Defensive climate　Inhibits the interaction between people.

Defensive communication　A reaction, either verbal or nonverbal, to a communication situation in which he or she feels personally threatened or uncomfortable.

Democratic leader　Demonstrates his or her confidence in the group by involving group members in decision-making matters.

Demographics　Easily identifiable characteristics such as age, sex, and ethnic/cultural/religious background.

Demonstration　Method for explaining a point or idea to an audience.

Denial　Refusal to acknowledge that a problem exists.

Denotative meaning　Specific reference of a word; it is what we would find if we looked in a dictionary.

Description　An image created verbally using concrete or abstract language.

Descriptive language　Employs specific words that represent observable behavior or phenomena.

Descriptiveness　The ability to focus on observable behavior.

Differentiating　The sixth stage of relationship development; characterized by the need for independence and autonomy.

Discreteness　Quality of being separate.

Distancing　Keeping others away by acting cold, conceited, and aloof.

Dyadic communication　The interaction between two people.

Dynamism　Degree of excitement that the speaker brings to the presentation.

Dysfunctional or negative roles   Hinder the group's ability to meet its goal or objective.

E

Emblems   Body motions that take the place of words.

Emergence phase   Groups grow anxious to reach a decision.

Emotional appeals   Are used to trigger the emotions or feelings of an audience.

Empathy   The ability to understand what someone else is feeling, involves looking at a situation from the other person's perspective.

Empowered   Power to make decisions, be creative, and explore their own potential.

Encoding   The process of putting thoughts, ideas, or feelings into meaningful symbols that another person can understand.

Equality   Treating others on a par with ourselves, represents a supportive climate.

Esteem needs   The desire for influence or status within the social structure.

Ethics   Rules that govern moral behavior.

Etymology   History of a word's development or use in the language where it is found.

Euphemisms   Words that substitute for other words because they are more pleasant.

Evaluative behavior   Judgmental; it attacks the individual rather than that person's actions.

Examples   Statements that attempt to illuminate the facts.

Experimenting   The second stage of relationship development; characterized by more in-depth topic discussion.

Expert power   One's superior knowledge in a particular field.

Extemporaneous delivery   Speaker delivers the presentation from notes; spontaneous, yet prepared.

External noise   Includes sounds or visual stimuli that draw our attention away from the intended message.

F

Factual example   Something that you have observed.

Fallacies   Flawed arguments.

Family   People who are related to you (parents, siblings, etc.).

Faulty analogy   Invalid comparison.

Faulty cause-and-effect argument   No proof offered to show that one event caused the other to happen.

Feedback   The receiver's response to the sender's message; it provides information about the way the message is being interpreted.

Fillers or vocal interruptions   Sounds used to fill in the gaps between the words that comprise our messages.

Focus groups   Used to discover what people are thinking and feeling and are primarily used by advertisers and marketers.

Formula communication Safe, nonthreatening communication that involves little or no risk.

Forum The group presents its ideas to an audience.

Frame of reference Allows us to create and interpret messages; our unique view of the world and everything in it.

Full-sentence outline Full sentences to list the major and minor points, as well as the different forms of support in the presentation.

Functional perspective Leadership focuses on the kinds of leadership behaviors that any member of the group can exhibit, which collectively result in the group's making progress.

G

Gatekeeper One who attempts to regulate the flow of communication within the group.

General purpose The overriding goal of a presentation is to inform, to persuade, or to entertain.

Generalization The use of nonspecific language to describe objects, events, and feelings.

Graduated scale Also known as the Likert scale, gives individuals the opportunity to rank their feelings on a continuum.

Groupthink The illusion of consensus among the group members.

H

Halo and horns stereotyping Based on our observations of an individual in a particular situation or setting, we develop either a positive or negative perception about that person; we then allow our initial perception to transfer to other situations.

Hidden quadrant One window in the Johari window; represents the part of self we keep to ourselves.

Highly structured body Includes all the questions that the interviewer plans to ask.

Hypothetical example Invites the audience to imagine a situation created expressly for the speech they are listening to.

I

Ideal individuals People who feel comfortable with themselves and with others.

Illustrators Nonverbal symbols that reinforce a verbal message.

Impression management How we want others to perceive us.

Impromptu delivery Speaker delivers a presentation without preparation.

Inclusion needs Desire to be part of a group.

Indexing A technique that takes into account the individual differences among people, objects, and places.

Inductive reasoning One moves from specific instances to generalizations.

Informational interview To acquire facts about a specific topic.

Informational listening   Allows you to focus on the content of the message in order to gain knowledge.

Informative speech   To impart knowledge.

Initiating   First stage of relationship development; characterized by small talk and the development of first impressions.

Integrating   The fourth stage of relationship development; characterized by coupling.

Intensifying   The third stage of relationship development; characterized by the expression of feelings for one another.

Interference   Noise.

Internal noise   Thoughts or feelings that prevent us from processing a sender's message.

Interpersonal communication   The informal exchange that occurs between two or more people.

Interpersonal conflict   An expressed struggle between at least two interdependent parties who perceive incompatible goals, scarce rewards, and interference from the other parties in achieving their goals.

Interpret   To clarify the message and offer an alternative perception.

Interview   A planned and purposeful interaction between two parties in which questions are asked and answers are given.

Interviewee   The party who responds to questions from the interviewer.

Interviewer   The party who asks questions of an interviewee.

Intimacy   Sense of closeness and trust shared with others.

Intimate distance   That distance at which it is appropriate for highly personal communication encounters to occur.

Intrapersonal communication   Communication with ourselves.

Introduction   The first part of a public presentation or interview.

J

Jargon   Terminology of a specialized group or activity.

Johari window   Visual representation of self.

Journals   Contain research findings carried out in a particular field.

K

Key-phrase outline   Abbreviated version of the full-sentence outline that is intended as a cue to each point in the presentation.

Kinesics   The study of bodily movements.

Knowledge-gaining groups   Come together to learn or experience new things.

L

Laissez-faire leader   Gives minimal direction or instruction to group members; rather, members have complete freedom to make decisions.

Leadership   The ability to exert influence on a group by providing a sense of direction or vision.

Leading questions   Designed to move the interview in a specific direction.

Legitimate power Derived from one's position of authority.

Line graph Useful in demonstrating change over a period of time.

Linear model The linear model argues that communication can only move in one direction, from the sender to the receiver.

Logical argument Giving one or more good reasons for a plan or proposal.

Loosely structured body Provides maximum flexibility for both interviewer and interviewee; the interviewer works from a list of possible questions or a list of possible topics and subtopics.

M

Maintenance roles Deal with the relationships within the group.

Manuscript delivery Delivery of a speech word for word from a prepared statement.

Median The middle point of a set of numbers.

Memorized delivery Speaker delivers the presentation from memory; notes are used only as a reference.

Message The thought, feeling, or action that is sent from the source to the receiver with the use of symbols.

Message overload Attention to details instead of the main ideas of the message.

Mode The number that occurs most frequently in a set of numbers.

Moderately structured body The interviewer determines the primary questions ahead of time.

Motivated sequence Design, advanced by Alan H. Monroe, that focuses on creating a sense of need and then explaining how that need can be satisfied.

Multi-channeled Use of body, voice, and, appearance to convey a message.

N

Narrative Story or an account of an event told orally.

Need to belong The desire to be part of a group.

Needs Physical or emotional desires that grow out of circumstances in our immediate environment.

Neutral One that does not "take sides."

Neutral questions Questions that reveal nothing of the interviewer's biases, preferences, or expectations.

Neutrality Indifference toward another individual.

Noise Often thought of as interference to the communication process.

Nonsequitur The minor points are not related to the major points, or the conclusion does not logically follow the points that precede it.

Nonverbal communication Encompasses the broad spectrum of messages we send without verbalizing our thoughts or feelings.

Norms Rules that dictate how group members ought to behave.

O

Open quadrant A window in the Johari window that represents the aspect of our self we share with others.

Open questionnaire   Gives respondents the opportunity to fully express their feelings.

Open questions   Nonrestrictive questions designed to give the respondent maximum latitude in formulating an answer.

Oral citation   Give credit orally to a source used in the presentation.

Organization   Another phase of the perception process; in other words, we perceive that certain items belong together, and therefore we tend to organize them that way.

Orientation phase   Beginning of a group discussion; members attempt to get to know one another.

Outdoing others   The need to constantly top the achievements of others.

Overgeneralizations   Add a dramatic effect to your speech, but are not logical.

Overly critical communication   Judging the behavior of others.

Overpersonal individuals   People who fear intimacy and who overcompensate by establishing many relationships.

Oversocial individuals   People who feel uncomfortable in social situations and overcompensate by excessive group participation.

P

Panel   Individuals attempt to solve problems or inform an audience about a topic.

Paralanguage   The vocal aspect of delivery that accompanies speech and other nonverbal utterances.

Paraphrasing   Restating another person's message in our own words.

Passive aggression   Subtle and covert aggression.

Passive listening   Only the sender is involved; no feedback is provided.

Peers   A group of significant others, also can profoundly influence our self-concept.

Perception   The process of assigning meaning to stimuli.

Perception checking   Using questions to clarify the understanding of the verbal and/or nonverbal message.

Periodicals   Written sources published at regular intervals (that is, weekly, monthly, quarterly, or semiannually).

Personal constructs   The characteristics we use to judge others.

Personal distance   The area most appropriate for interpersonal interactions dealing with personal matters, that is, approximately eighteen inches to four feet.

Personal growth   Groups focus on the individual and his or her personal well-being.

Personal individuals   People who feel comfortable with their ability to handle personal relationships.

Personal space   The area that exists between ourselves and others.

Persuasion   The act of convincing an audience through verbal and nonverbal communication.

Persuasive speech   Purpose is to change an attitude.

Physiological needs   The most basic needs, such as food, water, and air.

Physical setting   Such factors as seating arrangements, time of day, degree of privacy, room size, temperature, and lighting affect how people communicate with each other.

Pie graph   A pie shape divided into wedges, helpful in demonstrating to an audience the way something whole is divided into parts or the way one part of a whole relates proportionately to the other parts.

Power   Control, authority, or influence over others.

Powerlessness   Feeling not in control or having no power to make decisions.

Presentational aids   Visual or audio support for the verbal message.

Primary questions   Questions that introduce a major area of discussion to be guided by the interviewer.

Primary sources   Documents such as letters, manuscripts, or interviews.

Problem orientation   The parties involved realize that several people contribute to the problem and that adjustment of behavior is necessary on all fronts.

Problem/solution   Approach to organizing a speech that involves identifying a conflict and then offering a potential course of action that will correct the problem.

Problem-solving or task-oriented groups   Come together to answer a question or provide a solution to a problem.

Process-related leadership behaviors   Those behaviors concerned with maintaining a positive climate within the group.

Prototypes   Representatives of our ideal; we use this ideal as a means of comparison.

Provisionalism   A willingness to explore new ideas.

Proxemics   The study of physical space as it relates to human interaction.

Proximity   Closeness to one another; way to organize stimuli.

Psychological climate   The attitudes and feelings we have about ourselves and the other people involved in the communication.

Psychological withdrawal   We are forced to stay in a situation that makes us feel uncomfortable. We mentally escape from the situation.

Public communication   An individual shares information with a large group; the usual structure has a speaker presenting ideas to an audience.

Public distance   A distance exceeding twelve feet is most appropriate for public communication.

Q

Questioning   Requesting additional information from the sender in order to help us understand the message.

Question of fact   The group argues whether or not a statement is true or false.

Question of policy   The group must decide if any specific action is in order.

Question of value   Morality is at issue.

Quotation   Someone else's words used as support in the presentation.

R

Reaction formation   We behave contrary to the way we really feel.

Receiver   The individual to whom the message is sent.

Referent power   Derived from one's feeling of identification with another.

Reflective appraisals   Also called the "looking glass self" because we see ourselves through other people's eyes.

Regulative rules   Unspoken rules that guide our use of language.

Regulators   Nonverbal behaviors used to control, or regulate, communication between people.

Reinforcement phase   Final phase of the decision-making process; consensus is achieved.

Relational messages   Sent nonverbally; hidden messages.

Resume   A short account of one's qualifications for a particular position.

Reward power   One's perceived ability to provide things like money, objects, or love.

Rhetorical question   Posed to the audience and later developed or answered in the talk.

Roles   A set of expected behaviors each member of the group must follow.

S

Safety needs   The second level on Maslow's hierarchy, which refers to our desire to feel secure.

Sarcasm   Biting sense of humor designed to keep people away and to maintain control of a situation.

Secondary questions   Designed to gain additional information from the interviewee.

Secondary sources   Interpretations of primary material.

Selective attention   The process of determining what we pay attention to and what we ignore.

Self-actualization   Perceiving that you are at the highest level of what you believe to be your potential.

Self-concept   Our perception of ourselves, or how we picture ourselves in a very broad sense.

Self-disclosure   The conscious decision to share personal information

Self-esteem   Our measure of self-worth; as such, it is the evaluative dimension of our self-concept.

Self-fulfilling prophecy   Our behavior matches someone else's expectations.

Self-serving bias   Occurs when we see ourselves in a positive light by blaming others or external forces for problems.

Sequence   Order of ideas in a presentation.

Significant others   Those individuals to whom we are emotionally close and whom we allow to influence our lives.

Signposts   Help the audience know where you are in the speech.

Silence   The absence of using your voice.

Similarity   Stimuli that resemble one another are commonly grouped together.

Similes   Like analogies, they compare two things; but unlike analogies, similes compare similar objects or situations using the words "like" or "as."

Situational perspective   Each group creates a new situation, and this situation dictates which style of leadership is most appropriate.

Slang   Used by a specific group; can be cultural, geographic, or generational.

Small-group communication　A small number of people who share a common goal or objective and interact face to face.

Social distance　Distance most appropriate for communication of a non-personal nature.

Social groups　Not to solve problems or accomplish specific tasks, but to interact.

Social power　Potential for changing attitudes, beliefs, and behaviors of others.

Source　The person who creates and sends a message.

Spatial order　Refers to organizing the parts of a topic according to the relationship of their positions.

Specific purpose　Takes into account the following factors: (1) what you hope to accomplish, (2) which aspect of the topic you will cover, by narrowing your topic, and (3) your intended audience.

Spontaneity　An open discussion of feelings

Stagnating　The eighth stage of relational development; characterized by little or no self-disclosure.

Startling statement　Shocks, arouses, or surprises an audience.

Statistics　Ideas presented in numerical terms; used as supporting material.

Status　Relative standing of one party in relation to another.

Stereotyping　Placing or categorizing people, places, objects, or events into groups based on generalized characteristics; also contributes to the way we perceive others.

Strategy　To manipulate interactions between people.

Subordinate points　Minor points that grow out of the major ideas.

Summation　Reinforces the main points in your speech.

Superiority　An attitude that an individual is better, more important, or more valuable than someone else.

Suppression　We acknowledge that a problem exists, but we attempt to minimize its importance.

Supportive climate　Encourages free and open interaction between people.

Symbols　Things, names for the objects around us.

Symposium　Small group of speakers who share a topic, but who discuss it individually, often focusing on a specific aspect of the topic.

Synonyms　Different words that have the same or nearly the same meaning.

T

Task roles　Used when concerned about meeting the group's goal or objective.

Task-related leadership behaviors　Those actions whose purpose is to keep the group focused on the problem or question.

Technical language or jargon　The specialized terms associated with a particular discipline, skill, or career.

Terminating　The last stage of relational development; characterized by the end of the relationship.

Territory　The space we stake out as our own.

Thesis statement　The major ideas of the speech; at the same time, it refines the specific purpose.

Time order　Ideas arranged in a chronological framework.

Topic order Involves breaking down your main topic into smaller points that are pertinent to the main idea.

Touch A form of nonverbal communication that conveys a wide range of emotions.

Trait perspective Certain individuals are "born leaders" because they possess such qualities as a forceful personality, marked intelligence, and dynamic communication skills.

Transactional model Describes communication as an interdependent process where the speaker and receiver are simultaneously sending and receiving messages.

Transition Provides a link between the main parts of your speech.

Transitional preview Gives the audience an idea of what is to come.

Transitional summary Recaps all the coordinate points.

Trustworthiness Refers to the kind of "character" communicated to the audience by the speaker.

U

Underpersonal individuals People who shy away from intimate relationships.

Undersocial individuals People who find it difficult to participate in realtionships; those who have a lack of confidence.

Unknown quadrant Window in the Johari window that represents to ourselves and others parts of our self we have yet to discover.

V

Vague language Language that lacks directness and specificity; it is void of details.

Value Determines the morality of an issue; that is, either something is good or bad, right or wrong.

W

Walking transition Taking a small step to indicate the presentation is moving to another point.

References

Abernathy, R. (1977). Martin Luther King's dream. In L. Rosen, ed. *The Sixties: the decade remembered now, by the people who lived it then.* New York: Random House.

Anderson, P. A. (1999). *Nonverbal communication: forms and functions.* Mountain View, CA: Mayfield.

Annenberg Public Policy Center. (1996). *Call-in political talk radio: background, content, audiences, portrayal in mainstream media.* Philadelphia: University of Pennsylvania.

Armstong, C., Rubin, A. (1989). Talk radio as interpersonal communication. *Journal of Communication,* 39, pp. 84-94.

Beaver, H. D. (2000, June). Visual aids: how much is too much? *ABA Banking Journal,* 92, p. 80.

Beebe, S. A., Masterson, J. T. (1997). *Communication in small groups,* 5th ed. New York: Longman Press.

Bergen, K. (2000, February 24). Debt load looms as danger for many families. *Chicago Tribune.* Retrieved March 4, 2001, from chicagotribune.com/business/businessnews/article/0,2669,2-42494,FF.html.

Biggs, M. (2000, September) Assessing risks today will leave corporate leaders well-prepared for the future of work. *InfoWorld* 22, p. 100.

Black, H.C. (1979). *Black's law dictionary,* 5th ed. St. Paul, MN: West Publishing.

Boss, S. (1999, December 20). Face to face won't soon bow to technology. *Christian Science Monitor,* p. 15.

Brilhart, J. K., Galanas, G. J., Adams, K. (2001). *Effective group discussion,* 10th ed. New York: McGraw Hill.

Brokaw, T. (1999, July 15). Information and communication. *Vital Speeches of the Day,* pp. 607–608.

Browne, M.N., Freeman, K. E., Williamson, C. L. (2000). The importance of critical thinking for student use of the internet. *College Student Journal* 34, pp. 391–399.

Burrell, N. A., Koper, R. J. (1994). The efficacy of powerful/powerless language on persuasiveness/credibility: a meta-analytic review. In R.W. Preiss and M. Allen, eds. *Prospects and precautions in the use of meta-analysis.* Dubuque, IA: Brown & Benchmark.

Bush, G. W. Address to a joint session of congress and the American people. (2001, September 20). Retrieved October 20, 2001, from www.whitehouse.gov/news/releases/2001/09/20010920-8.html.

Bush, G. W. (2001, December 28). President, General Franks discuss war effort. Retrieved January 29, 2001 from whitehouse.gov/news/releases/2001/12/print/20011228-1html.

Carmichael, S. (1969). Stokely Carmichael explains black power to a white audience in Whitewater, Wisconsin. In R. L. Scott and W. Brockreide, eds. *The rhetoric of black power.* New York: Harper & Row.

Carmichael, S. (1969). Stokely Carmichael explains black power to a black audience. In R. L. Scott and W. Brockreide, eds. *The rhetoric of black power.* New York: Harper & Row.

Center for Disease Control. (2000). Health report 2000. Retrieved May 10, 2001, from www.cdc.gov/Nchs/data/hus.

Cline, R. J. Welch. (1990, Spring). Detecting groupthink: methods for observing the illusion of unanimity. *Communication Quarterly,* 38, pp. 112–126.

Clinton, W. J. (2000, January 27). State of the union address. Retrieved March 13, 2000, from www.pub.whitehouse.gov/uri-res/I2...pdi://oma.eop.gov.us/2000/1/27/15.text.1.

CNN.com. (2000, May 7). Serious crime shows eight-year decline, says FBI. Retrieved March 28, 2001 from www.cnn.com/2000/US/05/07/fbi.crime/index.html.

Coleman, J. (2000, March 27). Is technology making us intimate strangers? *Newsweek,* p. 12.

Cooley, C. H. (1912). *Human nature and the social order.* New York: Scribner.

Cronen, V., Pearce, W. B., L. Snavely, L. (1979). A theory of rule structure and types of episodes and a study of perceived undesired repetitive patterns. In D. Nimmo, ed. *Communication yearbook, 3.* New Brunswick, NJ: Transaction Books.

Cuomo, M. (1984, August 15). Keynote Address. *Vital Speeches of the Day,* p. 649.

Davich, J. (2001, March 22) E-mail explosion. *The Times,* pp. C1–C2.

Davidson, J. (1996, June 1). The shortcomings of the information age. *Vital Speeches of the Day* 62, pp. 495-502.

Department of Telecommunications Program, Ball State University. (n.d.). David Letterman Scholarship. Retrieved February 19, 2001, from www.+com.bsu.edu/program3.htm.#letterman.

Duvall, B., Duvall, T. (n.d.). The Everly Brothers homecoming. Retrieved February 19, 2001, from on-the-square.com/muhlenberg_ky/evernts/everly.htm.

Ekmin, P., Friesen, W. V. (1969). The repertoire of nonverbal behavior: categories, origins, and coding. *Semiotica* 1, pp. 49–98.

Ekmin, P., Friesen, W. V. (1975). *Unmasking the face.* Englewood Cliffs, NJ: Prentice-Hall.

Flynn, M. (n.d.). Credit card debit high among undergraduates. *The Post-Ohio University: Athens Campus U-Wire.* Retrieved March 4, 2001, from www.studentadvantage.com/article/print/0,4281,c6-i70-t0-a23768,00.htm.

French, R. P., B. Raven, B. (1968). The bases of social power. In D. Cartwright and A. Zande, eds. *Group dynamics.* New York: Harper & Row.

Frost, J. H., Wilmot, W. W. (1978). *Interpersonal conflict.* Dubuque, IA: William C. Brown.

Garcia, K. (1999, December 12). Technology survey: students are students. *Community College Week* 12, p. 16.

Gibb, J. (1961). Defensive communication. *Journal of Communication* 11, pp. 141–148.

Gilligan, R. (1999). Enhancing the resilience of children and young people in public care by mentoring their talents and interests. *Child and Family Social Work* 4, pp. 187–196.

Goett, J., Foote, K. (2000, March). Cultivating student research and study skills in web-based learning environments. *Journal of Geography in Higher Education* 24, p. 92.

Goss, K. (2000, May/June). Creating a generation of internet worshipers. *Book Report* 19, p. 47.

Grob, L., Meyers, R., Schuh, R. (1997). Powerful/powerless language use in group interactions: sex differences or similarities? *Communication Quarterly* 45, pp. 282–303.

Hall, E. T. (1969). *The hidden dimension.* Garden City, NY: Anchor Books.

Hofstetter, C. R., Gianos, C. (1997). Political talk radio: actions speak louder than words. *Journal of Broadcasting and Electronic Media* 41, pp. 501-515.

Hunt, E. (1996). Communicating in the information age. *Canadian Business Review,* p. 23.

Internet's illusion of intimacy leaves a lot of red faces. (1998, October 29). *Christian Science Monitor,* p. B4

Jackson, L. (March 2001). Gender roles and the Internet: women communicating and men searching. *Sex Roles: A Journal of Research.* Retrieved from www. findarticles.com/cf_0/m2294/2001_March/78361733/print.html.

Jaffe, G. (2000, April 26). What's your point lieutenant? Just cut to the pie charts. *The Wall Street Journal,* pp. A1, A6.

Johnson, D. (2000, Sept./Oct.). New words in English. *Futurist* 5, pp. 6–7.

Knapp, M., Hall, J. A. (1992). *Nonverbal communication in human interactions.* New York: Holt, Rinehart & Winston.

Knapp, M., Vangelisti, A. L. (1992). *Interpersonal communication and human relationships.* Boston, MA: Allyn & Bacon.

Kupfer, A. (1995, March 20). Alone together. *Fortune,* pp. 94–99.

Larson, C. (2001). *Persuasion: reception and responsibility,* 9th ed. Belmont, CA: Wadsworth.

Leader, E. (2000). So you want to be a mentor? *Journal of Child and Adolescent Group Therapy* 10, pp. 119–124.

Lieberman, J. (2000, September 1). Address to the Democratic National Convention. *Vital Speeches of the Day,* pp. 679–681.

Lipnack, J., Stamps, J. (2000). *Virtual teams: people working across boundaries with technology,* 2nd ed. New York: John Wiley & Sons.

Luft, J. (1970). *Group processes: an introduction to group dynamics.* Palo Alto, CA: Mayfield.

Magnuson, E., et al. (1984, July 30). Drama and passion galore. *Time Magazine,* p. 26.

Maney, K. (1999, May 12). Armed with PowerPoint, speakers make pests of themselves. *USA Today,* p. 3B.

Marcus, J. (2000, March 26). Karate kids: martial arts training can bring out the best in everyone. *Chicago Tribune,* pp. 3–4.

Maslow, A. (1970). *Motivation and personality.* New York: Harper & Row.

McCarthy, A. (1994, November 4). The child comes first. *Commonwealth* 121, pp. 9–10.

McLearn, K. T., Colasanto, D., Schoen, C. (2000). Child health: mentoring makes a difference. *Commonwealth Fund.* Retrieved February 10, 2001, from www.cmwf. org/programs/Child/mclea277.asp.

Melia, M. K. (2001, January 16). The hole story of getting out of debt. *Chicago Tribune.* Retrieved March 4, 2001, from chicagotribune.com/business/business-news/article/0,2669,ART-49256,FF.html.

Merrifield, D. (1997, March). The x files. *Bank Marketing, 29,* p. 46.

Miller, H. (n.d.). The presentation of self in electronic life: Goffman and the Internet. Retrieved December 15, 2001, from www.ntu.ac.uk/soc/psych/miller/goffman.htm.

National Institute of Consumer Education. (n.d.). Getting out of debt. Eastern Michigan University. Retrieved March 4, 2001, from http://www.emich.edu/public/coe/nice/Debtma1.html.

Nolo.com. (n.d.). Using credit and charge cards FAQ. Retrieved March 4, 2001, from www.nolo.com/Encyclopedia/faqs/dc/dc2.html#FAQ-38.

Nucifora, A. (2000, March). Generation Y makes appealing target. *Business Journal* 15, p. 16.

Nunberg, G. (1999, December 20). The trouble with PowerPoint. *Fortune,* pp. 330–331.

Office of Mentoring Programs of Maryland. (n.d.) What is mentoring? Retrieved February 10, 2001, from www.pgcps.org/~mentor.htm.

Ogden, C. K., Richards, I. A. (1923). *The meaning of meaning.* New York: Harcourt Brace.

Osborn, A. (1979). *Applied imagination: principles and procedures of creative problem solving,* 3rd ed. New York: Scribner.

Oxygen Media. (2000). Five easy steps to get out of debt. Retrieved January 31, 2001, from wysiwyg://159/http://ka-ching.oxyg...ics/ym/managing-orama01 steps.html.

Platt, L. (1999, September). Virtual teaming: where is everyone? *Journal of Quality and Participation,* p. 41.

Powell, Colin. (1997, June 1). Sharing in the American dream: the task may seem staggering. *Vital Speeches of the Day* 63, pp. 484–485.

Rademacher, L. (2001). Effective note taking techniques. Unpublished manuscript.

Reagan, R. (1984, September 15). Acceptance speech. *Vital Speeches of the Day,* p. 706.

Reno, J. (1999, July 1). Stand for what you believe in. *Vital Speeches of the Day,* pp. 548–549.

Robson, D. (1998). Intimacy and computer communication. *British Journal of Guidance and Counseling* 26, pp. 33–42.

Rubin, A., Step, M. (2000). Impact of motivation, attraction, and parasocial interaction on talk radio listening. *Journal of Broadcasting and Electronic Media* 44, pp. 635-654.

Samter, W. (1994). Unsupportive relationships: deficiencies in support-giving skills of the lonely person's friends. In B. Burleson, T. L. Albrecht, and I. G. Sarason, eds. *Communicating of social support: messages, interactions, relationships,and community.* Thousand Oaks, CA: Sage.

Sapir, E. (1921). *Language: an introduction to the study of speech.* New York: Harcourt, Brace & World.

Schantz, J. (1999, November 29). The limits of internet research. *Community College Week* 12, p. 4.

Schneider, M. (n.d.). Credit card activation: the beginning of the end. *The Pitt News-*

University of Pittsburgh U-Wire. Retrieved March 4, 2001, from www.studentadvantage.com/article/print/0,4281,c6-i69-+311-a15898,00.html.

Scholarship Research Network. (n.d.). A discussion on scholarships. Retrieved, 31 January. 2001, from srnexpress.com/discuss.

Scholarship Research Network. (n.d.). Federal programs. Retrieved January 31, 2001, from snexpress.com/federal.htm.

Schutz, W. (1966). *The interpersonal world.* Palo Alto, CA: Science & Behavior Books.

Skeat, W. (1958). *A concise etymological dictionary of the English language.* Oxford: Clarendon.

Skertic, A. (2001, September 30). Crossing the wires. *The Times,* pp. E1–E2.

Solomon, C. (2001, June). Managing virtual teams. *Workforce* 80, pp. 60–65.

Sowle, T. (2000, September 19). State legislators lobby for credit card policies for students. *Knight-Ridder Newspapers, 2000.* Retrieved January 31, 2001, from www.mankato.msus.edu.edu/Dept/reporter/reparchive/09_19_00/news5.html.

Stelzner, M. A., Egland, K. L. (1995). Perceived understanding, nonverbal communication, relational satisfaction, and relational stage. Paper presented at the Annual Convention of the Western States Communication Association, Portland, OR.

Stewart, C. J., Cash, W. B. (1997). *Interviewing: principles and practices.* Madison, WI: Brown & Benchmark.

Stewart, T. A. (2001, February 5). Ban it now! Friends don't let friends use Power-Point. *Fortune,* p. 210.

Stohr, K. (2000, November 7). Financial lifelines: drowning in debt? Or does it just feel that way? In either case, the Internet can help you get out of deep water. *Time digitalmagazine.* Retrieved March 4, 2001, from www.time.com/time/digital/magazine/articles/0,4753,59303,00.html.

Sullivan, H. S. (1953). *The interpersonal theory of psychology.* New York: Norton.

Taub, E. A. (2001, November 26). Shared cell calls spawn loathing. *Chicago Tribune,* p. 4.

Taylor, A. (1999, February 15). Women and men communicating: who's from Mars? *Vital Speeches of the Day,* pp. 270–273.

Taylor, N. (n.d.) Is your college student ready for a credit card? Consumer Affairs Department of the Institute of Certified Financial Planners. Retrieved 31 January 31, 2001, from protectassets.com/news/art/1999/student2499.html.

Teret, S. P., et al. (1998, Summer). Making guns safer. Issues in science and technology online. Retrieved May 10, 2001, from www.nap.edu/issues/14.4/teret.htm.

Thibaut, J. W., Kelley, H. H. (1959). *The social psychology of groups.* New York: John Wiley & Sons.

Turkle, S. (1995). *Life on the screen.* New York: Simon & Schuster.

U.S. Census Bureau. (1999). Vital statistics: births to teens, unmarried mothers and prenatal care: 1985–1997.

U.S. Census Bureau. (2000). *Historical income tables—people.* Retrieved March 26, 2000, from www.census.gov/hhes/income/histinc/p16.html.

U.S. Census Bureau. (2000). Poverty in the United States. Retrieved May 10, 2001, from www.census.gov/Hhes/poverty/poverty99/pov99hi.htm.

Urban Institute. (2000). America's homeless II: population and services. Retrieved March 21, 2001, from www.urban.org/housing/homeless/numbers/sld002.htm.

Verderber, R., Verderber, K. (1995). *Inter-Act: using interpersonal communication skills.* Belmont, CA: Wadsworth.

The very best source of employment information. (2000). Retrieved October 20, 2001, from collegegrad.com/book/9-4.shtml.

White, M., Dorman, S. (2000, April) Confronting information overload. *Journal of School Health* 70, pp. 160–161.

Whorf, B. (1956). The relation of habitual thought and behavior to language. In J. B. Carrol, ed. *Language, thought, and reality.* New York: John Wiley & Sons.

Willer, L. (2001). Warning: welcome to your world baby, gender message enclosed. An analysis of gender messages in birth congratulation cards. *Women and language* 24, pp. 16-23.

Winter, K. (n.d.). *Questionable web sites.* Retrieved January 7, 2002, from thorplus.lib.purdue.edu/`techman/review.html.

Wood, J. (2000). *Communication in our lives.* Belmont, CA: Wadsworth.

Wuorio, J. (2001, March). Digging into debt. *Good Housekeeping,* pp. 55–57.

Zuckerman, L. (1999, April 17). Words go right to the brain, but can they stir the heart? Some say popular software debases public speaking. *New York Times,* pp. B9, B11.

Index